Heart to Heart

Do emotions happen inside separate hearts across the spaces between individuals? This book focuses on how emotions affect other people by changing their orientation to what happens in the social world. It provides the first sustained attempt to bring together literature on emotion's social effects in dyads and groups, and on how people regulate their emotions in order to exploit these effects in their home and work lives. The chapters present state-of-the-art reviews of topics such as emotion contagion, social appraisal and emotional labour. The book then develops an innovative and integrative approach to the social psychology of emotion based on the idea of relation alignment. The implications not only stretch beyond face-to-face interactions into the wider interpersonal, institutional and cultural environment, but also penetrate the supposed depths of personal experience, making us rethink some of our strongly held presuppositions about how emotions work.

BRIAN PARKINSON is Professor of Social Psychology at the University of Oxford, UK. He has served as Chief Editor of the *British Journal of Social Psychology* and Associate Editor of *Cognition and Emotion* and *Transactions in Affective Computing*.

STUDIES IN EMOTION AND SOCIAL INTERACTION

Second Series

Series Editors

Brian Parkinson
University of Oxford

Maya Tamir
Hebrew University of Jerusalem

(Continued after the index)

Heart to Heart

How Your Emotions Affect Other People

Brian Parkinson

University of Oxford

CAMBRIDGE
UNIVERSITY PRESS

CAMBRIDGE
UNIVERSITY PRESS

University Printing House, Cambridge CB2 8BS, United Kingdom

One Liberty Plaza, 20th Floor, New York, NY 10006, USA

477 Williamstown Road, Port Melbourne, VIC 3207, Australia

314–321, 3rd Floor, Plot 3, Splendor Forum, Jasola District Centre,
New Delhi – 110025, India

79 Anson Road, #06–04/06, Singapore 079906

Cambridge University Press is part of the University of Cambridge.

It furthers the University's mission by disseminating knowledge in the pursuit of
education, learning, and research at the highest international levels of excellence.

www.cambridge.org
Information on this title: www.cambridge.org/9781108484503
DOI: 10.1017/9781108696234

© Brian Parkinson 2019

First published 2019

Printed in the United Kingdom by TJ International Ltd. Padstow Cornwall

A catalogue record for this publication is available from the British Library.

ISBN 978-1-108-48450-3 Hardback
ISBN 978-1-108-73598-8 Paperback

This book is dedicated to the memory of my father,
Alan Parkinson, 1928–2019

Contents

Figures

x   *List of Figures*

Preface

Is retrospective hubris a thing? Or is there no satisfactory name for that inflated sense of accomplishment that comes only after further reflection? Sometimes subsequent events confer added significance on any minor mark you might have made. History happens to work out in your favour, making you seem wiser and more prophetic than you really are. You start to believe some of the flattering stuff people have been saying.

A couple of decades ago, I wrote a book whose theme was that emotions are social. As far as I recall, it was an easy book to write, partly because the literature on many of the key topics was so sparse back then. I was free to speculate. I could make wild claims and follow intuitions that were informed by the barest smattering of undergraduate philosophy. The final sentence of the book ran as follows: 'I see a whole new territory of social psychology waiting to be explored, into which I have taken only a few tentative steps.' Whatever you might think about this pronouncement, I didn't really believe that I had reached some kind of summit after my forty days in the wilderness. I was just scrabbling to end on a high note. But looking back, it still sounds like I was surveying the tempting territory stretched out below.

My book didn't open any floodgates. It wasn't me who carved a channel for the trickle of papers on social aspects of emotion that soon followed or the broader streams that later welled up. Other gravitational forces had already turned the tides and I was simply riding one of the waves. But at least I was around before the flood. At least that old book anchored a marker buoy somewhere out at sea, some arbitrary point of reference.

Writing this book has been a greater struggle and I've got myself into deep water many more times. It has become increasingly difficult to wade through the growing literature and find any distinctive point of reference. Pretty much everyone has now come to accept that emotions are social in some way or other, but no one seems to agree about exactly how.

And when they do agree, it's only about the fact that the sociality of emotions is somehow partial or secondary. Something essentially non-social is still thought to reside somewhere at their heart.

Stubborn as I am, I continue to resist this familiar conclusion. I still want to maintain that emotions are social through and through. They cross any boundaries between people and permeate interpersonal and intergroup contexts. They don't start out as private states struggling to find expression. They don't need to leap across from one beating heart to another.

Suspending the individualistic assumptions of mainstream social psychological emotion research presents practical as well as conceptual problems. It's not easy to maintain a sceptical attitude when presenting the otherwise intriguing results of psychological studies whose procedures presuppose the truth of the very metatheory you are trying to unsettle. You need to be careful not to buy into the whole story.

My attempts to review the contemporary literature on its own terms introduce a central tension to the narrative of this book. It's even there in the title. Asking how your emotions affect someone else assumes that they are entirely yours to begin with. It makes it harder to think of them in primarily relational terms.

While writing, I've often felt that it might be better to consider how emotions operate between people who are either working together or pushing and pulling against one another in a reciprocal dynamic system. Any interpersonal effects would then be built into emotion's constitution rather than something that gets tacked on afterwards.

I didn't follow my own advice on this issue. Instead, I opted to suspend disbelief and keep scepticism in check. However, the nagging doubts sometimes sneak through the cracks, tugging at the snags in the interwoven narrative. I hope that readers will be tolerant of my occasional dizzying lapses into metatheory and epistemology, especially as the book approaches its conclusion.

Leaving aside these slippages and discontinuities, the plot line of this book runs roughly as follows:

In Chapter 1, I present a general approach to emotions based on the idea that they align relations between people and objects and contrast this view with more traditional single-minded accounts. I try to turn the prevalent approach to emotion inside out.

Chapters 2 and 3 discuss research on two of the main ways of communicating emotions to other people. Chapter 2 focuses on words that describe and otherwise present emotional orientations and considers their associations with emotional concepts. I argue that language provides a means of exerting emotional influence and not just a private representational system. Chapter 3 similarly contests the view that facial movements express underlying emotions, focusing instead on facial activity as a means of signalling relational orientations and cuing other people to important aspects of the situation.

Chapter 4 turns to the central issue identified by the book's title and considers the various processes that might underlie emotion's interpersonal effects. Although communicated emotions can provide inferential information about the appropriate appraisal of objects, events and people, other kinds of emotional influence are less dependent on the categorical meanings of emotion words and expressions. For example, emotions can present incentives and communicate promises and threats. They can cue, shape and reinforce other people's behaviour without any registration of their conceptual implications.

Chapter 5 considers how people exploit the interpersonal effects of emotion for the purpose of interpersonal influence. For example, someone may stoke up their anger in order to intimidate someone else who is refusing to cooperate with them. This kind of strategic interpersonal regulation clearly doesn't work in all circumstances and I discuss some of the ways it can go wrong.

Chapter 6 takes a step back by raising the possibility that emotions exert strategic effects on other people even when they are not explicitly regulated. I argue that one of the reasons that people need to have the capacity to experience and express emotion is to align, maintain and regulate their relations with other people. In support of this view, I present evidence that certain kinds of emotion are specifically attuned to their interpersonal consequences.

Chapters 7 and 8 broaden the focus to the strategic and functional effects of emotions in larger social collectives and social institutions. Chapter 7 addresses emotions that are experienced in groups of more than two people. Sharing emotions with other group members can enhance group solidarity and consolidate norms about appropriate appraisals of group-relevant events. Emotions can also spread automatically around crowds of people who are gathered together in close proximity and engaging in activities with a clear and coordinated temporal structure and rhythm.

Chapter 8 reviews research into the ways that managers, service employees and caring professionals work on their own and other people's emotions (emotional labour). The central message is that organisational structures and resources shape the presentation and regulation of emotion and their interpersonal effects on clients and colleagues. Emotional tension and dissonance may arise when conflicting roles and allegiances encourage mutually discrepant orientations to work events.

Finally, Chapter 9 summarises the arguments and evidence presented in the book and considers how emotion's various interpersonal effects and functions coalesce over the course of a child's development into a socialised adult. Because infants operate in environments that are populated with other people whose behaviour towards them is infused with cultural implications, their emotions carry articulated meanings and bring coordinated interpersonal effects. And this happens even before babies are capable of understanding what they are doing when they get emotional. I therefore argue that emotions are fundamentally social right from the start of life.

I tried to write the chapters in their correct sequence, building cumulatively on the groundwork laid down by the earlier ones. However, Chapter 2 was a relatively late addition to the structure, slipped in when I could no longer ignore the fact that words are just as important a means of communicating emotions as facial displays. I already knew that I wanted to say something about emotional concepts somewhere in the book and this extra chapter provided a good place for that discussion too. Perhaps because of the disrupted chronology, the second chapter turned out to be the most difficult chapter to write, and I kept coming back to it when I was working on later sections of the book. As a consequence, it may also be the most difficult chapter to read, so please skip ahead if you find it too heavy going.

It's a strange feeling to reach the end of a project that has occupied so much of my time and attention over the last eighteen months or so. I suppose I'd have to say that my satisfaction is tinged with a kind of premature nostalgia, not only for the moments when recalcitrant conceptual or structural issues somehow seemed to resolve themselves, but also for the sense of direction that working away at words, which ultimately turn into sentences, paragraphs and chapters, can't help but provide. It's mostly been a rewarding experience to put the whole thing together. I just have to hope that some of that pleasure gets across from me to you.

Acknowledgements

I did most of the writing for this book in my little office at the end of our small back garden in Jericho. Although friends and family members insist on calling this office a shed or worse a man-cave, I personally prefer to think of it as a studio. The connotations of artistic isolation and endeavour appeal to me. From my studio, I can get back to the kitchen in less than thirty paces, so coffee is always on tap. And I don't usually get too wet during my commute even when it's pouring with rain outside. If the computer hadn't got so sluggish, I'd have to say it was a practically perfect environment for wrestling with words and ideas.

My studio provided the space for writing, but I couldn't have spent as much time there without the full year of sabbatical leave generously provided by Christ Church and the Department of Experimental Psychology at the University of Oxford. My colleagues there have also mostly respected my attempts to keep my head down and get on with the task at hand and I should apologise for any of my unwarranted resentment about their occasional incursions into an otherwise open schedule.

I started with romantic ideas about how the sabbatical year would pan out. I imagined jetting around the world to find inspiration in far-flung places rather than staying holed up here. As it happens, I did manage to spend a few precious days in Berlin, Boston and Geneva. I'm not sure how much sense of place penetrates prose style, but I do know that I can identify precisely which passages of text I was typing away at in each of those locations. I am sincerely grateful to the academics who hosted these visits for sparing the time to discuss issues related and unrelated to what I was working on at the time.

Ursula Hess and Christian von Scheve offered warm and welcoming company during a sub-zero snap which I mainly spent under the shadow of the brutalist Fernsehturm near Alexanderplatz. Jim Russell managed to read through a full draft of the longest and most impenetrable chapter before meeting me in the lobby of the Hyatt Regency next to Macy's in Downtown Crossing. Although we still don't agree about Wittgenstein, Jim's insights, as always, were invaluable. Danny Dukes invited me to an illuminating workshop on different readings of relevance at the Swiss Centre for Affective Sciences out in semi-suburban Genthod, just a twenty-minute walk from the lakeside Hotel President Wilson where I was lucky enough to be staying. He also let me come along to the restaurant dinner in Parc des Bastions afterwards, despite the fact that it was specifically intended for those people who actually participated in the discussions instead of just lurking and listening. We even managed to catch United player Marcos Rojo scoring the winning goal for Argentina on one of the outdoor big screens in the Plainpalais World Cup fan zone later that night. Unfortunately, I was really supporting Nigeria.

My son left for University in Bristol as I was working on the final chapter of this book. Jamie's not really that interested in reading anything I've ever written (or indeed anything at all) but I doubt I'd have been able to motivate myself in the same way without him around. Having said that, my Starbucks bills have certainly gone down since he went away.

Having reached this stage of parenthood has made me appreciate how much I owe to my own Mum and Dad. I'm forever grateful for their tolerance of my eccentricities, without which this book would tell a very different kind of story. For similar reasons, appreciation also goes to my brother John, and to my sister Carol, brother-in-law Malcolm and their two daughters, Emma and Hannah. This book's for all of you too.

And as for Gillian, it shouldn't go without saying that I deeply appreciate the love and emotional support that you continue to provide, and feel thoroughly guilty that it often does. Everyone imagines that two professors living together must spend most of their time in deep intellectual discussion about one another's work, but the truth is we never do.

This is beginning to sound like one of those embarrassing Oscars speeches and I'm wary of succumbing to that kind of self-congratulation. For some reason, a few lines from an old song have been looping round my mind for the last several weeks as I've been adding these final touches. David McComb of the Triffids repeatedly intones the following words in that sonorous baritone of his:

> *You are not moving any mountains*
> *You are not seeing any visions*
> *You are not freeing any people from prison*
> *Just an aphorism for every occasion*
>   (Stolen Property, from the album *Born*
>   *Sandy Devotional* by The Triffids, 1986)

I've always felt that the intended target of these accusations was the singer himself. There's a mournful and resigned quality to his voice that undermines any apparent spite or bile. And if my reading's right, I totally get how McComb (junior) must have been feeling when he wrote the lyrics. I can relate to how he is relating to things. Except for the bit about aphorisms.

Someone once told me that the best way to get an earworm out of your head is to listen to the catchy cadences of Elvis Costello's *Watching the Detectives*. It always has the distinctive vim and syncopation to take precedence. *I get so angry when the teardrops start, but he can't be wounded 'cause he's got no heart.* So now I know who else to thank (Elvis) and what I need to do next (listen to his song). It's a less ambitious project than this one has been, but still privately satisfying in its own way.

CHAPTER 1

What's at the Heart of Emotions?

Are emotions simply private experiences concealed inside individual minds and bodies? Psychologists often search for their distinguishing characteristics in these internal locations. But focusing on physiological responses and cognitive appraisals distorts our understanding of emotion's relations to the contexts in which it occurs. In fact, emotion is a form of relational activity. Unfolding transactions between people, objects and events give structure to our emotional orientations to what is happening. And these orientations in turn influence other people and their own reciprocal orientations. Some social emotions, such as anger and embarrassment, directly target other people's responses as ways of dealing with current concerns. Other emotions are oriented at non-social objects but still serve social functions by affecting other people's orientations to those objects. Although emotions are often experienced privately, this is only possible because we have learned how they work in more public arenas.

It's not uncommon to ponder the true nature of love, resist accusations of hate and envy, or dispute the sincerity of expressed gratitude. We may be uncertain that apologies or denials are genuinely heartfelt. But when it comes to our own emotions, the doubts disappear. Personally experienced passions seem like incontrovertible and obvious things, 'so close to, and so entirely within our soul, that it is impossible to feel them without their being actually such as it feels them to be' (Descartes, 1649, p. 343). When talking about them in everyday conversation, we are pretty sure we know what they are.

Less so in academic psychology. Scholarly disagreement about emotion's definition has persisted for centuries, and shows little sign of reaching resolution (Russell, 2012). The age-old question 'what is an emotion?' (e.g., James, 1884) still lacks a definitive answer. Does this mean that we are approaching it the wrong way? Perhaps this seemingly straightforward issue is not so straightforward after all.

Part of the problem comes from our sense that emotion is somehow out of the ordinary. This encourages us to look for an added ingredient that makes it special (Parkinson, 2013). We ask ourselves what transforms everyday experience into something qualitatively different, something emotional rather than mundanely non-emotional. Maybe a kiss from the right princess could perform the alchemical trick. Perhaps a king somewhere has the Midas touch. But the hunt for the goose that lays the golden eggs (James, 1898, p. 448) may simply be a wild goose chase.

Setting aside myth and fairy tale, psychologists typically search for emotion's special ingredient inside the human mind, brain or body, trying to get to the heart of things. But maybe the confusion arises because they are looking in the wrong places. What if there is no core component or transformative element deep within? What if emotions get their meaning and purpose from connections with the people in the world outside, not what they feel like inside?

In this chapter, I consider the various physiological and cognitive factors that are said to distinguish emotion from non-emotion and different emotions from each other. I then attempt to develop a socially oriented alternative approach to these issues of differentiation. I shall argue that emotion's special ingredient is its capacity to align and realign people's relations with each other and with objects and events in the shared environment.

Interoceptive Signals

What makes emotions emotional? In attempting to answer this question, William James (1884) developed an explanation that is widely regarded as the first genuinely psychological theory of emotion. He started by considering which aspects of emotional experience are essential for its emotional quality. This thought experiment led him to conclude that bodily changes of various kinds add the emotional heat to what we are feeling. Without them, our experience 'would be purely cognitive in form, pale, colorless, destitute of emotional warmth' (p. 190), leaving only 'a cold and neutral state of intellectual perception' (p. 193).

According to James, then, emotions are subjectively felt experiences that depend crucially on internally sensed bodily reactions. From this perspective, the literal heart might well be one of the organs whose activities help to generate emotion. The feeling of it pumping or skipping a beat might provide the heat behind our reaction.

However, it soon became apparent that these interoceptive signals showed less-differentiated patterns than the emotions they were supposed to produce. According to James's ex-pupil, Walter Cannon (1927), very similar bodily changes occurred across a wide range of different emotional and non-emotional states. He believed that the brain generates a coordinated and unified arousal response in the autonomic nervous system (ANS: see Figure 1.1) whenever any kind of emotional challenge is detected. This leads to the release of metabolic energy to muscles and organs. The heart speeds up and pumps more blood.

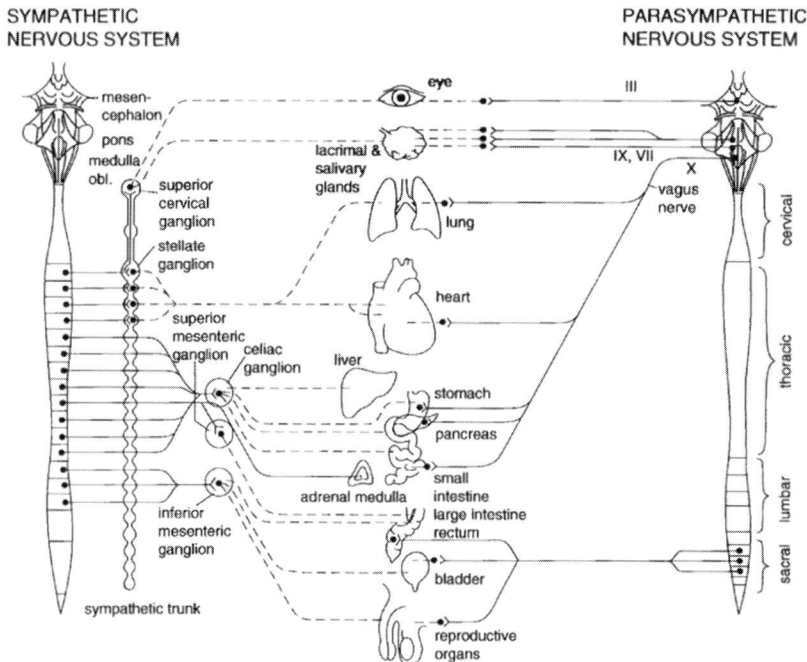

Figure 1.1 The sympathetic and parasympathetic divisions of the autonomic nervous system (Jänig, 2006)

Breathing quickens. The purpose of this activation is to prepare the body for any action that might be required. And it doesn't matter whether that action is fight or flight, approach or withdrawal.

If Cannon is correct, checking our bodily response cannot tell us what emotion we are experiencing. It cannot even indicate whether we are emotional at all. Autonomic arousal can produce the same interoceptive symptoms across a wide range of very different circumstances, including visits to the gym as well as more affectively charged victories and defeats, challenges and threats. Our arousal could just as well be angry arousal or fearful arousal. It might reflect either excitement or simple exertion.

Not everyone agrees with this conclusion. Some researchers argue that autonomic activity generates more distinctive patterns than Cannon's account implies (e.g., Ekman, Levenson & Friesen, 1983), allowing perceivers to make finer emotional discriminations. Others point out that the bodily changes discussed by James not only include autonomic changes but also muscular activity in the face and elsewhere. Perhaps then, people can detect the quality of emotion from a more integrated pattern of response across the whole body (e.g., Laird & Bresler, 1992).

However, neither of these attempts to rescue James's theory quite does the trick. The problem is that there is no distinctive bodily signature for any emotion, however many sources of interoceptive feedback are considered. It is true that autonomic responses are not as unitary or coordinated as Cannon believed. Different parts of the ANS can respond separately, producing different patterns (Folkow, 2000; Levenson, 1988). It is also true that the ANS response profiles of some emotions are often different from those of others (e.g., Kreibig, 2010). Your blood pressure is generally more likely to increase when you are angry than when you are sad, for example. But these differences are not clear enough to produce the obvious subjective distinctions between these two emotions. They don't seem to match their contrasting feelings or qualities.

And the autonomic differences are not consistent either. No pattern of bodily changes characterises every instance of anger, sadness or any other emotion (Siegel et al., 2018). And there is no solid evidence that any pattern of ANS activity only occurs during the experience of any particular emotion but never at other times. In other words, there are no autonomic fingerprints for emotions. The body cannot tell us precisely what emotion we are experiencing, period.

The reason is obvious. ANS responses depend on the situation and the kind of action that situation requires. And these requirements don't stay constant across all examples of any emotion. When I am angry, the way my body reacts depends on where my anger is directed, the person or thing I am angry with, what that person or thing is likely to do and what actions are available to me in the situation I happen to be in at the time. The autonomic response will be different if someone has a tight grip on my arm, if someone is about to punch me, or if they say something sarcastic in a formal meeting. In each case, the body needs to prepare for different actions in different ways. A fixed ANS pattern wouldn't work.

Or at least it wouldn't work perfectly. Some theorists argue that emotions prepare the body for the specific actions that were most likely to serve reproductive fitness at the time they first evolved. In other words, each distinct emotion might be associated with a default bodily response that once worked best on average when dealing with the situation that prompted the emotion (e.g., Scherer's, 2001, notion of a 'decoupled reflex'). If being ready to hit someone or something generally increased the prospect of survival across all kinds of provocation, then such a response might become prevalent in the population as a function of natural selection. Perhaps early hominids whose muscles were poised for punching whenever they were exposed to frustrating circumstances ended up being more likely to live to fight another day.

But how tightly would we need to specify the characteristic form of a behaviour to make this account work? Even an apparently delimited response such as punching has various possible profiles. It takes different forms when the antagonist is taller or shorter, at arm's length or closer and behind or in front of you. How your arm needs to move in order to hit the necessary target differs and changes depending on the situation and how it develops. No single set of muscular movements could provide any adaptive advantage, even if life really was so much simpler out on the savannah. So no default bodily signature seems viable.

And even if some elemental preparatory changes actually did always accompany any given emotion, how clearly would we be able to detect the internal signals they produced? Would we be able to focus our attention selectively enough to pick them out against the background of other things that our bodies happened to be doing at the time (cf. Stemmler et al., 2001)? Unless the signature symptoms override every-thing else the body is doing, the associated signals are likely to get lost in the noise.

What would detecting an autonomic signature tell us in any case? What extra emotional information could it provide? At some level, we must have already known what the emotional requirements of the situation were in order to produce the required pattern of bodily changes. Before reacting with fearful bodily changes, for example, we need to first perceive that something frightening is happening (e.g., Dewey, 1894). Isn't that initial emotional perception enough? Why would the body need to tell the brain what the brain must already know to make the body react in that way?

Two-Factor Theory

Another way of rescuing an interoceptive theory is to supplement it with additional principles. Schachter (1964) agreed with James that autonomic changes are crucial to emotional experience, but also accepted Cannon's evidence that they provided no diagnostic indication of the presence or quality of emotion. According to this view, generalised ANS arousal provides signals that need to be interpreted by reference to the current situation rather than ready-made information about the quality of experi-ence. Perceivers work out what external factors provoked the internal response in order to make sense of its emotional implications. Thus, arousal attributed to an uncertain threat is felt as fear, arousal following an insult is felt as anger, and arousal experienced after receiving exciting news is felt as joy (Figure 1.2).

In a famous experiment, Schachter and Singer (1962) tested this theory by assessing the emotional consequences of independently manipulating autonomic arousal and information about the situation. The students

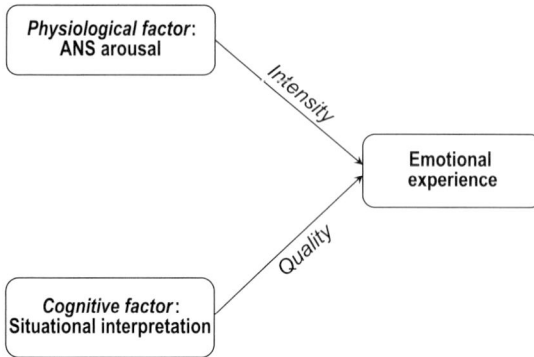

Figure 1.2 Schachter's two-factor theory (Parkinson, 1995, reproduced with permission from Routledge)

who participated believed that they were receiving an injection of a newly discovered vitamin compound called *Suproxin*, and that their perceptual performance would later be tested in order to assess its effects. In fact, the injection was either adrenaline, which leads to increased autonomic arousal, or a neutral saline solution that should not have produced any physiological effects. Among participants injected with adrenaline, one group was warned that they would experience side effects corresponding to adrenaline's genuine consequences (dry mouth, racing heart, etc.), so that they would have a non-emotional explanation for their experienced arousal. Participants injected with adrenaline without this warning of side effects were expected to explain their symptoms in terms of the situation, and consequently experience whatever emotion that situation implied.

Schachter and Singer (1962) stage-managed two alternative social situations that were specifically designed to provide contrasting emotional explanations for any unexplained arousal. The first was intended to encourage an angry interpretation. Participants were left in the waiting room with an accomplice of the experimenter who was posing as another participant. Their task while waiting was to fill out a questionnaire which asked increasingly personal questions. For example, there were requests for information about their mother's extra-marital relations and the bathing habits of close family members. While answering these questions, the accomplice made a show of getting increasingly cross before eventually tearing up the questionnaire and storming out of the room. In the second 'euphoria' condition, the accomplice instead improvised a series of games using objects that the experimenter had left lying around the room and encouraged the real participant to join in the fun. Paper planes were thrown and hula hoops spun.

The results of this experiment fail to justify its subsequent impact on the literature. There was no clear support for two key predictions. First, participants injected with a placebo did not report experiencing significantly less emotion than those injected with adrenaline and not warned of side effects. In other words, there was no evidence that unexplained arousal made any difference to emotional experience. Schachter and Singer argued that this failure to support their hypothesis arose due to their inability to exert full control over participants' autonomic responses and their explanations of those responses. In other words, some participants in the placebo condition may have experienced direct emotional reactions to the stage-managed situation and consequently experienced arousal ('self-aroused' participants), and some participants in the unexplained arousal conditions may have concluded that their symptoms were caused by the injection despite receiving no warning of side effects ('self-informed' participants). Only by removing these participants from their designated conditions, were the investigators able to make the predicted difference in emotional response statistically significant.

But why did 'self-aroused' participants have higher heart rates in the placebo condition in the first place? Presumably because of their stronger emotional reactions to the accomplice's behaviour. This means that selectively removing them from the placebo conditions leaves a group of participants who are generally less emotionally reactive. Correspondingly, self-informed participants may have been unconvinced that their arousal was due to the situation because they knew that their bodies would not normally react so strongly. Selectively removing them from the unexplained arousal condition therefore leaves a group of participants who are generally more emotionally reactive. So the comparison between the reconstituted placebo and unexplained arousal conditions now becomes a comparison between relatively less and relatively more emotionally reactive groups of participants. No surprise then that the difference in reported emotionality increased. More generally, tampering with random allocation to experimental conditions clearly invalidates statistical conclusions in this or any other study.

Implications of the second unsupported prediction are even more fatal. Participants injected with adrenaline and given inaccurate information about side effects on average reported themselves to be mildly happy in both euphoria and anger conditions (Zimbardo, Ebbeson & Maslach, 1977). Their ratings did not suggest that they were in widely divergent emotional states depending on their situational explanations for autonomic symptoms.

Given the inconclusive results, and the strong claims made for them, other researchers have since tried to replicate the experiment (e.g., Erdmann & Janke, 1978; Marshall & Zimbardo, 1979; Maslach, 1979).

None of these later studies provided unequivocal support for the theory either (see Manstead & Wagner, 1981; Reisenzein, 1983). This does not necessarily mean that Schachter was wrong. The problem may lie with the methodology rather than the theory behind it. Perhaps manipulating emotionally plausible situations independently of physiological arousal doesn't work because certain combinations of the two factors don't match or gel. People rarely experience bodily reactions that are disproportionate to what else is happening and may be confused by the incongruity. They may react in atypical ways to an atypical set of circumstances. Perhaps then arousal that better fits the emotional situation actually could contribute to our emotional experience. But in that case, the situation already provides an equally good explanation for the emotion anyway.

Schachter's theory implies that the special ingredient making emotion emotional does not lie wholly inside the body, but instead depends on arousal's connections with whatever is happening in the outside world. For him, emotion boils down to an interpretation of internal signals that is guided by cognitions about their causes. But our bodies don't react simply to provide information about what we are feeling. They provide energy and impulses that prepare us for action. Any internal signalling function seems secondary to this more practical purpose. Arousal helps to drive emotional behaviour, not to add emotional colour or heat to experience.

Perceptual Simulation and Emotion Construction

Barrett (e.g., 2017) developed a more sophisticated account of how internally perceived metabolic activity might contribute to emotional experience. In her view, context-specific perceptual simulations integrate available information coming from both inside and outside the body, providing a basis for distinctive emotion concepts (see also Chapter 2). Thus, someone might conceptualise their experience as the kind of 'anger' experienced when filling out an insulting questionnaire when the external and internal signals fit with a matching multimodal representation retrieved from memory. The situated anger representation in turn guides the individual's perception, attention and action, giving it its experienced angry quality.

According to this theory, different patterns of interoceptive signals might characterise different instances of the same emotion across different situations. It is only the application of the emotion concept that links these different instances together and makes them count as, and feel like, the emotion in question. So, unlike James, Barrett makes no claim that the body tells us what emotion we are experiencing, only that the changes we register are a key part of what the brain categorises to generate emotional experience.

Schachter's and Barrett's theories imply that bodily changes provide internal signals that help specify the felt quality of emotion. They both treat emotions primarily as inwardly focused personal experiences whose representation is what makes the main difference to their identification. As we shall see in the next section, other theorists put relatively more emphasis on emotion's object-orientation, and its dependence on appraisals of what is happening in the external environment.

Appraisal

Schachter (1964) implied that situational information clarifies the emotional meaning of experience in retrospect. By contrast, appraisal theorists such as Arnold (1960) and Lazarus (1991a) argue that interpreting and evaluating situational information is what activates emotional reactions in the first place. Bodily changes typically depend on things happening in the person's dealings with the world. They rarely pop up out of the blue as events in need of disambiguation. In most circumstances, we are already focused on whatever our emotion is about before any bodily changes begin to register. Perhaps, then, the way we perceive and interpret the current transaction provides the initial spark for any heat behind our response.

James's (1898) introspective focus diverted attention from the object-directedness and external orientation of most emotions. Although he acknowledged that the 'perception of an exciting fact' (such as seeing a wild bear in the woods) initially provokes the emotional bodily changes, he failed to explain why that fact (e.g., the bear's appearance) is perceived as exciting or emotionally provocative in the first place.

Instead of asking what makes internal experience emotional experience, Arnold's (1960) alternative thought experiment considered what makes the perception of what is happening in the person's life an emotional perception. Her conclusion was as follows:

> To perceive or apprehend something means that I know what it is like as a thing, apart from any effect on me. To like it or dislike it means that I know it not only objectively, as it is apart from me, but also that I estimate its relation to me, that I appraise it as desirable or undesirable, valuable or harmful for me, so that I am drawn to it or repelled by it.
>
> (p. 170)

According to Arnold, appraising what is happening as personally significant is what adds emotional heat to our response. To feel an emotion is not only to feel certain changes happening inside our bodies, but also to perceive the situation as having emotional qualities (Frijda, 2005). To feel angry means experiencing someone else as annoying just as much as it means sensing internal turmoil. To feel pride means registering a personal achievement as well as feeling inflated or in high spirits.

Arnold's appraisal approach emphasises the 'intentionality' or about-ness of emotion: the fact that it always focuses on some particular thing that concerns us (e.g., Gordon, 1974; Ortony, Clore & Collins, 1988). We don't just get angry; we get angry with someone about what they have done. We don't just feel afraid; we are frightened of a potential event and about what its consequences might be. In philosophical terminology, whatever we are angry with, or frightened of, is known as the emotion's intentional 'object', even when that 'object' is a person, event or imagined abstraction rather than a physical thing. According to Arnold, it is our perceptual orientation to this object that gives colour to our emotion rather than our perception of what is happening inside the body. In other words, it's not bodily changes that specify emotional quality, but rather appraisals of the personal meaning of events.

Dimensions of Appraisal

According to Arnold, appraisal is not only what makes emotion emo-tional, but also what makes different emotions different from each other. In other words, distinctive patterns of appraisal give distinct emotions their specific qualities. Subsequent theorists have attempted to specify more precisely what these emotion-differentiating appraisal patterns might be (e.g., Frijda, 1986; Lazarus, 1966; 1991a; Roseman, 1979; Scherer, 1984; Smith & Ellsworth, 1985).

According to Smith and Lazarus (1993), the appraisal of motivational relevance determines whether a person experiences any emotion in the first place. In other words, unless what is happening relates to something that makes a difference to our plans, goals or concerns, we will not get emotional about it. The appraisal of motivational congruence further assesses whether events help or hinder progress towards our goals and determines whether our emotional reaction is positive or negative. We feel good when things are going our way and bad when they are not. The specific quality of our positive or negative emotion additionally depends on appraisals assessing who or what is responsible for the thing we are emotional about ('self- and other-accountability'), our capacity to cope with both that thing ('problem-focused coping potential') and the way it makes us feel ('emotion-focused coping potential') and the anticipated likelihood of negative and positive outcomes ('future expectancy').

Thus, anger is specifically prompted by appraisals of motivational relevance, motivational incongruence and other-accountability: the per-ception that someone else is responsible for the thing that is interfering with your goals (see Figure 1.3). This pattern of appraisal need not be

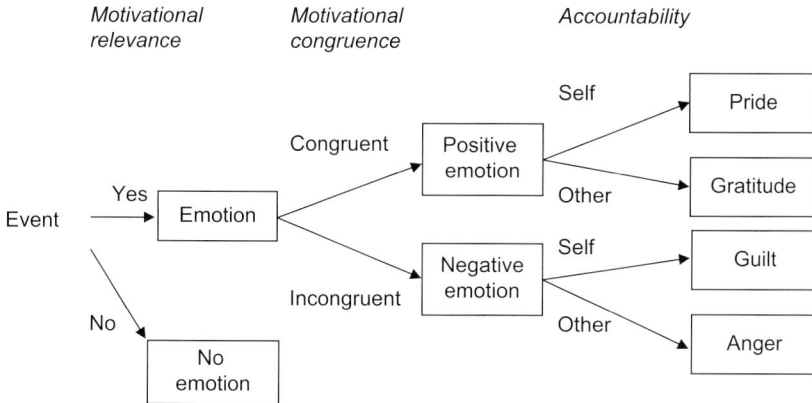

Figure 1.3 Appraisals characterising four different emotions according to Smith and Lazarus's (1993) model (Parkinson, 2018, with permission from Wiley)

computed bit by bit, or registered explicitly. Any conscious or unconscious process that produces the holistic meaning (or 'core relational theme') of 'other-blame' automatically activates anger. Indeed, according to Smith and Lazarus, the emotion cannot be activated in any other way: anger *always* depends on first arriving at the other-blame appraisal pattern. Correspondingly, arriving at this appraisal pattern *always* leads to anger.

Given such tight interdependence between appraisal and emotion, we might start to wonder whether the core relational theme genuinely reflects a separable appraisal pattern preceding emotion's onset, or simply the relational meaning of an emotion that is already underway (e.g., Parkinson, 1997; 2001a). Perhaps the sense of other-blame is so tightly intertwined with the sense of being angry that the two things cannot realistically be disentangled. Leaving aside the question of whether appraisal causes or characterises emotions, most appraisal theories agree that distinctive patterns of appraisal are directly associated with different emotions.

However, the evidence for emotion-defining appraisal signatures is far from perfect. Appraisal reports certainly differ across different kinds of recalled (e.g., Smith & Ellsworth, 1985), imagined (e.g., Smith & Lazarus, 1993; and see Parkinson & Manstead, 1993), reported (e.g., Smith & Ellsworth, 1987) and experimentally manipulated (e.g., Roseman & Evdokas, 2004) emotion. However, prediction of emotional quality based only on appraisals leaves a substantial amount of variance unexplained.

There is also evidence that the same emotion is not always associated with the same profile of reported appraisals (Nezlek et al., 2008; Parkinson, 1999; Parkinson & Illingworth, 2009; Parkinson, Roper & Simons, 2008). For example, anger does not seem to involve reported other-blame across all situations or for all people (Kuppens et al., 2003). Of course, this apparent inconsistency in appraisal pattern might simply reflect the fact that self-report measures of appraisal do not perfectly capture underlying appraisal processes, which may often operate at an unconscious level. Perhaps people always direct blame externally when they get angry but aren't always aware of it. However, appraisal researchers have yet to validate viable methods for assessing people's appraisals without directly asking them about their experience, making it difficult to substantiate this kind of claim. Indeed, how would we be able to tell that someone was making an unconscious other-blame appraisal except by assessing their angry orientation to events?

Do Appraisals Cause Emotions?

No single event has precisely the same emotional effects on all people regardless of context. For example, a wild bear may be exciting for a hunter, but frightening for a picnicker. One of the main selling points of appraisal theory is that it can account for this variability in emotional effects (e.g., Roseman & Smith, 2001). Instead of explaining the nature of the emotional reaction in terms of the event's intrinsic characteristics, appraisal researchers focus on how the event relates to the person's current concerns (Frijda, 1986), how it helps them get where they are trying to go, or hinders their progress.

But does the relation between events and personal concerns need to be appraised by the individual's mental system before an emotion can be activated? Does emotion's apparent dependence on relational considerations mean that people need to decode those considerations in order to become emotional?

No-one disputes that this sometimes happens. There are clearly occasions when information about an experienced outcome is evaluated and interpreted before any emotional consequences take hold. For example, we may only get angry when we finally work out that someone's apparently offhand remark was in fact a disguised insult, or only start to feel afraid after appreciating further potential consequences of an impending event. But do appraisals mediate all effects of perceived events on emotions in all cases and under all circumstances?

The answer partly depends on what we mean by 'appraisal' and what we mean by 'emotion' (Leventhal & Scherer, 1987; Parkinson & Manstead, 1992). If the defining characteristic of emotion is a recognition that what is happening is personally significant, then clearly the cause of emotion must be something that gets us to that point of recognition. And if any process that gets us to that point counts as 'appraisal', then appraisal becomes a *sine qua non* for emotion. You simply can't have that kind of 'emotion' without that kind of 'appraisal'.

Lazarus's (1984) claim that emotion necessarily depends on prior appraisal rests on exactly this kind of argument. He wrote that 'cognitive activity is a necessary pre-condition of emotion because to experience an emotion, people must comprehend – whether in the form of a primitive evaluative perception or a highly differentiated symbolic process – that their well-being is implicated in a transaction, for better or worse' (p. 124). Note that Lazarus does not propose that a *particular* kind of process is necessary for emotion, but that any of a range of possible processes can do the job equally well, as long as it leads to the conclusion that what is happening is personally significant. And if it does, that process qualifies as 'appraisal' precisely for that reason. In other words, 'it is meaning that counts in emotion, not how that meaning is achieved' (Lazarus, 1991a, p. 160). The specific kind of meaning required for emotion is one that involves implications for personal well-being, and appraisal necessarily produces that meaning. If the correct kind of meaning is not achieved by the process, the response does not count as an emotion. From inside this circle, it is logically impossible to get an 'emotion' as defined without an 'appraisal' as defined (Zajonc, 1984). Appraisal becomes such an elastic concept (cf. Scarantino, 2010) that it can be stretched or squeezed to fill or fit into any gap between an eliciting event and the supposed emotional response to it (Parkinson, 1995; Parkinson & Manstead, 1992). And that response is emotional precisely because it involves the kind of meaning that only appraisal can produce.

Not all appraisal theorists take the view that appraisals are the exclusive causes of all emotions. Many acknowledge that emotions or components of emotion can also be induced by other means, including taking drugs or getting tired (Roseman & Smith, 2001). Critics of appraisal theory are even more sceptical about appraisal's causal priority. For example, Zajonc (1980) argued that seeing emotion as the output of an information-processing sequence involving prior appraisal gets things back to front because emotional reactions change our appraisals rather than vice versa.

In response to critiques such as this, Lazarus (1991b) conceded that appraisals can be constituents and consequences of emotion as well as causes. In his view, appraisals lead to emotions that not only include those appraisals but also influence subsequent appraisals. However, he continued to argue that no emotion begins without a prior appraisal. In his view, even effects of drugs on emotion depend on the appraisal changes they induce. Pharmacological agents can make you perceive, interpret or evaluate the world in different ways. According to Lazarus, this is how they affect your subsequent experience. But how can we tell whether a drug produces changes in appraisal before it produces changes in emotion? How can we substantiate appraisal's supposed mediating role?

In the absence of definite criteria specifying precisely when an emotion begins, it is difficult to imagine any evidence that could directly support Lazarus's claims about appraisal's causal priority. How could we ever zero in on the exact moment between the onset of an emotional stimulus and the activation of the emotional response to it? Lazarus implies that in that instant there must be an appraisal that is not already tinged with the emotion it is about to activate. But how could we catch that nascent appraisal before the emotion takes over? In everyday emotional episodes, things rarely, if ever, unfold in such clear and separable stages (e.g., Ellsworth, 2013).

Cumulative Appraisal

Let's suppose that we can break down an emotional episode into a series of stimuli. Each successive stimulus simply adds to the cumulative effect of previous stimuli that have already put the system into a state of emotional readiness. The last straw may break the camel's back but only because of the extra pressure it adds to the weight of preceding straws. Our emotional response consolidates bit by bit as we make adjustments to small changes that happen in sequence.

In cases such as this, there is no need to generate an integrated appraisal at the putative instant immediately before experience transitions into emotional experience. There is no one-step transformative process that adds emotional heat to our cold perception of an object, but rather an accumulation of lower-level adjustments. At no point in such a process do we need to ask ourselves abstract questions such as: 'Does this situation affect me personally?' (motivational relevance: Lazarus & Folkman, 1984, p. 23) in order to work out whether to respond emotionally. Nor do we need to wonder 'What if anything can I do in this encounter, and how will what I do and what is going to happen affect my well-being?' (secondary appraisal: Lazarus, 1991a, p. 134) in order to determine what particular emotion should be selected. These are not questions that directly concern us at the time. Indeed, we often neither know nor care about their answers when in the throes of an emotionally engaging episode.

Scherer's (e.g., 2001) version of appraisal theory provides a more dynamic and temporally articulated account of the processes leading to the consolidation of emotional orientations. In his view, appraisal operates as a cumulative series of rapidly cycling stimulus evaluation checks that detect events requiring emotional response. Thus, the appraisal system makes successive sweeps of the environment like a radar system designed to detect potential sources of pain or pleasure on the horizon. First, the mental apparatus checks whether anything novel is happening, then whether it is intrinsically pleasant, then whether it is conducive with current goals and compatible with norms, and so on.

Rather than assuming that appraisal coordinates patterned emotional response all in one go, Scherer argues that the different components of the response are separately activated by each successive stimulus check. For example, as soon as novelty is detected, attention is alerted to the novel event, and the autonomic system generates appropriate activation preparing the body to respond. These changes occur before the overall relational meaning of what is happening has been computed. Bit by bit the separate responses coalesce into a coherent, coordinated emotion as the transaction unfolds.

Despite Scherer's appreciation of the cumulative nature of developing emotional orientations, his alternative formulation of the appraisal process is still not fully attuned to the dynamic content of unfolding emotional transactions. Stimulus evaluation checks run cyclically in a fixed sequence rather than operating in parallel or coming online flexibly as the situation unfolds. Further, the information they extract is at a similarly abstract level to less dynamic theories (e.g., Roseman, 1979). From either perspective, appraisal orients to generic concerns such as novelty, evaluation, coping potential and norm compatibility rather than the specific practical matters that confront people in everyday situations. This means that micro-adjustments to local circumstances remain partly unexplained. Like core relational themes, stimulus evaluation checks can get the system into a strategic mode of action readiness appropriate for dealing with generic challenges or threats, but cannot specify the precise tactics required in any particular emotional situation. For example, an emergent appraisal of uncertain threat prepares you for escape, but the manner of that escape, and the associated vigilant attentiveness depend on whether a bear is chasing you, a lover is about to leave you or you are struggling to answer an essay question in a decisive written examination. In each of these cases, your specific emotional orientation builds up in attunement to specific changing circumstances as the situation approaches the point where the emotion consolidates. The detection of novelty, motivational congruence and so on may well contribute to your present state of action readiness but does not allow you to address the more concrete concerns that need addressing. For that, you need a more grounded and flexible mode of dynamic sensitivity.

Distributed Appraisal

Lazarus's (1984) theory specifies a spatial as well as temporal location for appraisal. Emotional meaning is seen as a mental conclusion about personal significance, something that takes place inside the skull. It is as if the relational considerations producing emotional consequences somehow need translating into something intrapsychic before emotion can be produced. If the events leading to emotion happen outside and the emotional reaction happens inside, then a process that converts the outer to the inner seems to be required. And the obvious place to look for it is within an individual person's mind.

Elsewhere, Lazarus (1991a) acknowledges that emotions emerge from transactions between the person and the environment rather than being elicited by any purely external cause. It is not events themselves that get appraised but rather their relation to whatever we are doing at the time. It's not seeing the diamond in our hand that makes us happy, but the sense of having managed to grab hold of it. It's not seeing it fall away into the abyss that prompts disappointment or despair but the fact that it slipped from our grip. Correspondingly, emotional 'reactions' to relational events such as these are not purely subjective states, but modes of event-oriented action readiness. We clasp the diamond protectively, or prise ourselves away from fruitless attempts to retrieve it. Why then do we need to funnel relational events through a localised private appraisal process in order to generate this kind of attuned relational activity? Why must we draw private conclusions about our relation to the environment and the other people in it before our orientation counts as an emotion?

Because emotions focus on specific objects, we tend to see them as reactions prompted by those objects. And because the objects taken alone cannot determine the nature of our emotional reaction, it seems as if something that determines their relational significance must intervene between stimulus and response. Thus, appraisal theory postulates a mental process that computes relational meaning and then outputs an emotional reaction. But maybe personal significance is already specified by our active orientation to the emotional object. Perhaps we don't need to register meaning at all in order to have a meaningful emotional orientation to what is happening. Indeed, meaning might even be an effect rather than cause of becoming emotional. It may get picked up by someone other than the person who is emotional. Or it may never get picked up at all.

From this perspective, the low-level responses that accumulate as emotions develop are not primarily constituents of appraised meaning, but instead practically oriented operations that make a material difference to what is happening. Many emotions emerge gradually in attunement with the changing pressures and openings presented by the thing at which action is directed. Let's say that I am tying a shoelace that gets tangled into an ever-tightening knot. My tugging hands and prising fingernails meet increasing resistance as the strands tighten and refuse to come loose. At some point my frustration may turn to anger. But what is the specific stimulus for this response? Do I have to conclude implicitly that the lace is to blame for my struggle before I can get angry with it? Or are the anger and the blame both part and parcel of my escalating struggle against increasingly recalcitrant or intractable forces?

Developing emotions orient to social as well as practical actions. When an emotional episode involves other people, those people's orientations feed into the consolidating emotion too. Your changing activities can guide my attention and shape my evaluation of what is happening. Your worried glance at the clock may convey urgency without me having to make the related appraisal on my own. In other words, any emotion-shaping appraisal processes may be distributed not only between the person and environment but also between the different people on the scene (Parkinson, 1996; 2001a; and see Griffiths & Scarantino, 2009; Hutchins, 1995). Emotional orientations can consolidate and meanings emerge as a function of interpersonal interaction and negotiation as well as private sense-making.

Relational Activity

Although Arnold (1960) emphasised the importance of appraisal in determining the emotional quality of perceptions of the world, she saw emotions themselves as distinctive forms of action readiness rather than merely mental orientations. Indeed, the central point of appraisal in many appraisal theories is to prepare the person for dealing with the appraised situation, and to get the body ready for whatever kind of action may be necessary. According to Arnold, appraisals immediately and automatically prompt externally directed states of action readiness, that poise the individual physically and mentally to do certain things to, with or against the things they are emotional about. The resulting sense of attraction or repulsion involves a disposition to behave in a certain way towards the emotion's object rather than a more detached evaluation and interpretation. In other words, an emotion is a physically embodied stance or orientation and not simply a mental state.

For example, when angry with someone, we direct blame at that person with the aim of stopping them doing whatever blameworthy thing they are doing. In some circumstances, this may even involve squaring up for a fight, and getting ready for physical attack. And adopting such a stance can have powerful effects on how the other person is likely to react, which often make fighting unnecessary after all (see Chapters 3 and 9). Simply showing that you are ready to retaliate may sometimes be enough to deter further misbehaviour. Action preparation can serve communicative as well as practical functions.

An important implication is that emotion is not just something that goes on inside a person but instead involves the relation between a person and the object of the emotion. Anger focuses us on an obstacle or insult and gets us ready to attack or push it away. Fear makes us vigilant, cowering, and avoidant. In both cases, the emotion operates across any boundary between the person and object rather than simply at one side of it.

Practical Relations

Extending Arnold's version of appraisal theory, Frijda (1986) explicitly argued that emotion is a form of relational activity 'that establishes or modifies a relationship between the subject and some object or the environment at large' (p. 13), and that is manifested in 'the manner in which the subject positions himself with respect to the environment' (p. 24). Like Arnold, Frijda believed that each distinct emotion is characterised by a distinctive mode of action readiness, specifying the person's relation to the surrounding situation.

Action readiness modes do not dictate particular behavioural responses to emotional situations. For example, the body's specific preparation for angry attack (and the associated autonomic profile) may take different forms depending on the particular object and context. No single set of muscles is poised or tensed across all situations. Indeed, anger may involve preparation for punching someone during a physical confrontation, hitting a ball at them hard during a tennis match or saying something insulting or sarcastic in a conversation. What is important is the common function served by these very different movements (equipotentiality: Campos, Frankel & Camras, 2004).

The flexibility of action readiness also implies responsivity to changing circumstances. When pushing against something, increasing resistance will be met by escalated effort. Similarly, when a readied action is directed at another person, its specific manifestations may also change depending on that person's unfolding responses. For instance, if an antagonist squares up to you physically in response to your sarcastic comment, pursuing the angry agenda is likely to involve shifting from verbal to more physical resistance. In other words, the specific behaviour that is prepared is partly determined by changing relations between people rather than by either individual in isolation.

The dynamic context-sensitivity of action readiness explains not only why autonomic patterning is inconsistent across instances of the same emotion (e.g., Stemmler et al., 2001) but also why appraisal patterns can vary too (e.g., Nezlek et al., 2008; Parkinson, 1999). What gives an emotion its identity is not how the individual is evaluating and interpreting what is happening, but how their actions and communications are oriented to unfolding events. We don't need to blame someone else for getting in the way of what we are doing in order to push against the particular blockage that they are presenting (Frijda, 1993).

Frijda's (1986) relational approach allows us to distinguish the motivations associated with different emotions, but what about their distinctive subjective aspects? Do those also depend on patterns of relational activity? When we think about our own emotions, it often seems that the internal symptoms take priority over any connections with what is going on outside. But perhaps this is precisely because we are trying to abstract our emotional response from its relational basis (like James, 1884, in his famous thought experiment). Perhaps it is because we are applying our attention to how our emotion feels to us internally rather than what it feels like when we are emotionally oriented to ongoing events.

In the heat of the moment, our conscious experience is more likely to focus on the object of our emotion than on how our mind and body are reacting to it. When angry, our anger is often not what directly commands our attention. Instead, our thoughts and perceptions are fully occupied by the other person's annoying or insulting behaviour towards us (Frijda, 2005; Lambie & Marcel, 2002). We may not be aware of our bodily responses or even that we are experiencing any particular emotion at the time. If anywhere, the emotional experience spans any divide between us and whatever is happening to us. It consists of the embodied sense of being ready to act on some object or event that is perceived as emotionally charged. In Frijda's (2005) words, 'such emotion experience is best characterised as a perception of a meaningful world that is filled with calls for action' (p. 474).

Interpersonal Relations

De Rivera's (1977) structural theory differentiates emotions on the basis of relational activity operating between people, rather than between individuals and non-social objects. In his view, different emotions embody different social relationships rather than different experiential qualities or appraisal dimensions (see Figure 1.4). For example, de Rivera and Grinkis (1986) argue that anger should not be seen 'as a particular facial expression or as any particular set of instrumental behaviors, physiological responses or internal sensations, but as a particular social relationship between the angry person and a provocateur. The person who is angry *wants to remove* the challenge posed by the other's behaviour' (p. 352, emphasis in original).

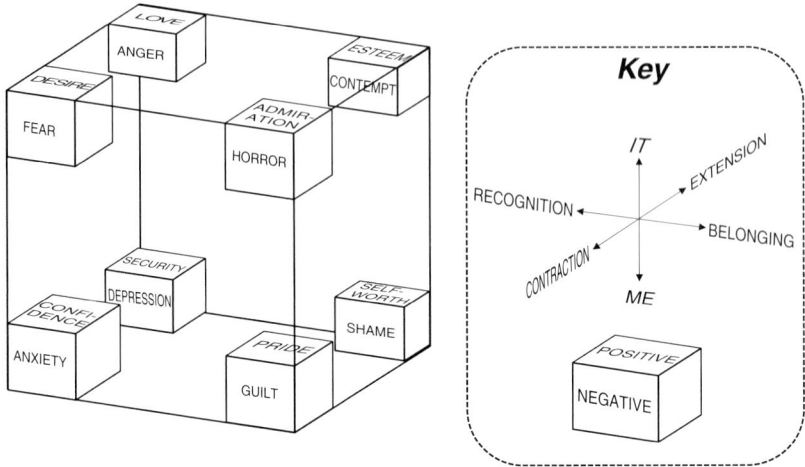

Figure 1.4 Distinguishing emotions on the basis of social-relational activity (de Rivera & Grinkis, 1986, reproduced with permission of Pergamon Press)

More generally, de Rivera argues that emotions involve attraction to, or repulsion from, other people or correspondingly their attraction to, or repulsion from, the self (extension vs. contraction in de Rivera's terms). The other is drawn towards or pushed away from the self, or the other draws the self towards them or pushes them away. Thus, anger is an other-directed repulsion emotion that involves pushing the other person away from the self, whereas shame is a self-directed contraction emotion that involves the other person pulling away from the self. Early in development, these relational movements may be literal displacements of the two bodies that are involved. However, approach and withdrawal can operate at a more abstract level in socialised adults. For example, distancing from someone else's intellectual position might involve the use of complicated sentences rather than physical separation.

Socialisation also allows us to shift our position in relation to people who are not physically present (see Chapter 9). We learn to anticipate or imagine how other people might orient to our actions and make corresponding emotional adjustments. For example, guilt may involve the expectation that someone else will recoil from us following a transgression. In other words, we may feel guilty not simply because we blame ourselves for what we have done to someone else, but also because we imagine the blame that they would direct at us were they to find out (Parkinson & Illingworth, 2009). As argued by de Rivera and Grinkis (1986, p. 367), 'in the case of any self-directed emotion, there is a corresponding other-directed emotion held by an implicit other'. Thus, another person does not need to be actually on the scene to be the target, object or cause of our emotional orientation.

In de Rivera's model, the relations that matter when distinguishing different forms of relational activity are relations between people. Rather than preparing a single individual to act on what is happening, emotions involve two or more people relating to each other. They operate between rather than within those individuals. But are all emotions distinctive forms of social-relational activity or only some? The next section addresses this question.

Non-social Emotion Objects

De Rivera proposes that emotions involve distinctive patterns of social relational activity, where people either get closer or move further from each other, reach out or pull back, offer something or take it away. These distinctions apply best to emotions that are oriented primarily at another person or what that person is doing. However, not all emotions work in this way. Can other less obviously social emotions also be characterised by distinctive relational patterns? Before answering this question, we need to think more about what makes an emotion a social emotion.

Some emotions focus directly on another person in relation to the self (e.g., love, hate, contempt and admiration) or on the self in relation to other people (pride, shame). Other emotions are oriented to what someone else has done and how it affects us (e.g., anger), or what we have done and how it affects them (guilt, embarrassment). These all clearly count as 'social' emotions (Hareli & Parkinson, 2008), because they concern other people in one of these four possible ways (they are directed at the other person, the other person's actions, the self or the self's own actions). In each case, the emotion's intentional object is something social.

Even these social emotions can sometimes take non-social objects. Many of us love or hate things other than people. We sometimes feel angry with resistant hardware (computers, cars) rather than humans, or guilty about things that affect no one but ourselves. However, all these cases seem to involve redirection of a primarily social emotion to a non-social object. Our ability to treat an object as if it were another person probably depends on prior experience of having the same emotion in genuinely social circumstances. Indeed, it seems unlikely that our earliest encounters with love, hate, anger or guilt involved purely private events.

So what about emotions whose primary object seems to be non-social? Many of our fears concern physical and practical dangers rather than social threats: spiders, snakes or precipices, for example. The things we most often find disgusting also lack any obvious interpersonal aspects.

Does that put emotions such as fear and disgust outside any classification based on social-relational considerations?

Even apparently non-social emotions can also take social objects. We can be disgusted by what someone does rather than by rotting food or dirty toilets (e.g., moral disgust: Tybur, Lieberman & Griskevicius, 2009). We can be awestruck by a person's achievements as well as dramatic landscapes (e.g., Keltner & Haidt, 2003). And we can certainly be afraid of other people and what they might do or think as much as wild animals or vertiginous precipices (e.g., Leary, 1983). The question then is which instances of these emotions take primacy when deciding how to classify and distinguish them. Is fear a primarily non-social emotion with some secondary social instances or is it primarily a social emotion that is often directed at non-social objects?

One consideration is whether these emotions start out as non-social emotions that subsequently take social objects. Many theorists believe that human beings are genetically predisposed to respond (or to learn to respond) to potentially dangerous objects with fear (e.g., Öhman, Eriksson & Olofsson, 1975) and to possible sources of biological contamination with disgust (e.g., Rozin & Fallon, 1987). If so, the primary instances of these emotions need not involve social-relational activity.

But even if our earliest experiences of fear, disgust or any other kinds of emotion are directed at non-social objects, the close availability of a caregiver to help deal with the emotion-provoking situation already adds a social dimension. If the function of fear is to escape from a threatening object, this function cannot easily be served by activating internal responses that prepare the infant's mind and body to run away or hide. At early stages of development, neither of these escape strategies can be implemented without social assistance. It is far more effective for the infant to signal the danger to any adult who is nearby, someone who is in a better position to provide an effective solution.

The more general point here is that emotions need not be directed at social objects to involve characteristic patterns of social-relational activity. Many emotions function to change other people's relations towards objects (which may be either social or non-social) rather than to address those objects more directly. These triadic situations are discussed further in the next section.

Communicating Relational Information

An individual's object-directed relational stance affects other people who are around to see or feel it, even if those other people are not the direct object of the emotion. For example, it is difficult to take a detached perspective when witnessing a heated argument between friends. You usually want to take sides or find an appeasing middle ground. Similarly, if someone's eyes keep darting to the door whenever there is a sound of movement outside, it is difficult not to pick up a sense of impending threat, and to direct your own attention to the same place. These examples are central to the topic of this book. They show how your emotions can affect other people even when those people are not the direct focus of your emotion. Emotions align relations not only with other people at whom they are directed, but also with other people who may come to share or contest your own orientation to what is happening.

One of the clearest cases of this kind of social-relational activity is the phenomenon known as social referencing (e.g., Klinnert et al., 1983). At around the age of twelve months, toddlers' attentional capacities and representational abilities broaden significantly. They begin to focus not only on other people and objects as separate entities but also on the relations between people and objects in the shared environment. This allows toddlers to learn from other people's orientations to objects, including their emotional orientations. Indeed, toddlers actively seek out this kind of relational information when unsure about how to make sense of what is happening.

The classic demonstration of social referencing is Sorce and colleagues' (1985) experiment. Each toddler taking part was separated from an attractive toy by a vertical precipice covered by thick glass (visual cliff). The floor in front of them suddenly became visibly lower. The precipice was not deep enough to scare the toddler off completely, but also not shallow enough to be ignored. From the other side, the toddler's mother either smiled back or showed a fear face. All of the toddlers crossed the cliff towards their mother when she smiled, but very few ventured out across the glass when confronted by their mother's fear expression. Thus, the mother's apparent emotion changed the toddler's orientation to the visual cliff, making them more or less willing to crawl onto it. When she expressed fear, the toddler decided at some level that moving forward was too dangerous to risk.

In social referencing, both parties to the exchange share compatible orientations to what is happening. The mother has the toddler's best interests at heart and the toddler implicitly appreciates that fact. They cooperate with each other in the process of calibrating their perspectives. In other cases, the nonverbal negotiations leading to emotional influence may involve greater levels of conflict and different orientations to the same event (see Chapter 4). This may lead to divergence as well as convergence of object-directed emotions.

Do emotions that are oriented to non-social objects only become social following the onset of social referencing? That seems unlikely given that caregivers constitute such an important part of the environment within which infants operate from birth onwards. In fact, caregivers specifically attune their behaviour to the sensitivities of babies with whom they interact, producing exaggerated facial expressions (e.g., Gergely & Watson, 1996) and highly salient gestures ('motionese': Brand, Baldwin & Ashburn, 2002), speaking in sing-song tones ('motherese': e.g., Ferguson, 1977), and co-ordinating movements and vocalisations with the activities of those under their charge (e.g., Stern et al., 1985). They make events more directly meaningful to infants by responding to them in distinctive ways.

Parents and guardians also encourage certain kinds of relational orientation and discourage others using smiles, hugs and other means of social reinforcement that are appropriately timed to capitalise on infants' engagement. In a sense, then, emotion-related object orientations have a social component long before children learn to coordinate their attention interpersonally or engage in joint action. The development of social referencing is just another step on the road to their subsequent articulation as other-oriented communications (see Chapter 9).

Calibration of object orientations need not involve explicit social referencing processes when adults interact with other adults either (Parkinson, 2019). Instead of an exchange of nonverbal information where clarification is sought by one party and provided by the other, mutual influence may involve more direct adjustments to the two parties' respective orientations that develop cumulatively between them. The various communicative and practical processes whereby two people's emotions can become aligned or misaligned are considered in more detail in later chapters.

Characterising Emotions

This chapter has considered a number of factors that might account for the distinctive qualities of emotions, including interoceptive perceptions, appraisals and practical or social relational activity. I have argued that attributing emotional quality to either bodily feelings or our interpretations of them underestimates the impact of the relational context of emotion. Appraisal theories represent a positive step forward because they acknowledge that emotions depend on relations between persons and objects including social objects. However, they still tend to localise emotion and its causes within the individual, locked away somewhere in a single person's mind, instead of operating across boundaries between people and unfolding environmental events.

This book presents the case that emotions are oriented to their social consequences and serve social functions. Some social emotions directly align relations with other people. Other non-social emotions can align two or more people's relations with objects in the shared environment, including other people. In all these cases, emotions constitute a means of social influence. This does not mean that people usually adopt emotional orientations voluntarily and deliberately in order to produce interpersonal effects. On many occasions, emotional orientations are instead pieced together over time by cumulative low-level adjustments to what is happening. However, emotions are not simple reactions to stimuli or momentary events in either of these cases. They are positions taken in relation to other positions (cf. Billig, 1987), oriented to anticipated consequences as much as to the immediate eliciting situation.

In trying to get to the heart of emotion, researchers often look for special ingredients inside the mind or body of the individual. But the essential features of the phenomenon may lie elsewhere, in the relational activities people perform together or against each other, or in the ways that they present and represent their experiences to one another. In subsequent chapters, I will explore the consequences of adopting this kind of social orientation to emotional episodes.

Conceptual Differences

Throughout this chapter, I have tried to pin down the basis for differences between emotions. But are different emotions really different in the first place? This might sound like a stupid question. After all, we can easily distinguish cases of anger from cases of joy or embarrassment. Surely we don't need to worry about whether it makes sense to contrast what it is like when we feel like hitting someone from when we want to hug them.

However, when we distinguish anger from fear, joy or embarrassment, we are applying English-language concepts that may not perfectly capture the nature of the psychological realities they are supposed to represent. People who have learned to use different languages might divide up the emotional world in different ways (Parkinson, Fischer & Manstead, 2005). The emotions that seem obviously different to us might not be the same as those that seem different to them. This raises a further possibility that one of the bases for emotional differences is conceptual rather empirical, something to do with our representation of things, rather than the internal, external or relational things we are representing (e.g., Barrett, 2017).

Pursuing this possibility, some emotion theorists are sceptical about whether words such as 'anger' and 'fear' really refer to distinct objects, states, processes or events at all. They argue that the apparently clear differences between different emotions partly reflect the fact that we put our experiences into different conceptual boxes (e.g., Russell, 2003). For this reason, the emotion names I have used in this chapter should be seen as provisional placeholders rather than precise labels for conceptually rigorous descriptive concepts. Exactly how the language of emotions refers to psychological phenomena and performs other psychological functions is the topic of the next chapter.

CHAPTER 2

Words and Concepts

This chapter focuses on how emotions are expressed, enacted and communicated in language. Although words such as 'anger', 'joy' and 'fear' sound like names for precisely defined psychological objects, their exact descriptive meaning is hard to pin down. Disagreements about which words count as emotion names are common both within and across societies, with language encoding emotional events in different ways depending on circumstances. Emotion words also serve a range of pragmatic and performative functions in conversations and arguments. They can convey blame or assign credit, and establish, maintain or break social connections as well as merely describe personal experience. No all-purpose representational system seems capable of explaining this diversity. Indeed, the main purpose of emotional language may be to facilitate various forms of social influence rather than merely to codify emotional distinctions relating to personal experience.

Putting emotions into words is not always easy. Language can seem inadequate to the subtlety of an internal twinge or the enormity of a personal upheaval. Perhaps painting, composing music or performing an interpretive dance would be a more effective way of communicating what we really mean. Or maybe the problem is that we are mistaken about what it is that we are supposed to be representing when we try to represent emotions.

If emotions are things happening deep inside us, in a realm that is inaccessible to others, then the task of communication seems to involve dredging those things up and bringing them out in the open for all to see. Does that mean that we need to detail the changing chemical concentrations of neurotransmitters in the dark corners of our nervous system, or specify exactly what might be tugging at our guts to make them wrench in that peculiar way? Or should we try to document exactly how our perception of what is happening around us is somehow coloured with a different tinge or taint?

There are so many literal and metaphorical ways of describing what goes on when we get emotional that it is unsurprising that we can't always decide which is most appropriate. But do any of them fully capture what we really want to convey? Or are the shifts, tremors and landslides in our dealings with the social and practical world where the real emotional action happens? Is talking emotionally actually just another of the ways of aligning relations with other people? This chapter considers how emotional language is used to represent, communicate and construct emotions. The goal is to understand one of the ways in which emotions can affect other people, namely by being conveyed in language.

Naming Private Objects

This chapter is not about emotions, at least not directly. It is about the ways that emotions are represented in words and concepts. Writing about these words and concepts involves lots of quotation marks. The topic is 'anger' or 'fear' rather than whatever those words refer to in the psychological world. Keeping this distinction in mind is likely to prove tricky. Words often make little sense unless we can relate them to the things they are supposed to represent.

So why even bother trying to separate them? If emotional language provides direct access to our inner world, then studying its operation is just another way of studying emotional phenomena. Readers who find this point of view appealing may simply decide to skip this otherwise unsettling chapter.

Although this short cut might seem attractive, it ignores two crucial points. First, emotions may not be the kinds of thing that easily translate into words and concepts. They might be too diffuse, messy or difficult to pin down. Second, the concepts associated with many kinds of words, including emotion words, don't always specify precise objects or classes of objects either. Having a word for something doesn't always mean that there is a definite something corresponding to that word.

Some things seem eminently nameable. Their distinctive form or appearance provides a clear basis for applying a categorical representation, allowing us to say that they are one kind of thing rather than another. Imagine looking into a room containing a variety of differently coloured geometric shapes. The red ones are distinctively red rather than orange, pink or crimson. The square ones have perfect right angles and sides that are exactly equal in length. To describe these objects, we can simply pick out their characteristic features using words whose meanings we already understand. And if all the square objects in the room are red, we might come up with a new word that captures the fact that their shape and colour go together (e.g., 'squed' or 'rare'). It's appealing to think that emotion concepts work just like that, identifying the distinctive characteristics of mental rather than physical objects. Then, we could just look into the internal room of our mind and pick out the separable objects that are inside.

From this perspective, representation and reality match perfectly, so thinking about either carries direct implications for the other. Our concept of 'anger' would mean exactly what that concept refers to, just as 'squed' means a red square. More generally, emotion words would have precise agreed meanings that perfectly capture the emotions that they describe. The lines on our conceptual maps would run along actual divisions between distinct territories in the real world, carving nature at its joints. Why then doesn't the story simply end there, tied up with a neat bow?

But is looking into our minds at subjectively experienced emotions really the same as looking into a physical room containing objects laid out for public inspection? Do the things inside actually have distinctive properties that can potentially be calibrated or measured? What if they are murky and hard to distinguish? What if the door is closed or the window misted up?

Wittgenstein (1953) came up with a neat analogy for the problem of naming purely internal experiences such as putatively private emotions. His thought experiment was a little like our earlier idea of looking into a room containing colourful geometric shapes. But if there is a doorway or window, other people can look through it too, undermining the analogy with a private mental location. And if we can see that the objects are square or red, then their characteristics are already things we agree about rather than purely subjective features. Wittgenstein's analogy therefore imagines a guessing game in which everyone has their own matchbox which only they can look inside. The point of the game is to work out whether everyone else has the same thing inside their box. However, the rules specify that you are not allowed to look inside anyone else's box. Otherwise what's in the box would not really be private in the first place. And for similar reasons, you are not allowed to take the secret object out of your own box and show it to anyone else.

The first thing you might do when playing this game is look inside your matchbox to see what's there. This sounds simple enough, but how do you then tell what it is? It may seem that you can identify the contents just by inspecting them. But whatever's inside has no name yet. There are no definite characteristics that might be detailed or classified. You cannot take the contents out to compare them with the contents of other people's boxes. You cannot measure whatever is inside, determine what colour it might be, or sketch an outline of its shape, because that involves getting it out of the box and inspecting it in the light of day, applying the established procedures for putting something into a familiar category.

Wittgenstein (1953) used another analogy to clarify the nature of this problem: 'Imagine someone saying: "but I know how tall I am!" and laying his hand on top of his head to prove it' (p. 96). Saying 'I'm *this* tall' means nothing unless you can point to the right place on the tape measure. Similarly, you might perform a mental act of pointing at whatever is in the matchbox and say something like 'it's *this* thing!' But that means nothing unless you can show the thing you have in mind to someone who can check it against other objects (or pictures or descriptions of them). At minimum, they need something that tells them what it ought to look like.

Let's say that the thing inside the matchbox is actually a beetle. Let's say that everyone else has a beetle too. But could anybody know they had a 'beetle' just by looking into their own box. Could they ever work out that anyone else had a beetle too? No direct comparison between the beetles in different boxes is possible. Everybody's beetle seems to be a thoroughly secret beetle with no determinable features. No one has any way of knowing whether other players have anything similar.

Could this kind of private object ever be pinned down for the purpose of attaching a name? You might imagine that you could at least recognise the beetle next time you played the game, offering the possibility of a private language. The first time you see the thing in the box, you might say to yourself something like: '*I'm* going to call this a "beetle" even if no-one else understands what that word means'. But how would you know it was the same beetle (or even the same anything) next time you looked? What criteria could you use for determining whether it corresponds to what it seemed to be the last time? Seeming familiar is never going to be enough. Familiarity doesn't match recognition to whatever you think you are recognising or the time and place it was last encountered. Words can't get any footing or purchase under these conditions.

The general point here is that descriptive language doesn't work without some externally available yardstick against which it can be measured, or another standard procedure for grounding meaning. Learning to call something a 'beetle' or 'anger' or 'confusion' depends on other people having access to criteria for establishing that the description correctly applies. If everyone spoke in terms that only they personally understood, then no meaning could ever crystallise or come across. And that means that even private meaning would be effectively meaningless in the first place.

So what are the implications for emotion words? Wittgenstein's reasoning suggests that we cannot have worked out the meanings of 'anger', 'fear', or 'embarrassment' simply by looking into the private matchbox of our mind. The words cannot refer to *purely* subjective experiences. Using them consistently for communicative purposes requires shared access to their public manifestations. Perhaps then emotion words are calibrated to visible expressions or discernible patterns of relational activity. Perhaps the concepts develop to represent spatial displacements between people such as those identified by de Rivera (1977; see Chapter 1), the ways we pull away or press closer to someone or something.

Or perhaps we picked up emotional language during the process of learning how to conduct ourselves emotionally. Our caregivers may have helped channel our relational activity along lines suggested by existing cultural concepts, teaching us how to use the relevant words along the way. In either case, any criteria for application of the words must depend (at least partly) on what goes on in the social world, between people rather than only inside.

None of this means that there are no private aspects to the relational movements involved when people experience whatever the things that we call 'emotions' might be. The point is simply that these purely subjective considerations played no direct role in deciding whether or not the word fit the experience in the first place. In short, emotion words don't simply describe what goes on inside an individual's mind. That might be one of the things they do but only as a secondary consequence of other more primary relational functions.

Culture and History

If emotions were directly perceptible objects with distinctive characteristics, and emotion words simply described those objects, then we might expect people from different places and times to use similar words. After all, it would be useful for them to tell other people about those objects in the clearest possible terms. However, it turns out that emotion words are neither universal nor historically fixed. In fact, the English word 'emotion' was first used in the seventeenth century, only applied to mental states in the eighteenth century, and only crystallised around the contemporary psychological concept in the nineteenth century (Dixon, 2012). Obviously, English speakers had words for many of the phenomena that are now conceptualised as emotions long before then. But terms such as 'anger', 'happiness' and 'fear' previously fell under the headings of 'passions', 'sentiments' or 'affections' rather than the unified banner of 'emotion'.

Many other languages still have no single word corresponding to the emotion category, and some do not have any word for emotion at all. The anthropologist Lutz (1988) was unable to find a direct translation in the language spoken on Ifaluk, an atoll among the Caroline Islands north of Fiji in the Pacific Ocean. The closest general term was 'niferash' meaning (roughly) 'about our insides' but this included sensations and bad feelings resulting from illness alongside apparently emotional phenomena covered by words such as 'song' (roughly 'justifiable anger') and 'metagu' (roughly 'fear/anxiety'). There is also no non-technical term matching English-language 'emotion' in either Russian or German (Wierzbicka, 1999). Wierzbicka (1994) contends that even the French word 'émotion' does not cover conditions such as those described as 'tristesse' (roughly 'sadness') because they are not considered overwhelming enough to count as proper instances of the conceptual category.

Words used to denote distinct emotions in English often have no direct translations in other languages either. For example, Levy (1973) reports that Tahitians lack any concept of 'sadness'. Correspondingly, other languages name apparently emotional experiences using words that do not translate into English. Thus, Japanese people refer to the cosy sense of basking in quasi-parental dependency and tenderness as 'amae' (Morsbach & Tyler, 1986), and the Ifaluk language uses the word 'fago' to refer to caring states involving love, compassion and sadness, thus drawing equivalences that seem unusual to Anglo-Americans.

Emotion words can also go out of fashion and become forgotten. English medieval monks once talked of the morally reprehensible emotion of 'accidie' (Harré & Finlay-Jones, 1986), a slothful, enervating state of mind that makes people experience religious duties as a miserable chore. But they probably wouldn't have understood what it meant to be 'chipper', 'grossed out', 'hangry' or 'chilled'.

It is difficult to determine whether these idiosyncratic emotion terms genuinely refer to distinct emotions that people consistently experience. Languages might just as easily have names for experiences that happen to fall together without any inherent interconnections or shared essence (feeling 'post-conversational', 'oceanic' or 'eleven-o'-clockish', for instance; see also Barrett, 2006; Griffiths, 1997). And correspondingly, there might be 'real' emotions in the psychological world that are not named in any language, such as the uncomfortable sense of having failed to put in enough time or effort (see also Barrett, 2017). In either case, the availability of the word is not the decisive consideration in identifying a corresponding emotion.

The extensive literature on these and other cultural and historical differences would take us beyond the scope of the present book (see Parkinson, Fischer & Manstead, 2005, for a review). However, the central point is clear. There are alternative ways of drawing boundaries around the contested territory of emotion and alternative ways of dividing it up. At minimum, this means that words can't provide consistent criteria for making emotional distinctions across all humans. We should be careful about assuming that any word, English or not, directly picks out a corresponding universal object in the psychological world (Wierzbicka, 1994). Our words for things may mislead us about what those things are.

Conceptual Geography

When contemporary English speakers talk about emotions, they use a variety of words and phrases, some of which are more obviously metaphorical than others. We say we are 'over the moon', 'gutted' or 'on tenterhooks'. Or that we are 'elated', 'disappointed' or in a state of 'anxious expectation'. Some of these descriptions seem to have more similar meanings than others, but exactly how they match up and inter-relate is not always straightforward. Can we lump them together into a smaller number of categories or map out underlying dimensions representing their meaning?

In this section, I discuss two ways of mapping the conceptual territory of English-language 'emotion'. The first distinguishes categories of emotional meanings. The second looks for underlying dimensions that account for similarities and differences between those meanings.

Categories

Shaver and colleagues (1987) collected together 135 nouns that a sample of psychology students in the USA generally agreed named emotions. They then asked another group of 100 US students to sort cards showing the names of these emotions into separate piles on the basis of their similar meanings. One participant put all cards naming pleasant emotions into one pile and all cards naming unpleasant emotions into a second pile. Another participant used 64 separate piles. Despite this variability, there was some consistency in how people sorted the emotion terms, with many participants putting at least some of the same words together.

Similarity scores were computed by counting how many participants put each word in the same pile as each other word. Thus, any two words that every participant put together in a common pile received a similarity score of 100, and any two words that none of the participants put together received a similarity score of 0. Similarity scores for each possible pair of words were then subjected to a statistical procedure known as hierarchical cluster analysis, which brought together emotion words that participants most often had in the same piles as each other but kept apart those that participants most often had in different piles. The results therefore provide a representation of the categories used by the group of participants as a whole.

Cluster analysis identified six distinct categories, whose meanings were then checked by inspecting the words that they included and by looking at participants' own descriptions of card piles containing similar sets of words (see Figure 2.1). Shaver and colleagues

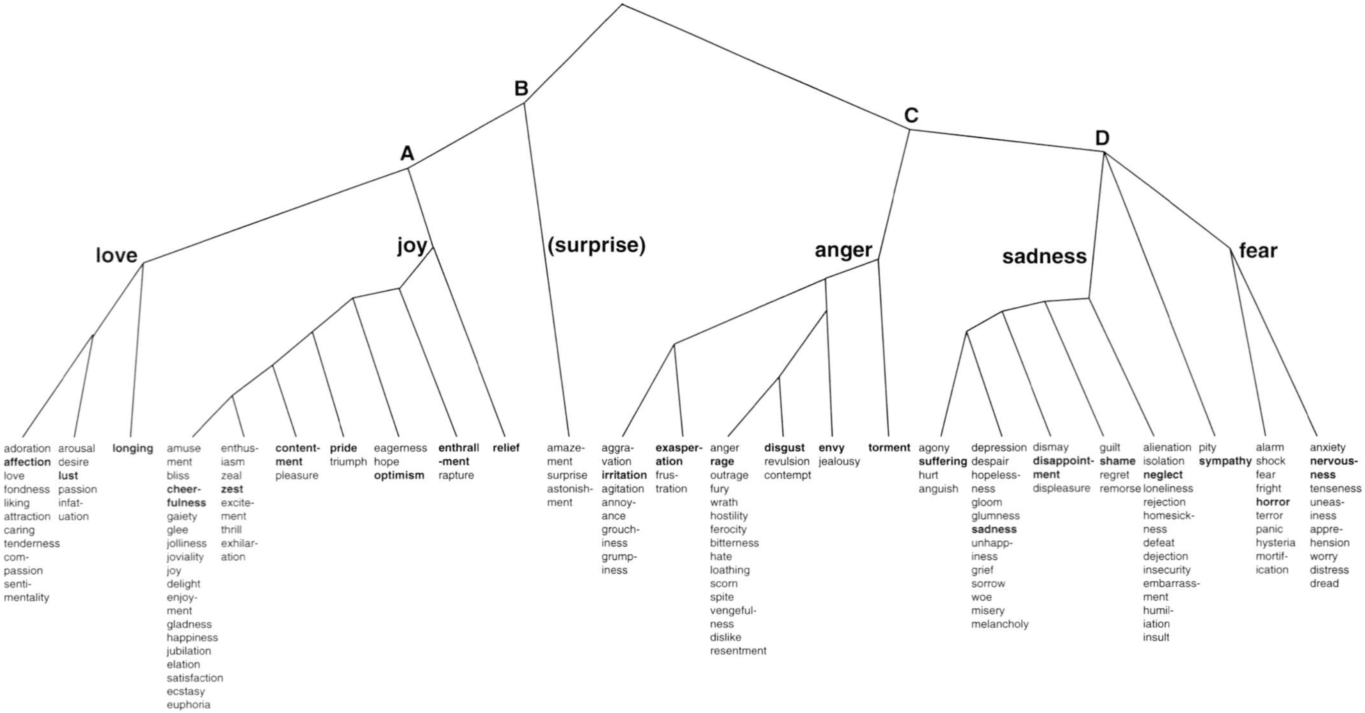

Figure 2.1 Hierarchical cluster analysis of emotion words (Shaver et al., 1987, reproduced with permission of the American Psychological Association)

concluded that the emotion clusters represented love, joy, surprise, anger, sadness and fear. However, the surprise cluster contained only the three words surprise, astonishment and amazement, none of which had been rated as definitely describing an emotion by a majority of participants in the earlier study. This uncertainty may depend on the fact that feeling 'surprise', unlike other things we call emotions, need not be either a pleasant or unpleasant experience (Ortony, Clore & Collins, 1988). Thus, the researchers were reluctant to include surprise as one of the key categories of emotional meaning, leaving only love, joy, anger, sadness and fear.

You might be tempted to conclude that these five groups of emotion names pick out corresponding mental states that people experience, and that five (and only five) basic kinds of emotion exist in the psychological world. However, that would be premature. What the results actually show is that these US students divided English words into these categories, and that differences between these emotion concepts generally made sense to them. This certainly tells us something about how these participants had learned to think about word-cued emotion concepts, and about how the English language represents them. But we should not conclude that people from all societies and using all languages think in exactly the same way (Shaver, Murdaya & Fraley, 2001). Indeed, inhabitants of Ifaluk atoll classified 'emotion' words from their language quite differently when performing a similar task (Lutz, 1982), making distinctions based on the situations in which the emotions were experienced rather than feelings associated with those situations. Whether either the Ifaluk or US conceptual system corresponds to the emotions actually experienced by members of each society is not a question that this kind of study could ever answer.

Dimensions

Shaver and colleagues (1987) identified emotion categories by directly instructing participants to put emotions into categories, and by analysing the resulting data in a way that specifically extracted a categorical structure. But the distinctions they uncovered were not absolute. There are overlapping similarities and differences between the emotions represented in the five clusters that are concealed by treating them as wholly separate categories. We can get some indication of these conceptual relations by looking at the results in more detail.

Cluster analysis works by an iterative process known as agglomeration. At the first stage, the computer program looks for the two most similar items. In Shaver and colleagues' study, this means identifying two words that participants put into the same pile as each other most often.

Let's say that almost everyone puts the card saying 'fear' in the same pile as the card saying 'fright'. This suggests that they see these words as having similar meanings, so cluster analysis puts them into the same initial cluster.

Next the program looks for two of the remaining words that participants put together most often and combines them into a second cluster. If it turns out that participants put a third word (say 'terror') together with the initial cluster of 'fear' and 'fright' more commonly than they put any two words together, then the program instead produces a three-item cluster at this second stage. The process of combining words into clusters, and clusters into larger clusters, continues step-by-step until all the words and clusters are combined into a single common cluster. You can see how the process progressed by working up from the bottom of the tree diagram shown in Figure 2.1.

Working back down from the final one-cluster stage, the penultimate stage tells us how the emotion words can be grouped into two clusters, the stage before that tells us how the emotion words can be divided into three clusters and so on. Shaver and colleagues' five-cluster representation therefore only applies to one stage of the analysis, chosen because it seemed to capture the most important similarities between emotional meanings without also ignoring important differences.

The investigators also acknowledged that other stages of the analysis produced meaningful emotion clusters. For example, along the bottom row of Figure 2.1 are twenty-five lower-level clusters of more differentiated emotions, and higher up the letters A, B, C and D correspond to clusters that Shaver and colleagues label 'joy', 'cheerfulness' and two kinds of 'sadness' respectively. Moving still higher, the top two branches of the tree diagram distinguish 'pleasant' and 'unpleasant' emotions.

The hierarchical representation thus contains information not only about distinct emotion categories but also about the relations between these categories. In particular, clusters that get combined sooner are more similar to one another than those that get combined later. The ones that get combined last of all are those perceived as most different ('pleasant' and 'unpleasant' emotion concepts). As a simple rule of thumb, emotions and emotion clusters that are furthest apart from each other horizontally at any of the vertical levels shown in Figure 2.1 are perceived as most different by participants.

Applying this reasoning to Shaver and colleagues' five clusters tells us that they differ in their relative similarity to one another. For example, 'fear' and 'anger' share the characteristic of unpleasantness, and so get combined at the penultimate stage of cluster analysis, but 'fear' and 'joy' don't share this characteristic, and therefore don't get combined until the final stage of the analysis (which puts all the emotion names together regardless of how participants sorted them). In other words, the cluster analysis results tell us that 'fear' is relatively more similar to 'anger' than to 'joy', and that this similarity relates to unpleasantness.

Unlike cluster analysis, some statistical procedures are designed to extract information about relations between items, objects or categories more directly. When Shaver and colleagues processed their data using one of these techniques (multidimensional scaling, or MDS), they found that the dimensions of pleasure and arousal provided an economical representation of the similarities and differences in emotional meanings identified by their participants. This suggests that the conceptual territory of emotion can be mapped by plotting the coordinates of each word in a two-dimensional space as well as by demarcating boundaries around clusters.

The pleasure–arousal representation of emotion has a long history in psychology (e.g., Abelson & Sermat, 1962; Averill, 1975; Block, 1957; Gladstones, 1962; Schlosberg, 1952; Wundt, 1897), but its most influential contemporary formulation was developed by Russell (e.g., 1978). Russell (1980) argued that emotion terms can be arranged in a circular representation known as a *circumplex* (see Figure 2.2), with their specific positions defined by the degree to which they are experienced as pleasant or unpleasant and the degree to which they involve high or low levels of arousal. Items that are opposite one another on the circle have maximally contrasting meanings as defined by these dimensions (e.g., 'happiness' and 'sadness' have opposite values on the pleasure dimension). Items close to each other share similar values on the two dimensions (e.g., 'fear' and 'anger' have similar scores on both pleasure and arousal). When Russell (1980) asked participants to arrange emotion words representing each octant around a circle, they mostly put them in the places predicted by the circumplex model. And when they didn't, they were more likely to put them in adjacent octants rather than in octants that were a full diameter apart. In other words, participants generally agreed about how the eight emotion concepts related to each other.

Do cultural differences in specific emotion concepts also apply to the dimensions of pleasure and arousal? Russell (1983) showed that English-speaking participants from a wide range of different countries rated the similarities between twenty-eight English emotion words in ways that generally fit the circumplex representation. Other studies have shown that pleasure and arousal dimensions capture important aspects of emotion representation in languages other than English too (e.g., Fontaine, Scherer & Soriano, 2013; Russell, Lewicka & Niit, 1989). However, Lutz (1982) argued that the inhabitants of Ifaluk atoll use different dimensions. Her multidimensional scaling of their card-sorting data revealed a primary 'evaluation' dimension that focused more on the situations associated with

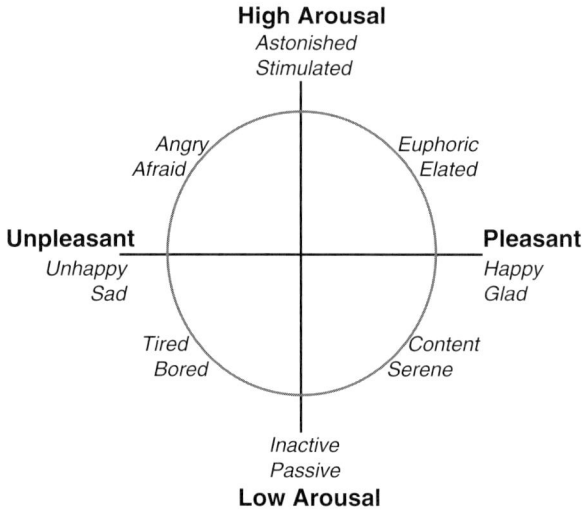

Figure 2.2 Circumplex model of affective meaning (adapted from Russell, 1980)

emotion concepts than the feelings those situations might induce. Words scoring high on this dimension related primarily to events that the person wanted to happen whereas those scoring low related to events they didn't want to happen. Perceptions of how good it felt during these events seemed secondary to this externally oriented meaning. Lutz's other MDS dimension concerned the extent to which the word related to events that put the person experiencing them in a strong or weak position (similar to the 'potency' dimension found in other studies, e.g., Averill, 1975; Osgood, Suci & Tannenbaum, 1957) rather than arousal.

Outside societies such as Ifaluk, why do pleasure and arousal feature so heavily in people's representations of emotional meaning? One influential answer is that they directly reflect underlying affective qualities, representing how emotions actually feel (e.g., Russell, 1978). However, another possibility is that they provide maximally flexible resources for making comparisons between different concepts. Indeed, Osgood, Suci and Tannenbaum's (1957) semantic differential studies extracted similar dimensions of evaluation and activity from participants' ratings of words such as 'nurse', 'success' and 'sincere'. Osgood (1962; 1969) argued that participants need to think metaphorically when dealing with the task of rating diverse objects along multiple scales, which often ask for judgements with little direct relevance to the practical meaning of the relevant concepts (e.g., how fair or unfair is 'music'? How hard or soft is 'defeat'?).

The only meaningful comparisons available to them are therefore based on emotional connotations. In other words, evaluation and activity emerge as common factors because they allow non-specificity and looseness of reference, and not because they pick out intrinsic characteristics of rated objects. Correspondingly, pleasure and arousal may be predominant affective dimensions because they are sufficiently diverse and flexible to apply to a broad range of emotions.

So, do all representations of pleasure or arousal really refer to the same underlying experiential quality? Or do different kinds of goodness and different activating urges apply to different emotion concepts? Let's think about 'anger' and 'fear', for example. Both imply that something is happening that you don't like, and both are associated with wanting to do something about it. At this abstract level, there is certainly commonality. But do anger and fear both involve the same unpleasant feelings or the same kinds of arousal? Certainly not always. Being 'angry' can feel good as well as bad when indignation is righteous (e.g., Hess, 2014). And some varieties of 'cold' anger don't seem to involve high arousal or at least not the same kind of high arousal. But these may be atypical cases. It remains possible that normal anger and normal fear share the same displeasure and high arousal.

Even here there is room for doubt. Do bad angry feelings have all the same qualities as bad frightened feelings? Is the kind of activation we experience really identical in both anger and fear? Perhaps there is a common displeasure or arousal component mixed in with any emotion-specific differences, something that could be distilled if we boiled everything else away. Or perhaps the only commonality is the fact that loose and abstract concepts of pleasure and arousal continue to apply across the different cases.

Parkinson and Lea (1991) allowed participants to generate and articulate their own distinctions between different emotion concepts such as 'anger' and 'fear'. As usual, analysis of these distinctions yielded an evaluation dimension related to pleasure. However, precise interpretation of this dimension was complicated by the fact that participants used a range of different evaluative distinctions between different overlapping sets of emotions. Some of these distinctions referred specifically to how good it felt to experience the emotion, but others concerned the positivity of the emotion's consequences for the self or other people, and whether it was considered a morally good thing to feel. Intercorrelations between these distinctions do not necessarily imply that they have a common underlying meaning. Different emotions may get similar scores on different evaluative dimensions for different reasons.

So, is there really an internal mental pleasure gauge or hedonometer that registers how nice or nasty things feel along a single dimension? And is there a unified arousal system that energises emotional responses across the board? Or instead, might there be different kinds of reward, desire, approach, activation and inhibition mechanisms that often (but not always) operate in conjunction with one another? In the latter case, statistically coherent factors may in fact disguise diverse but broadly correlated subprocesses (e.g., Mackintosh, 2011; Parkinson & Lea, 1991).

Some researchers have searched for specific substrates of pleasure and arousal inside the brain. Evidence from scanning techniques such as functional Magnetic Resonance Imaging (fMRI) suggests that participants' ratings on these dimensions are reliably predicted by patterns of neural activity measured across the brain as whole (e.g., Chang et al., 2015; Kragel & LaBar, 2016), but do not correlate with neural activity in any specific region. The level of prediction is far from perfect even when widely distributed neural networks are coordinated with responses to restricted sets of emotional stimuli. For example, Bush and colleagues (2017) were only able to correctly predict whether reactions to pictorial stimuli were rated as pleasant or unpleasant on 59 per cent of occasions using measurement of activity across all accessible brain regions (when chance prediction would yield 50 percent accuracy). Prediction of whether arousal was rated as low or high was slightly less accurate at 56 per cent. If emotions experienced across a wider range of contexts had been sampled, these levels of accuracy would likely have dropped still further. So far, no one has been able to detect a distinctive profile of neural markers that closely tracks either pleasure or arousal levels. Of course, neural activity need not map directly onto psychological phenomena in all cases. But where should we look for evidence of unified pleasure and arousal systems if both brain mapping and psychometry are inconclusive?

If pleasure and arousal were nothing but internal experiential qualities, that would make them inaccessible to language according to Wittgenstein's (1953) beetle-in-a-box analogy. Linking the concepts with more clearly relational considerations such as approach and withdrawal, attraction and repulsion or intensity of engagement would give them better communicative traction. In other words, perhaps pleasure- and arousal-related concepts are abstractions based on diverse experiences of positively or negatively evaluating what is happening and of focusing more or less intensively on objects in the shared environment respectively.

Regardless of their specific interpretation, pleasure and arousal are certainly concepts that meaningfully apply to most if not all possible emotional states, at least at an abstract level. Using these concepts helps us to distinguish different emotion concepts from each other. However, a two-dimensional representation of the conceptual space does not allow fine-grained distinctions between all of the emotion words used by speakers of any language. For example, 'anger' and 'fear' are both characterised by practically identical values on both dimensions.

How should we understand differences in meaning that are not fully captured by pleasure and arousal? Russell (1978) argued that emotion terms 'often, but not always, convey additional meaning regarding the circumstances surrounding the emotional state' (p. 1166). In other words, the distinctive connotations of emotion words might not relate directly to the experience itself. For example, 'anger' might simply be a name for the combination of displeasure and arousal that is associated with an urge to retaliate or caused by someone else offending you. If we want to get at the mental state conveyed by the word, then these extrinsic connotations concerning contexts, causes and effects are not directly relevant. However, if emotion words correspond to relational processes rather than momentary private experiences, their meanings cannot be prised away from contextual factors so easily.

One way of introducing additional conceptual content to specific emotion representations is to consider further dimensions (see also Cowen & Keltner, 2017; Fontaine et al., 2013), including dimensions based on the appraisals associated with different emotions (e.g., Smith & Ellsworth, 1985; and see Chapter 1). Another is to use categorical distinctions. However, categories can only provide additional information about emotional meaning if they include specification of features that cannot be represented dimensionally. Otherwise their main advantage lies in identifying commonly co-occurring patterns of values across different dimensions, which leads to clustering of emotions in particular sectors of the multidimensional semantic space (e.g., Scherer's, 1994, notion of modal emotions; see also Cowen & Keltner, 2017; 2018).

Boundaries

Both dimensional and categorical approaches to emotional meaning focus on the internal structure of the conceptual domain of emotion. But how do we decide what is inside or outside that domain in the first place? Russell (1980) found that words such as 'sleepy' and 'relaxed' occupied important positions on the two-dimensional pleasure–arousal circumplex alongside more obviously emotional words such as 'anger' and 'joy' (see Figure 2.2), thereby raising questions about whether these dimensions are specifically emotional, and whether it matters if they are not. Shaver and colleagues' (1987) categorical analysis questioned whether the identified category of 'surprise' should really count as an 'emotion', thus raising issues about whether that higher-order category itself constitutes a coherent cluster. Where then should we draw the line between emotion and non-emotion? How can we resolve any border disputes?

Classical Concepts

Ortony, Clore and Collins (1988) proposed a systematic set of definitions precisely demarcating English-language emotion concepts. They argued that 'emotion' refers to pleasant or unpleasant mental states caused by a person's appraisal of what is happening. Meanings of more specific emotion words can then be distinguished in terms of the particular appraisals that are involved. For example, 'anger' means an unpleasant mental state caused by appraising someone else's actions as blameworthy.

Adopting these definitions permits clear decisions about whether something is or is not an example of 'emotion' (and whether something is or is not an example of 'anger'). By checking off a list of necessary features, we can make a firm determination about what we are experiencing or what someone else is experiencing. Is there a mental state? Is it pleasant or unpleasant? Is it caused by appraisal? If the answer to all these questions is yes, then the experience counts as an 'emotion'. If the appraisal takes a certain form and produces feelings of the right valence, then it counts as the particular kind of emotion corresponding to that appraisal. For example, if another person is perceived as blameworthy and this blame perception leads to bad feelings, then this is a case of 'anger'. In other words, there are necessary conditions for applying emotion names to experience, and when all of them are present, the phenomenon in question automatically qualifies as a category member. Taken together these individually necessary and jointly sufficient conditions provide a *classical* definition.

Classical definitions mean that language can draw clear boundaries around phenomena. If any of the necessary conditions fails to apply, the phenomenon lies outside the category, period. However, this does not mean that it is always straightforward to decide if something counts as a proper instance in practice. There is still the problem of working out whether or not the conditions apply to the case in question. And we may not always have access to all the information that is necessary for making a clear decision. For example, I may be unsure whether someone is appraising someone else's action as blameworthy based on their observable behaviour making it difficult to determine whether they are really 'angry'. Indeed, given that appraisal may operate unconsciously (e.g., Lazarus, 1991), I may even be unsure about whether I am myself angry at any given moment. I may go on acting in an 'angry' manner without realising that I am experiencing that emotion (Frijda, 1986; 2005).

If people are often uncertain about emotion classification in practice, how can we tell if they can do it systematically in principle? Ortony, Clore and Foss (1987) present evidence that people are consistent in making at least some kinds of emotion-related categorical judgements. For example, they proposed a practical criterion for deciding whether words genuinely refer to emotions. If an adjective has an equally emotional meaning when linked to the word 'being' and the word 'feeling' then that adjective is an intrinsically emotional adjective (see also Bedford, 1957). For example, competent English speakers would agree that 'being angry' and 'feeling angry' equally represent emotional states. This implies that the word 'angry' describes an emotion without needing additional linguistic context. By contrast, 'feeling alone' seems to describe an emotion but 'being alone' does not, so 'alone' is not a description of an emotion (even if 'feeling alone' might be). The word 'alone' only conveys emotional meaning when linked to 'feeling' but not 'being' and therefore doesn't itself contain all the necessary affective information. The idea of feeling needs to be added to make it emotional.

If Ortony and colleagues' criteria can be applied consistently to all words that are possible candidates for membership of the emotion category, then we can draw a clear and classically defined boundary around it, and make consistent judgements about which words are inside and which are outside. But is the possibility of clear, systematically defined boundaries enough to support a classical approach to the conceptual domain of emotion? Isn't it also important to know whether these boundaries map onto distinctions people use in practice when representing emotional phenomena? What if I decided only to call something an 'emotion' if the word for it has five letters and two syllables? I could then mark out a defined territory and teach other people how to use the distinction in the same way. However, my version of 'emotion' would no longer have any serious resemblance to the concept used by people in everyday language. It would include 'anger', 'upset' and 'panic', but also 'apple', 'lorry' and 'lasso'.

Ortony and colleagues' suggested distinctions have more direct relevance to the ways most people actually talk about emotions. Any slippage between their technical specification and participants' untutored categorisations is clearly less dramatic than we'd get from applying my flippant definition. The lay concept might only need some tidying up at the edges for the purposes of scientific clarity. But even so, how can we be sure that any proposed category perfectly matches what people really mean when they talk about emotions (assuming that they always mean the same thing)? We'd need to find some way of determining whether the criteria for membership staked out a territory that overlaps substantially with the colloquial domain of 'emotion'. And only then could we draw meaningful classical boundaries.

Fuzziness

If we need to calibrate distinctions against those used in everyday language, why not simply work from those distinctions in the first place?

One of the problems is looseness of reference. It's not clear that people always use the same words in the same ways or whether they always agree with each other about how they should be applied. Perhaps, then, the edges around people's emotion concepts are fuzzy rather than distinct. Maybe there is no well-defined conceptual category underlying 'emotion' talk.

Many of us resist this idea because we feel that we can easily recognise an emotion when it comes along. However, we'd probably also agree that there are times when we are unsure whether our own or other people's experience really counts as emotional. Is this simply because the information we are trying to classify is not clear enough, that we are grasping at something just out of reach in a darkened room? Are we simply unsure whether classical criteria properly apply in particular cases? Or are there no classical criteria to start with? Is the concept itself ill defined? Indeed, if people really use classical criteria to decide whether something is an emotion, then why do they usually find it difficult to say what those criteria are?

According to Fehr and Russell (1984), 'everyone knows what an emotion is, until asked to give a definition' (p. 464). So what kind of knowledge must emotion knowledge be to resist clear and consistent articulation? To answer this question, Fehr and Russell asked 200 Canadian psychology students to list words that describe emotions. Another group of fifty-five students then rated the extent to which the 'feelings' described by these words were good or bad examples of 'emotion'.

Results of these two tasks revealed agreement about the emotional status of some of the words. In the first study, more than half of participants included 'happiness', 'anger', 'sadness' and 'love' on their emotion lists. In the later study, these same words were rated as picking out good examples of emotion, with an average score above 5 on a 6-point scale. However, other words did not seem to be as clearly or consistently 'emotional'. For instance, only a few of the first study's participants listed 'pride', 'awe', 'calmness' or 'respect' as 'emotions', and the later study's participants rated these same words as relatively poorer examples. This seems to indicate that judgements about membership of the 'emotion' category are not simple binary decisions which allow participants to say definitively whether something does or does not qualify. Does this mean that the 'emotion' concept has no clear boundaries, and that it is not susceptible to classical definition?

Not necessarily. Armstrong and colleagues (1983) asked undergraduate US students similar questions about potential examples of classical as well as non-classical categories and found comparable results for both. The non-classical categories lacked any clear technical definitions (e.g., vehicles, sports), leading to fringe cases which are obviously less clear examples than others (e.g., To what extent is a skateboard a 'vehicle'? To what extent is chess a 'sport'?). The classical categories were defined by clear and well-known criteria allowing definite decisions about whether something belonged inside or outside. For example, anyone with a basic knowledge of math can correctly allocate both 3 and 447 to the category of 'odd number' and 6 and 806 to the category of 'even number'. But Armstrong and colleagues found that participants still rated different odd or even numbers as better or worse examples of the category, just as they did for different examples of vehicles and sports. Thus, 447 was rated as a worse example of an 'odd number' than 3 or 7. And this difference applied even when participants had explicitly stated at an earlier stage of the study that membership of the 'odd number' category was an all-or-none matter. In other words, participants were perfectly aware that numbers were either odd or even with no possibility of a middle ground, but still rated oddness and evenness as matters of degree.

On what basis did participants make distinctions implying different degrees of oddness or evenness? Perhaps 447 is slightly more difficult to identify as an odd number than 3 or 7 (Armstrong et al., 1983), especially when you haven't had to think about the concept for a while. Correspondingly, if we want to present a 'good example' of an odd number to someone struggling to understand the concept, we would probably pick 3 or 7 rather than 447 because those smaller numbers make it easier to clarify what's odd about them. In other words, these examples are relatively 'good' because they work better when explaining the concept's meaning. Potentially, this might also be why participants said that 'pride' and 'calmness' were worse examples of 'emotions' than 'anger' and 'fear'. The latter cases may simply work better for illustrative purposes (even if they qualify equally well as category members more generally). Regardless of precisely why ratings varied, the important point for present purposes is that they varied for both odd numbers (in Armstrong and colleagues' study) and emotions (in Fehr and Russell's study). This means that differences in the rated goodness of emotion examples cannot rule out clear boundaries around the 'emotion' concept.

Fehr and Russell (1984) collected additional data to provide more conclusive evidence of fuzzy boundaries. Participants were asked simple yes/no questions about the category membership of various conceptual objects, including odd numbers and supposed emotions (e.g., 'Is pride an emotion?'; 'Is 447 an odd number?'). Participants consistently agreed that the 'good' examples of each category were members of that category. For example, everyone said yes when asked if 'happiness' was an 'emotion' and if 3 was an 'odd number'. However, judgements of relatively poor examples were less consistent across the two kinds of concept. Although almost all participants agreed that 447 was an 'odd number', fewer than three quarters said that 'pride' or 'awe' were 'emotions'. Agreement was even lower for 'calmness' with roughly half of participants saying that it was an 'emotion' and roughly half saying it was not. Fehr and Russell concluded that the boundaries around the emotion category are blurred, making it difficult to agree about whether fringe cases are really inside or outside.

However, disagreement might reflect interpretation of the items being classified rather than the category to which they may or may not belong. Even if people know exactly where a boundary lies, they may still find it difficult to tell whether something ill defined, nebulous or otherwise diffuse is entirely inside or out. Imagine, for instance, trying to decide if a roughly sketched four-sided figure is really a square. Perhaps then deciding whether 'pride' is an emotion is difficult because it is a fuzzy concept itself (cf. Russell & Fehr, 1994), unlike the precise numbers that participants agreed were either odd or even. Perhaps the meaning of 'pride' is only partly emotional, or sometimes emotional and sometimes not (Johnson-Laird & Oatley, 1989). Maybe some participants were thinking about 'feeling proud' and others about 'being proud' (Clore, Ortony & Foss, 1987).

Russell (1991) addressed criticisms of this kind in a follow-up study. He provided participants with definitions that either did or did not imply the feeling variety of pride. Twenty-three per cent of those specifically asked whether 'pride (meaning satisfaction or pleasure taken in one's work, achievements or possessions)' (p. 43) is an emotion still said it was not. But even reading a precise definition does not necessarily help participants think of a clear example. They may still have been caught up with their unclarified understanding of the target word itself or they may have imagined a level of satisfaction or pleasure that they considered too weak to qualify for emotional status. If so, fuzziness might still depend on lower-level concepts such as 'pride' (or its defined varieties) rather than the higher-level concept of 'emotion' itself. In this case, asking participants to classify directly observed phenomena rather than verbal descriptions of general cases might yield higher levels of agreement.

Although these caveats suggest that classical representations may potentially be hiding behind apparent fuzziness, so far no one has been able to provide direct evidence for their existence. Laypeople don't seem to use classical definitions either when categorising emotions or reasoning about them. If they have precise criteria for deciding whether or not something is an emotion, they seem unable or unwilling to say what those criteria are. So, what other forms might their representations take? In the next section, I consider some of the alternatives.

Representation

Having tried to draw boundaries around the concept of 'emotion', we now turn to the question of how people represent its content. What do people have in mind when they use emotion words? Do the kinds of representation they use explain why the edges of the category often seem fuzzy?

Prototypes

Building on earlier work on cognitive processes of pattern classification (e.g., Posner & Keele, 1968), Rosch (1973) developed prototype theory to account for the fact that instances of many ordinary language categories seem to share only family resemblances (Wittgenstein, 1953) rather than the consistent defining features implied by classical approaches. The notion of family resemblance alludes to the fact that different members of any group of genetically related individuals might share the same shape of nose, the same prominent chin or bushy eyebrows, but none of these features is common to all members. And yet we can still see the similarity in their facial features and make generally consistent judgements about whether they belong to the family. Rosch explains our ability to classify in the absence of defining characteristics by proposing that we have acquired a cognitive prototype that represents frequently co-occurring features. We have in our mind a kind of idealised family member, who embodies the clearest possible representation of the family's distinctiveness. Potential instances of the category are then compared to this prototype to assess the likelihood of their membership.

Judgements about family members based on resemblances in their appearance can sometimes be wrong. You might be surprised when someone introduces a person who looks nothing like them as a long-lost sister or brother. You might falsely conclude that two friends with similar facial features are related to each other. And if you resort to genetic testing, that too might reveal unsuspected familial connections or undermine previous beliefs about paternity or sibling status. In all these cases, it is possible to make a determination about family membership using information other than that specified by perceived 'family resemblances'.

Russell (1991) argues that such a process of independent fact-checking would be impossible in the case of emotion because there is nothing more to the concept than the prototype (Clore & Ortony, 1991). It's no good checking separate technical specifications because there aren't any. There are no defining characteristics shared by all members of the category, only varying degrees of family resemblance. From this perspective, it is unsurprising that people disagree about what is inside and outside the 'emotion' category. Judgements will always be probabilistic and fuzzy when cases only resemble the prototype to a limited degree. For example, pride may not have enough common features with the 'emotion' prototype to permit consistent decisions about its category membership.

Scripts

What precise form does the prototypic representation of 'emotion' take? The object categories investigated by Rosch (1973) could be characterised by lists of features. For example, a prototypical bird has feathers, can fly, lays eggs and so on. If emotions are simply mental objects, then we can similarly represent them in terms of their probable attributes, including appraisals, changes in heart rate, facial expressions, urges to act, etc. However, emotions are better conceived as events, processes or episodes than as static objects or collections of symptoms that just switch on and off. Perhaps then prototypes for emotion concepts are not simply feature lists, but scripts specifying the typical sequence in which features follow one another (Fehr & Russell, 1984).

Shaver and colleagues (1987) explored this possibility by collecting narrative accounts of typical experiences of different emotions. Six raters then coded participants' emotion stories in order to identify their most common features and the usual order of their occurrence (see Figure 2.3). Unsurprisingly, narrators often started by saying what events and thoughts triggered the emotion, including appraisals. They then characterised what the emotion felt like, what its facial, bodily and cognitive effects were and how the situation ultimately turned out. For example, anger narratives focused on responses to situations appraised as unfair. These responses involved feelings of nervous tension, narrowed attention, thinking you are in the right, frowning, gritted teeth, swearing and shouting and imagined or actual aggression. In many cases, the protagonist also tried to control or regulate the situation and their response to it.

Kövecses (1990; Lakoff & Kövecses, 1987) investigated prototypical structure by considering common idiomatic expressions rather than narrative reports. He argued that certain common metaphors underlie our understanding of how emotional events unfold (like our understanding of other categories, Lakoff, 1987). For example, a popular metaphorical representation of anger compares the emotion to the heat of the fluid in a container, such as a saucepan or pressure cooker. Thus, people often say things like: 'you make my blood boil', 'I got hot under the collar', 'I reached boiling point', 'I got all steamed up', 'I had to let off steam', 'I tried to simmer down' or 'I blew a gasket'. These formulations of what

*Predisposition to anger, either because of previous similar or related experiences or because of stress, overload, fatigue, etc.

*Reversal or sudden loss of power, status, or respect; insult
*Violation of an expectation; things not working out as planned
*Frustration or interruption of a goal-directed activity
*Real or threatened physical or psychological pain

*Judgment that the situation is illegitimate, wrong, unfair, contrary to what ought to be

*Obscenities, cursing
*Verbally attacking the cause of anger
*Loud voice, yelling, screaming, shouting
*Complaining, bitching, talking about how lousy things are

*Hands or fists clenched
*Aggressive, threatening movements or gestures

*Attacking something other than the cause of anger (e.g., pounding on something, throwing things)
*Physically attacking the cause of anger
*Incoherent, out-of-control, highly emotional behavior
*Imagining attacking or hurting the cause of anger

*Heavy walk, stomping
*Tightness or rigidity in body; tight, rigid movements
*Nonverbally communicating disapproval to the cause of anger (e.g., slamming doors, walking out)

*Frowning, not smiling, mean or unpleasant expression
*Gritting teeth, showing teeth, breathing through teeth
*Red, flushed face

*Crying
*Feelings of nervous tension, anxiety, discomfort

*Brooding; withdrawing from social contact

*Narrowing of attention to exclude all but the anger situation;
not being able to think of anything else
*Thinking "I'm right; everyone else is wrong"

*Suppressing the anger; trying not to show or express it
*Redefining the situation or trying to view it in such a way
that anger is no longer appropriate

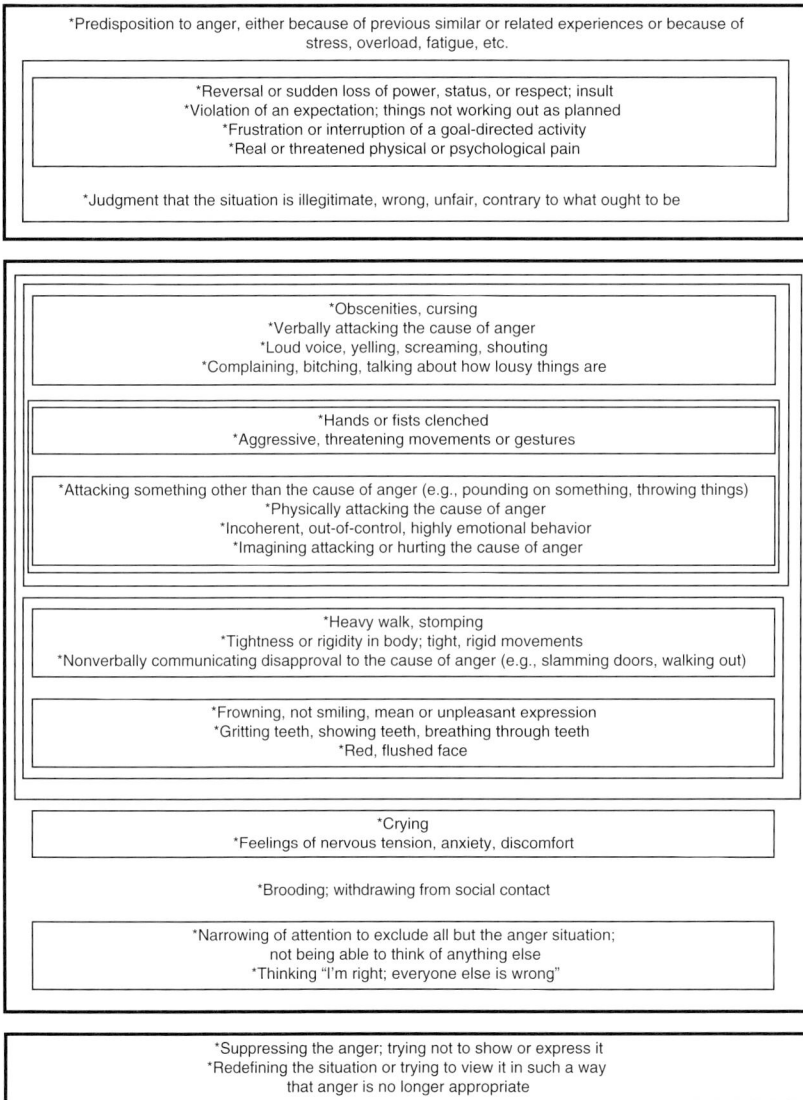

Figure 2.3 Anger script based on participants' narrative descriptions (Shaver et al., 1987, reproduced with permission from the American Psychological Association)

happens when a person gets angry fall into a clear temporal sequence, with heat applied to the container, pressure building up, attempts to contain pressure and a possible explosion at the end.

Working from this heated-container metaphor, Kövecses set out the chain of events characterising the prototypical script for anger. First there is an 'offending event' (heat is applied to the container). Second, anger is experienced (pressure builds up inside). Third, the angry person attempts to control their anger (to keep a lid on it or simmer down). Fourth, control attempts fail (and the angry person flips their lid). To be a recognisable instance of anger, the episode need not pass through all these stages in exactly this form. There might be no attempt to control, for example, or no final outburst. However, when roughly these events happen in approximately this order, we are likely to conceptualise the episode in angry terms.

In Kövecses' (1990) view, anger is a prototypical case of emotion. This means that the script for 'anger' also provides the template for a more abstract script representing 'emotion' more generally. According to this script, some event causes us to experience an emotion, which we then attempt to regulate, but ultimately lose control. Again, not every episode that we call an emotion has exactly this temporal structure, but unfolding in pretty much this way makes it more likely that we use that word to describe what happens.

Encoding

Deciding whether something counts as 'anger' or if it is really an 'emotion' by comparing it to a script-based representation sounds straightforward. We can just check what is happening at each stage and see how well it matches what the script says should happen. But exactly how does the comparison process work? The features that need to be represented include autonomic changes, facial expressions, appraisals and action impulses, among other things. How do they all get combined into a unified mental representation?

Imagine carrying around a written list of these features and ticking off words whenever you detect the feature they describe. Something in the way? Check. Heart pounding? Check. Eyes fixed? Check. This checking task is easiest when information about the specified features is already presented in words, especially if those words are exactly the same as the ones written on the list. This might happen occasionally in psychological studies assessing emotion concepts, or during conversations when another person describes emotional symptoms in terms that happen to correspond to your own specific representation. However, it is not a common situation elsewhere.

The emotional events that we more usually conceptualise are presented not only linguistically but also as visually detected facial movements, aurally detected tones of voice and contextual information coming from a range of different sensory modalities. In the case of our own experiences, there may also be other kinds of symptoms, impulses or relational factors to consider. How then are those different kinds of information checked off against our mental concepts? If those concepts are analogous to feature lists, scripted or otherwise, then we need to translate incoming sensory information into the language used on those lists before any direct comparison is possible. If the list is written in English, then we need to represent the things that are happening in the right English words in order to work out whether to insert a tick or cross next to the corresponding items.

Such a process seems to require conversion of multisensory perceptions into a common code. For related reasons, theorists such as Fodor (1975) believe that our mental representations specify features in a common 'language of thought' that permits information in different forms and modalities to be integrated and processed by general-purpose modules and mechanisms. If so, emotion-related features can't directly activate emotion concepts. Instead they first need to be represented in the same abstract code.

An alternative is simply to abandon the idea that concepts use a common language of representation. Barsalou (1999) argues that conceptual representations use the same perceptual code as the incoming information to which they are applied. In this case, we categorise simply by matching patterns instead of checking off features from a list. In other words, the concept directly specifies the sensory and perceptual experience of the events or objects that it represents, allowing more direct contact between the two parts of the process. In the case of emotion, the relevant concepts would then be represented as interoceptive patterns of bodily response, including pounding hearts, feelings of warmth and increasing muscle tension, coupled with exteroceptive information from seeing, hearing, smelling, tasting and touching (Barrett, 2017). In other words, emotion representations might remain distributed across various sensory and perceptual systems rather than integrated in any amodal mental module.

Specificity

One likely function of concepts is to permit the treatment of different things as equivalent in important respects. Instead of having to approach every event as something entirely new, we can see it as one of a familiar kind, and prepare ourselves for what is likely to happen. Perceiving an object as an 'apple' tells me something about what it will feel like when my teeth penetrate its skin, how it will taste and at what point I should stop biting to avoid chewing on the core. Perceiving an episode in 'angry' terms similarly allows approximate prediction of what I am about to feel, think and do (or what someone else is about to feel, think and do). It sets out a prototypical chain of events or activates perceptual simulations of what is happening. However, an apple may turn out to be sour or soft rather than sweet and crunchy, and 'anger' may be passive-aggressive rather than simply aggressive. At what point, then, does a generic concept stop being a useful guide to the probable nature of what it represents? When do we need to individuate exemplars instead of treating them as functionally equivalent?

Barsalou's (1985) view is that category representations aggregate exemplars stored in memory, but different exemplars are selectively retrieved in different contexts. For example, the criteria for deciding what counts as 'anger' might differ for a formal meeting, a physical confrontation or a DIY job. In each case, the context attunes the perceiver to a different subset of exemplars that are more likely to match what then unfolds (Barrett, 2017).

But how specific would emotion representations need to get before they provided a workable mapping of the dynamic environment? There is an obvious trade-off between economy of processing and sensitivity to contextual particularities. In other words, some of the potential benefits of categorisation may be negated when people need to respond to specifics rather than generalities. And when our representations drill right down to the shifting currents, eddies and grains of unfolding situations, do they still count as categorical? Are they even representations? Or are we simply picking up dynamic information from the relational stream of our dynamic transaction with the world (e.g., Gibson, 1979)?

Predictive Coding

Because prototypic scripts for emotion concepts are abstract and generic, they do not permit precise local prediction of unfolding events. We can anticipate that someone who we perceive as 'angry' is likely to want to push against obstacles, but we don't know what those obstacles might be or exactly how they are likely to push. The more context-attuned perceptual representations proposed by Barrett (2017) are precisely designed to serve the purpose of localised prediction. They serve as simulations of what is about to happen and thus permit direct preparation for immediately anticipated events.

From this perspective, emotion representation is a form of predictive coding (e.g., Rao & Ballard, 1999; Srinivasa, Laughlin & Dubs, 1982). It involves generating working models that function as perceptual simulations. This means that conceptual understanding is embodied in a form that permits direct assessment of anticipated matches with incoming perceptual information. In the case of emotional episodes, we construct expectations not only about how external events might soon unfold but also about how our bodies will prepare for, and adjust to, those events (Barrett, 2017).

Assuming that our transactions with the environment proceed as our working models have learned to expect, then we continue to navigate successfully through the world. Indeed, we may not even notice minor discrepancies between what we anticipate and what actually happens, because we are operating from within our perceptual simulation rather than processing every bit of information that is available in the internal and external environment (cf. Cacioppo, Berntson & Klein, 1992). However, if there is a salient and intrusive mismatch between prediction and perceptual feedback, this leads to corrective learning. Theoretically, then, the process of predictive coding allows us to develop representations that are broadly accurate (or at least practically workable) because of their grounding in experience.

Goal-Directed Categorisation

Accurate anticipation of unfolding events is not the only relevant consideration when assessing the utility of categorical representations, especially when these representations are directly self-relevant. Sometimes our motivation for using a particular representation is that it fits with other concepts we like to use or helps us defend a valued orientation to the world (cf. Sedikides & Strube, 1997). Sometimes, our concepts need to facilitate transmission of information to others rather than help us individually navigate the practical world. We may be oriented to their understanding of events rather than how those events affect us personally (e.g., Grice, 1975; Sperber & Wilson, 1986). Indeed, in conversational contexts, we may be applying emotion concepts to someone else's formulation of events presented in words rather than encoding sensory information of other kinds. For example, when someone describes behaviour in aggressive terms, we might respond by representing it as a particular kind of unjustified 'anger', thus refining the other person's formulation while still conveying our shared understanding.

Application of emotional concepts can also serve self-presentational or self-defensive purposes. We can make excuses for ourselves by attributing our impulsive response to anger. We can make someone else seem more blameworthy by representing our interpersonal orientation in angry terms. Under these circumstances, the concept is intended to influence other people's representations and change their behaviour towards us rather than simply to facilitate predictions about what is about to happen (as we shall see).

In all these cases, currently active goals may influence the formulation or application of emotion concepts. One way in which this might work is by biasing the search for stored exemplars so that we selectively retrieve those that match our motives (Barsalou, 2005). For example, when we suspect that another person has aggressive intentions, we may selectively retrieve memories of unreasonable anger to make sense of what they are experiencing in a way that puts the blame on them rather than ourselves.

Do people ever categorise objects in an entirely neutral context where no goals or contextual considerations intrude? If not, there may be no unifying representation for the category, only a range of different possible context-based prototypes that can be assembled on the fly as the situation requires. As Barsalou (2005) puts it: 'Rather than a single abstraction representing a category, diverse abstractions may be constructed online to represent a category temporarily . . . If so, then studying the *skill* to construct temporary abstractions dynamically may be more fruitful than attempting to establish one particular abstraction that represents a category' (p. 394).

Barrett (2017) takes a similar approach to emotion concepts. According to her, the specific multimodal representation of any emotion category depends on the circumstances in which it is generated and the current goals of the person generating it. In other words, we do not usually apply an unmarked concept of 'anger' to our experiences or those of other people, but instead use more specific, contextually attuned emotion representations, such as 'anger to get one's way in an argument with a relationship partner', 'anger during a debate with a political opponent' or 'anger that the train is late'.

Unlike prototype theorists, then, Barrett (2017) does not assume that emotion concepts can be crystallised into defining instances, around which exemplars loosely cluster. The same emotion word may have quite different meanings and representations depending on the perceiver's goals and the prevailing context. Aggregating different instances would then yield no conceptual core. In other words, there might not be anything at the heart of the emotion concept. Whether such an unstructured concept could ever gain linguistic currency is another question.

Alternative Representations

In this section, we have reviewed some of the different ways in which emotion concepts might be represented. Classical definitions may be applied to appropriately delimited sets of phenomena when precise technical specifications are required. People may identify or communicate emotional information by reference to prototypes that specify either an ideal or average case. And they may have a store of context-specific multimodal memory traces that allow them to simulate emotions during imagination, planning and prediction.

These alternatives are not mutually incompatible. Emotions may be represented in different ways and at different levels, allowing us to reason about them, distinguish and identify them, and to anticipate moment-by-moment how ongoing emotional episodes will unfold. In other words, a range of different kinds of representation may be used under different circumstances and for different purposes.

One of the primary purposes of emotion representations is to influence other people. For example, saying that they are making us 'angry' may be a way of trying to get them to change their behaviour towards us. To what extent then do our emotion concepts need to be attuned to the requirements of these kinds of social influence? The next section addresses this question.

Communication

So far, we have considered how emotion concepts represent the structure of emotional life, loosely or precisely picking out states, processes or relations. In this section, the focus shifts from isolated emotion words to sentences and utterances, and from how language describes things to the many other ways it is used when spoken aloud with someone else around to hear (or written down for someone else to read).

Pragmatics

Even apparently descriptive statements serve functions other than simply describing what is happening. When I point out that the thing in your hand is a 'gun', the message may be intended to make you or someone else act in a way that prevents me getting shot. Correspondingly, when I say that you are 'angry', or that I am 'angry', this usually involves more than simply categorising a psychological state or episode. I may also be criticising or agreeing, blaming or denying blame, trying to make something happen or not happen. Perhaps, then, the word 'anger' is not only a name for a sequence of events or pattern of dynamic perceptual information but also a tool for achieving certain kinds of conversational effect.

Austin's (1962) classic book *How to Do Things with Words* sets out some of the ways in which speech acts can serve pragmatic functions. Talking can directly perform actions when we christen a baby, take marital vows, plead 'guilty', resign from a job or accept a wager or offer of employment. And performative speech acts are not restricted to these formal uses of language. We can also use words to accuse or condemn someone, and to make promises, bets or commitments outside the courtrooms, churches or casinos where ceremonial or officially sanctioned linguistic practices take place. In each of these cases, saying something means doing something. And it means doing more than simply providing a description. Speaking is an activity that relates to the other activities we perform, not just a commentary that goes on separately from the things it is about.

What kinds of activity are performed by emotion talk? What functions does it serve? One possible answer was offered by the philosopher, Bedford (1957), who wrote that 'emotion words form part of the vocabulary of appraisal and criticism' (p. 294). From his perspective, speakers use first-person emotional language to interpret and evaluate what is happening. For example, saying 'I am angry' allocates blame to someone or something, and saying 'I am afraid' confers threatening qualities on an object, event or person. Both utterances encourage any person to whom they are directed to adjust their own orientations accordingly, by also blaming the object of communicated 'anger' or attending to the threat identified by communicated 'fear'.

If emotion talk is simply a means of appraising things, then why can't the same function be served by more directly evaluative language? Why not simply say 'I blame you' rather than 'I am angry with you'? One answer is that emotional language also implies a commitment to back up appraisal by directly acting on the identified concern. Saying 'I am angry' means that I am ready to hit out or retaliate in other ways and saying 'I am afraid' means that I want to run away or hide. And not only am I ready to act in these ways, but my action readiness takes 'control precedence' (Frijda, 1986). The reference to emotion sends the message that I may not be able to stop myself from following through if the situation does not change, that my action impulse has a momentum of its own. Thus, my angry warning of aggression may constitute a compelling threat, and my fearful commitment to escape may be an overtly last-ditch appeal for your protection.

Functional Description

How do the evaluative and commitment-making functions of emotional language relate to its descriptive uses? Is saying that 'I am angry' still primarily a report of what I am experiencing in the context of a prototypical scripted episode? Does the utterance only serve as a threat or criticism as a secondary consequence of this descriptive meaning? Perhaps I inform you about my 'anger' and you adjust your interpretation of my mental state and behavioural readiness accordingly. You work out that I must be evaluating things in a certain way and that I am likely to act in corresponding ways. This in turn encourages you to modify your own orientation and action.

Although this kind of articulated process may sometimes happen (see Chapter 4), it implies a level of detachment that seems incompatible with most directly involving emotional situations. When I say that 'I am angry' right now about some urgently pressing matter, the blaming and the threatening take precedence. Similarly, telling you that 'I love you' is never a neutral characterisation of a state of mind or sequence of psychological events. You wouldn't be tempted to check whether the statement was accurate by taking my pulse or observing whether the episode unfolds in accordance with the script. Instead, my subsequent indifference or betrayal might be the key factors that demonstrate failure to honour the implied commitment ('but you told me that you loved me'). You'd be more alert to breach of promise than misrepresented symptoms.

Do descriptive functions ever take priority in emotion talk? Are there language games where describing our experience is the central task? In a counselling session or psychological experiment, we might sometimes do our best to detail the true nature of our emotions. But even in these rarefied settings, the descriptions we produce refer primarily to our relation to the object of the emotion, and that relation always already implies evaluation and a commitment to act. 'I am angry' means that I don't like having something blocking my actions and am ready to push against whatever is blocking them. Under normal circumstances, this descriptive content is peripheral to what the invocation of 'anger' is really doing, namely allocating blame and threatening retribution.

Subjects and Addressees

The point of communicating emotion partly depends on who it is communicated to (the addressee of the communication or target of social influence). When presenting my anger to the person blocking my progress, the point is to ward or warn them off, to threaten serious consequences if they don't budge, shift, or buckle. Or to make it obvious that they are in the wrong. When presenting my anger to a potential ally, the point is to bring them onside, to agree that someone else is in the wrong or help dislodge the blockage that I am confronting.

Verbally representing someone else's orientation in emotional terms serves functions other than simple description too. These functions partly depend on whether emotion is attributed to a second or third person (whether the subject of the emotion verb is 'you' rather than 'he', 'she' or 'they'). Saying that *you* are emotional may be an accusation of irrationality or an offer of sympathy. Saying that *he* or *she* is angry can warn others about how the person in question is poised to react. In either case, attributing the other person's reactions to emotions carries further implications about the controllability of the forces motivating it. Thus, a lawyer may ask for mitigation on the basis that their client acted in the heat of the moment. Even murder may be presented as a crime of passion. In less formal contexts, we can similarly discount the apparent implications of someone's actions by invoking emotional explanation. We can say that it's just the anger talking.

These examples of first-, second- and third-person emotional language all point to the same conclusion. Description is only one of the things that people do with emotion words, and often not the most important thing. When talking about our own or other people's emotion, most of what we say implies evaluation and commitment to action in some shape or form. It works on the relations between us.

Conversations

As we have seen, many psychologists use controlled experimental tasks to investigate emotion language (e.g., Clore et al., 1987; Fehr & Russell, 1984). They present participants with individual words taken out of their everyday contexts of use so that they can zero in on underlying concepts. They try to create a neutral and uncontaminated situation for comparing and classifying meanings. But to what extent does this kind of research tell us how emotion words and concepts operate in settings other than sterile laboratories, or in sentences that don't make their specific meaning the topic? Can any unitary descriptive representation underlie the various pragmatic uses to which emotion words are put in the messy conversations that take place outside the lab?

The previous section broadened the focus somewhat by putting words into plausibly realistic sentences and considering interactive social situations in which these sentences might be delivered as utterances. However, the linguistic examples were still concocted and contrived precisely to make certain points. They did not directly quote any specific person talking to any specific other person on any specific occasion. There is a limit to how far this kind of armchair speculation or conceptual analysis can take us. To better understand how emotion talk functions in more directly involving contexts, we need to get out of the armchair and step back from the lab bench. What, then, does emotional talk actually do when delivered outside these artificial settings? Relevant data can be found from qualitative studies that analyse naturalistic discourse.

Discursive psychologists have extended Austin's pragmatic approach to language by questioning the integrity of the descriptive concepts routinely used in quantitative social science (Potter & Wetherell, 1987), including the concept of 'emotion' (e.g., Edwards & Potter, 1992). Edwards (1999) specifically criticises the common assumption that emotion words are associated with pre-existing mental concepts that pick out more or less definite objects in the psychological world. He argues instead that emotion talk always presents a specific formulation of events that is selected from a range of possible alternatives to achieve particular conversational functions. The formulation may then be accepted, reworked or contested by whomever we are talking to. From this perspective, 'emotions' are constructed online in verbal interactions. Using an emotion word is not about finding the most accurate description of something that is already there. Instead, it helps to build a version of events that supports your argumentative position.

As an example of this approach, Edwards (1999) analysed conversations recorded during relationship counselling sessions. Talk was first transcribed using the Jefferson (2004) system which adds annotations indicating pauses (brackets) and their duration in seconds (numbers in brackets), volume (°° surrounding quieter stretches), speed (>< surrounding slower stretches, colons for stretched vowel sounds), intonation (e.g., ↓ for falling intonation, underlining for emphasis), and audible breaths (.h for breathing in, h for breathing out with repeated hs to indicate duration, e.g., hhh). These annotations give a better sense of *how* what is being said is being said, and what the utterance is doing as part of the unfolding context of the dialogue.

The extract below presents Jimmy's account of an episode following an evening spent at a bar, when his wife Connie had invited some friends back to their house. Jimmy is explaining what happened during this episode to their relationship counsellor:

1 *Jimmy*: Uh: I was (.) boiling at this stage and
2 I was real angry with Connie (.). And
3 uh went up to bed 'n (.) I lay on the bed.
4 (0.7) °got into bed.° (0.6) I- uh (.) could
5 hear giggling ('n all that) downstairs and
6 then (0.5) the music changed (0.5) slow
7 records. (1.2) And um: (1.2) >and then they
8 changed to slow records< (0.8) I could
9 hea::r (1.0) that Connie was dancing with
10 (0.2) this blo:ke downstairs. (1.0) And
11 Caroline turned round and said (.) something
12 (.) about it (it was wha-) it was oh Connie
13 look out I'm going to tell (.) Jimmy on you.
14 (1.0) And (.) next thing I hear is (.) °what
15 he doesn't know (doesn't) hurt him°.
16 (0.2)
17 *Counsellor*: °I'm sorry?°

18 *Jimmy*: What he: doesn't know: doesn't hurt him.
19 (0.8) Soon as I heard that I went- (1.6)
20 straight down the stairs. (0.8) 'n uh (0.6)
21 threw them out. (1.2) Took Connie up the
22 stairs and threw her on the bed. (1.6) I kept
23 trying to ru:n to jump out the window. (1.6)
24 But y'know: I I couldn't. (.) I couldn't (.)
25 get myself (0.4) to go out. (.) I couldn't
26 (.) do it.
27 *Counsellor*: So that's what you felt like.
28 *Jimmy*: Oh ye:h.

In the first line of this extract, Jimmy presents his 'anger' in terms familiar from Kövecses' (1990) heated-container metaphor, as something 'boiling' and threatening to burst (Edwards, 1999). His account then emphasises how a series of cumulative provocations led in stages to his final aggressive response. The initial reference to 'boiling' anger helps him deflect some of the possible responsibility for his actions. It presents his anger as something impossible to contain. And the fact that the specific expression of this anger involved potential violence to himself ('I kept trying to run to jump out the window', l. 23) also reduces the chance that his aggression is seen as specifically directed against other people, including Connie in particular.

Connie's own account of things provides a counter-narrative by attributing Jimmy's apparent anger and aggression to his prior emotional disposition and oversensitivity rather than her own allegedly provocative behaviour on the evening in question. In her version of events, Jimmy's actions were a familiar manifestation of his deep-seated jealous tendencies, and part of a long-standing pattern of irrational overreaction:

1 *Connie*: At that poi:nt, (0.6) Jimmy ha- (.) my-
2 Jimmy is extremely jealous. Ex- extremely
3 jealous per:son. Has a:lways ↓been, from
4 the da:y we met. Y'know? An' at that point
5 in time, there was an episo:de, with (.) a
6 bloke, (.) in a pub, y'know? And me: having
7 a few drinks and messin'. (0.8) That was it.
8 (0.4) Right? And this (0.4) got all out of
9 hand to Jimmy according to Jimmy I was
10 a:lways doin' it and .hhh y'know a:lways
11 aggravating him. He was a jealous person
12 I: aggravated the situation. .h And he
13 walked out that ti:me. To me it was (.)
14 totally ridiculous the way he (0.8) goes o:n
15 (0.4) through this problem that he ha:s.

The two key parties involved in these events use emotion talk to describe and present what happened in different ways. Each account is oriented to potential accusations and counter-accusations from the other partner and is designed to defend a particular view of what was going on and who was to blame. For example, Jimmy's characterisation of himself as 'boiling' with anger serves the purpose of emphasising the personal impact of what Connie was doing, while Connie's account uses the emotional concept of 'jealousy' to present Jimmy's 'angry' reactions to her behaviour as disproportionate and inappropriate. Thus, formulation of conduct in emotional terms may be used to demonstrate its justifiability as a reaction to emotionally provocative events, or, by contrast, to undermine its rationality (e.g., Lutz, 1988; Shields & MacDowell, 1987).

One of Edwards' central points is that the flexibility of emotional discourse is an interesting and important feature of how it works in real interactions between people. Rather than trying to recover a true underlying version of events, we should acknowledge and investigate variability as a phenomenon in its own right. Instead of saying that emotions are really rational or irrational (or consistently perceived as such), we need to acknowledge that they can be represented in either way depending on the conversational concerns that we are attending to at the time. Questions then arise of whether other aspects of emotion representations are similarly flexible, and whether open-endedness is what makes prototypical scripts or goal-dependent categories useful conceptual devices in the first place. Emotional descriptions may be particularly effective precisely because their malleable specifications allow them to meet the varying demands of different conversational tasks.

In the extracts presented above, Jimmy and Connie talked about Jimmy's emotions some time after the events in question. Their conversations with the counsellor may therefore tell us more about how people describe emotions in hindsight than how they present them in ongoing interactions. After all, people often make up stories that help them provide excuses or retrospectively rationalise their conduct. Does emotion talk also work in similar ways when it relates to what is happening at the time it is delivered?

Evaldsson and Melander (2017) investigated 'reproach-response sequences' during ongoing interactions between teachers and students diagnosed with Attention Deficit Hyperactivity Disorder (ADHD) in Sweden. For example, they focused on a series of interchanges between a student named Mattias and his two teachers. Mattias's lack of cooperation and argumentativeness lead one of his teachers to say to him at an early stage in the interaction: 'you seem: a bit (.) hypersensitive today' (p. 76, authors' own translation from Swedish). However, Mattias simply slams down his desk lid and continues to grumble and complain. Things

Excerpt 4b

```
 8   OLOF:      ja: vill inte bli arg. (.) å de:: som-
                I:  don't want to become angry. (.) and tha::t like-

 9              du har sett mej arg.=
                you have seen me angry.=

10   Mattias 2. =å JA E REDAN ARG.=
                =and I AM ALREADY ANGRY.=
```

```
11   OLOF:      =du har SETT mej a[rg,     ]
                =you have SEEN me    angry,

12   Mattias:                     3. [om du-] om du blir arg på mej
                                      if you-  if you get angry at me

13              då smäller ja till dej.=
                then I'm going to hit you.=

14   OLOF:      =du har ↑sett (.) mej a[rg.
                =you have ↑seen (.) me    angry.

15   Mattias:                          [få fetaste smällen av mej.=
                                        get the fattest smack from me.=

16   OLOF:      =du har sett mej arg en gång.=
                =you have seen me angry once.=

17   Mattias 4. =håll käften [(    )
                =shut up

18   OLOF:                    [de vil- de vill du inte se en gång till.
                               that wa- that want you not see one time more.
                               'you don't want to see that one more time.'
```

Figure 2.4 Transcript from Evaldsson and Melander's (2017) study
(reproduced with permission from Elsevier)

escalate after he spits on the classroom floor and starts shouting, first at another student and then at his other teacher, Olof.

Specifically emotional language is first used after Olof suggests that Mattias should wipe up the spit and apologise for screaming at him (see Figure 2.4). It is Olof who raises the topic of 'anger' at this point by issuing a veiled threat: 'I: don't want to become angry. (.) and tha::t like- you have seen me angry'. (p. 82). Note that the emphasis on 'I' implies that Mattias, unlike his teacher, is already angry, and therefore guilty of not similarly controlling his temper. Before Olof finishes speaking, Mattias interrupts by shouting: '= and I <u>AM</u> ALREADY ANGRY. ='

Mattias's interjection is an interesting one, partly because of the emphatic way it is delivered and its particular stress on the present-tense verb ('AM'). There is an overt contrast between his own immediate and directly involved emotional orientation and the calm promises of possible emotional retaliation delivered by Olof. But why is Mattias telling Olof something that Olof has already implied he knows? The shouted description seems intended to reinforce in as clear a way as possible the message that Mattias is in the throes of a potentially uncontrollable angry reaction. The point may be to contest Olof's ability to talk him out of it. Or it may be a last-ditch attempt to direct blame at someone who is evidently refusing to participate in any reciprocation, an explicit provocation intended to push Olof over the edge. In any case, Olof refuses to rise to the bait, maintaining his distance by repeatedly saying that Mattias has seen him angry, thus reemphasising that this is a reaction properly reserved for extreme and deliberate transgressions.

The results of this study support the general conclusion that speakers' emotional formulations of both their own and other people's concurrent as well as recalled behaviour are oriented to the argumentative positions taken by other people involved in the conversation. Olof's training and experience lead him to present Mattias's real-time 'anger' as a problem indicating lack of appropriate control and respect for others. Mattias resists Olof's authority by claiming this same anger as his own authentic response to being told how to behave. There are obvious parallels between this dialectic of control and resistance and Edwards' earlier discussion of rationality and irrationality. In both cases, presenting experience in 'angry' terms is an argumentative move whose interpretation depends on understanding the conversational context. We need to know what alternative formulation is being rejected to make sense of it.

None of the emotion talk analysed in either of the studies discussed so far explicitly refers to the object or target of the emotion that is presented. Mattias emphasises that he is angry, and not that he is angry about being ordered around or that he is angry with Olof specifically. Jimmy says that he was boiling with anger, and not that his anger was about Connie flirting with other men or even that it was primarily directed at her. There are at least two possible reasons for this lack of specificity. First, the practical and linguistic context implicitly provides much of the relevant information to both parties as common ground (e.g., Clark, 1985), making any explicit reference to object or target partly redundant. Second, characterising an emotion as a personal condition that you simply have serves its own rhetorical purposes. It is in both Jimmy's and Mattias's interests to make their 'anger' seem like something with its own intrinsic and undirected momentum rather than something focused on any specific object or targeted at any specific person.

The researchers also have their own reasons for focusing on non-specific and untargeted emotion talk. It allows them to develop arguments about the rhetorical functions achieved by direct descriptions of supposed mental states, which often seem like the purest and most straightforward uses of the concepts in question (cf. Wittgenstein, 1953). It turns out that neither Jimmy nor Mattias is simply describing how they feel, even though the grammar of their sentences suggests that is exactly what they are doing. However, the researchers' focus on direct emotion descriptions draws attention away from cases where emotion talk evaluates objects or commits speakers to interpersonal actions. To understand how these pragmatic functions operate in the wild, we need to consider a wider range of conversations, and we need to look at what else is going on around those conversations.

Nonverbal Discourse

Discursive approaches foreground participants' talk as a way of getting at its rhetorical functions. However, what talk achieves also depends on nonverbal aspects of utterances such as volume, intonation and timing. Accordingly, transcription conventions include annotations representing these paralinguistic cues alongside the words themselves. Jefferson (1985) even specified codes for specific characteristics of different forms of 'laughter' in order to explore their role in conversation. But is even this enough to get a clear sense of how emotion talk operates in real-life social settings? Facial movements, people's orientations to each other and their interpersonal actions may also make a difference to interpretation of what is being said and its interpersonal intent and effect. Indeed, Mattias's screaming and spitting in the example above provide the initial basis for the attribution of 'anger'.

Evaldsson and Melander (2017) use various devices to supplement their textual transcripts (Figure 2.4). Captions indicate actions and diagrams indicate the relative positions of the participants and their movements over time. For example, a bird's eye view of the classroom shows footprints marking out Mattias's trajectory as he walks out the door. This information is added specifically to clarify certain parts of the social interaction, so that the words can be understood in the context of their delivery. The implication is that words alone don't perform speech acts. The pragmatic work is done by delivering those words with a specific intonation, volume and pitch, accompanied by specific gestures and body movements, which in turn unfold in relation to a specific dynamic context.

Does this mean that the real emotional action takes place in a non-discursive realm? In the transcript above, Olof evidently concludes that Mattias is behaving angrily before Mattias personally acknowledges it, but even Olof does not use that word directly at this earlier stage. Should we therefore see anger as something prior to talk that simply gets formulated in a certain way when people start to speak about it? Or is Mattias's nonverbal (or preverbal) presentation already part of his angry formulation of what is happening?

Hepburn and Potter (2012) analysed different forms of 'crying' exhibited by an unsuccessful contestant in the UK reality TV show *Pop Idol* and by distressed callers on a telephone help-line run by the UK's National Society for Prevention of Cruelty to Children (NSPCC). Their conclusion was that crying consistently serves a number of identifiable functions during conversation. In particular, it often licences a failure to provide an expected verbal turn such as a direct reply to a question (a disruption of progressivity), eliciting replies such as 'it's alright' or 'take your time'. Or it encourages the hearer to affirm or empathise with the crier, or to break through the formality of an otherwise bureaucratised encounter.

Hepburn and Potter (2012) argue that none of these cases imply that crying intrudes into talk as an independent outpouring of individual emotion. Instead, crying is part of an interactive achievement that emerges as part of the conversation rather than outside it: It 'is something that typically inflects talk, sometimes interferes with, dramatizes, or underscores talk, and sometimes replaces talk, rather than appearing as an action or set of actions in its own right' (p. 208). In other words, crying is a conversational move and not an expression of being moved by something going on elsewhere.

Goodwin, Cekaite and Goodwin (2012) present an alternative view that helps explain why nonverbal behaviours are able to perform the kinds of function identified by Hepburn and Potter. According to them, people use their bodies not just to supplement or clarify talk but also to achieve distinctive emotional functions that talk itself would not directly permit. For example, physical positioning and orientation allow people to take up particular stances in relation to other people. Interactants coordinate the timing of their respective movements and move closer or disperse as ways of presenting their degree of convergence with, or opposition to, other people and their actions.

Goodwin and colleagues illustrate their analysis with an annotated transcript of an interaction involving four adolescent female pupils having lunch in their school cafeteria (see Figure 2.5). Three of the girls sit on one side of a shared table, while the other student, Angela, sits on the other side, eating her chocolate pudding without a spoon. When Angela dips her tongue into the pot, one of the other girls describes what is

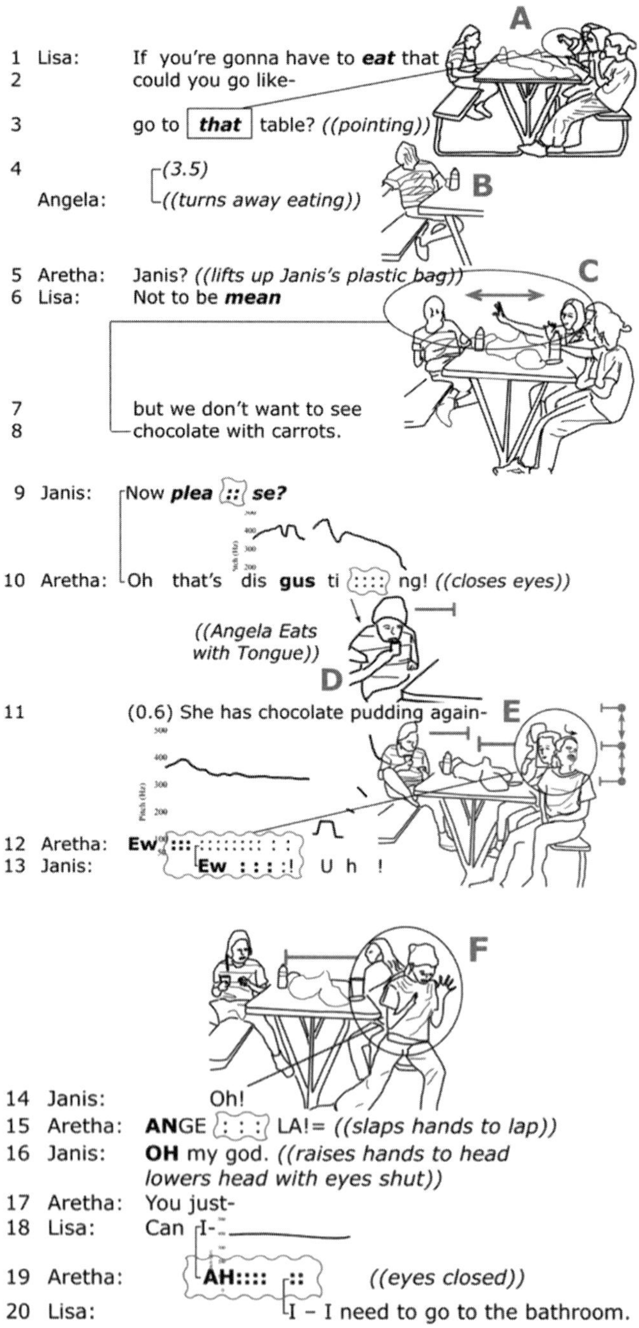

1 Lisa: If you're gonna have to **eat** that
2   could you go like-

3   go to [*that*] table? ((pointing))

4   ⎡(3.5)
   Angela: ⎣((turns away eating))

5 Aretha: Janis? ((lifts up Janis's plastic bag))
6 Lisa: Not to be **mean**

7   but we don't want to see
8   chocolate with carrots.

9 Janis: ⎡Now **plea** :: **se?**

10 Aretha: ⎣Oh that's dis **gus** ti ::::: ng! ((closes eyes))

          ((Angela Eats
          with Tongue))

11   (0.6) She has chocolate pudding again-

12 Aretha: **Ew** :::::::::::::
13 Janis: **Ew** ::::! U h !

14 Janis: Oh!
15 Aretha: **ANGE** ::: LA!= ((slaps hands to lap))
16 Janis: **OH** my god. ((raises hands to head
          lowers head with eyes shut))
17 Aretha: You just-
18 Lisa: Can I-:
19 Aretha: **AH**:::: :: ((eyes closed))
20 Lisa: I – I need to go to the bathroom.

Figure 2.5 Annotated transcription of conversation in school cafeteria (Goodwin et al., 2012, reproduced with permission from Oxford University Press)

happening in explicitly emotional terms ('Oh, that's disgusting'), but the public presentation of her emotional orientation also involves her and her two friends pointedly turning away, closing their eyes, moving hands in front of their faces and making shrieks. This coordinated set of actions visibly presents the three girls as aligned in shared opposition to Angela, thus communicating a humiliating form of social rejection. Adoption of these positions also excludes Angela from the group more directly.

In this episode, it is not the girls' individual movements that separately achieve their social effects, but rather their joint orientation away from Angela and her point of view (see Chapter 7). Meanwhile, Angela herself turns away from the three girls shielding the action that they are treating as 'disgusting' from their sight. In other words, embodied relational activity operating between people is what seems to be making the difference to their respective emotional positions (cf. de Rivera & Grinkis, 1986; and see Chapter 1). Words alone could not easily serve the same evaluative functions (or at least not in the same ways).

In fact, none of the girls directly presents their own experience as emotional terms in Goodwin and colleagues' excerpt. One of them describes Angela's conduct as 'disgusting' but does not describe her own reaction to that conduct as 'disgusted'. The fact that people can present their orientation to emotional events more directly using movements and nonverbal expressions may make more explicit presentation of their own emotion unnecessary. Further, openly attributing an emotion to yourself in words runs the risk of criticisms from interlocutors of irrationality and lack of control. For both these reasons, saying explicitly that you are emotional may actually happen relatively rarely in everyday conversation.

Concepts in Context

What implications does discursive research have for our understanding of emotion concepts represented by words such as 'anger'? One lesson is that emotion words usually function as part of more articulated conversational moves that may also involve nonverbal signals and movements towards or away from the other people involved. The two streams of communication and social influence may or may not be integrated with each other and may or may not achieve similar effects on other people.

A second conclusion is that emotion talk is often specifically oriented to what other people have already said and done or what they might be about to say or do. Interpretation therefore depends on attending to the unfolding content and context of the surrounding talk and action. Saying that you are 'angry' may be my way of undermining the rationality of your version of events, a request or demand for you to regain composure or an acknowledgement that I have done something that might justifiably make you 'angry'. But telling which means checking how it relates to whatever else is, has been and will be going on.

Conclusions

This chapter has discussed a range of different approaches to emotion language. We first looked at laboratory research that focuses on the meanings of individual emotion words, specified either as dimensions or categories with clear or fuzzy boundaries, and represented by proto-types or context-specific perceptual simulations. We next turned to the pragmatic uses of emotion words in utterances that perform a range of actions in addition to simple description. Finally, we reviewed discursive studies showing that people formulate emotion descriptions as ways of defending their argumentative position against actual and potential counter positions.

   Is it better to keep these diverse approaches separate or should we try to integrate their various insights? One possibility is to start from the bottom and work up. Let's say that words are the common currency linking the different levels of analysis. Perhaps, then, the various prag-matic functions and discursive effects achieved by utterances containing emotion words depend on the descriptive meanings that those words convey. In that case, we can break down the higher-level operations to lower-level component processes. For example, pragmatic functions may be reducible to the deployment of descriptive concepts for specific purposes.

   Along these lines, it might be possible to explain the pragmatic function of evaluation by reference to an underlying descriptive dimension of 'pleasure' and action commitment by reference to an underlying descrip-tive dimension of 'arousal'. Perhaps emotion words are only able to evaluate because they represent pleasure, and only able to commit people to action because they represent arousal.

   However, reductions such as this are only achieved at a cost. Using emotion words to evaluate something implies much more than describ-ing your reaction to that something as 'pleasant'. Correspondingly, mak-ing a verbal commitment to act for or against that something is not just about describing the arousal it provokes. The pragmatic point of any expression of emotion-related pleasure is to ascribe goodness to the object at which the emotion is directed, and not to characterise how you are feeling. The pragmatic point of any communication of arousal is to demonstrate embodied engagement with the current concern and readiness to back up the action commitment. Descriptive specification is only a small part of either of these functional operations.

Should what words mean or what they do take priority in our understanding of their operation? What if we were to turn the reductive argument on its head? Perhaps, pleasure and arousal are descriptive representations that derive from experience of diverse performative acts of evaluation and action-commitment (respectively) rather than underlying dimensions of meaning that allow the performance of those acts in the first place.

Another possible linkage between levels of analysis links the apparent fuzziness, goal-directedness and context-dependence of descriptive emotion concepts with their flexible uses in emotional discourse. Here again we face questions about which level takes priority, and about what underlies what. According to Edwards (1999) the point of conceptual fuzziness is precisely to facilitate flexibility when making and countering arguments. Rather than seeing descriptive concepts as elementary carriers of emotional meaning, he concludes instead that they take their particular form because of pragmatic requirements. So flexibility is the origin rather than consequence of semantic indeterminacy.

Is there any way of determining definitively which level of analysis is more basic? One possible answer is that their relative priority depends on what kind of phenomena you are seeking to understand or explain. However, for present purposes, the most relevant issue is not whether emotion words have primarily descriptive meanings, but what role those words play in processes of interpersonal emotional influence. Some of the ways in which your emotions affect other people depend on the words that you use. And the effects of those emotion words may sometimes depend on their activation of descriptive concepts in whomever you are talking to. The other person may use their mental representation of the relevant emotion script when deciding how to respond. Alternatively, they may contest your description with a counter-formulation of their own. Or they may respond more directly to the pragmatic force of your implied evaluation or action commitment. Which of these processes operates most strongly partly depends on the nature of the interaction between the different people who are involved. It is certainly possible to create tasks that foreground the articulated descriptive meanings of emotion concepts. However, these may be relatively atypical cases (see Chapter 4).

There is at least one bottom line to all this. Emotion words don't originally acquire their meanings from any simple naming process (e.g., Wittgenstein, 1953). We first learn how and when they work in intersubjective contexts, when engaged in communion or shared activity, while pulling away from other people or pushing against them (de Rivera, 1977;

and see Chapter 9). Evaluation and action commitment are implicated in these relational alignments from the very start. Under these circumstances, it seems more plausible that descriptive concepts emerge from pragmatic uses of language than vice versa. Whether description ever takes precedence later in development is another matter.

CHAPTER 3

Facial Activity and Emotion Expression

How do faces convey emotional information? Some psychologists believe that private emotions automatically surface as facial expressions. Others argue that the main purpose of facial activity is to communicate social motives and influence other people's behaviour. This chapter evaluates these competing accounts using evidence from judgement and production studies. Judgement studies ask participants to decide what emotion is being expressed in photos or videos of facial expressions. Production studies assess facial activity in emotional situations more directly. Findings obtained using these two methods do not always converge but neither kind of study provides direct support for universal or consistent emotion-expression connections. A range of different factors seems to influence facial activity, only some of which relate to emotion. However, some forms of emotional influence clearly do depend on facial communication and calibration.

Although emotions are said to reside somewhere in the metaphorical heart, we often look for them on people's faces. Even when someone doesn't say what they are feeling, we may pick up clues from their smile or frown. In face-to-face interaction and more remote forms of interpersonal contact, we watch people's eyes to see where they are looking and their mouths to follow what they are saying. And we read all kinds of things into any lip curl, brow furrow or nose wrinkle that we detect. Sometimes it seems as if these movements make whatever is going on in their minds directly visible to us.

The idea that the face provides a window onto an internal world of emotion has a long history, and there are a number of good reasons for its appeal and persistence. Tracking another person's eye movements provides information about where and how their attention is directed, whether they are actively taking in or rejecting information from a definite location in the shared environment, or from the person with whom they are interacting. Facial movements can also tell us about what someone is about to do, whether they are poised to act, whether they are braced against some impending event and so on. These cues to action readiness are certainly relevant to emotion, even if only indirectly.

However, facial information makes most sense when linked to whatever else is going on. Seeing that someone is looking at something tells us much more when we can also see what it is that they are looking at. Noticing that they are getting ready to act is more useful when we can also discern where their prepared action is directed, and what it is intended to get them. We often register these kinds of contextual information automatically as part of the unattended background. Thus, faces can seem intrinsically meaningful and transparently expressive because we readily pick up their relation to other things that we implicitly know are already happening. Because our focus falls on the faces themselves rather than their surrounding context, we often think they are the only source of the information we are extracting. But we may be reading emotional meaning into them, rather than reading it out from what they actually show.

What happens then when we have less complete knowledge of the other person's orientation, perspective and action trajectory, when we catch sight of a grimace or scowl made by someone we don't know in a situation that is unfamiliar or contains few meaningful cues? What information can we extract from faces under these circumstances? How much can they tell us about a person's emotions? Before attempting to answer this question, it is worth making a few observations about the terms psychologists use to describe what faces do.

Terminology

'Facial expression' may seem like an easily understandable and unproblematic description of whatever shows on people's faces. However, it is also a loaded term. It already implies something more specific about what faces are doing. If they are expressions, they must be expressing something, something that started out inside and then gets out (Ekman, 1997; Ekman, Friesen & Ellsworth, 1972; Hinde, 1985). As we shall see, many theorists argue that the facial movements that are usually interpreted as expressions in Anglo-American societies, may in fact be performing different functions (Russell & Fernández-Dols, 1997). For example, they may be communicating something to other people rather than simply expressing it (Crivelli & Fridlund, 2018). And what they are communicating may be something other than emotion, such as relational information or object orientation (Parkinson, 2017). For this reason, I will mostly adopt the more neutral term 'facial configuration' to describe a static pattern held by facial muscles or a still picture of a face, and the terms 'facial activity' and 'facial movement' to describe changing patterns of muscular tension and relaxation. There may still be occasions when it is appropriate to describe something as a 'facial expression'. However, from now on

I will try to use this phrase only to refer to faces that are (supposedly) expressing something, and not those whose muscles just happen to be configured in a certain way.

We should also be careful about how we describe particular forms of facial configuration and movement. Many researchers talk about sad and angry faces, again implying that they directly carry information about particular emotions. This more specific claim is also hotly contested by researchers for reasons that will soon become clear. At any rate, it is important not to presuppose that any particular face is necessarily related to a particular emotion. I therefore follow the lead of researchers such as Russell and Fernández-Dols (e.g., 1997) by labelling different facial configurations in terms of their patterned muscular movements rather than the emotions they supposedly express. Thus, I will call the so-called angry expression either a scowling face or an 'anger' expression (with appropriate scare quotes). Even these revised descriptions can never be entirely theoretically neutral. That would involve somehow specifying the precise degree of tension in each individual facial muscle rather than trying to summarise the overall pattern. However, an appropriate balance needs to be struck between succinctness and theoretical over-interpretation.

A final loaded term that needs unpacking is 'accuracy'. When research participants make judgements of scowling, smiling or pouting faces, the extent to which they see them as indicating anger, joy or sadness (respectively) is often taken to reflect correct perception of their actual meaning. In fact, the people posing those faces are often not experiencing any of those emotions at the time. For example, they may have simply been asked to pull and hold their facial muscles in a certain way or to act as if they were experiencing the emotion for the camera. Thus, attaching predicted emotion labels to facial stimuli does not necessarily reflect accuracy or correct attribution of underlying meaning. For this reason, I shall refer to consistency in judgement or its correspondence to predicted categories when describing the results of studies where participants attach emotion labels to faces.

Having got these terminological issues out of the way, let's turn to the real business at hand. What can faces communicate and what other things do they do in relation to emotion's interpersonal effects?

Neurocultural Theory

Many psychologists share the commonsense intuition that faces can tell us what emotion someone is experiencing. Perhaps the clearest attempt to explain how this might work is Ekman's (1972) neurocultural theory (see also Ekman, 2003; Izard, 1971; Tomkins, 1962). As implied by its concatenated name, the theory addresses the ways in which brain processes and societal processes combine in the production of facial activity. By putting neuro first, Ekman's aim was to tip the balance of explanation away from cultural factors, which he saw as taking undue precedence in other theories that were popular at the time (e.g., Birdwhistell, 1970). The neuro part of neurocultural theory defends the priority of biological factors against these perceived challenges to their priority in two ways.

First, it proposes that a small number of so-called basic emotions are pre-programmed into the human central nervous system as a consequence of natural selection. The English names for these emotions are 'happiness', 'sadness', 'anger', 'fear', 'disgust' and 'surprise' (and perhaps also 'interest' and 'shame', according to Ekman's mentor, Tomkins, 1962).

Second, it contends that each of these basic emotions is directly linked to a characteristic, biologically determined facial configuration (see Figure 3.1). Experiencing the emotion automatically activates a pre-wired 'facial action program' that produces the corresponding expression

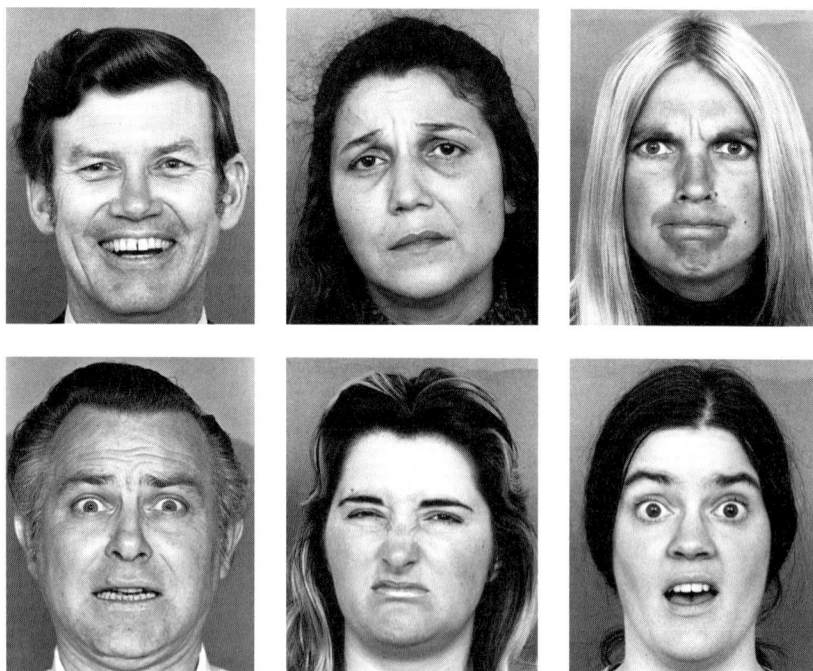

Figure 3.1 Six basic emotion expressions (clockwise from top left: happiness, sadness, anger, fear, disgust, and surprise (reproduced with permission from the Paul Ekman Group)

by sending efferent impulses to muscles in the face. Thus, happiness spontaneously leads to smiling, and disgust to nose-scrunching.

The cultural part of neurocultural theory makes two proposals intended to explain variability in facial expression across societies without undermining the claim that they are hard-wired. First, Ekman argues that basic emotions are not uniquely tied to their original biologically specified elicitors and may acquire associations with other culturally specific stimuli as a result of local social learning. For example, fear may start out as a preprogrammed response to sudden and intense stimulation, looming objects or direct threats to survival. However, children soon learn about other potential sources of danger, some of which arise primarily because of the cultural conditions surrounding them. They may become attuned to threats to reputation, face or honour, or start to watch out for harbingers of divine retribution, for example. In other words, different things acquire emotional relevance as people become socialised into different cultural practices and belief systems. Cultural differences of this kind thus explain why the same situation doesn't universally lead to the same facial expression even if that expression remains closely linked to the emotion.

Ekman's second proposal about cultural influence is that society-specific norms about what it is appropriate to express (display rules) sometimes lead people to alter or disguise what shows on their faces. For example, different countries and regions have different conventions about smiling in public. In most of the US and UK, it is considered polite to greet someone else with a smile even if you do not know them and are not currently feeling particularly sociable or happy. However, most Russian people do not routinely smile at strangers, even if they are positively inclined towards them. In recognition of this display rule, local authorities mounted a publicity campaign immediately prior to the 2018 FIFA World Cup to ensure that foreign visitors felt more welcome when attending the tournament. Smiling became a civic duty for Russian citizens living near the towns and cities where the matches were taking place. Thus, instructions and conventions about what to show on your face may loosen any connection between emotion and its usual expression. Display rules can stop people from directly revealing what they feel.

The operation of display rules means that entirely spontaneous facial expressions may be relatively rare in many public contexts. According to Ekman (1997), habitual control of facial activity may even extend into our private lives. This makes it much harder to prove or disprove the existence of the underlying facial configurations supposedly activated by facial action programs (see also Crivelli & Fridlund, 2018). After all, how can we tell whether any observed expression is unadulterated?

Neurocultural theory recapitulates the everyday idea that emotions are internal states, buried within an individual's brain (see Chapter 1). Although they may sometimes manifest themselves in publicly observable facial movements, the link between their inner essence and outward man- ifestations is disrupted whenever display rules get in the way of expres- sion. This complicates the task facing any observer (such as a psychological researcher) who wants to find out what is really going on inside. Whatever emotion is in this account, it stays largely insulated from the social world (a bit like Wittgenstein's imagined beetle in a matchbox).

Unmasking

Is it possible to distinguish spontaneous expressions of basic emotions from those whose appearance is distorted by the influence of display rules? According to Ekman and Friesen (e.g., 1975), a number of poten- tially detectable cues indicate emotional authenticity. Attempts to contain the impulse to express may be incomplete or unsuccessful, thus allowing some of the emotion to leak out onto the face, like a trickle of water through the crack in a dam.

Correspondingly, spontaneous facial movements may have specific characteristics that distinguish them from regulated ones. Probably the most famous example is the apparent difference between smiling 'with the eyes' and simply saying 'cheese'. One of the pioneers of facial anat- omy, Duchenne de Boulogne (1862), codified this distinction following a series of experiments involving 'localized electrization' (p. 10) – a procedure in which live electrodes were pressed to the skin of volun- teers' faces to activate muscles below the surface. One of Duchenne's favoured participants was a toothless man whose gaunt ageing features allowed more precise targeting of specific muscles and clearer recording of their movements (and whose lack of facial sensitivity made him rela- tively more willing to endure repeated electric shocks, see Figure 3.2).

Duchenne's observation of the different smiles induced in these studies led him to the following conclusions:

> [T]he emotion of frank joy is expressed on the face by the combined contraction of m. zygomaticus major ... and the inferior part of orbi- cularis oculi ... The first obeys the will but the second (the muscle of kindness, of love, and of agreeable impressions) is only put in play by the sweet emotions of the soul. Finally, fake joy, the deceitful laugh, cannot provoke the contraction of this latter muscle. (p. 126)

The zygomatic major muscle in the cheek simply lifts the corners of the lips, but the orbicularis oculi sphincter muscle tightens the eyelids to add the distinctive appearance of crow's feet wrinkles, and it is the combination of these two movements that Duchenne interpreted as an expression of authentic happiness (see Figure 3.3).

Duchenne's photographs were subsequently used by Darwin in some of the first reported experiments on emotion judgement (Ekman, 2009).

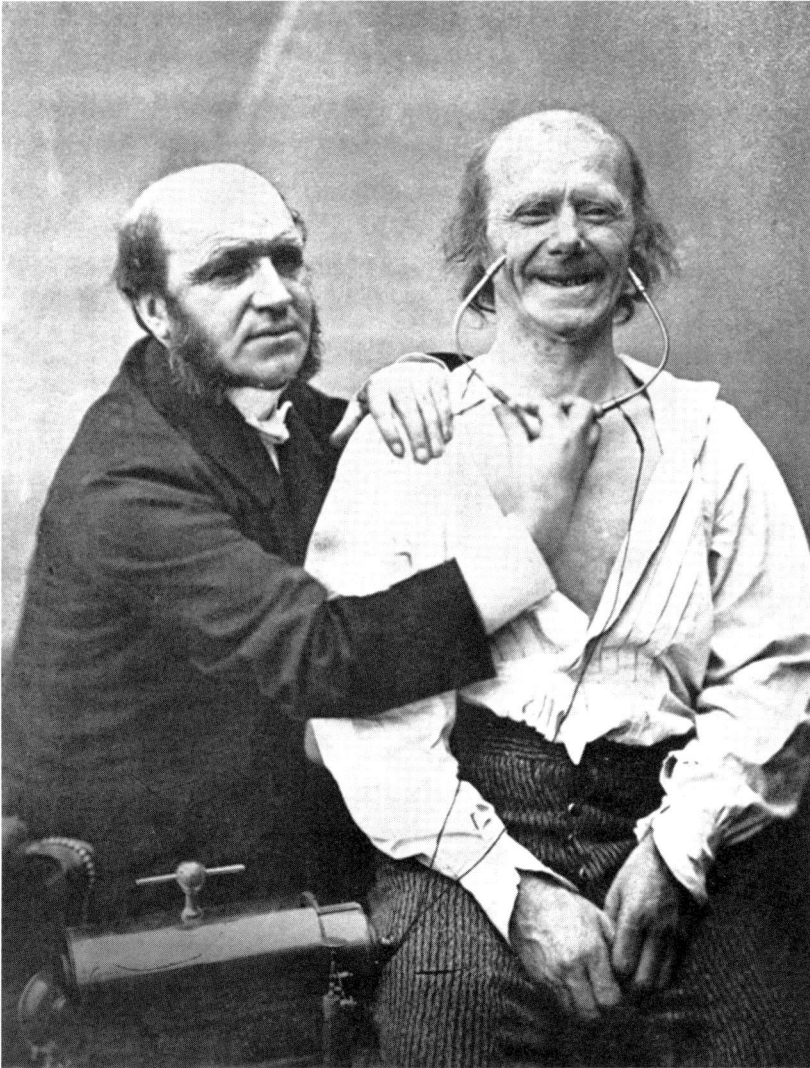

Figure 3.2 Duchenne de Boulogne with research volunteer (public domain)

They were also included in his landmark book *The Expression of the Emotions in Man and Animals* (Darwin, 1872) after painstaking use of airbrushing to remove the unsightly electrodes (in the days before Photoshop). Later still, Ekman (e.g., 1989) dubbed the combination of lip-corner raising and eyelid-tightening the 'Duchenne smile'. Like its eponymous originator, Ekman believed that this facial configuration reliably indicates the presence of genuine happiness and cannot easily be faked.

Although Duchenne (1862) argued that contraction of orbicularis oculi 'does not obey the will' (p. 72), more recent research has shown that many of us can actually control this muscle voluntarily (e.g., Gunnery, Hall & Ruben, 2013; Krumhuber & Manstead, 2009; and see Figure 3.3), making its status as a marker of spontaneity suspect. Further, so-called genuine smiles rapidly transition into so-called false smiles and back again over the course of brief stretches of behaviour (Messinger, Fogel & Dickson, 1999). Unless we want to argue that people also alternate abruptly between being genuinely happy and pretending from one millisecond to the next, the Duchenne eye wrinkle does not seem to be as reliable a cue of underlying emotion as once supposed.

However, leakage might still be detectable in other ways. For example, Ekman and Friesen (1969) suggest that the voluntary muscle control required to produce 'false' expressions disproportionately affects the right-hand side of the face (e.g., Ross & Pulusu, 2013) making the resulting expression asymmetrical. Similarly, deliberate movements may begin

(a)   (b)

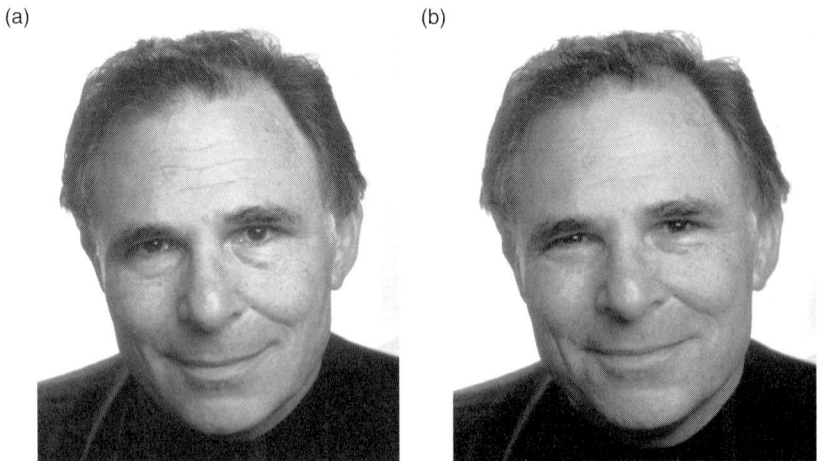

Figure 3.3 Paul Ekman posing a 'polite' smile (A) and a Duchenne smile (B) (reproduced with permission of the Paul Ekman Group)

more slowly and be less smoothly executed than spontaneous move-ments, leading to distinctive temporal dynamics (e.g., Schmidt, Bhattacharya & Denlinger, 2009). Lapses of control might also allow micro-expressions to slip through a person's defences for a brief instant, allowing trained observers to detect underlying emotion, especially when equipped with the technology for slow-motion recording.

Given that people don't have full and perfect control over the move-ments of their facial muscles, it seems plausible that faking or feigning is not always successful. However, this does not necessarily mean that genuine emotions can be reliably diagnosed and distinguished using information about symmetry, dynamics or micro-expressions. In parti-cular, it is not clear how often these cues are also produced under non-emotional conditions, regardless of any fakery.

One of the few studies that has directly assessed micro-expressions asked participants to neutralise or mask their facial responses to pre-sented slides that were selected to be strong or weak elicitors of various emotions (Porter, ten Brinke & Wallace, 2012). The idea was that micro-expressions (lasting between 0.04 and 0.2 seconds) should surface most commonly when participants are trying to cover up the expression of a strong emotion. In fact, none of the 1,711 facial configurations recorded in this study involved a full-face micro-expression. Eighteen of the configurations that were brief enough to qualify showed only in either the top or bottom half of the face. Only six of these corresponded to the predicted pattern associated with the emotion participants were trying to cover up, and only seven of the eighteen were observed in the strong (rather than weak) emotion condition. In other words, the recorded facial configurations that came closest to micro-expressions did not seem to be responses to any leakage or overflow of intense emotion.

Yan and colleagues' (2013) study used videos instead of slides to elicit emotional reactions. Twenty-two participants were given a monetary incentive to neutralise their expressions throughout a thirty-minute per-iod during which disgusting, fear-inducing, sad and happy film clips were presented. Two of the participants managed to keep their faces immobile throughout the procedure. The other twenty showed facial movement at some point, yielding a dataset containing over 1,000 recorded facial expressions. When the investigators tried to identify examples of micro-expressions, they found only twelve that met Porter and colleagues' duration criterion (lasting less than 0.2 seconds) and none that lasted less than 0.1 seconds. However, relaxing this criterion yielded a sample of 109 facial configurations lasting less than 0.5 seconds. Again, the majority of these 109 brief facial movements only involved partial and low-intensity versions of one of the pre-specified basic emotion expressions, and even those often did not match the pattern theoretically associated with the intended emotional content of the movie clips.

These findings certainly suggest that people's deliberate control of facial responses can lapse, but do not directly support diagnostic micro-expressions of the kind postulated by Ekman and Friesen (1975). The relatively brief facial movements recorded in this research happened rarely, often lasted for too long, and mostly failed to fit the predicted configuration associated with the supposedly concealed emotion. If micro-expressions observed outside the laboratory also have similar parameters, then their utility in determining when someone is experiencing something they are trying not to express is highly limited. On the few occasions that brief flashes of something appear on the face, their specific form usually tells us little about the nature of any underlying emotion (see also Durán, Reisenzein & Fernández-Dols, 2017).

Su and Levine (2016) used a computer vision approach to generate an algorithm that maximised detection of lying from facial movements recorded in situations involving high-stakes deception, where fear about getting caught out might potentially leak out. For example, they processed videos of family members making televised appeals for information about a missing person or crime victim. In some cases, the people making these appeals were subsequently convicted of the crime in question, giving the researchers a reasonable indication about whether deception was involved. Human observers typically perform no better than chance when judging whether a suspect is lying (e.g., Porter & ten Brinke, 2008), but Su and Levine's algorithm correctly detected lies at rates above 75 per cent. However, the algorithm's performance mainly depended on facial movements other than micro-expressions. Including micro-expressions in the identification process only improved the algorithm's accuracy by about 3 per cent, and using micro-expressions alone produced detection at levels that only marginally exceeded chance. In other words, trying to catch evanescent facial clues is apparently not the best way of uncovering concealed emotions or intentions in realistic settings, despite what TV dramas such as *Lie to Me* might seem to imply (Su & Levine, 2016).

Looking for symptoms of control or failure of control may be the wrong approach to emotion detection in any case. Controlled facial movements may often be intended to communicate what we are really feeling to someone else rather than to cover up a conflicting emotion. Correspondingly, uncontrolled facial responses may result from various factors other than leaked emotions, such as concentration, effort or action preparation (as well as twitches, twinges, yawns, partial sneezes and so on). Ruling out some of these alternative causal factors is often possible in laboratory settings where researchers can limit the possibilities of contamination by keeping the environment clear, contained and simple. However, outside the laboratory, the task of facial coding is often precisely to work out which of the many possible causal factors might be relevant in the first place. Under these circumstances, determining that one movement is controlled and another uncontrolled does not necessarily tell us whether either of them corresponds to an underlying emotion.

Reformulated Basic Emotion Theories

Neurocultural theory has been highly influential both within and outside psychology. Surprisingly, however, no one (including Ekman himself) fully subscribes to its original 1972 form any longer. Contemporary versions of 'basic emotion theory' or the 'facial expression program' (Russell & Fernández-Dols, 1997; Fernández-Dols & Russell, 2017) add qualifying clauses and soften some of the earlier model's more extreme claims. For example, Ekman (e.g., 2003) now sees basic emotions as families of inter-related lower-level emotions rather than single unitary states. This more flexible approach potentially allows facial expressions to vary across different cases of anger, fear and so on. In some cases, the pattern of facial blood flow may produce distinctive colouring in addition to any discriminative information provided by muscular position (e.g., Benitez-Quiroz, Srinivasan & Martinez, 2018; Thorstenson et al., 2018). Many latter-day researchers also doubt that the presence of a basic emotion automatically prompts the corresponding expression across all contexts (e.g., Hess, Banse & Kappas, 1995). And when it does, the expression need not involve a static facial configuration in isolation but rather a multimodal dynamic sequence of movements including other communication channels such as the body and voice (Keltner & Cordaro, 2017).

Predictions arising from these reformulated theories are more nuanced and less specific, making it harder to be sure exactly what data might permit falsification. It starts to seem as if the only definite claim that remains is simply that emotion expression is not entirely learned, not exclusively the product of nurture. However, it's not clear that anyone actually said that it was in the first place (see Russell, 1995). Indeed, the cultural relativists whose ideas Ekman's theory was originally intended to dispel were hardly biology-denying extremists (e.g., Birdwhistell, 1970; Klineberg, 1940, see Crivelli & Fridlund, 2019). To some commentators, then, neurocultural theory now seems like an overreaction to a position that no one ever really held, with little residual substance apart from a misplaced critique of a straw person. Correspondingly, supporters of reformulated basic emotions theory accuse their opponents of attacking a view that has since been revised, even when the revisions seem too diverse or too flexible to permit contestable claims or specific predictions.

Where does this leave us? There are clearly a range of alternative opinions about how closely facial movements and positions relate to emotions, and about how distinct those emotions are in any case. Let's look at the key evidence before deciding which angle makes most sense.

Cross-Cultural Judgement

Isolating Pan-Cultural Elements

In 1969, Ekman, Sorenson and Friesen published one of the most influential papers in the psychological literature on facial expressions. The studies reported in this paper used still photographs showing Western people pulling faces intended to express the six 'basic' emotions of happiness, sadness, anger, fear, disgust and surprise (see Figure 3.2). Participants from several different countries had to look at these pictures and say which of the emotions they represented.

Ekman's team wanted to show that facial expressions had the same emotional meanings for all human beings because of their shared biological heritage. However, cross-cultural agreement in facial judgement might also depend on learning by observation during intercultural contact. Even seeing Hollywood movies might teach members of other societies which American expressions are supposed to go with which emotions. To reduce the possibility of this kind of cultural contamination, the researchers sought to recruit participants who had minimal prior contact with Westerners, because only their judgements would remain unaffected by knowledge about how Western faces react. The researchers therefore visited New Guinea and Borneo to study relatively isolated small-scale communities.

How did participants from these small-scale societies perform on the judgement task? Could they tell what emotion was being expressed by each of the different American faces? These sound like simple questions, but the answers turn out to be complicated and controversial.

There were two bottom-line findings. The first provided the headline that made the studies so influential in the first place. Participants from New Guinea and Borneo selected the predicted emotion label for the presented faces more often than we would expect purely on the basis of chance (one out of six, or 17 per cent). In other words, there are 'pan-cultural elements in facial displays of emotion'. The second bottom-line finding is that these pan-cultural elements really are only elements. Participants from the least Westernised societies selected the predicted emotion label significantly less often than participants from the USA, or societies with more Western contact (Nelson & Russell, 2013; Russell, 1994; and see Figure 3.4). Putting these two findings together, it seems

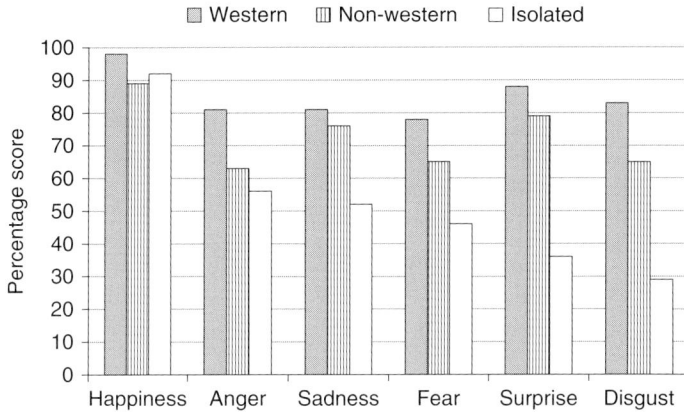

Figure 3.4 Performance in judgement tasks by participants from different societies (Russell, 1994; see also Nelson & Russell, 2013 for similar findings from subsequent studies, figure adapted with permission of the American Psychological Association)

that people from small-scale non-Western societies can discern enough information from American faces to point them in the direction of their supposed emotional meanings, but not enough to get them directly to those meanings themselves (or at least not in all cases).

How big were the differences between the facial judgements made by members of the different sampled societies? Ekman and colleagues emphasised the fact that the intended emotion word was the most commonly chosen option for all presented expressions in all but two of the sampled societies. However, these two exceptions were precisely those societies that had the least prior contact with Westerners. Members of the Fore ethnic group in New Guinea commonly labelled the pouting 'sad' face as 'anger' (56 per cent), and the open-mouthed, wide-eyed 'surprised' face as 'fear' (45 per cent). Participants from the Sadong group in Borneo more commonly labelled the nose-scrunching 'disgust' face as either 'sadness' (26 per cent) or 'happiness' (23 per cent) rather than 'disgust'. More generally, Fore and Sadong participants gave the supposedly incorrect response around half the time or less for all faces except for smiles, which received consistent responses across all sampled societies (Figure 3.4). This contrasts with the performance of Western participants, who gave the predicted response in around 80 per cent or more cases for all presented facial configurations.

Why were there such obvious cross-cultural differences in consistency of judgement if all humans universally recognise the same faces as expressing the same emotions, as neurocultural theory implies? Given the distinctiveness of the pre-selected photographs and the limited number of response options provided, the judgement task seems straightforward, especially if basic emotions really do automatically produce the expressions in question during everyday life. You might well assume that an expression designed by natural selection to convey specific emotional information would do the job pretty well when presented in isolation and without distraction. If you know that a scrunched nose is an expression of the basic and commonly experienced emotion of 'disgust', what would stop you from picking the closest available translation of that term when shown a clear picture of the face?

One possible complication is that the judgement task was unfamiliar and confusing to participants from small-scale societies with little knowledge of Western ways. If so, this may have made their performance less consistent than otherwise. However, participants from Borneo managed to label smiles as 'happy' at rates above 90 per cent. If the problem was with understanding the task, how did they answer the question so consistently for this face but not for the others (Russell, 1994)?

A more recent study in a small-scale society in the Trobriand Islands used a simpler task where participants simply had to point at or put their hand on the visual stimulus that matched an aurally presented word (Crivelli et al., 2016). When participants were asked to indicate the picture of a familiar local animal (dog, pig, fish or rooster), they got the correct answer every time (Crivelli, 2016). Similarly, when asked to indicate which was the happy face, all participants picked the smile. However, when asked to indicate the angry face, only 6 per cent selected the supposedly correct answer (as we shall see). In short, misunderstanding of task requirements does not seem a viable explanation for the lower rates of predicted emotion judgements in societies with little Western contact.

If the general structure of the task is not the problem, could there be an issue with the specific terms used to make emotion judgements? As discussed in Chapter 2, English words for basic emotion categories may not translate directly into different languages (e.g., Wierzbicka, 1991). This means that choosing the right word might be more difficult in societies where the emotional meanings of words are most different from the closest English language equivalents. But how big a problem would this be? Participants don't need to find a word that perfectly matches the emotional quality of the presented face. They only need to find the one that fits better than the five other alternatives that are available. If pouting faces universally express sadness, why then would the majority of Fore participants reject the best available translation for 'sadness' as a description of their meaning and choose instead the best available translation for 'anger'?

Maybe then it was the facial stimuli rather than the response alternatives that confused them. The photographs were carefully selected to have clear and consistent emotional meanings for US participants. Indeed, Ekman and colleagues (1969) did their best to filter out any effects of display rules or mixed emotions (p. 87) so that any underlying basic emotional meaning could shine through. However, what if viewers from different cultural backgrounds were less sure that the picture was intended to convey the emotion in an unadulterated way? What if they still suspected that display rules were distorting its underlying emotional meaning? Perhaps then, they read a face showing one basic emotion as more likely to reflect a different one. Although this remains a remote possibility, it cannot easily account for many of the specific findings. For example, how plausible is it that a Sadong participant would conclude that a person scrunching their nose was actually covering up their sadness or happiness? If nose-scrunching is naturally associated with 'disgust', wouldn't the closest translation for that term still be the more reasonable response?

Rather than worrying whether cross-cultural judgements converged enough to provide direct support for neurocultural theory, Ekman and colleagues (1969) focused on the fact that they converged at all, thus apparently ruling out any extreme cultural relativist account. For them, the glass was half-full rather than half-empty. Indeed, their findings certainly do show that something universal must relate to some aspects of the judgement task. The question is what that something might be.

In fact, evidence that classification scores for most facial stimuli were significantly above chance levels in samples with little Western contact only tells us that participants were not simply guessing at the answer (Russell, 1995). In other words, they must have been able to extract enough meaningful information from the faces to rule in or out some of the possible emotional interpretations. Anything providing any clue that one possible answer was more likely (or another possible answer less likely) would help push performance above baseline levels. For example, inferring pleasure rather than categorical emotional quality from faces would already introduce sufficient response consistency to rule out randomness. Knowing that a scowling face is not happy means that only five rather than six response options are now possible. And seeing that the muscles are tensed and eyes are narrowed may suggest a readiness for imminent action towards an object, ruling out avoidant forms of emotion such as disgust. Bit by bit, participants might piece together the more or less likely answers.

Even in the case of smiles, participants need not have recognised that they expressed happiness in order to make highly consistent judgements. 'Happiness' was the only emotion name listed with an unambiguously pleasant meaning, so participants may have simply worked out that a smiling face was not experiencing any of the available negative options to arrive at the predicted answer by a process of elimination (Russell, 1994). Alternatively, they may have seen the smile as an interpersonal greeting or invitation to interact and concluded that 'happiness' was the most likely of the listed emotions to accompany that social motive (e.g., Fridlund, 1994).

The general point here is that consistent labelling of any of the presented faces does not necessarily mean that participants spontaneously extracted its intended emotional meaning. Instead, they may simply have judged that the selected response alternative was the one that was most likely to be correct or the least likely to be incorrect (the best of a bad bunch).

Subsequent Studies in Small-Scale Societies

Because cross-cultural research in societies with little Western contact is so difficult and time-consuming, only a handful of subsequent studies have used comparable samples to those tested by Ekman's team (see Gendron, Crivelli & Barrett, 2018, for a review). Tracy and Robins (2008) collected data in rural settlements in Burkina Faso, West Africa. Their stimuli included faces intended to correspond to the six originally investigated basic emotions plus two new photo sets, one of which showed a supposed 'shame' expression (eyes pointing down and away from the camera, head bowed forward) and the other of which showed face and torso, with the face showing a slight smile, the head inclined backwards, hands on hips, and arms with elbows pointing outwards (see Figure 3.5). US participants consistently choose the response option of 'pride' for these latter pictures, and Tracy and Robins' study was intended to demonstrate that participants unfamiliar with Western culture agreed about their emotional meaning.

Consistency of responding in this study was at similar low to moderate levels to those found in Ekman and colleagues' (1969) earlier research. Only 30 per cent of participants labelled the wide-eyed gasping face as 'fear' and only about a third labelled the scowling face as 'anger' (compared to chance levels of 12.5 per cent). Frequencies of predicted judgements were a little higher for the nose-scrunching 'disgust' face (44 per cent), the pouting 'sad' face (51 per cent) and the open-mouthed wide-eyed 'surprise' face (58 per cent), but a substantial number of participants still got the supposedly 'incorrect' answer. As before, smiles were labelled most consistently (84 per cent). Unlike in Ekman and colleagues' earlier research, this relatively higher consistency score did not depend on 'happiness' being the only available pleasant response option, because 'pride' was also a possible answer. However, 'pride' also has potential negative connotations of boastfulness or hubris, which may have been cued by viewing the expanded posture shown in the 'pride' stimuli (Figure 3.5).

Figure 3.5 Example of 'pride' expression from Tracy and Robins' (2008) study (reproduced with permission of the American Psychological Association)

More than half of participants classified this posture as 'pride' (57 per cent), and about a third classified the bowed 'shame' face as shame (34 per cent). The fact that these percentages are no lower than those for other supposedly 'basic' emotions suggests either that these two additional emotions are equally basic or that basic emotions do not have such a special status in the first place. Again, consistency of response might still depend on the clues these new stimuli provide about possible emotional meaning, rather than their capacity to directly express the emotions themselves. For example, the expanded 'pride' posture may imply that the person wants to be visible to other people whereas the bowed shame face suggests the opposite. Participants may have inferred the most likely of the available response options on the basis of this kind of information rather than any encapsulated message about underlying emotional state.

Crivelli and colleagues' (2016b) study modified Ekman and colleagues' experimental task to make it more manageable for participants in small-scale societies with minimal Western contact. Instead of picking an emotion name for each face from a range of available alternative names, participants were given a single emotion name and asked to pick out the face of the person who was experiencing that emotion from a range of presented faces. The findings of this study provide a striking demonstration that facial configurations do not all have consistent emotional meanings across cultures. Fifty-six per cent of participants from the Trobriand Islands pointed at the gasping 'fear' face when asked to indicate an angry person. In a related study, Crivelli and colleagues (2016a) directly compared the face selections made by Trobriander and Spanish participants. While Trobrianders were much more likely to select the gasping face than the scowling face when asked to point at the angry person, this pattern was reversed in the Spanish sample.

In his 2017 chapter, Ekman set a high bar for any study seeking to contest his conclusion that all humans can directly read out basic emotions from facial expressions: 'evidence against universality … would have found that the expressions that the majority of people in one country judged as showing one emotion (let us say anger) were judged as showing another emotion (fear) by the majority in another culture. This never happened' (Ekman, 2017, p. 42). If the Trobriand Islands counts as the first country (or part of a country) and Spain as the second, then these conditions that 'never happened' in earlier research by Ekman's team were apparently met in Crivelli and colleagues' (2016a) study.

Why were the Trobrianders' judgements of the gasping face so dramatically different from those of Westerners? Fridlund (e.g., 1994; Crivelli & Fridlund, 2018) has argued that different faces may communicate similar social motives across different contexts. Correspondingly, the same facial configuration may feature in different sequences of action. We already know that similar muscle movements may be involved in getting your hand ready to punch someone and in getting your hand ready to grasp hold of a small object. Why shouldn't the same principle also apply to facial muscles? Along these lines, the 'gasping' movement associated with taking a sharp breath in preparation for dealing with a sudden threat may be morphologically similar to the movement required to fill your lungs in preparation for shouting. Similarly, the widened eyes associated with anxious vigilance may resemble the exaggerated stare associated with threatening someone.

Look again at the so-called fear face in Figure 3.1. Couldn't it also be seen as menacing given the right context (Carroll & Russell, 1996)? Doesn't it look a little like the faces pulled by the All Black rugby team in their pre-match intimidation ritual (Hakka)? Perhaps the interpretation of the configuration in terms of 'fear' is more prevalent in Western societies because their prototypical representation of that emotion specifies the personal aspects of a reaction to perceived threat to a relatively greater extent. Maybe Westerners have learned to use the gasping face as a shorthand way of communicating fear for similar reasons, and its conventional meaning has consequently been codified in these terms (see Chapter 9). By contrast, the Trobriand prototype for anger may feature shouting and an interpersonally directed focused stare relatively more strongly, possibly as a consequence of its ritualistic uses of this facial configuration as a display of menace (Crivelli et al., 2016a). The general point here is that the emotional meaning of faces may depend on the trajectories of action that they indicate or foreshadow and the centrality of these trajectories to our culturally specific prototypical representation of the emotion in question.

Most cross-cultural judgement studies depend on participants' explicit interpretations of the meaning of different emotion terms. However, it is also possible to assess perceptions of facial stimuli without using direct verbal cues. Gendron and colleagues (2014) asked participants from the USA and from the Himba ethnic group in Namibia to classify photos of African-American actors posing basic facial expressions by sorting them into piles. One set of participants from each society was provided with the basic emotion names used by Ekman and colleagues (or appropriate translations) and told that the faces might show these emotions (category-cued condition). The other set of participants was not provided with emotion words but simply told to 'sort the faces by feelings so that each person in a given pile was experiencing the same emotion' (free-sorting condition, p. 253). Americans sorted the photos in broadly similar ways across both these conditions, mainly relying on the familiar basic emotion categories. However, they only put the nose-scrunching 'disgust' faces into a separate category in the category-cued condition. In the free-sorting condition, they lumped together nose-scrunching 'disgust' with either scowling 'angry' faces or pouting 'sad' faces. This difference between free-sorting and category-cued conditions clearly shows that linguistic concepts affect judgements of so-called basic emotion expressions (see also Gendron et al., 2012).

Himba participants used different categories from US participants across both conditions. Although they consistently put smiling faces and wide-eyed gasping faces into distinct separate categories, their other categories all included faces that US participants sorted into two or more different piles. For example, pouting 'sad' faces, scowling 'anger' faces and nose-scrunching 'disgust' faces commonly ended up in the same categories as each other. When asked to provide labels for each of their freely sorted piles, Himba participants tended to use descriptions of behaviour such as 'looking at something' or 'laughing', whereas US participants tended to provide names for emotions.

The results of Gendron and colleagues' study potentially offer some support for the idea that Himba participants spontaneously distinguish smiling and gasping faces on the basis of their emotional meanings.

However, two methodological factors may have contributed to these apparent consistencies in emotional judgement. First, Gendron and colleagues specifically asked participants to classify faces based on emotional content, thereby attuning them to certain kinds of difference rather than others. Second and more important, the presented facial configurations were preselected to represent distinct basic emotion categories, meaning that their perceptual similarities tended to cluster in similarly distinct categories. This fact probably increased Himba participants' tendency to categorise the faces using cues that happened to correspond to the supposed categorical distinctions between the sampled emotional meanings, carving the stimulus set at its most obviously visible joints regardless of whether they actually picked up on any emotional implications.

Jack and colleagues (e.g., 2012) have pioneered a more data-driven psychophysical approach to classification that avoids issues that might otherwise arise as a consequence of stimulus preselection procedures. Participants in their studies are presented with a randomly generated set of animated facial movements and asked to rate them using various dimensions. This allows the researchers to work backwards from patterns of judgement in order to infer which movements are perceived as indicating which emotions. Using this technique in small-scale societies has the potential to uncover how native emotion concepts map on to movements that have not already been sorted into Anglo-American categories or shaped by US modes of expression.

Facial Accents and Dialects

The judgement studies considered so far were conducted in small-scale societies visited because of their limited contact with the Western World. Are there also cross-cultural differences between societies where contact is less restricted? A number of investigators have compared responses to the standard forced-choice judgement task across a range of cultural groups. Russell's (1994) and Nelson and Russell's (2013) reviews of this research suggest that culture still makes a difference. Even societies with ready access to Western facial activity and the portrayal of facial emotion in Hollywood films show significantly lower consistency in judgements of the basic emotion categories than samples from the USA where the categories and faces were originally specified (see Figure 3.4).

Elfenbein and Ambady's (2002) meta-analysis showed that cross-cultural differences in judgement partly depend on the cultural origins of the people whose faces are presented in the judgement task. Facial judgements were most consistent when participants judged faces of members of their own society, and least consistent when they judged faces of members of societies that were more remote and with whom they had little contact. These effects of the cultural match between the judges and the judged even applied across societies which shared the same language. This suggests that they cannot be explained by problems arising from the translation of the emotion words used in the judgement task. Elfenbein and Ambady concluded that societies develop their own distinctive dialects of the universal language of facial expression (see also Tomkins and McCarter, 1964). In other words, people with different cultural backgrounds make subtly different facial movements when expressing the same emotion (Elfenbein et al., 2007). Familiarity with these culture-specific movements makes it easier to decode them.

Marsh, Elfenbein and Ambady (2003) compared US participants' judgements of facial photos that were produced as part of a standardised stimulus set by Matsumoto and Ekman (1988). The pictures showed either native Japanese people or Japanese Americans displaying the supposed basic emotion expressions. Participants were able to tell which of these faces showed Japanese American (rather than native Japanese) faces, especially when the faces were intended to express sadness. In other words, there must be something noticeably different about the way Japanese people with different cultural backgrounds pull their muscles when trying to adopt a configuration representing particular emotions. And this difference is still detectable when facial stimuli have been carefully vetted to include only the predicted muscle movements. As Marsh and colleagues acknowledge, clearer interpretation of this finding depends on determining exactly what it is that is different about the two sets of faces – a problem that might potentially be solved using computer vision coupled with machine-learning procedures (e.g., Su & Levine, 2016).

Instead of working from six sets of faces intended to represent basic emotions, Jack and colleagues (2012) produced 4,800 1¼ second computer-animated video clips depicting a random sample of all possible movements of 'facial action units' (visible muscle changes). Both Caucasian and East Asian faces were used as models for the animations. Fifteen Caucasian European participants and fifteen recent arrivals to the UK from China then assigned one of the six basic emotion names (or no emotion) to each clip, and rated the intensity of that emotion. The resulting data allowed Jack and colleagues to work backwards in order to determine which clips were associated with which emotion judgements (at different intensities) for each cultural group.

European participants were relatively consistent in their allocation of different clips to the six different emotional categories. However, Chinese participants only showed comparable levels of consistency for happiness

and sadness, and not for the other four emotion categories, where allocations were more variable. This suggests that the six basic emotion categories that were provided as response options did not fit their perceptual
representations of facial movements as well as it did for the European
sample.

The reverse correlation technique also allowed Jack and colleagues to
determine which particular patterns of muscle movement were most
closely associated with emotion judgements in the two cultural groups.
One interesting finding was that Chinese participants were more
inclined than Europeans to see eye-muscle movements as indications
of emotional intensity. As noted by the researchers, this finding is
consistent with the different emoticons used to convey emotional meanings in European and Chinese text messages. Europeans typically use
emoticons that include the mouth as the key communicative feature
(e.g., :-) for happy, and :-| for angry). By contrast, Chinese emoticons
generally only indicate eye patterns (e.g., ^.^ for happy and >.< for
angry). Whether this difference represents how the emotions are actually expressed by members of the different societies or simply where
attention is directed when interacting with another person is another
question. However, if we assume that facial displays are typically
oriented to perceivers' responses, it seems reasonable to conclude that
processes of expression and decoding are aligned with each other. In
other words, the reported cross-cultural differences in judgement may
well reflect the impact of cultural dialects on the production as well as
the perception of facial activity.

Open-Ended Judgement

Results of judgement tasks not only depend on what facial stimuli are
sampled but also on what alternative responses are available (Gendron
et al., 2014). The forced choice procedure used in early universality
studies provided only six possible response options for six distinct
kinds of facial configurations. Repeated presentation of the facial stimuli
in conjunction with those response options allowed participants to calibrate the two over time (Russell, 1994). Of course, if participants knew
nothing about what faces might reveal, this would not have helped them
reach agreement. However, as we have seen, faces may provide enough
emotionally relevant information to give participants a foothold that
permits further progress in determining what the 'correct' response is
supposed to be.

For example, if participants start by assuming that faces with upturned
lips are greeting someone, they may conclude that none of the unpleasant
emotion words are appropriate descriptions (and that the affectively

ambiguous word 'surprise' doesn't apply either because it does not directly communicate positive intentions). This means that 'happiness' is the only remaining response alternative that plausibly matches the face. Even 100 per cent consistency in responses would only show that 'happiness' is clearly the best of the alternative interpretations provided, not that the facial stimulus directly carried that emotional meaning.

How can we tell what meanings participants extract from faces spontaneously? As argued in Chapter 2, it is impossible to solicit entirely neutral descriptions from participants because any communicative context carries its own specific demands. However, we can at least relax the constraints imposed by fixed response alternatives. It turns out that when participants are asked open-ended questions about their interpretations of facial stimuli, they do not always use emotion labels.

In the Netherlands, Frijda (1953) separately interviewed two female acquaintances and filmed their spontaneous facial reactions to a variety of emotionally relevant interventions, stopping the procedure after every apparently significant expression to ask what the interviewee was thinking and feeling. He then showed film clips (and still photographs) of the two interviewees' faces to forty participants, who gave their impressions of what had been going on in the person's mind when the shots were originally taken.

Viewers' descriptions mostly referred to what the interviewee was apparently doing or what situation she might be in rather than her emotional state at the time. For example, a short film clip showing facial movements during a shocked, fearful reaction to an unexpected (small) explosion was interpreted by one viewer in the following terms: 'You are telling her something, and she does not understand it. Then she suddenly says "Oh yes, that's it!"' (p. 309). Another viewer's impression of an interviewee's face while she was experiencing anxious expectation was that it appeared as if she were 'looking at something with fixed attention, a game or something, tense, two cars which almost get into collision, but nothing happens . . . Gosh, who would do anything so stupid?' (p. 314).

Clearly, these interpretations are informed by participants' personal memories and culturally shaped experiences of sudden realisations in tutorial-style situations and observed automobile accidents. Their narrative form probably also depends on the changing configuration of the faces as they moved over the course of the presented clips. Their dynamic characteristics make them more amenable to explanation in terms of unfolding processes rather than concurrent momentary states. However, it is still notable that references to thoughts, expectations, intentions and emotions were relatively rare, despite the experimenter's explicit instruction that viewers should say what was going on in the interviewee's mind.

When asked to provide open-ended descriptions of standardised basic emotion faces rather than spontaneously recorded facial movements (such as those used by Frijda), Western participants are relatively more likely to use emotion terms to represent their meaning (e.g., Gendron et al., 2014). There are obvious reasons for this. First, the preselected faces were chosen in the first place because they produce consistent emotional interpretations in Western cultural samples. Second, the link between these faces and so called 'basic emotions' is now so widely accepted as scientific fact that kindergartens in the USA and UK teach kids their categorical meanings. Hollywood movies use animated versions of the same facial configurations (often concocted in collaboration with affective scientists) to represent emotion categories. The title of Pixar's film 'Inside Out' even goes so far as providing an explicit metaphor for facial 'expression' as an exterior manifestation of what is happening in a person's private world. Exposure to all of these learning experiences further consolidates Western prototypical representations of emotions as characterised by specific facial expressions.

Westernised facial judgements are also guided by a more general cultural assumption that observed behaviour reflects mental processes. This means that the default interpretation for facial movements and other forms of activity is to attribute them to internal events. But this kind of mentalism is neither inevitable nor universal. Some societies in the Pacific area and elsewhere seem to assume instead that other minds are essentially opaque and private to their owners (e.g., Robbins & Rumsey, 2008). For example, explicit mind-reading abilities do not seem to develop in Samoan children in the same way or at the same rate as in UK or US children. Mayer and Träuble (2012) found that most ten-year-old Samoan children were incorrect about where another person would look for a hidden object that had been moved without their knowledge. Performance on such 'false-belief' tasks is considered the hallmark of having acquired 'theory of mind' (the ability to reason about other people's behaviour by inferring their internal mental states). By this token, Samoan children seem to lack that cognitive resource or belief system.

Cultural beliefs about opacity of other minds may also be related to judgements of supposed basic emotion expressions. Gendron and colleagues (2014) found that participants from small-scale societies were relatively more likely to describe these facial stimuli in terms of the actions the person in the picture was performing (e.g., staring, smelling, smiling) or the situations in which the face might be observed (e.g., crying at a death), and relatively less likely to refer to the emotions or other mental states that might be expressed in the presented faces (see also Crivelli et al., 2017; Gendron et al., 2018). Whether this reflects opacity beliefs or simply closer attunement to the situational and relational processes shaping facial activity is another matter.

Effects of Context on Judgement

In most of the studies reviewed so far, participants were shown still photographs of faces looking into the camera, with nothing but a blank wall in the background. No clues were given about where the person in the pictures might be, what they might be doing or at what object their attention might be focused. There was no indication of how quickly the face might be moving or how long it had remained fixed in its current full-on pose. Encountering such decontextualised faces is highly unusual in everyday life. Even when all we see is a photograph, we usually have some idea who the person might be and what is happening around them.

Ekman and colleagues (1969) preselected their facial stimuli to maximise consistency of emotional interpretation without the need for further information. The idea was that the depicted faces represented the pure and unadulterated expression that would be seen if all display rules and competing emotions were cleared away, distilling the essence of the emotional meaning itself. If the researchers had succeeded in finding faces that contain clear and direct information about emotion, it should not matter what else is going on around them. But if their meaning is more flexible and non-specific, then context should make a difference to how other people respond to them. Research on the effects of context on judgement therefore helps to clarify the extent to which facial configurations specify intrinsic emotional meanings regardless of what else might be happening.

'Context' is a term without a clear specific meaning and a range of different kinds of 'contextual' effects have been investigated by psychologists. To impose some order on this literature, Wieser and Brosch (2012) distinguish between contextual information relating to the situation surrounding the face (external features) and contextual information concerning the person whose face is being presented (within-source features). They also discuss two other kinds of information that are less obviously 'contextual'. Within-face features are a subset of within-source features that focus on aspects of the face other than its supposed emotion expression, such as its movements and the direction in which its eyes are gazing. Whether these should be seen as the context for the stimulus configuration or part of it is debatable. Finally, within-perceiver features include characteristics, states or processes located in the person making the facial judgements. In the following sections, I review each kind of contextual effect in turn.

External Context

The most obviously relevant contextual factors concern whatever is happening around the face. In some studies of external context, faces are presented together with verbal descriptions of the situation the person is supposedly facing. In other studies, contextual information is presented visually as a static image either alongside or surrounding the face, or as a video including the face or showing what the face is reacting to. In some studies, contextual information also includes information about other people and their faces.

Does the nature of the external context make a difference to judgements about faces? Not always. If the facial stimulus encourages a clear emotional interpretation and the context is open to different possible emotional interpretations, then facially conveyed emotion can override situational information (e.g., Ekman, Friesen & Ellsworth, 1972; Nakamura, Buck & Kenny, 1990). Indeed, Hess and Hareli (2018) showed that participants' interpretations of context may be influenced by the apparent emotional meaning of a simultaneously presented face rather than vice versa. For example, participants told that a nose-scrunching 'disgust' expression was a reaction to a cake covered in flies (shown in a separate picture) rated that cake as significantly less desirable than if the face showed a smile. These effects are analogous to social referencing where the mother's object-directed 'fear' face modifies the toddler's orientation to the visual cliff.

One of the reasons why standardised facial stimuli are relatively powerful determinants of interpretation arises from their direct orientation to the viewer. The eyes typically look straight at the camera conveying an intention to communicate (Fernández-Dols, Sierra & Ruiz-Belda, 1993). By contrast, contextual information is rarely communicative, let alone ostensive, and is often open to a range of possible emotional interpretations. Indeed, it is usually possible to imagine that something else is happening that overrides the apparent implications of the depicted situation. A wild animal or crock of gold might be positioned somewhere out of shot, for example.

However, contextual information can often modify interpretations of emotional meanings despite its lack of direct communicative power. For example, Carroll and Russell (1996) asked participants to read stories describing clearly specified emotional situations then presented standardised photographs that purported to show the protagonist's facial reaction. Most participants said that the person showing a gasping, supposedly 'fearful' face in an anger-inducing situation was angry (cf. Crivelli et al., 2016), and most participants said that the person showing a scowling, supposedly 'angry' face after frightening events was afraid.

Carroll and Russell concluded that scowling and gasping faces could be read as indicating any unpleasant emotion involving high levels of arousal, with the specific emotional interpretation depending on the context in which the face was encountered. In other words, the facial configurations only told participants how much displeasure and arousal the person was experiencing and not anything about the more specific quality of their emotional response (see Chapter 2). If this interpretation is correct, contextual information should be incapable of making participants interpret gasping or scowling faces as indicating happiness (which involves pleasure rather than displeasure) or sadness (which involves low rather than high levels of arousal). In other words, judgements of so-called basic emotion expressions are flexible but not infinitely flexible.

Facial stimuli that are not preselected to represent basic emotions may be even more susceptible to contextual effects (e.g., Munn, 1940). For example, Kayyal, Widen and Russell (2015) showed participants spontaneous facial reactions of athletes who had just won or lost their event in the Olympic games. Participants who were misinformed that a winner's facial reactions followed a loss or that a loser's facial reactions followed a win based their pleasantness judgements on the outcome information rather than the faces. The implication is that naturalistic facial movements are perceptually ambiguous enough to be interpreted as signs of an oppositely valenced emotion, even when the associated emotion is a strong and involving response to a career-defining event (see also Aviezer, Trope & Todorov, 2012).

Context not only affects interpretation of a face's emotional meaning, but also memory for what the facial configuration actually looked like in the first place. For example, Fernández-Dols and colleagues (2008) showed participants video clips or still photographs of two- and three-year-old children being vaccinated and provided accurate information about this painful context. Although none of the depicted children showed the canonical facial configuration associated with any basic emotion, over 80 per cent of participants incorrectly reported that they had seen the facial configuration prototypically associated with either fear or sadness when presented with comparison pictures afterwards. Apparently, interpreting facial reactions as reflecting one of these two emotions biased participants' perception or memory, making them believe that they had seen a facial configuration that had never genuinely appeared. In other words, the contextual information shaped their interpretation, which in turn changed their representation of the visual characteristics of the facial stimulus (see also Halberstadt et al., 2009). This kind of misrecognition may lead people to believe that basic emotion expressions generally accompany emotional situations more often than they really do.

Why does external context make a difference to emotional interpretations of faces? The most obvious answer is that it provides information concerning what the face is reacting to. Relatedly, knowing what the situation involves might indicate what message the face is trying to convey. If the message has emotional content, then the context provides clues about possible objects of the emotion that is being communicated. For example, if the situation contains a potentially threatening object, this makes it seem more likely that the face is reacting with fear or communicating an appraisal of threat. Thus, to the extent that emotions involve processes of relation alignment, knowing what relations are being aligned clarifies emotional meaning.

Social Context

A particularly useful source of clarifying information about relations between persons and objects is provided by the social context. Social factors may play at least three possible roles in the interpretation of facial configurations. First, other people, like non-social entities, may be the object of the emotion conveyed by the face, thus providing clarification of what any emotion might be about. Second, other people may be the intended recipients of any emotional message, thus helping perceivers understand the motives behind the facial movement (e.g., Nakamura et al., 1990). Third, other people's orientations to any social or non-social object may provide clues about how that object should be appraised, thus indicating the likely orientation of the person whose facial configuration is being judged too.

The contextual information presented in the studies reviewed in the previous section sometimes included information about other people. For example, Carroll and Russell's (1996) anger-inducing story described how restaurant staff delayed honouring the protagonist's table reservation yet still found tables for other guests who arrived later. After reading this story, participants probably concluded that the depicted facial display conveyed a message to the obstructive staff about the way they had behaved. Other studies have focused more directly on the effects of other people and their facial activity on emotion judgements.

Masuda and colleagues (2008) asked Japanese and US participants to rate the emotions expressed by a cartoon face surrounded by other cartoon figures with either the same or different facial configurations. Japanese participants judged the expressed emotion as stronger when the surrounding faces showed the same configuration as the central face than when they showed different configurations, but US participants gave similar emotion ratings regardless of what the other faces showed. Eye-tracking data revealed that Japanese participants also looked at the surrounding faces to a greater extent, suggesting that they were more oriented to social context than US participants. Similar findings have also been reported using photos of facial configurations rather than cartoons (e.g., Hess, Blaison & Kafetsios, 2016; Masuda et al., 2012).

Masuda and colleagues made little attempt to make the social context appear realistic. The faces all looked directly at the perceiver as if their photograph was about to be taken. There was no sense that they might be engaged in interaction with one another, or that the surrounding faces were providing an audience for whatever the central person was doing. However, common gaze direction and co-presence may have led participants to assume that they were all part of a single group, especially in the condition where they showed the same facial configurations as each other (e.g., Livingstone et al., 2011). Perceptions of shared group identity may have been especially strong among Japanese participants, because collectivistic societies such as Japan tend to focus on relations between people to a greater extent than individualistic societies such as the USA (Markus & Kitayama, 1991). Thus, Japanese participants may have seen the central person's emotion as stronger when it seemed to reflect a collective experience shared with other group members (see Chapter 7 for further discussion of group-based emotions).

Some studies of social context manipulate relations between the central face and other faces more directly. For example, Mumenthaler and Sander (2012) compared the effects of a single peripherally presented face whose eyes looked either towards or away from a centrally presented face, thus providing information about where the facial communication was directed and what the facial reaction was about. Both central and peripheral faces showed animated movements depicting basic emotion expressions. The investigators found that perceptions of the emotion expressed by the centrally presented face depended on the emotion-related activity of the peripheral face, but that effects were generally stronger when the eyes on that face turned towards the central face. For example, when the contextual face showed a scowling 'angry' expression, participants rated the level of fear shown by a gasping central face as higher, but only when the contextual face turned its gaze towards the central face. In other words, participants apparently interpreted the relational situation as one in which the central face was responding to the other person's directed anger, making the perception of fear more likely.

Within-Source Context

Within-source context (or within-sender context in Wieser and Brosch's, 2012, terminology) focuses not on the external situation or the other people in it, but rather on the person who is making the facial movement (the source of emotional information), and specifically on what else that source is doing apart from moving their face. The external context already provides clues about what they might be thinking about or engaged with. However, in this section we focus specifically on how the rest of the source's body is configured in terms of posture and gesture. Does it make a difference if the presented face is part of a body that is striking a particular pose or adopting a certain stance?

The impact of postural cues probably lies in their capacity to convey information about the source's orientation to what is happening. Perceivers are able to work out what attitude the source is taking to whatever is happening or how they are preparing themselves to respond to it. In realistic situations, combining postural information with external contextual information provides further clarity by linking the body's orientation with what the body is oriented to.

Aviezer, Hassin and colleagues (e.g., Aviezer & Hassin, 2017; Hassin, Aviezer & Bentin, 2013) pioneered and refined the most commonly used methodology for assessing effects of bodily context on facial judgement. Most of their studies have presented information visually, usually in the form of static pictures that have been doctored using photo-editing software. This permits systematic and independent manipulation of bodily and facial configurations. In other words, different faces can be attached to the same body and different bodies can be attached to the same face. Faces and bodies can also be presented in isolation from each other in appropriate comparison conditions.

For example, Aviezer and colleagues (2008) attached a nose-scrunching 'disgust' face to a body that took one of four different stances, each of which was consistently perceived as indicating one of four different emotions (anger, sadness, fear or disgust) when presented with the face blanked out (see Figure 3.6). In some cases, the pictures also included external contextual information in the form of objects to which these stances were directed. For example, the 'disgust' stance (panel a, Figure 3.6) showed a dirty diaper being held away from the body and gripped at the corner by only thumb and forefinger, thus implying that the source wants to keep it at a distance and minimise any chance of contact with its contents. In other cases, the depicted stance invited viewers to imagine a particular object whose nature was strongly implied by the body's orientation. For example, the angry posture (panel b, Figure 3.6) included a raised fist positioned in a way that suggested that the source was ready to punch whomever he was looking at.

The nose-scrunching face was most consistently interpreted as expressing disgust when accompanied by the disgust stance (with the dirty nappy), and least consistently interpreted as expressing disgust when accompanied by the angry stance (where the stimulus person looked ready to punch someone). Only 11 per cent of participants reported that the face expressed disgust in the anger stance condition, and 87 per cent

a

b

c

d

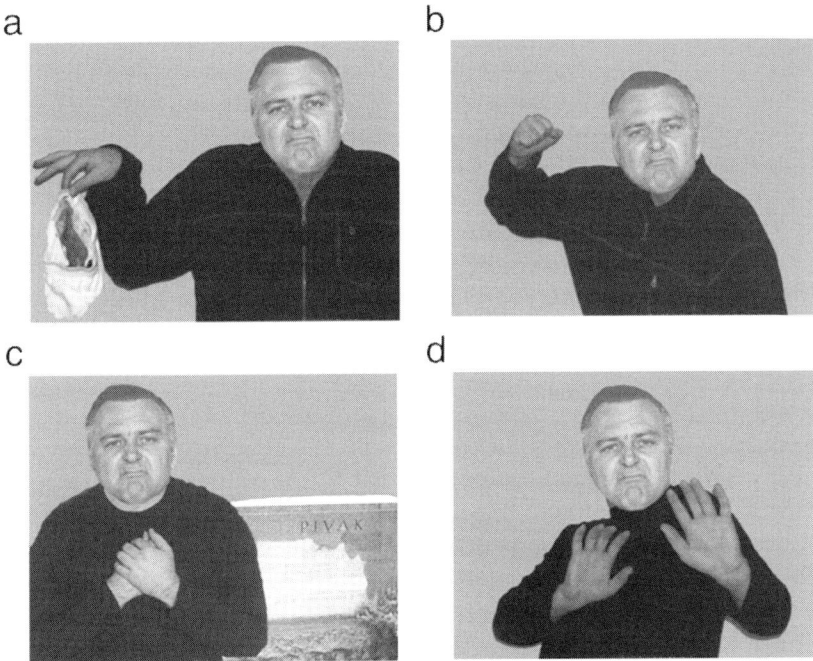

Figure 3.6 Nose-scrunched 'disgust' face attached to four different emotion postures (Aviezer et al., 2008, face reproduced with permission of the Paul Ekman Group)

said that it expressed anger instead. Fear and sadness stances also influenced viewers' facial judgements but to a lesser extent.

Aviezer and colleagues' findings again suggest that facial stimuli preselected to convey consistent emotional meanings are subject to a range of interpretations, but not an infinite range (see also Carroll & Russell, 1996). Judgements of so-called 'disgust' faces were influenced more by 'angry' bodies than by 'fearful' or 'sad' bodies. The differences in the effects of different postures cannot be explained by the levels of arousal associated with the corresponding emotions (Carroll & Russell, 1996) because both 'anger' and 'fear' have similar values on the arousal dimension, and therefore should be equally plausible alternative interpretations of the high-arousal 'disgust' expression. Instead, Aviezer and colleagues argue that the viability of an alternative emotional interpretation of the facial configuration depends on its perceptual similarity to the prototypical expression associated with the other possible emotion ('confusability'). In particular, scowling 'anger' faces resemble nose-scrunching 'disgust' faces more closely than gasping 'fear' faces do.

This confusability explanation implies that facial configurations may be interpreted as expressing emotions that differ in levels of either pleasure or arousal as long as these emotions are associated with sufficiently similar facial configurations. Aviezer and colleagues' second study provided direct support for this idea. Attaching a nose-scrunching 'disgust' face to a muscular body posing pride led 78 per cent of participants to say that this ostensibly displeased face expressed the typically pleasant emotion of pride. Correspondingly, attaching a 'sad' face to a 'fearful' body led 58 per cent of participants to say that this ostensibly unaroused face expressed the aroused emotion of fear.

Like information about external context, bodily information has even stronger effects on emotion judgements when facial stimuli are not pre-selected to have clear and consistent emotional meanings. Aviezer and colleagues (2012) showed participants naturalistic photos of high-ranking professional tennis players taken immediately after they had either won or lost a crucial point in a tournament match. The pictures showed just the face, just the body or both face and body in combination (see Figure 3.7). When participants only saw the face, they rated the player's emotions as equally positive regardless of whether they had actually won the point.

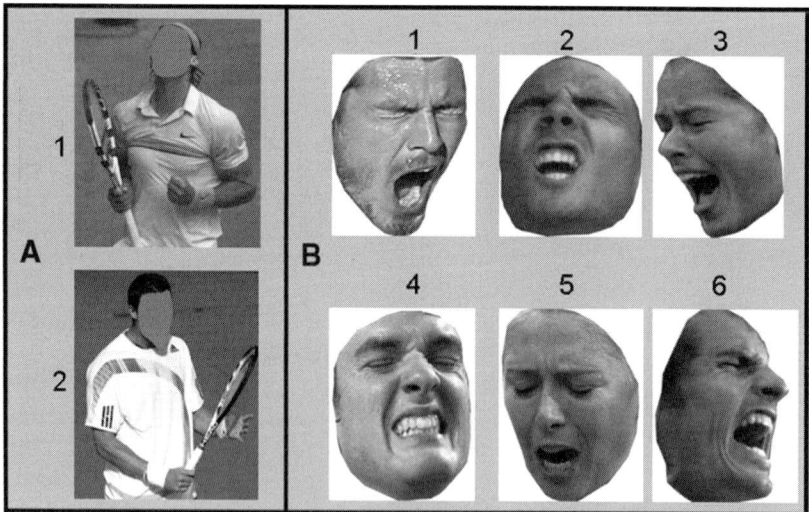

Figure 3.7 Tennis players' faces and bodies after winning (A1, B2, B3 and B5) or losing (A2, B1, B4 and B6) a crucial point (Aviezer et al., 2012, reproduced with permission of the American Association for the Advancement of Science. All photos credited to a.s.a.p. Creative/Reuters)

However, when they saw the body (either in isolation or attached to the face), they rated players' emotional state as significantly more positive when the player had won rather than lost the point. In other words, any diagnostic information about the pleasantness of the reaction seemed to come purely from bodily stances.

This conclusion was supported in a second study where participants viewed mismatched composite pictures produced by combining the facial configuration following a losing point with the bodily posture following a winning point or vice versa. Again, the emotional information conveyed by the bodies overrode any indication of pleasure provided by the faces. Aviezer and colleagues also asked participants to mimic the facial expressions they could see while viewing the mismatched composite pictures. The faces participants produced were then shown to a separate set of judges. When copying a face attached to the bodily posture following a winning point, participants produced more positive expressions than when copying the same face attached to the bodily posture following a losing point. In other words, participants apparently misperceived facial expressions in a way that made them appear more consistent with the emotion actually conveyed by bodily posture (cf. Fernández-Dols et al., 2008). Interestingly, participants seemed unaware of the overriding influence of bodily cues. When asked what information had guided their judgements of face–body composites, more than half said that they had relied on facial information, which in fact was non-diagnostic.

Why do bodily cues sometimes take priority in determining emotional interpretation? One answer is that some postures and gestures seem to have an overt communicative orientation that helps them to convey messages directly to perceivers. For example, the elbows-out, hands on hip posture stereotypically associated with pride (e.g., Tracy & Robins, 2004) or the raising of arms following victory appear to be intended to make the source as prominent and visible to others as possible. Bodies are also capable of conveying information about objects and events other than the self. They can present something for inspection by someone else. They can hold that thing close or at a distance, and be ready to pull it nearer or push it further away. They can even single something out for attention by pointing at it directly. Bodily stimuli with these explicitly communicative qualities are more likely to dominate emotional interpretation, perhaps explaining their relative advantage over certain kinds of facial cue in some of the published studies.

Within-Face Context

Even faces presented in isolation provide some information about context. For example, we may infer a stimulus person's ethnicity and other social attributes from their facial features or skin colour. And different faces may seem more or less attractive or dominant regardless of what emotion they might be expressing (e.g., Hess, Adams & Kleck, 2009). Facial features providing cues about gender may even encourage specific emotional interpretations, with masculine faces generally appearing more angry and feminine faces generally appearing happier or more afraid (Adams, Hess & Kleck, 2015; Hess et al., 2009).

It is not only a face's fixed features that shape our impressions. Facial movement and orientation can also provide cues about what the person is doing that set the context for emotional interpretation of what is happening. Indeed, the same pattern of muscular activity may be interpreted differently when gaze direction varies, when it is preceded or followed by different configurations or when transitions leading to it or following it are slower or faster. In the following subsections, I review evidence for these contextual effects of within-face features.

Dynamics

If perceivers are judging a specific facial configuration adopted at any particular moment, then what the face shows before that moment and how it changes as it gets to that moment set the context for judgement. Someone might smile for an instant, but that smile will look different if it follows a sustained scowl and if that scowl disappears quickly rather than slowly. Perception may also be altered by what the face does immediately *after* the judged configuration. If the smile disappears as quickly as it first flashed on, then its implications change.

Most studies that have investigated dynamic facial movements do not pinpoint a single still frame and check whether its emotional interpretation differs when presented in a temporally unfolding context. Instead, researchers compare judgements of dynamic and static facial movements to determine whether dynamic factors make a difference more generally. Strictly speaking, then, these studies do not directly assess contextual effects at all, but rather whether an additional source of information based on facial movement contributes to the overall impression that faces make.

Compared to still faces, dynamic faces seem to convey emotional information more clearly, especially when the facial stimulus is ambiguous or degraded (Krumhuber, Kappas & Manstead, 2013). Such a direct comparison may seem unfair given that dynamic stimuli are effectively composed of multiple still frames and therefore contain more information in the first place. However, Ambadar, Schooler and Kohn (2005) showed that consistency of emotion judgements for 'subtle expressions' was higher in a dynamic condition than in a 'multi-static' condition where the same full sequence of frames was presented sequentially with a visual mask interposed between each pair of frames, thus disrupting the perception of a continuously unfolding facial movement. Even though the presented facial information was equivalent in both conditions, the directly dynamic condition still increased discrimination.

Ambadar and colleagues also included a 'first–last' condition in which only two frames were presented in direct succession to yield the perception of a transition. Results in this condition were similar to those found in the fully dynamic condition. In other words, perceivers apparently did not capitalise on specific temporal cues provided by the unfolding movie (e.g., jerkiness or fluidity of movement) but simply oriented to the overall change in the facial configuration between the beginning and end of the sequence. What mattered was where the face started and where it got to, not the points in between.

However, Ambadar and colleagues' fully dynamic stimuli contained a maximum of just eight frames and lasted for only a fraction of a second before freezing on the final frame, thus limiting the possible variation over time. In a subsequent study, Bould, Morris and Wink (2008) found that twenty-five-frame dynamic stimuli produced clearer emotion perceptions than either nine-frame dynamic stimuli (comparable to those used in Ambadar et al.'s study) or first–last transitions. Slowing down or speeding up the film also reduced consistency of performance in some conditions (see also Kamachi et al., 2001), suggesting that the rate of change in facial movement is an important factor in determining emotion perceptions.

Dynamics may clarify the possible meaning of facial movements partly because they provide information about the temporal profile of the corresponding experience. Perceivers are able to detect when and how quickly things are happening by watching the way the face moves. Presenting dynamic external information that unfolds in parallel with facial changes would probably clarify perceivers' impressions still further.

In realistic contexts, perceivers are also able to calibrate dynamic facial movements with unfolding external events. For example, a rapid flinching movement or jaw-drop following a sudden loud bang or bright flash gives strong and hard-to-simulate cues about the sender's level of surprise (Tomkins, 1981). More articulated temporal profiles characterise complicated event sequences such as sports games. Here too the way in which spectators' facial responses track developing patterns of play clarifies their perception and interpretation. As a striker weaves around defenders and gets ready to shoot, supporters respond with similar changing contours of excited expectation, flipping into reactive elation if the ball is tipped over the cross-bar by the goalie.

As this example suggests, facial movements may track other people's facial movements as well as unfolding events. Indeed, part of the referential significance of the mother's fear expression in the classic social referencing experiment by Sorce and colleagues (1985) derives from the fact that the facial movements are attuned to the toddler's own directed signals concerning approach towards the visual cliff. Mutual interpersonal attunement of nonverbal behaviour is associated with a sense of rapport (Bernieri, Reznick & Rosenthal, 1988, and Chapter 4), which may provide a more direct basis for empathically tracking the other person's changing emotional orientations. Investigating facial dynamics in the context of unfolding social situations might well reinforce the conclusion that static configurations tell far from the whole story about what is happening at the emotional level.

Gaze Direction
The faces typically presented in judgement studies are turned towards the camera with their eyes directed straight forwards. They seem to imply that the source is reacting directly to the perceiver or trying to communicate something to them (e.g., Fernández-Dols et al., 1993). What difference does this make to our emotional interpretation? What if the eyes divert their gaze or look at something out of shot and away from the viewer?

Adams and Kleck (2003) presented facial stimuli that manipulated the source's gaze direction without altering the particular muscular configurations supposedly relating to the underlying basic emotion. Their idea was that direct eye gaze indicates the tendency to approach the viewer whereas deflected eye gaze indicates avoidance of eye contact and social withdrawal. Thus, direct gaze should be concordant with behavioural intentions associated with approach-related emotions such as happiness and anger, whereas averted gaze should be concordant with behavioural intentions associated with avoidance-related emotions such as fear and disgust. When gaze signals match the approach or withdrawal implications of the emotion that the facial configuration is intended to convey, this should strengthen the corresponding emotional interpretation. However, when the two sources of information conflict, gaze cues should weaken the face's usual emotional interpretation or make it less accessible.

Consistent with this shared signal hypothesis, Adams and Kleck (2003) found that the facial configurations associated with 'anger' and 'happiness' were categorised more quickly when the source's gaze was direct, whereas the 'fear' configuration was categorised more quickly when the source's gaze was averted. Similarly, anger and happiness were rated as stronger when the corresponding facial configurations showed direct gaze, but fear and sadness were rated as stronger when the correspond-ing facial configurations showed averted gaze (Adams & Kleck, 2005; see also Sander et al., 2007). Not only does gaze direction influence interpre-tation of facial configurations, but also facial configurations influence perception of gaze direction. For example, Adams and Franklin (2009) found that discrimination of gaze aversion was enhanced when the gaz-ing face showed the configuration associated with fear rather than a neutral expression.

Gaze direction also carries information that goes beyond general approach or avoidance. For example, averted gaze may indicate that attention is directed specifically at some object other than the perceiver (Sander et al., 2007). Thus, a gasping 'fear' display with deflected gaze may imply the need to be alert to some frightening event happening somewhere close by, making the face seem more fearful. Hadjikhani et al., (2008) suggest that a 'fear' face with downward-directed gaze is especially amenable to this interpretation because it indicates a potential threat on the ground such as a snake. Dynamic faces may provide even clearer indications of where attention is directed. For example, diverted gaze that is fixed while the rest of the face moves (Sander et al., 2007) is likely to be associated with attention towards an object with a definite environmental location, whereas diverted gaze that shifts or seems unfo-cused implies avoidance of a moving object, several different objects or the more general situation.

Direct gaze carries implications that go beyond approach too. It often also signals engagement and intention to communicate with the person at whom it is directed (e.g., Fernández-Dols et al., 1993). Thus, direct gaze on a scowling face may suggest that the source is angry with you as viewer, thereby increasing its emotional impact (cf. Dimberg & Öhman, 1983). By contrast, direct gaze on a gasping face may be read as an appeal for comfort or reassurance (Hadjikhani et al., 2008), soliciting calming responses from perceivers (Parkinson & Simons, 2012; Parkinson, Niven & Simons, 2016) that may reduce fear-related interpretations.

Combining gaze-direction cues with information about the objects at which gaze is directed can potentially clarify their emotional implications still further. Just as a nose-scrunching face attached to a body holding a dirty nappy at arm's length was perceived as relatively more disgusted in Aviezer and colleagues' research, gaze directed at a potentially frigh-tening object might well increase the impression of fear. Indicating a communicative intention using direct gaze before redirecting the eyes at the object may provide the perceiver with the additional information that the source wants them to attend to the object and notice what might be frightening about it (e.g., Sorce et al., 1985). Thus, a look towards an object may serve as a form of ostensive communication identifying objects of potential relevance (Sperber & Wilson, 1986).

What Counts as Context?

The idea of within-face context implies that we can make a clear distinction between the parts of a facial configuration that do and do not directly express emotion. The expressive parts are the focus of judgement and the non-expressive parts provide the context for judgement. This distinction works reasonably well when we contrast the changeable configuration of facial muscles with the more stable morphological characteristics of the face, including bone structure, skin tone, and so on. Facial features relating to age, gender and health can easily be seen as setting the context for judgements of the pattern of muscular contractions that transform the face's temporary appearance at any given moment.

However, things are not so straightforward when we turn to eye gaze and temporal dynamics. Where do we draw the line between the aspects of the face's muscular movement that relate directly to emotion expression and those that are part of the context? Both gaze direction and facial dynamics clearly make a difference to judgements about emotion, but is that because they modify a separable perception of the face's core emotional meaning? Or are the dynamics and orientational aspects of facial movements already part of what the face reveals to others, including what it reveals about emotions?

Neurocultural theory argues that a small number of universal facial configurations encode the basic elements of emotional meaning. From that perspective, other facial movements are not part of the underlying emotional code and only affect judgement by serving as contextual factors. But perhaps the canonical basic emotion expressions do not deserve this special status in the first place. Maybe they are just configurations that best represent our orientation to the kind of scenario represented in the prototypical script for the emotion in question. For example, a scowling face may consistently convey anger in Western societies because it provides a clear indication that the source is getting ready to attack someone who is stopping them doing what they want to do (see Chapter 9).

A wider range of facial movements convey emotional orientations when we look beyond prototypical situations. Usually, we don't just flash on and off basic emotion expressions but instead engage in more articulated forms of object-directed facial activity. Gaze patterns and distinctive profiles of temporal response are key aspects of this activity and not things separately added on as part of the surrounding context.

Emotionally meaningful orientations don't stop at the edges of the face either. Movement of the rest of the body may also be an integral component of the overall pattern. Making full emotional sense of this pattern requires seeing embodied activity embedded in an unfolding situation that specifies where that activity is directed. Thus, even the external context may be seen as part of the source's emotionally meaningful orientation. Relational activity is fundamentally situated activity.

Within-Perceiver Features

A final category of factors contributing to facial judgements concerns perceivers rather than the sources whose faces they are perceiving. Perceiver features may affect interpretation either of the face itself or the external context in which it appears. If a perceiver has prior knowledge of (or prior prejudices about) the meanings of different facial configurations, this is likely to affect their judgement. Similarly, cultural familiarity with dialects of facial expression may make people more sensitive to cultural nuances (Elfenbein & Ambady, 2002). Emotional intelligence and mindreading skills may also attune perceivers to diagnostic facial information or facilitate interpretation of specific features or configurational patterns (e.g., Elfenbein, Marsh & Ambady, 2002).

One reason why individual differences in cognitive or emotional style affect judgement is that they make perceivers more or less likely to use certain processing strategies. Extracting an intended emotional meaning from a face requires a specific focus on relevant features and their configural arrangement. This is because faces not only express emotion, but also carry other kinds of information that may or may not be emotionally relevant (Matsumoto & Hwang, 2017). For example, eye gaze indicates attentional patterns (e.g., Lee, Susskind & Anderson, 2013), brow-wrinkling indicates concentration or struggle (e.g., Scherer, 1992), and other aspects of facial appearance provide cues about dominance (e.g., Berry & McArthur, 1986), gender (e.g., Keating & Doyle, 2002) and race (e.g., Marsh et al., 2003). Some of these factors carry (direct or indirect) emotional implications whereas others do not. Emotion judgement therefore involves keying into certain aspects of facial stimuli while ignoring others.

Linguistic Concepts

As we saw earlier, the cultural availability of emotion concepts is another factor that can affect perceivers' judgements of emotion-related faces (Gendron et al., 2014). US participants readily classified facial configurations into basic emotion categories, whereas Himba participants did not spontaneously use the same categorical concepts and applied them less consistently when they were explicitly provided. Thus, cultural socialisation provides us with specific conceptual tools that may be applied when distinguishing facial stimuli.

Studies of categorical perception suggest that emotion concepts can also help to demarcate boundaries between different facial configurations. When presented with morphed facial configurations showing different mixtures of two different basic emotion expressions, participants seem to experience a perceptual shift in their emotional judgement when the level of one of the expressions passes a certain threshold (e.g., Etcoff & Magee, 1992). For example, a morphed face blending scowling and pouting configurations is seen as expressing 'anger' up to the point when its pouting aspects become predominant determinants of emotion perception, now making it look like a 'sad' face. If perception matched the continuous changes in the visual features of the presented stimuli, we would not expect such an abrupt transition from one expressed emotion to another.

Categorical perception is demonstrated most conclusively in experimental tasks where participants have to decide which of two consecutive blended facial stimuli (A and B) matches a third separately presented stimulus (X), that provides a standard against which they are compared (Fugate, 2013, see Figure 3.8). The degree of perceptual similarity between A and B is equal across all trials, but in some trials both A and B are at the same side of an emotion boundary (e.g., both relatively closer to the 'anger' end of the anger–sadness dimension), whereas in other cases A and B are on opposite sides of the boundary (e.g., one relatively closer to the 'anger' end and the other relatively closer to the 'sadness' end). Participants are more consistent in matching A or B with X when A and B are at opposite sides of an emotion boundary than when they are both on the same side, even though the perceptual distance from A to B is no greater in the latter condition.

Research using this method has shown that being able to access the linguistic representations of the emotion concepts associated with faces

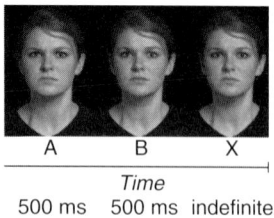

Figure 3.8 Comparison task for assessing categorical perception
(Fugate, 2013, reproduced with permission from Sage)
Note: Participants have to say which of A and B matches X (the correct answer is B).

(e.g., the words 'anger' and 'sadness') tends to make cross-boundary discriminations more pronounced. For example, Roberson and Davidoff (2000) gave participants a verbal interference task where they had to read aloud words naming emotions not expressed by the presented facial stimuli before making their judgement. This procedure removed the advantage for cross-category judgements. However, interference that targeted visual processing did not. In other words, being able to name a visually presented facial blend seems to reinforce the categorical distinction.

Although verbal concepts clearly make a difference to categorical perception, they may not be the only contributory factor. Kotsoni, de Haan and Johnston (2001) found that seven-month-old infants directed their gaze relatively more towards a morphed fear-happiness facial stimulus at the fear side of the categorical boundary than a simultaneously presented face at the happiness side of the boundary. However, there was no such preferential looking when both faces were at the same side of the fear-happiness boundary. Thus, it seems that these pre-verbal infants already had implicit knowledge about where the categorical boundary was located.

Kotsoni and colleagues' evidence does not decisively rule out a role for linguistic concepts because even children who are not yet able to speak may have picked up word–face associations from hearing adults talk. However, Sauter, LeGuen and Haun (2011) showed categorical perception effects for 'anger' and 'disgust' faces among native speakers of the Yocatec Maya language which does not distinguish between these two emotion concepts. In other words, they made categorical distinctions between two facial configurations they did not have different names for. Does this mean that these participants had a language-independent perceptual representation of the distinctive facial configurations associated with these emotions? One possible alternative is that they focused instead on specific facial features that showed clear differences across the two classes of stimulus. For example, there may have been categorical perception of whether or not the nostrils were flared, eyes narrowed or lips pressed together rather than whether or not the whole patterned configuration fit a built-in perceptual template for the corresponding emotion.

In sum, access to relevant linguistic emotion concepts seems to enhance perceivers' category discriminations but may not be the only factor contributing to categorical perception of facial configurations. According to Roberson, Damjanovic and Pilling (2007), when faces activate linguistic concepts this encourages participants to refer to a prototypical representation of the emotion, thus making the memory of the face more distinguishable from a face from a different emotion category (see also Huttenlocher, Hedges & Vevea, 2000).

Simulation

Perceivers' embodied representations of emotion concepts (see Chapter 2) may also make a difference to their facial judgements. When trying to identify an ambiguous or subtle facial configuration, people often have a spontaneous tendency to try to mimic it (Korb, Grandjean & Scherer, 2010, and see Chapter 4). One possible function of this process is to simulate what might be going on in the source's mind. In other words, producing a matching expression may facilitate evocation of the experience associated with that expression. Relatedly, adopting the same kind of facial orientation may help perceivers to see things from the stimulus person's perspective. In either case, interfering with the facial simulation should affect the clarity of the impression created by the facial stimulus. Supporting this conclusion, a number of studies have suggested that stopping participants from using facial mimicry by asking them to hold a pen between their teeth and lips (e.g., Maringer et al., 2011) or putting a rugby mouthguard over their gums (Rychlowska et al., 2014) can disrupt their judgements of facial stimuli that are otherwise difficult to decode or discriminate.

One explanation for the effects of facial simulation is that it activates verbal concepts associated with the resulting embodied sensations. However, Wood and colleagues (2016) showed that the internal signals produced by mimicking even improve discrimination of facial stimuli at the same side of an emotion category boundary (e.g., when both faces were seen as 'anger'). In this study, participants either covered their faces with a peel-off gel mask that dried on their skin as a thick crust, thus reducing their ability to make facial movements, or they applied moisturiser in a control condition. Those in the mask condition were less successful in matching morphed facial stimuli to a comparison stimulus even when the faces were at the same side of the emotion threshold. Linguistic concepts would not help with this discrimination because the same concept would be associated with both of the comparison faces. Thus, it seems that the sensations associated with unconstrained facial movement provide an embodied marker that clarifies perceptual as well as linguistic representations of facial stimuli.

The results of studies that constrain perceivers' facial movements remain controversial (e.g., Hess & Fischer, 2016). One issue concerns whether face masks, mouthguards and pens pressed tightly between lips and teeth actually do stop faces from moving in the first place. Instead they might simply introduce distracting proprioceptive signals that impact any perceptual and semantic judgements concerning facial configurations. Indeed, Wood and colleagues (2016) acknowledged that application of their gel-based face mask 'exaggerates feedback from slight facial movements, producing feedback "noise"' (p. 1152).

Mimicry does not need to provide diagnostic internal signals to facilitate emotional understanding in life outside the laboratory. In everyday social interactions, interpersonal calibration of facial movements may help people to arrive at a shared orientation to the unfolding situation (e.g., Bernieri et al., 1988, and see Chapter 4), which in turn facilitates the contextual interpretation of the facial movements each party is making. The use of a common emotional language to represent these facial movements may also contribute to the development of mutual understanding. More generally, the effects of many within-perceiver factors on facial judgement may ordinarily depend on their ability to promote either mutual calibration of attention or access to contextual information.

Summary

Contrary to the notion that facial expressions encapsulate self-contained emotional meanings, context effects reveal that faces derive much of their emotional meaning from their connections with whatever is going on around them. In particular, the source's gaze direction and bodily orientation indicate where their action is directed, temporal dynamics indicate the level of urgency and rate of situational change, and external contextual factors clarify what specific objects and events the source's action is targeting. In other words, it is the overall pattern of situated facial and bodily movement that specifies the relational significance of what is going on.

As well as indicating practical orientations to events, facial and bodily movements can serve as communicative acts specifically directed towards other people. Eye contact and the adoption of an open bodily posture may invite the perceiver to engage in communication, setting the stage for interpersonal negotiations about the significance of what is happening. Thus, sources may also use facial and bodily movements more actively to draw perceivers' attention to something that they want them to deal with.

Meanings and Functions

So far, we have focused on how consistently pictures or movies of faces convey emotional meanings to different perceivers in different contexts. But are the stimuli used in this research necessarily expressions of emotion in the first place? After all, they do not seem to provide direct information about the precise category of emotion that the source is experiencing across all cultures without additional contextual information. So exactly what information do basic emotion expressions carry? And what else might they do apart from express emotions?

Affect Dimensions

In Russell's (1997) view, the information that perceivers can universally extract from facial configurations does not specify any particular category of emotion. Instead it mainly relates to levels of pleasure and arousal. The more the lips turn up at the corners, the greater the level of perceived pleasure, and the more the mouth opens and the eyes widen, the greater the level of perceived arousal (see Figure 3.9).

Reliance on only pleasure and arousal information would allow participants to achieve better than chance performance on forced-choice judgement tasks even if they were unfamiliar with Western conventions about emotion expression. Perceived pleasure would make happiness the only plausible response alternative for smiles, explaining the high levels of consistency in judgement. Perceived levels of arousal would then help to discriminate some of the unpleasant response alternatives for the faces with downturned lips. For example, a face perceived as indicating displeasure and low arousal is more likely to be associated with sadness than with anger or fear.

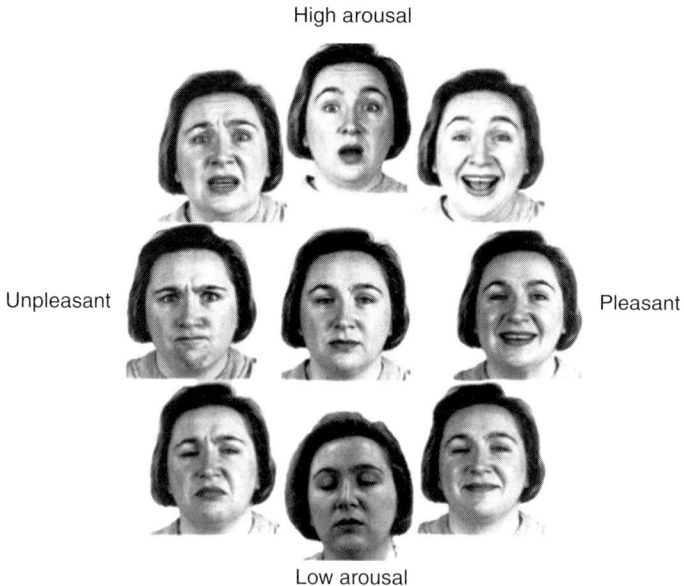

Figure 3.9 Circumplex arrangement of facial configurations (Russell, 1997)

Appraisal

Instead of assuming that facial configurations convey aspects of personal experience by expressing emotions or encouraging perceptions of pleasure and arousal, many appraisal theorists argue that they encode the source's appraisals of what is happening. Any pleasure conveyed by upturned lips may in fact reflect appraisals of the desirability or motivational congruence of what is happening (e.g., Smith, 1989).

Perceivers may piece together emotional meaning by extracting different kinds of appraisal information from different components of the source's facial configuration rather than picking up the encapsulated message all in one go (Scherer, Mortillaro & Mehu, 2017). For example, a lowered brow may encode goal obstruction and a raised upper lip may indicate a sense of unfairness and immorality. Putting these two components together increases the probability of seeing the source as angry. In principle, then, combinations of facial components need not reflect any of the so-called basic emotions (or blends of two or more of them), but simply specific patterns of appraisal that are not encoded by the most familiar emotion names.

A number of studies have shown that perceivers consistently associate some facial stimuli with specific appraisals (e.g., Scherer et al., 2018; Sergi et al., 2016). However, some appraisals such as coping potential seem to be linked with different muscle movements depending on other aspects of the facial configuration. It therefore seems possible that appraisal information (like emotion information) is more consistently extracted when faces are presented as part of a meaningful context, which makes the nature of the appraised object clearer. For example, de Melo, Carnevale, Read and Gratch (2014) found that avatars showing scowling faces while competing in a game were consistently perceived to be blaming the other player for what was happening (see also Chapter 4). Thus, faces presented in context may give perceivers some indication of how the source is appraising what is happening, which also relates to what they are prepared to do next.

Action Readiness

One of the reasons why faces adopt certain configurations is to get the person ready to engage in certain forms of action. Perhaps then the information they convey to perceivers relates more directly to action tendencies than to appraisals or emotions (Frijda, 1986; Frijda & Tcherkassof, 1997). For example, someone scrunching their nose appears to be rejecting a certain kind of noxious stimulus. Someone with a fixed stare and pressed-together lips looks ready to burst into action that is directed against you. In both cases, the facial movement embodies the relational mode that characterises the emotion rather than directly expressing the emotion itself.

In some cases, the main point of the facial movement is not to make the practical preparation for action but to indicate to perceivers that the source is ready to act in the implied way if necessary. For example, pulling an about-to-attack face may lead your antagonist to back off if they want to avoid an actual fight. Facial movements can thus be warnings, threats or invitations, as well as direct preparations for action. And they sometimes perform these communicative and practical functions at the same time.

Social Motives

A similar view about the action-related implications of facial activity was developed by Fridlund (1994), who took his inspiration from studies of the behavioural ecology of animal communication (e.g., Dawkins & Krebs, 1978; Hinde, 1981). Fridlund argues that so-called facial expressions are in fact displays that signal behavioural intentions or (more generally) social motives to conspecifics. Their function is communication not expression. According to him, displays could never have evolved to reveal a person's internal feelings for two basic reasons. First, information about someone's subjective state bears an uncertain relation to their future behaviour and so cannot be informative or helpful to the receiver (who would therefore ignore it, undermining any communicative functionality). Second, automatic expression would often lead to negative consequences for the expresser because it would reveal information that could benefit enemies. Thus, facial displays need to be sensitive to social context, only occurring when an appropriate addressee is present. Their function is to communicate useful information to particular people, not to provide a direct readout of emotional state regardless of who else is around to pick them up.

Social motives may relate either to what the person intends to do or what they want another person to do. Thus, the staring, scowling face with pressed-together lips conventionally interpreted as 'angry' might communicate to a potential antagonist that the displayer is ready to fight and wants the antagonist to back down. According to Fridlund, this display is only one among many possible threat faces that might be displayed in different contexts and when different addressees are present. Unlike neurocultural theory, then, the behavioural ecology approach assumes no one-to-one meaning-to-muscle mapping.

Fridlund's behavioural ecology theory contends that so-called emotion expressions are in fact facial displays that communicate social motives, thus implying that these two functions are mutually incompatible. If emotions are private and subjective states insulated from the social world, then their bearing on social motives seems tenuous at best. But what if emotions are in fact forms of relational activity (e.g., Frijda, 1986)? Perhaps facial movements convey social motives precisely because they embody emotional action readiness. In this case, the conflict between the emotion-expression and motive-communication views seems less pronounced (Parkinson, 2005).

Scarantino (2017) presents an integrative account of facial activity that develops this kind of approach. In his view, emotion expressions are analogous to the speech acts studied by Austin (1962; see Chapter 2). As with emotion talk, we do not need to see facial activity as performing a purely expressive function, representing something going on inside. It can also serve pragmatic functions similar to those served by performative utterances in spoken or written language (see also Fernández-Dols, 2017). For example, saying that 'I have to get up early tomorrow' not only presents you with facts about my schedule but may also be a hint that you should think about leaving and stop keeping me up so late. Similarly, Scarantino argues that a smile may express happiness, represent an event as pleasant, invite social interaction and promise cooperation, sometimes all at the same time. And other people may respond to smiles by registering any or all of these intended meanings. More generally, facial expressions can perform many of the same illocutionary actions as verbal statements. Indeed, according to Scarantino's account, they may provide a phylogenetic bridge between certain forms of animal communication and human spoken language. Being able to do things with faces may be a step towards doing things with words.

Production

Because information about affect dimensions, appraisals, states of action readiness or social motives could equally provide clues about a source's likely emotion (e.g., Shuman et al., 2017; Yik & Russell, 1999), evidence from judgement studies does not conclusively rule in or out any of these alternative explanations for facial activity. Indeed, this kind of evidence does not directly address questions of how, when or why facial activity occurs in the first place. Why then has there been such a strong focus on this perceiver-directed methodology for investigating facial activity?

The advantage of judgement methods is that they allow investigators to focus on stimulus features that make a difference to perception of emotions, appraisals, action tendencies or social motives, and to filter out extraneous factors such as display rules, mixed emotions or other potential causes of facial reaction. This also means that the facial stimuli used in these studies may not match the faces observed outside the laboratory, but this does not necessarily matter when the intention is to isolate the cues that make a targeted difference.

Deeper problems arise when findings from judgement studies are used as the sole basis for inferences about the processes that lead to the production of facial activity. Because participants judge smiles as indicating happiness, it is routinely assumed that happiness produces smiling. But the evidence from judgement studies does not directly support that conclusion.

Even the argument that perceivers know from experience what expressions go with which emotions is flawed. Learning about emotion-expression associations is necessarily selective, because it requires calibrating observations that are already biased. One of the reasons why we think that someone else is happy is because they are smiling, and our perception of that expression may similarly be distorted by our impression of their emotion (e.g., Aviezer et al., 2012; Fernández-Dols et al., 2008). So we notice an illusory correlation between two things whose perceptions are already interdependent. And we fail to factor in episodes when someone else might be happy and not express it, because we never find out about the other person's emotional state in those cases. We may even have a false impression of what our own face is showing when we are emotional ourselves (e.g., Barr & Kleck, 1995; Qu et al., 2017). In sum, any consistency of judgement may reflect the content of shared prototypical representations of emotions rather than the sampling of a representative range of emotional situations. To establish that judgements reflect deeper connections between emotion and expression, we need to assess the causes of facial activity more directly. Only then can we obtain clear evidence about what kind of activity facial activity really is.

Investigating the production of facial activity is not as straightforward as investigating its perception or judgement. Faces move in many different ways under many different circumstances for many different reasons. Trying to measure all possible facial reactions to all possible events in all possible contexts is simply not feasible. It is necessary to make difficult decisions about what facial movements to look for and when and where to look for them. Because the canonical basic emotion faces are the ones that judgement studies have used most commonly, production studies mostly focus on those too. Because their association with emotion and related factors is at the heart of the biggest controversies, most production studies also involve manipulation or measurement of emotion as well. Finally, because facial regulation is often explained in terms of social norms and other people's responses, social factors are the most commonly investigated contextual moderators of any emotional effects.

Emotion Dependence

The first and most obvious question about production of so-called emotion expressions concerns whether they actually depend on emotions in the first place. Even if people consistently think that smiles indicate happiness or scowls indicate anger, does that necessarily mean that people actually smile when happy or scowl when angry? Perhaps the perceived associations reflect conventions for representing emotions when they need to be communicated rather than automatic habits of expression. For example, even if we do not know the local language, we can show someone that we are hungry by rubbing our tummies and pointing at our mouths (Russell, 1994). But we very rarely perform this kind of pantomime or charade when we are hungry under other circumstances. It is certainly not a spontaneous expression of our internal state.

So how often do people show so-called basic emotion expressions when they are actually in emotional situations and experiencing the emotions in question? The first method for assessing emotion-expression associations is experimental. Researchers try to get their participants into specific emotional states and then measure how their faces react. Experimental studies face the potential criticism that the emotions they induce are too weak or too mixed to yield clear and distinct expressions. For practical as well as ethical reasons, it is often difficult to make participants experience strong and pure emotions in the lab. There is too little time to develop the levels of involvement required, and experimenters don't have a legitimate right to make people feel very bad (or indeed very good) in any case. We can't ask our participants to fall in love, and it is no longer considered morally acceptable to get them so angry that they want to hit someone, or so scared that they pray for their lives (at least not since Ax's 1953 study; see Chapter 1).

But people often do get strongly emotional in real-life situations and researchers have measured their facial reactions to those too. For example, Fernández-Dols, Carrera and Crivelli (2011) analysed facial expressions posted on a website devoted to facial expressions during sexual excitement and orgasmic ecstasy. None of the 100 videotaped participants showed Duchenne smiles at the point of orgasm and only 5 out of 100 showed them immediately afterwards. The most commonly observed facial movement corresponded more closely to one usually associated with pain rather than pleasure, confirming earlier observations by Masters and Johnson (1966). More recent evidence suggests that facial movements representing orgasmic pleasure are subtly different from those associated with pain but neither corresponds to the supposed expression of the basic emotion of happiness (Chen et al., 2018).

Durán, Reisenzein and Fernández-Dols (2017) conducted a meta-analysis of studies of facial production conducted both in the laboratory (as previously reviewed by Reisenzein, Studtmann & Horstmann, 2013) and in naturalistic settings (as previously reviewed by Crivelli & Fernández-Dols, 2013). This statistical procedure permitted them to estimate the general level of association between 'basic' emotions and their supposed expressions across a wide range of contexts. On average, the facial configuration predicted by neurocultural theory was observed in fewer than a quarter of those participants who were apparently experiencing the associated emotion. This measure of occurrence tells us whether the predicted face was visible at any point during the experience of the relevant emotional situation for each person, but not how often it was produced over that period or how long it lasted. In other words, it may still overestimate the prevalence of predicted facial configurations. An alternative measure of emotion-expression correspondence is to assess the extent to which the strength or frequency of the predicted facial activity corresponds to reported emotional intensity (either across different participants or across different time points for the same participants). The average correlation obtained using this latter approach was 0.35, which means that less than an eighth of the variance in facial activity could potentially be explained by the measured emotion. Both these statistical indices point to the same simple conclusion. During emotional experiences, faces are much more likely not to show the predicted configuration than to show it.

However, associations between emotion and facial activity were clearly not random. Although the predicted configuration occurred rarely, it still occurred more often while the emotion was being experienced than at other times. This tells us that factors that have some association with emotion influence facial activity. Clues about what these factors might be can be found by comparing situations where predicted facial activity was commonly observed with those where it was infrequently observed.

The highest levels of predicted facial activity were found in amusing situations where around half of participants showed smiling mouths (but not always eyes), and reported amusement explained about a quarter of the variance in this mouth movement. By contrast, only around an eighth of participants smiled in happy situations that did not involve amusement. One possible explanation for this difference is that amusement is often experienced in response to someone else's deliberate attempt to induce it, meaning that displaying a responsive smile is normatively appropriate. For example, the experimenter in Ruch's (1997) study of humour wore silly clothes, asked nonsensical questions and generally clowned around while directly interacting with the participant in order to induce 'exhilaration'. Other studies have presented participants with recorded jokes as humorous stimuli (e.g., Harris & Alvarado, 2005). In delivering jokes, comedians use various techniques to establish rapport with the audience and to get them involved with the social situation where the humorous incident they are recounting took place. The smiling observed in response to both clowning and jokes may be seen as cooperating with the intent of someone who is specifically addressing an intended addressee. That addressee may indeed feel pleasant emotions at the same time but those two responses need not be directly interrelated to account for obtained correlations between smiling and amusement.

Emotion-expression associations may also be higher when the emotion manipulation induces specific action tendencies that feature centrally in the prototypical script for the emotion category in question. For example, anger induction based on the possibility of direct physical confrontation may lead participants to adopt a ready-to-fight posture that includes the canonical 'scowling' face. However, the same face may not be shown in anger-inducing situations where there is no direct contact with any possible antagonist (such as reading about injustices or seeing photographs of lynchings).

Both of the examples of context-dependent emotion-expression association that I have discussed in this section imply that an important factor provoking diagnostic facial activity is the possibility of direct communication with someone else and the related prospect of exerting social influence. Indeed, if facial movements serve the function of displaying motives to others (Fridlund, 1994), they are more likely to be associated with emotions when there is a suitable audience at hand. In the next section, I review more direct evidence for this hypothesis.

Audience Sensitivity

The most distinctive aspect of Fridlund's (1994) behavioural ecology theory is his claim that facial displays are not direct reactions to external stimuli or internal states but instead depend on communicative opportunities. Without a potential recipient for the signal, there is no need to display anything. And unless that recipient's response is likely to benefit the displayer, displaying the motive is potentially costly (e.g., Dawkins & Krebs, 1978). So, a facial display depends on a social motive directed at a perceiver whose response is likely to benefit both parties. My fixed stare and pressed-together lips might signal that I am prepared to attack the person I am staring at, and if that person then backs down, both of us have avoided the potential costs of engaging in a fight.

Fridlund's account of audience sensitivity stands in stark contrast to Ekman's idea of display rules. For Ekman, the emotion carries its own impulse for expression, but that expression may be blocked or distorted in response to social pressures. The social world presents a separate set of forces that gets in the way of spontaneous expression. For Fridlund, the display is already oriented to the intended addressee, who is part of its cause in the first place. Social factors do not distort displays; they either activate them or not.

How can we distinguish empirically between these competing accounts? Ekman's theory implies that the presence of an emotion in the absence of competing emotions or display rules should automatically produce the corresponding expression. Fridlund's theory says that the display depends on the availability of a suitable audience. So, in situations where there are emotions and associated social motives but no suitable audiences, Ekman's theory predicts an expression whereas Fridlund's does not. However, the complication is that audiences for displays may be imagined or anticipated rather than physically co-present. In other words, showing a supposed emotion expression while alone does not rule out Fridlund's theory because the source may be thinking privately about a potential addressee for communication (Fridlund, 1991).

Distinctive predictions are even harder to derive for situations where emotion and associated social motives are experienced in the presence of other people. Both theories imply that those other people can either increase or decrease facial activity depending on other factors. For Ekman, other people may or may not invoke display rules, and those display rules may either encourage or discourage the expression of the emotion. In settings where societal norms prescribe emotional composure, the presence of others may lead to active suppression of expression. In settings where societal norms prescribe emotional involvement, the presence of others may lead to active exaggeration of expression. For example, British funerals encourage contained grief and although sobbing is common, there is rarely loud bawling even among close family members of the deceased. By contrast, Iranian funerals often involve exuberant wailing, especially from the professional mourners who attend.

For Fridlund, the impact of other people on facial activity depends on your relation to them at the time. The presence of appropriate addressees makes display more likely, whereas the absence of appropriate addressees makes it unnecessary. Predictions are less clear in multiple-audience situations (e.g., Fleming, 1994), where the immediate social environment includes a mixture of appropriate and inappropriate addressees. The theory provides little scope for regulated presentation of displays that are targeted at some addressees but selectively avoid others because such an account would come perilously close to acknowledging the impact of display rules. The following sections review the available experimental and observational evidence to get a better handle on whether specific findings are more consistent with either the emotion-expression or motive-communication accounts of facial activity (see also Parkinson, 2005).

Experimental manipulations

The earliest studies of the effects of other people on facial activity were specifically intended to demonstrate the operation of display rules. Friesen's (1972) unpublished Masters thesis described research on Japanese and US students' facial responses to an unpleasant film depicting painful accidents (see Ekman, 1972, for a partial report, and Fridlund, 1994, for a more detailed account of procedures and findings). When the students watched the film alone in the first phase of the experiment, facial activity was coded as equally negative across both national samples. However, in the final phase, when participants watched the film for a second time with an interviewer who asked questions about its content, Japanese students' facial activity was coded as more positive than that of American students.

Although these findings provide evidence of a cultural difference, it is not clear what kind of difference it is. Ekman (1972) and Friesen (1972) explain the effect by reference to different display rules activated by the presence of the interviewer. They argue that Japanese participants are socialised to avoid expressing negative emotions in front of other people, especially authority figures, and therefore concealed their unpleasant reactions. However, it seems equally possible that the interviewer's presence had different direct effects on the social motives of members of the two cultural groups, with Japanese students showing relatively greater deference and interpersonal attunement. In that case, the apparently more 'positive' facial movements displayed by Japanese participants might reflect their relatively more cooperative intentions in the interpersonal context. In other words, they might be seen as acknowledgements of status addressed to the other person rather than false smiles covering up any negative reactions to the film. The general point here is that introducing another person to the scene not only incentivises moderation of facial responses to other emotional stimuli, but also brings its own independent effects on socially directed facial activity.

A number of studies show that being with friends is relatively more likely to increase facial activity, whereas being with strangers is relatively more likely to decrease facial activity (e.g., Wagner & Smith, 1991). For example, Fridlund (1991) showed that participants smiled more when watching humorous films in the company of friends. This effect even extended to friends who were not physically present but supposedly watching the same films at the same time in a different room. This implicit sociality effect suggests that even facial activity in private settings may be affected by audience effects. Merely imagining a friend sharing the situation provides a potential addressee for social motive displays.

Imagined audiences also significantly increased smiling in subsequent studies by Hess, Banse and Kappas (1995) and Jakobs, Manstead and Fischer (1999). However, Hess and colleagues (1995) found no comparable effects of actual or imagined social presence when the other person was a stranger rather than a friend, presumably because participants did not feel that they were sharing the situation in the same way with strangers. It is also possible that participants were unsure about how strangers would evaluate their expressions potentially evoking either a display rule or an alternative social motive (Wagner & Smith, 1991).

Sociality seems to have different effects in situations evoking sadness. Jakobs, Manstead and Fischer (2001) showed sad films to participants who were alone, or in the actual or imagined presence of friends or strangers. Facial activity corresponding to a pouting 'sad' expression was strongest in the alone condition and weaker in all social conditions regardless of whether the other person was physically present and of whether that other person was a friend. Although 'sad' expressions were stronger in response to a film that induced stronger self-reported sadness, they did not correlate significantly with self-reports of sadness in any condition. On the surface, these findings seem to present problems for both emotion-expression and motive-communication accounts. However, there are two possible explanations that are potentially consistent with Fridlund's theoretical approach.

First, because the film clips used to induce sadness involved the suffering of the depicted protagonists, any facial communication may have been addressed to those actors rather than actual or imagined co-viewers. Indeed, the actual or imagined presence of friends or strangers may have decreased participants' level of involvement with the interpersonal narrative of the film and consequently reduced their motivation to offer empathic support for the central character. Second, participants in the alone condition may have been imagining an idealised confidant at whom displays soliciting comfort might be directed.

It is also possible that the presence of either friends or strangers induced display rules inhibiting the expression of sadness. However, this would require the assumption that people even suppress their expressions when imagining a potential negative evaluation from someone who cannot actually see what their face is showing, and who need never know whether sadness was expressed or not.

Naturalistic Research

How does facial activity change in non-laboratory situations that switch from private to public? A classic study by Kraut and Johnston (1979) filmed facial movements at a bowling alley. Smiles were recorded at two time points after the bowler had achieved either a strike or spare. The first phase was the period immediately after the pins fell while the successful bowler still had their back to everyone else. The second phase was when they turned away from the pins to face the other players waiting their turn to bowl. If smiling is an immediate and direct reaction to happiness, we would expect to see it most strongly at the key moment when players saw that they had successfully knocked down all the pins (or all but one of them). However, only 4 out of 116 participants actually smiled before turning to face their friends, at which point 42 smiled. This pattern of results seems to suggest that smiling is a socially oriented communication rather than a direct expression of emotion.

However, can we be certain that the observed bowlers were genuinely happy following their success in knocking down the pins? Perhaps some of them were so confident in their skills that their performance simply fulfilled their expectations rather than producing genuine joy. To rule out this possibility, Ruiz-Belda and colleagues (2003) asked bowlers to say how they felt after each bowl. When participants reported being happy and not experiencing any other emotion, they still smiled much less before than after they turned to face their friends. Even the frequency of 'authentic' Duchenne smiles was higher during the second social phase.

The results of these two studies are easy to explain using Fridlund's theory because the bowlers' displays seemed to be directly attuned to the availability of suitable recipients. Facing the skittles without an audience, there was no point in communicating anything. Facing friends, there were various possible social motives to display. But can Ekman's theory also explain the findings? It is possible that the social situation invoked display rules encouraging bowlers to express happiness towards their friends, but that would not explain the Duchenne smiles reported by Ruiz-Belda and colleagues (2003), which Ekman claims are expressions of genuine happiness.

Another possibility is that the initial joy about the strike or spare was at too low a level to induce smiling (e.g., Matsumoto & Willingham, 2006). Seeing friends' reactions might then have added to the experienced pleasure, pushing it over the necessary threshold for facial expression.

According to this account, stronger emotional reactions should produce clear expressions even in private situations.

Fernández-Dols and Ruiz-Belda (1995) investigated smiling among competitors at the 1992 Olympic games, where stakes were much higher than in informal bowling games, and emotional reactions should be consequently stronger. Video footage of victorious athletes was coded for three stages of the ceremony when the medals were awarded. Each stage involved different kinds and levels of interpersonal contact, each of which might be expected to influence either display rules or the availability of suitable audiences for communication of social motives.

During the first stage, athletes waited while the podium was being prepared and officials gathered to organise the awards ceremony. None of the competitors interacted with anyone else at this stage, and the crowd's attention was directed elsewhere. Were the gold medallists happy at this stage? After having trained and prepared for their event for four years, they now knew that all their work had paid off and they had achieved their central goal. Strong happiness seems inevitable. Indeed, other medal-winning athletes rated their own level of happiness as having been close to the top of the scale across all the ceremony stages investigated in this study.

Did the athletes smile at the first stage? Hardly at all. Were they covering up their expressions because of display rules? Unlikely, given that no one was really watching them at the time. And in any case, why would concerns about other people's judgements override the acknowledged right to rejoice and celebrate on such an occasion?

During the second stage, athletes stood on the podium conversing with officials before the medals were finally awarded. An appropriate recipient for communication of social motives was directly available. And there were frequent smiles.

During the third stage, athletes stood silently on the podium after receiving their medal, with their country's National Anthem playing over the PA system. There was no direct interaction with either officials or the crowd of spectators. And again, there was hardly any smiling.

So smiling seemed to depend not on the level of the athletes' happiness, but rather on interacting directly with someone who is congratulating you. Potentially, neurocultural theory might explain the observed differences in smiling between stages 2 and 3. Display rules might be absent while interacting with a sympathetic official. They might even encourage exaggerated smiling to meet social expectations. By contrast, standing silently while a National flag is raised might have invoked norms about appropriate respect rather than celebration, or might have encouraged sober reflection about the wider context of the athlete's achievement.

But stage 1's findings remain a problem for the emotion-expression view. In a situation where happiness is clearly strong and display rules are either absent or encourage expression, why did the athletes not smile? Why make the effort to stop themselves?

Matsumoto and Willingham (2006; 2009) argued that methodological limitations undermine the results of this and other studies showing that private smiling is uncommon following sporting victories. For example, they argued that some previous researchers coded facial activity before smiles had time to develop or otherwise failed to track immediate emotional responses precisely enough. Using different recording methods, their own study showed that judo players competing in an international tournament smiled both immediately after victory and during subsequent social interaction with officials.

However, the data presented by Matsumoto and Willingham allow no direct comparison between the different sampled time periods. Instead of coding intensity or frequency of smiling over time, the investigators worked through a series of successive still photographs to find the point at which facial movement showed a meaningful pattern, ignoring the amount of time that had elapsed up to that point and disregarding other facial patterns either before or afterwards. The results therefore tell us whether smiles were observed at any point during the periods selected for comparison but not how often they occurred or how long they lasted.

The immediate reaction to victory recorded by Matsumoto and Willingham did not occur at an entirely private moment for the successful contestant in any case. During public judo tournaments, competitors remain in full view of the crowd at all times. Other potential addressees for any facial display include the other competitor and the referee who are both close by during and immediately after each match. Because of the position of the photographer, Matsumoto and Willingham were not able to specify which pictures were taken at more or less interactive or more or less public moments, making it difficult to draw clear conclusions about the effects of sociality.

Crivelli, Carrera and Fernández-Dols (2015) coded facial activity from video records of judo matches rather than still photographs. They found that victors displayed Duchenne smiles significantly less often immediately following victory than during the more interactive phases of the event that came later even when time windows for recording were extended to meet Matsumoto and Willingham's suggested guidelines. Their findings thus substantiate the earlier studies of Olympic athletes and bowlers.

Why do these findings seem surprising? The idea that happiness and smiling go together is deep-rooted. But perhaps the fact that people often smile when they want to communicate their happiness to us misleads us into thinking that there is a stronger association than there actually is. When someone else is happy and doesn't smile, do we ever work out that they are happy at all? And when they are not happy but still smile, maybe we think they must be happy anyway. In other words, we may be working from a biased sample of smiling-related happiness that ignores cases of happiness that do not involve smiling and cases of smiling that do not involve happiness. Perhaps focusing more on possible counter-evidence from everyday life would disabuse us of our illusions about smiling.

So, think about it for moment. Try to remember an occasion when everything went right and you were truly happy. And your happiness continued for minutes or even hours. Did you smile? If so, did you keep on smiling throughout the period of your happiness? Or did your facial activity change over time, adjusting to the social situation and the other things you were doing?

Think too about the different ways sportspeople react on TV when they win something – the crying, the victorious punches in the air, the gaping mouths (Aviezer et al., 2012; Kayyal et al., 2015). Does it still seem obvious that intense happiness automatically produces smiles? Perhaps you want to say that different kinds of happiness, such as pride, awe, gloating and relief each have their own distinctive expressions. Maybe winners cycle between these reactions, experiencing a whirl of intertwined emotions. But then how many emotions are we going to need before we can fully explain what really happens? And couldn't it equally be the case that different communicative possibilities arise as the social context develops and changes? Wouldn't that provide a better explanation of the absence of facial activity in more private contexts?

Interestingly, modes of expression during Olympic awards ceremonies seem to have changed since Fernández-Dols and Ruiz-Belda (1995) conducted their research. The biggest historical change is in the degree of informality, here and elsewhere. The podium is now much lower, leaving little sense of a backstage area. Conversations happen all around, between officials and athletes, athletes and media-people, even athletes and other athletes. It has become far more difficult to isolate social and non-social phases in the ceremony. And smiles, laughter and tears all seem to be very common throughout. None of this tells us much about how facial activity works, however. It just shows that opportunities for field research change and evolve in the public arena.

Beyond Displays and Expressions

Faces do many things apart from communicating social motives or expressing emotions (e.g., Parkinson, 2017; Parkinson et al., 2005). Indeed, both Ekman and Fridlund explicitly restrict their preferred explanations to specific varieties of functional facial movements, and exclude others from their theoretical accounts. For example, neither theory is intended to cover facial reflexes (Ekman, Friesen & Simons, 1985). People sneeze when exposed to allergens or irritants, and gag when something blocks their throat or tastes foul. Although some of these reactions may sometimes be exaggerated to attract the attention of other people who might be able to intervene (e.g., Jäncke & Kaufmann, 1994), those other people don't need to be around to make them happen in the first place. Faces often move in these ways without any real or imagined addressee and regardless of how the source happens to be feeling at the time.

At the other end of the spectrum, some conventionalised facial movements are produced deliberately in order to communicate information or regulate conversation (e.g., Ekman, 1979). We may nod our heads to show assent or shake our heads to withhold it. We redirect our gaze to indicate when it is someone else's turn to speak (e.g., Bavelas, Coates & Johnson, 2002; Kendon, 1967), or when we want to draw their attention to something (facial pointing, Fernández-Dols, 2017). These movements are clearly socially oriented and usually depend on the availability of suitable audiences. But they need not carry any direct emotional implications.

The facial movements considered by both Ekman and Fridlund mostly fall somewhere between reflexes and deliberate communications. However, the coverage of their two theories does not perfectly overlap. Motive-communication accounts easily extend to some kinds of conversational signal (e.g., Bavelas et al., 1986; Chovil, 1997). Correspondingly, emotion-expression theories may reach further towards the reflex end of the facial spectrum. Emotion-related processes that are a little more articulated than pangs, tickles or pains may produce direct facial responses regardless of whether anyone is around to see them.

For example, some of the facial movements directly involved in action preparation or execution might well occur in private even when the actor is not explicitly imagining a particular audience. Effort and concentration on specific practical tasks such as fitting an electrical socket or climbing a ladder may produce distinctive patterns of movement including movements of the face. In these cases, we could potentially get information about what the person is doing and how much they are struggling with it by secretly observing their face, even if watching their whole body perform the task in context would give a clearer picture. Although none of the facial information available in these situations directly or consistently indicates emotion, it may still help perceivers to draw indirect emotional inferences. Thus, faces may sometimes provide clues about emotion even in non-social settings, and when they are not directly expressing or communicating anything.

Practical and Communicative Functions

In this chapter, I have argued that expressing emotion is not the central function of any kind of facial activity. However, this does not mean that facial movements are unrelated to emotions. The fact that people from many societies attach emotional meanings to faces is not simply a historical accident. So where does the intuitive emotion–face connection come from?

Darwin (1872) proposed three reasons why facial activity might acquire the function of expressing emotions. First, it might serve direct practical functions in performing emotionally relevant actions such as rejecting a stimulus using eye closure or turning away (principle of associated serviceable habits). Second, it might indicate that someone is in a state of mind opposite to that which provokes a practically oriented action, as happens when a person looks away from something they are not about to confront (principle of antithesis). Third, the face may reveal symptoms of an underlying physiological state associated with emotion, such as flushing due to raised blood pressure (e.g., Thorstenson et al., 2018), or muscular tension associated with action preparation (principle of actions due to the constitution of the nervous system).

None of these principles implies a direct connection between emotion and expression. In each case, the face provides information with potential emotional relevance because it is doing something that is primarily non-emotional. Faces may play a role in preparing for or executing practical action, signalling that practical action is unlikely or showing side effects of the body's internal condition, but emotion need not be implicated at any point. Indeed, Darwin's general conclusion was that facial configurations acquire their emotion-expressing power from other non-emotional processes.

In this chapter, I have also argued that facial movements play a practical role in preparing and performing actions, and that those actions may be more or less closely related to emotions. This means that perceivers can derive some information about what emotion someone might be experiencing by looking at what their face does, even when their knowledge of context is limited. For example, someone staring hard in a fixed direction seems likely to be monitoring something that is happening or about to happen. Knowing that they are doing this imposes constraints on possible emotional interpretations. Other information from the face or elsewhere can then fill in the gaps, leading us to conclude that the staring person is anxious or angry about something.

We have also seen how facial movements can be used communicatively to produce effects on other people. I can direct your attention to something by looking at it myself (Fernández-Dols, 2017; Parkinson, 2017) or indicate my disapproval by deflecting my attention. Thus, the practical functions of facial activity may be co-opted for the purpose of social influence (Mead, 1934). The resulting facial displays are likely to be attuned to the availability of suitable addressees, as implied by Fridlund's (1994) motive-communication theory.

Most displays primarily communicate social motives and only provide indirect evidence of any associated emotion as a secondary consequence of their social influence function. However, in some cases, facial activity conveys information about actions that feature in prototypical represen-tations of a particular emotion. For example, people scrunch their noses when something smells bad, and smelling something bad (either literally or metaphorically) is central to many societies' shared conceptualisation of disgust (see Chapter 9). Thus, nose-scrunching not only provides clues that restrict possible emotional interpretations, but also cues the more specific concept of 'disgust' in certain contexts.

This kind of conceptual association allows people to use their faces specifically to indicate an emotion to others. As an Englishman, I may scrunch my nose to let you know that something disgusts me. You will get the message because you share my prototypical representation of 'disgust' and its metaphorical association with bad smells. In one sense, then, some facial movements may actually 'express' emotions, or at least emotion concepts. However, they don't do it because of some prewired connection between the internal experience and its external manifesta-tion. And they only do it when the point is to communicate a culturally articulated emotional meaning to someone else.

Taken together, these practical and communicative functions can account for all available evidence from judgement and production studies, including those that assess effects of context and culture. Participants who share similar prototypical representations of basic emotion categories are able to associate certain stylised facial configurations with those categories, especially when given rating tasks that key them in to the required emo-tional interpretations. Providing contextual information that activates the relevant representational script or otherwise disambiguates the underlying relational orientation also helps. Participants unfamiliar with Western emotion concepts may instead need to work from the source's apparent action readiness or relational orientation to rule in or out possible emo-tional interpretations. And in some cases, the facial cues may even indicate a quite different emotional script, as happens when a gasping 'fear' face gets read instead as a stereotypical threat display (Crivelli et al., 2016b).

Turning from perception to production, supposed basic emotion expres-sions are more likely to be generated when events closely match the prototypical scripted episode for the relevant emotion, when the relational orientation associated with that script needs to be communicated to someone else, and when participants want to explicitly convey an emotional meaning using their face in Anglo-American contexts. In none of these cases, does the emotion itself directly produce the facial movement. What the face is doing is not expressing an internal state but performing an action or communicating something to somebody.

CHAPTER 4

Explaining Emotional Influence

This chapter discusses how and why emotions affect other people's actions, appraisals and emotions. One popular explanation of inter-personal influence is primitive emotional contagion. According to this account, people arrive at similar emotional states because they copy one another's gestures and expressions (mimicry). The feelings and sensations produced by these gestures and expressions then produce convergent emotional experiences (interoceptive feedback). However, mimicry effects are too selective and feedback effects too weak to make this process work consistently. An alternative process is social apprai-sal, which involves calibrating emotional orientations to objects or events in the shared environment. Most studies of social appraisal present participants with verbal or facial information about someone else's emotion and assess their inferences about that information. However, relation alignment may also operate at a more implicit level when people adjust to each other's developing object-directed signals and movements. Similar processes may also produce diver-gent or conflicting emotional orientations when two people approach the same event from different angles or interpret its consequences in different ways.

Other people's emotions are difficult to ignore. Think of the last time someone got angry with you or showed enthusiasm about something you were doing. Think of how you feel when someone close is hurt or upset, or when their worst fears suddenly evaporate. Their reaction carries a kind of gravitational pull regardless of how unjustified or dispro-portionate it might seem at the time. You can't help getting drawn in.

We don't need to be the target of someone else's emotion for it to affect us. And we don't need to be close to the person expressing an emotion for it to make us care about something that we would not otherwise care about. At times, the constant barrage of news about disasters, bereave-ments and other tragedies might start to seem overwhelming or mind-numbing. We might want to detach or otherwise switch off. But then some reporter inevitably presses a microphone into the face of any sur-viving victim or witness to ask how they feel. That's what they always want to know even if the interviewee is too close to the heat of the moment to really tell them. Often, the best that can be managed by way of reply is 'I don't know what to say'. But we still sense the trauma behind the words. And that's what makes things matter to us.

Why are emotions so socially compelling? How do they achieve their interpersonal effects? It turns out that a wide range of different processes are involved, depending on what the emotion is about, who it is directed to and how it relates to whatever else is going on. But before getting to that, it's worth making some basic distinctions between the various effects that other people's emotions actually have on us.

Interpersonal Effects

No single explanation can account for all possible interpersonal effects of emotion because emotions affect other people in such a wide variety of ways. In this section, I distinguish some of these effects to give a better sense of what might need explaining.

Emotional Effects

Convergence

The most obvious cases of emotional influence happen when another person comes to experience similar emotions to yours. Excitement and happiness sometimes seem infectious. Empathy may lead someone else to share your sorrow or emotional pain. In these cases, two people's emotions come closer to each other or converge. Convergence is not usually total, however. The other person's emotion is rarely identical to the one you are experiencing in all respects. They may feel sympathy with your situation without completely sharing your sadness, for example. They may be disappointed by your failure without directly feeling the same sense of loss. Their emotional response may be weaker than yours or may involve subtly different emotions. The degree of interpersonal convergence partly depends on the extent to which you are mutually aligned to what is happening around you both. If you saw everything from precisely the same perspective as each other, then your emotions might match perfectly. However, given that no two people ever occupy exactly the same physical or psychological coordinates, some residual differences are likely to remain.

Emotion matching can also happen when two people arrive at similar orientations to different objects. You may get angry about something I have done, and I may get angry back. I may resent being blamed for doing something you are accusing me of doing. Perhaps I don't agree that I was in the wrong. Maybe I didn't actually do what you think I did, and you somehow got the wrong end of the stick. In either case, you are blaming me for one thing, and I am blaming you for something else (namely, blaming me by getting angry). In other words, convergent emotions don't necessarily reflect convergent orientations to events. Sometimes they reflect conflict instead.

Divergence

Both convergent and conflicting orientations can lead to divergent as well as convergent emotions. Your anger may make me feel guilty rather than provoking reciprocated anger. Your disappointment may make me gloat rather than empathise. There is an obvious difference between these two examples. In the first case, my emotional response is consistent with your relational agenda and emotional orientation even though the nature of the emotion itself is different. When angry with me, you usually want me to feel guilty for what I have done (Parkinson, 2001b). In order to respond with guilt rather than reciprocated anger or resentment, I need to be able to see things from your angry perspective. My emotional response is thus complementary to yours. Other examples of complementary emotions include pity in response to someone else's grief, shame in response to someone else's contempt and admiration in response to someone else's pride.

By contrast, schadenfreude in response to disappointment implies competitive or antagonistic interpersonal or intergroup relations, involving goal conflict or incompatible orientations. For example, supporters of opposing teams in football matches have conflicting reactions not only to game events such as fouls, goals, victories and defeats, but also to each other's emotional reactions to these game-related events. Gloating celebrations by supporters of one team may make supporters of the other team angry. Thus, divergent emotional responses may be conflicting as well as complementary. Other examples of conflicting divergent emotions include malicious envy in response to someone else's pride, and pride in response to someone else's malicious envy.

Non-Emotional Effects

Emotions may also have non-emotional effects on other people. Let's say someone notices that you look a little sad without really thinking too carefully about it. They still might draw conclusions about what is happening. In fact, this situation is not so different from what happens when research participants are shown photographs of strangers' faces and asked to make judgements about them or about what else is happening (Chapter 3). If the faces genuinely convey the source's emotions, their effects on participants' perceptions and interpretations count as interpersonal effects of emotion.

Do participants experience emotions when making judgements about the face of someone they don't know? As we shall see, some theorists argue that identifying facial expressions sometimes involves subtly moving your own face to produce a matching expression and reconstructing what it feels like in that configuration (e.g., Niedenthal et al., 2010). This may lead you to experience a corresponding emotion in attenuated form. It may be that you recognise anger because copying a scowling face reignites a spark of your own anger. But people can also use abstract knowledge to infer the meanings of emotional stimuli, and this does not necessarily involve noticeable levels of emotion.

Some non-emotional effects run in parallel to emotional ones. Toddlers who hold back instead of crossing a visual cliff may well be more anxious after seeing their mother's wide-eyed gasping face (Sorce et al., 1985; and see Chapter 1), but their hesitation need not depend on personally experienced anxiety. Instead it might simply reflect an implicit conclusion that the cliff is potentially dangerous. In other circumstances, emotions can direct other people's attention, affect their perception and interpretation of what is happening or change their behaviour. And all these effects need not imply any emotional response, although they may sometimes come together to produce emotional effects of their own.

Influence Processes

Having outlined the kinds of interpersonal effect we want to explain, it is now time to think about how to explain them. In this section, I set out different processes that might underlie emotional influence based on what aspects of the situated emotion are exerting that influence. To understand these distinctions, we first need to clarify our terminology.

Terminology

Psychologists use a variety of terms to describe the processes whereby one person's emotion can influence another's. These include affective linkage (e.g., Levenson & Gottman, 1983), interpersonal emotional transfer (Parkinson, 2011), emotional contagion (Elfenbein, 2014), and social appraisal (Manstead & Fischer, 2001). To complicate matters further, different writers have different views about how these terms should be defined, and how wide their coverage should be. For example, there is disagreement about whether 'contagion' covers the full range of cases in which people come to experience similar emotions (Wróbel & Imbir, 2019) or refers more specifically to a particular kind of process that produces emotional convergence ('primitive emotional contagion': Hatfield, Cacioppo & Rapson,

1994). Similarly, 'social appraisal' may include all social effects on appraisal (e.g., Fischer, Manstead & Zaalberg, 2003) or only those caused specifically by someone else's perceived appraisal (e.g., Parkinson, 2011). Further, social appraisal may either be seen as distinct from social referencing (Clément & Dukes, 2017) or equivalent to it (Walle, Reschke & Knothe, 2017). These inconsistencies and slippages in the application of concepts can create confusion. They can give the appearance of theoretical disagreement when there is none (Parkinson, 2017). Or they can make different theoretical views seem more similar than they really are.

In the absence of any legislative body empowered to enforce terminological edicts, I will content myself with saying as clearly as I can how I intend to use the relevant words and concepts. Starting with the general topic of this chapter, 'emotional influence' is meant as a theoretically neutral description of the phenomena to be explained. 'Influence' should not be read as implying that one person is actively trying to influence another (although this may certainly happen). Instead, the emotion is doing the influencing regardless of the intentions of the emotional person.

I also tried to use neutral terms when describing the possible emotional outcomes of emotional influence in the discussion so far. Emotional convergence and divergence, complementarity and conflict are not intended to refer to explanatory processes. They set out effects that these processes need to explain.

Two additional terms allow me to avoid repeatedly implying that it is your emotions that are influencing mine, my emotions influencing yours, or someone else's emotions influencing you, me or yet another person. From now on, I refer to the person whose emotions are exerting influence (person A) as the 'source' and the person being influenced (person B) as the 'target'. These too are intended as neutral terms. The target is not necessarily someone targeted by a specific influence attempt, but simply the target of any emotional influence that might happen for any reason. Targets are broadly equivalent to 'recipients' (e.g., Elfenbein, 2014; van Kleef, 2016), but I am avoiding that multisyllabic term because it tends to imply that sources' emotions are presented to targets as encapsulated information.

Finally, it is worth noting that the roles of source and target are not exclusive or permanent. Sources can become targets, and targets can become sources. Indeed, sources and targets often take both these positions at the same time in reciprocal influence processes. My excitement makes you more excited while your excitement does the same to me. Reciprocity of emotional influence turns out to be an important feature of interactions outside laboratory settings.

Active Ingredients

It's not only imprecise terminology that complicates distinctions between emotional influence processes. The processes themselves also overlap, interpenetrate, and merge into one another. My automatic empathic reaction to your expressed worry may lead me to focus on different aspects of the situation that also make me feel more worried. I may then try to regulate my worry in order to alleviate yours (see Parkinson et al., 2016) and so on. These overlapping phases can be distinguished in principle but isolating their distinctive mechanisms may be challenging in practice.

One way in which we can separate out different processes is to focus on where the influence is coming from. How is the source's emotion presented? Which of its aspects or manifestations are responsible for producing interpersonal effects? When we have worked out what activates the process of emotional influence, we should be in a better position to understand how it might work.

Emotional Events

Some cases of emotional convergence and divergence have nothing to do with interpersonal emotional influence. We may just end up having the same or different emotions at the same time for other reasons. When watching a football match, for example, all your team's supporters may react with delight when the winning goal is scored. And all the opposing team's supporters may react with disappointment, anger or despondency. However, neither of these effects involves the transfer of emotion from one person to another, at least not at first. It is certainly true that emotions may intensify because allies nearby are sharing them, and because enemies who are also within sight or earshot are feeling the opposite (see Chapter 7). However, what provokes both groups' emotions at the outset is the fact that your team scored.

Even when emotion is explicitly communicated, it may be the associated event that drives the interpersonal response. You may react to what has happened rather than the other person's conveyed orientation towards it. For example, a friend may send an excited text conveying the news that the team you both support has just scored. Let's say you were sleeping while the match was on, and only pick up this text the next morning. Again, if your delayed reaction is to your team's goal rather than your friend's emotional reaction to it, this would still not count as emotional influence. In practice, it may sometimes be difficult to draw a clear line between the situation and a person's emotional orientation to it, or to determine which of these interrelated factors brought two people's emotion into line or put them out of alignment (see Elfenbein, 2014).

However, in order to isolate relevant processes, we should at least attempt to distinguish between effects of common exposure to emotional events and effects of other people's emotional orientations to those events (Hess & Fischer, 2013; Totterdell, 2000).

But what does it mean to say that the emotions themselves are having the effects? I have argued that whatever does the influencing has to be something about the emotions rather than the situations in which those emotions occur. But what exactly is it about the emotions that makes the difference? The metaphor of heart-to-heart conversation implies that people somehow make direct contact with each other's emotions. But no purely subjective experience could ever be registered by anyone else (see Chapter 1). The emotion needs to be detectable in some way before it can have any influence on another person. Something about what the source is saying, expressing or doing (or something about the way they are saying, expressing or doing it) must be what produces interpersonal influence. In the following sections, I consider what that something might be.

Categorical Emotion Information

Some of the clearest cases of emotional influence involve one person telling or showing another person that they are experiencing a particular emotion. For example, you may say that you are 'angry' or pull a scowling face. Based on the prototypical script for Anglo-American anger, I may conclude that you blame someone for something bad that has happened, that you have an urge to retaliate, that your blood pressure is high and so on. In this case, your explicit communication about a particular emotion is what transmits its influence. The active ingredient is your descriptive representation of what you are experiencing.

A similar process may operate when someone else tells me that you are experiencing an emotion or otherwise directs my attention to your emotional expression or behaviour. Indeed, this is often what happens in psychological experiments investigating emotion's interpersonal influence. Participants are informed (or otherwise led to believe) that another person is experiencing a certain kind of emotion instead of being put in direct contact with that emotion. Again, any interpersonal effect is likely to depend on the target categorising the source's emotional experience.

Information about a discrete emotion is most obviously the active ingredient of emotional influence when either the source or another person explicitly communicates that information (and only that information) to the target. However, information-based effects need not involve direct communication of any kind. I may work out that you are angry simply on the basis of your raised voice, fixed stare or directed aggression, and my conclusion about the specific angry quality of your emotion may mediate its effects on me.

Componential Information

In the cases considered in the previous section, emotion's interpersonal effects depend on the target picking up on the fact that the source is experiencing a specific emotion. Your anger affects me once I realise that you are angry. I integrate the available information from words, facial movements, orientations and context by applying a more abstract representation such as that contained in an emotion prototype. This then allows me to draw other conclusions about what you might do. But does the target need to draw conclusions about the particular emotion experienced by the target before that emotion can have an interpersonal effect?

In some cases, the information that the target extracts from the source's emotional orientation relates to the emotion's lower-level components rather than its integrated meaning. For example, by observing your scowling face and fixed stare, I may work out that something is happening that you do not like, or simply that there is something I should watch out for. And I may reach this conclusion before I have attributed any anger to your facial movements. In some cases, neither you nor I may even realise that your orientation to events might be categorised in angry terms. But that doesn't stop your anger affecting me. In other words, different aspects of the source's emotional orientation may provide information that influences the target's response even when the target has not apprehended their wider emotional meaning. Emotional influence does not require categorisation of the emotion that is doing the influencing. The active ingredient may be information about emotion components rather than emotion as a whole.

Cues, Nudges and Adjustments

If emotional influence can happen without emotion attribution, can it also bypass inference and meaning extraction altogether? We certainly respond to some aspects of other people's emotional orientations without having to think about it. For example, humans automatically track each other's eye gaze (e.g., Driver et al., 1999) and adjust their position and posture to each other's movements while interacting (e.g., Bernieri, Reznick & Rosenthal, 1988). Further, when these processes of adjustment involve reciprocal influence from source to target and target to source, more coherent patterns of orientation may emerge between people, building convergent or divergent emotional orientations bit by bit from the bottom-up. This still counts as emotional influence because each person's movements and adjustments are part of more general emotional orientations. But it doesn't seem to depend on communicating and decoding emotion, and need not involve mental representation of what is happening in either emotional or non-emotional terms.

Of course, this does not mean that no form of implicit categorisation or perceptual simulation plays any role at any stage of interpersonal episodes of this kind. However, what seems to drive influence is the relation between the target's and source's dynamic orientations and how they adjust to each other rather than any separate attachment of meaning. The structure of the emotional interaction emerges and coalesces from lower-level adjustments, rather than being imposed from top-down mental representation and planning.

Some aspects of a source's emotional orientation may even be unconditioned elicitors of target responses. Smiles may have intrinsic reward value (e.g., Rolls, 1999) and high-pitched shrieks or loud screams may directly capture other people's attention (see Hatfield et al., 1994). Being hugged may be inherently comforting under the right circumstances. In all these cases, one person's emotion-related responses serve to incentivise or energise someone else's behaviour in ways that do not depend only on their informational content. The perceptual qualities of the interpersonal stimulus are what make the difference.

Orientation
The preceding sections have tried to zero in on the active ingredients that bring about the interpersonal effects of emotions. The implication was that something inside the source's emotion provides information, cues or incentives that prompt the target's response. Indeed, I explicitly distinguished emotional influence from situational influence as if the two processes always operated independently.

In practice, emotions can never be entirely decontextualised. Even in controlled laboratory experiments, information that another person is angry or disappointed is always delivered at a certain time in relation to a certain kind of stimulus or task. Research reviewed in Chapters 2 and 3 already tells us that participants' emotion judgements about emotion-related words and faces are affected by the surrounding context. It therefore seems likely that context also makes a difference to other interpersonal effects of emotion, making emotion's relation to whatever else is happening another candidate for an active ingredient of influence (or at least a moderator of influence exerted by other active ingredients).

The most relevant contextual features concern where the emotion is directed and what it is about. For example, your anger may be about my own action or inaction or someone else's. In the first case, I am more likely to apologise or respond with reciprocated anger. In the second case, I am more likely to sympathise or leap to the defence of the person with whom you are angry. If we see emotions as relational orientations, then their capacity to affect other people is likely to depend on how those other people are implicated in the relations they embody. Taking an angry stance towards someone would then already be part of an influence process.

Information about where emotions such as anger are directed may be available from the dynamic orientation of bodily movements or sensory adjustments. Alternatively, it may be conveyed in statements made by the emotional person or someone else. Some experiments provide explicit details about where emotion is directed using verbal information. For example, Lelieveld and colleagues (2011) found that telling participants that a source was angry with them produced stronger emotional reactions than telling them that the source was angry about the outcome they had experienced (see also Steinel, van Kleef & Harinck, 2008). Thus, information about object-directedness can clarify or otherwise modify an emotion's relational meaning. Less explicit interpersonal effects may also occur when the source's object-directed emotional orientation helps channel or redirect the target's orientations to the same object.

Separable components of emotion may also be more or less object-directed. It may not be the directedness of your anger that affects me, but rather the fixed stare associated with that anger, or the information that you are staring at me or something else in a fixed way. Some aspects of emotion are more overtly object-directed than others, and their inter-personal influence is therefore more likely to be affected by their direct-edness. For example, eye gaze directs attention to where the person is looking and gestural movements can push or pull others in the direction of whatever is being approached or avoided. By contrast, blushing, trem-bling and slumping are not intrinsically directional responses. Nevertheless, their dynamic temporal association with ongoing events can still yield contextualised perceptions and produce context-sensitive interpersonal effects that are separable from those of the directed or undirected emotion itself. For example, if I blush immediately after catching your eye, the contiguity of the two events carries clear implica-tions about the orientation of my blushing.

Processes

Identifying active ingredients not only helps us understand where emo-tional influence comes from, but also provides clues about how it might operate. In this section, I turn to possible distinctions between emotional influence processes relating to their dependence on different kinds of information about the emotion and its intentional object and on whether information is directly involved at all.

Inference

An initial distinction can be drawn between processes that work on emotion-related information and those driven more directly by emotional orientations or aspects of those orientations. Information-based effects mainly depend on the target making inferences or deriving conclusions about what a source is feeling, thinking or doing, whereas directly orientation-based effects bypass emotion attribution and explicit reasoning processes. Thus, backing off because I have worked out that you are angry counts as an inferential process, and making direct adjustments to gaze patterns or bodily movements counts as a non-inferential process (see van Kleef, 2008, for a related distinction between inferential and affective routes to emotional influence).

It is worth noting that these different kinds of processes are not wholly determined by how the source's emotion is presented to the target. Although explicitly communicated emotion information may activate an information-based inferential process in the target, it may also lead that target to attend to different aspects of the source's object-orientation, leading to non-inferential effects. You telling me that you are angry may attune me to your fixed stare and where it is directed, making me attend to that object too. Correspondingly, a deflection of gaze or tightening of muscles may lead me to make inferences about how you are feeling even when no one has explicitly communicated your emotion to me. Despite these complications, emotions that are presented as encapsulated information are more likely to produce inferential effects than those to which we are exposed more directly without explicit categorisation. Things are more likely to work as active ingredients when they are foregrounded.

Directionality

It is also possible to distinguish emotional influence processes depending on whether or not they factor in the object-directedness of the source's emotional orientation. When the active ingredient of emotional influence is an object-directed emotion, emotion component or information about it, the immediate effects are directional too. A source's emotional orientation can push or pull the target's action and attention towards or away from the object at which it is directed. Aspects of that orientation may bring component-based or integrated interpersonal effects. Correspondingly, information about a source's overall emotional orientation or its components can change perceptions, interpretations and appraisals of the specified objects.

By contrast, when targets are responding to object-independent aspects of emotions or components, their object-orientations are less likely to be directly affected. Non-directional effects may instead involve drawing inferences about what the person is like or what they are feeling, thinking or doing. Or they may involve non-inferential transfer of either affective state or more specific non-directed movements. The target may simply pick up something about what the source is experiencing without registering what that experience is about.

Directional emotional influence processes are more diverse than non-directional ones. Differences depend on various factors relating to the nature of the emotional object and how the source and target are oriented to it. For example, I am likely to respond more defensively to anger directed at me than to anger directed at someone else especially if we are in the middle of an argument about something that matters to both of us. These more specific distinctions should become clearer in subsequent sections of this chapter. But first, let's consider an apparently non-directional process of emotional influence.

Contagion

In emotional contagion, it is the emotion itself that spreads from person to person rather than anything to do with its orientation to what else might be happening. The idea is that we simply catch other people's feelings when they come into contact with us, much as we might catch a disease.

Although different formulations are possible (Elfenbein, 2014; Hatfield et al., 1994), most of the things that are described as emotional contagion share three broad characteristics. First, contagion involves two or more people arriving at matching rather than different emotions, convergence rather than divergence, conflict or complementarity. You wouldn't call an illness contagious if interpersonal contact led another person to experience an entirely different syndrome of symptoms (a phobic reaction to someone else's asthma, for example), so why do it for an emotion?

Second, the active ingredient in contagion is the undirected emotion rather than its specific orientational aspects. Contagion does not depend on where or on what the source's emotion is directed, whether the target is oriented to the same object, or indeed any object at all (Parkinson, 2011). It is the feeling or evaluative tone that gets transferred from person to person and not the contextualised emotion. Thus, what makes excitement contagious is nothing to do with what the excited person is excited about. It may be that contagion ultimately leads to two people becoming excited about the same thing, but that thing plays no direct role in the contagion process itself (Parkinson, 2011; Parkinson & Simons, 2009).

Third, contagion happens immediately and automatically, without any need for appraisal or interpretation of the source's emotion. In other words, it seems to be a non-inferential process (see also van Kleef, 2008). For example, emotional influence would not count as contagion if I heard later about what you were feeling, drew conclusions about your plight and arrived at a similar emotional reaction on that basis. Other kinds of emotional convergence may depend on the target taking an emotional orientation towards the source's perceived emotion (interpersonal meta-emotion: Elfenbein, 2014; Parkinson & Simons, 2012). I can be happy that you are happy, sad that you are sad or embarrassed by your embarrassment. In each of these cases, your emotion leads me to experience a similar emotion. However, I am not catching your emotion but reacting to its relational meaning (cf. Hess & Fischer, 2013). It is not contagion if the target's emotional response is focused specifically on the target or the target's emotion.

Although contagion does not require coordination of source and target's orientations, and operates independent of their focus, there needs to be some level of contact between the two people involved. We cannot easily catch another person's emotion if it is happening somewhere far away, outside our current sphere of activity. Indeed, reported cases where supposed 'contagion' depends on sharing of emotional content on social media would not count as contagion at all using the present formulation. Surreptitious monitoring of people's use of Facebook may show that they tend to share more negatively toned content in response to receipt of negatively toned content from others (Kramer, Guillory & Hancock, 2014). But this only means that they are responding either to the bad news conveyed by that negative content or to their changed evaluation of that news in response to an object-directed emotion communication. In the first case, it is exposure to common events that causes emotion convergence, thus taking things outside the realm of interpersonal emotional influence. In the second case, the object-directedness of the emotion communication makes the influence something other than contagion (e.g., social appraisal).

Varieties

How does contagion work? Direct physical contact is not required and there is no airborne virus that carries emotion from person to person. So what is the vehicle of transmission? How does the source's emotion get to the target and make them emotional too?

Hatfield and colleagues (1994) distinguished three kinds of process. The first involves active perspective-taking. The target imagines what it would be like to be in the source's shoes, and experiencing the things that they are apparently experiencing. This in turn leads to empathic emotions. Whether such a process counts as contagion depends on whether the target factors in whatever the source is emotional about. If they do, then the process is not strictly contagion according to the present formulation. Instead it involves arriving at a convergent orientation to a particular object, or feeling empathic concern about the source's orientation. In other words, the object-directedness of the source's emotion is implicated. Excluding these cases leaves us only with the unlikely situation that the target takes on the source's undirected emotional perspective in some shape or form, imagining what it must be like to feel something without knowing what that feeling is about. But whatever the target might be imagining in such a situation doesn't really seem to be a perspective that they are now taking. Indeed, removing a perspective's object-directedness leaves nothing of any real substance.

The second contagion process proposed by Hatfield and colleagues concerns social reinforcement. Throughout their lives, people are exposed to other people's facial expressions and bodily gestures and learn to associate certain outcomes with them. For example, children may come to learn that parents' gasping 'fear' faces are associated with danger of some kind, just like Pavlov's dog learned that a bell signals delivery of food. Because of this associative learning, gasping faces become conditioned threat stimuli, eliciting fear responses in the same way that a bell makes a suitably conditioned dog salivate. Thus, one person's expression of an emotion may come to directly evoke a matching emotion in other people because of classical conditioning. Although this seems a plausible non-inferential account of some contagion-like effects, it works better for some aspects of emotion than others. It makes sense to see autonomic and orienting responses as classically conditionable (or innately tied to unconditioned stimuli), but not more integrated emotional orientations including transaction-attuned modes of action readiness or relational activity. Many aspects of emotion require more flexibility and context-sensitivity than reflexive accounts allow (e.g., Ekman et al., 1985; Scherer, 2001; Smith & Ellsworth, 1985). In other words, the social reinforcement account seems to explain interpersonal effects of emotion components rather than integrated emotion syndromes. It is not the emotion itself that gets transmitted from person to person.

Hatfield and colleagues' (1994) third process, referred to as 'primitive emotional contagion' is the one they discuss in most detail and the one that has been investigated most extensively in subsequent research. A similar process was originally proposed by Lipps (1907; see Hatfield et al., 1994) in his discussion of 'einfühlung', which roughly translates as 'empathy'. Lipps was especially interested in the question of how we come to perceive the physical movements of other people's bodies and faces as expressions of an underlying emotion, allowing us to make psychological contact with them. In other words, what adds experiential depth to our impressions of those environmental objects that happen to be other people? According to Lipps, the answer involves a form of

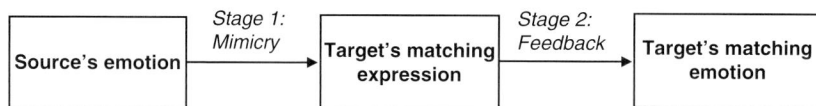

Figure 4.1 Primitive emotional contagion according to Hatfield and colleagues' (1994) model (Parkinson, 2011, reproduced with permission from Blackwell/Wiley)

projective identification. We recreate the other person's experience internally and then attach it to our perception of their bodily movements. How we see the other person is coloured by our reconstruction of what they are feeling. Thus, we see others as emotionally expressive rather than simply moving in meaningless ways because we have projected our own internal simulation of their emotions onto their faces. Such an empathic process can only work if we can first conjure up a matching internal experience in ourselves. According to Lipps, achieving this involves moving our own bodies in similar ways to the other person to check how that makes us feel. Empathy therefore depends on a prior contagion mechanism.

Based on the same kind of reasoning, Hatfield and colleagues argue that the first stage of primitive emotional contagion involves copying the other person's expressions. This mimicry is activated automatically by innate mechanisms that attune us to other people's faces and induce matching facial reactions. These matching facial reactions in turn induce a corresponding emotional state (see Figure 4.1). Thus, if I mimic your smile, my smiling tends to make me happy too.

The initial premise of Lipps' account is that perceivers are confronted with decontextualised bodily movements which can only be made to make sense by working out what internal mental processes are controlling them. If bodies move in relation to observable objects and events, then this apparent 'problem of other minds' becomes more tractable (cf. Reddy, 2008). Perhaps we don't need to dredge up another person's private experience on the basis of indirect cues or symptoms. Instead, we may simply need to engage with them or the events they are engaged with more directly in order to pick up on their orientation. When they are already oriented to our own responsive actions, this doesn't seem like such a difficult process.

Setting aside the conceptual necessity for remote mind-reading, what is the empirical evidence for the two stages of the primitive emotion-contagion process? In the following subsections, I separately review the literature on mimicry and feedback effects, before considering how they might combine to produce emotion convergence.

Mimicry

Innate Imitation

Lipps' (1907) account of empathy assumed that humans have an innate instinct predisposing them to imitate each other's gestures and expressions. This assumption continues to be widely but not unanimously held. Before reviewing the evidence, it is worth considering what capacities infants might require for them to achieve this kind of mimicry. They somehow need to translate a perception of someone else's movement into a matching response, but how is that translation achieved? The stimuli are visual, but the responses are muscular. It therefore seems that the infant needs to register the visual configuration presented by the model's face, then generate a pattern of muscle movements that produces a matching configuration, without at any point being able to see what their own face is showing.

To solve this 'correspondence problem' (Heyes, 2005; Ray & Heyes, 2011), the infant must know at some level what their own face looks like when the muscles are in a particular position. Some cognitively oriented accounts conclude that the brain generates an abstract representation of bodily configurations which can then be converted into muscle commands (e.g., active intermodal matching: Meltzoff & Moore, 1997).

Alternatively, embodied perception theories argue that the target's perception of the source's movement is achieved by an internal simulation process which involves corresponding muscle signals in the first place. But this too implies that infants know what movements to make in order to simulate what they see. It seems as if they could only learn this by watching themselves in a mirror, which is beyond their experience or capacity.

So maybe humans are innately prepared to represent their own body movements in visual terms. Perhaps the so-called mirror neuron system in the brain (e.g., Rizzolatti & Craighero, 2004) provides a biological basis for social engagement. Or perhaps infants learn to imitate on the basis of their early social experiences of receiving encouragement for responding appropriately to other people's faces. In that case, they wouldn't need any cross-modal representation, only the ability to try out different kinds of movements and to register their interpersonal effects during interaction (see Chapter 9).

To test whether learning is necessary for the development of imitation, we need to check how soon after birth infants start to imitate. The sooner imitation occurs, the less likely it becomes that it depends on learning, and the more likely it begins to seem that it has an innate basis. However, very young infants have limited motor control and start out lacking the ability to make a wide range of muscular movements. This means that researchers need to focus specifically on those particular movements that they are already capable of making. Unfortunately, the fact that they can make these movements implies that they already serve some useful function, meaning that they must also be produced for reasons other than imitation. Researchers therefore need to demonstrate that infants produce these movements selectively as imitative responses, as well as more spontaneously. In other words, it is necessary to compare the frequency of production across appropriate comparison periods.

Working within these constraints, some researchers investigating early imitation claim to have demonstrated imitation of some specific facial movements before infants are three days old (e.g., Meltzoff & Moore, 1983). At this age, it is unlikely that much prior learning has taken place (at least outside the womb). However, these reports of very early imitation are not universally accepted. To understand why, we need to consider the relevant methods and findings in more detail.

The paradigm most commonly used in this kind of research was developed in a classic study by Meltzoff and Moore (1977). These researchers tested whether infants under three-weeks-old imitated the two specific facial movements of tongue-protrusion and mouth-opening after they had been enacted by an adult experimenter. However, Meltzoff and Moore did not test whether infants automatically copied these movements immediately every time they saw the experimenter making them. Instead, they counted instances during a 150-second period that followed the modelling period. The prediction was that tongue-protrusion would be observed more often after modelled tongue-protrusion than after modelled mouth-opening (and vice versa). The comparison between conditions was necessary because merely showing that tongue-protrusion became more frequent after modelled tongue-protrusion may simply demonstrate that modelled tongue-protrusion simply increases the probability of a range of behaviours that happen to include matching ones. For example, physiological arousal arising from any change in stimulation may make tongue-protrusion and other responses more likely (see Jones, 1996).

Results were consistent with differential imitation of tongue-protrusion. The overall frequency of mouth-opening was much lower across all observation periods, and the apparent imitation effect for mouth-opening was also weaker. Tongue-protrusion effects have been replicated relatively more consistently in subsequent research too (see Ray & Heyes, 2011). Although some studies report apparent imitation effects for mouth-opening, differences in the relative frequency of this behaviour across observation periods may in fact reflect decreases in its frequency when infants are imitating tongue-protrusion rather than increases in its frequency following modelled mouth-opening. In other words, the more often an infant protrudes their tongue the less often they are able to open their mouths because the two kinds of response are in direct competition with each other (Ray & Heyes, 2011). Infants can't easily stick out their tongues and open their mouths at the same time.

Oostenbroek and colleagues (2016) assessed the response-specificity of infants' capacity for imitation by comparing tongue-protrusion with ten other comparison behaviours including mouth-opening. There was no evidence of differential imitation for any of these behaviours at any of the four sampled age-points. At one week and nine weeks, tongue-protrusion was more frequent following modelled tongue-protrusion than following modelled mouth-opening. However at both of these age-points, tongue-protrusion was equally frequent following each of the other modelled behaviours apart from mouth-opening, suggesting that the differential effect in comparison to mouth-opening was not the result of imitation processes. At the other two time-points, tongue-protrusion was no more frequent following modelled tongue-protrusion than following any of the other modelled behaviours including mouth-opening. This suggests that the earlier positive evidence for differential imitation of tongue protrusion may have depended on a specific selective comparison between modelling of tongue-protrusion and mouth-opening. At any rate, it does not seem to be the specific configuration of the modelled behaviour that prompted the tongue-protrusion response.

Despite this failure to replicate imitation of tongue-protrusion, controversies persist. Some researchers continue to argue that there is something special about tongue-protrusion that makes it more susceptible to imitation. Others maintain that any differences in behavioural frequency reflect factors such as response competition and effects of arousal rather than any innate imitative tendency. However, even if such a tendency exists, it only seems to work for specific behaviours such as tongue-protrusion, which often happens for other reasons in any case. Babies clearly do not automatically and immediately copy whatever someone else's face does. Any hardwired imitative capacity seems at best highly selective. None of the evidence suggests that humans are biologically equipped with any all-purpose mechanism that facilitates contagion or empathy.

Although it seems unlikely that humans are born with automatic tendencies to respond to facial stimuli with matching facial movements, this does not negate the conclusion that infants quickly come to use imitation communicatively to engage with their parents and other adults and children (Reddy, 2008). Supporting this communicative orientation of early mimicry, De Klerk, Hamilton and Southgate (2018) showed that four-month-old infants only mimicked movements by videotaped models when the model directed their gaze towards the camera rather than away from it. In other words, young infants are already sensitive to signals that indicate that another person's orientation is being shown to them. In unconstrained caregiver-infant interactions, the infant's responses and self-generated movements are specifically encouraged or discouraged by caregivers' responses which are attuned to synchrony and interdependence, and which may be exaggerated for the purpose of soliciting appropriate responses (e.g., Gergely & Watson, 1996). Mothers and fathers try to make and maintain contact with babies who are also trying to make contact with them (see Chapter 9). Mimicry of certain kinds emerges relatively early in development as part of these interlocking relations. But it may be highly person- and context-sensitive. And it may get replaced by more sophisticated forms of communion and communication over time.

In conclusion, although infants selectively imitate adult movements from a relatively early age, this capacity seems to emerge as a developmental outcome from the relational system operating between infant and caregiver rather than from any innate executive capacity within the infant's individual mind. Further, the primary function of infant imitation is to communicate and regulate interpersonal contact not to generate internal signals indicating the other person's emotional state. Imitative capacity thus develops as a side effect of engaging with others rather than being the thing that facilitates engagement in the first place.

Adult Mimicry

When and what do people mimic in later life? Studies of adult mimicry often focus on movements that carry no intrinsic meaning in order to avoid the complicating influence of factors such as emotion expression or intentional communication. For example, tongue-protrusion has obvious unwanted connotations in interactions between adults in many human societies that make it an unsuitable topic for imitation research. Chartrand and Bargh's (1999) influential studies instead focused on the mimicry of face-rubbing and foot-shaking. Each of these behaviours was performed continuously by one of two different experimental confederates while they engaged in one-on-one interactions with individual participants during a task that involved taking turns to describe photographs. As predicted, foot-shaking was relatively more common while the participant interacted with the foot-shaking confederate and face-rubbing was relatively more common while the participant interacted with the face-rubbing confederate. In other words, seeing someone else performing each behaviour made participants more likely to perform it too. When interviewed afterwards, participants seemed unaware that the confederate was engaging in either of the modelled behaviours, suggesting that any interpersonal influence was automatic and unconscious.

Chartrand and Bargh explained this finding in terms of a 'chameleon effect' which predisposed participants to blend in with their social environment. More specifically, they argued that the stimuli presented by the confederate's modelled behaviour directly activated participants' impulses to enact matching behaviours themselves. However, one issue with this supposedly automatic perception–behaviour link concerns its apparent selectivity. If people uncontrollably copied everything they saw anyone else doing, everyone would quickly end up acting in an identical manner to everyone else. So how does the mental system decide when and what to mimic?

In Chartrand and Bargh's first study, the confederate's continuous face-rubbing only increased participants' own frequency of face-rubbing from just under once every two minutes to just over. The face-rubbing model led them to rub their face roughly one more time over the whole ten-minute interaction, on average. In other words, face-rubbing was mostly spontaneous rather than copied. Participants were clearly not mimicking all the time, so what prompted them to mimic on the rare occasions that they did it?

One obvious answer is that mimicry depends on registering the modelled behaviour. Perceivers clearly need to detect another person's movement at some level before they can copy it. In an interpersonal interaction, gaze gets directed and redirected to different stimuli and events at different times. Indeed, participants performing the photograph-describing task used in Chartrand and Bargh's study were sometimes looking at the pictures rather than the other person in the room. The confederate's face and foot were probably outside participants' field of vision for much of the time. If the behavioural stimulus was not available to their perceptual apparatus during these periods, then they had no opportunity to copy it.

But people don't copy all of the movements that they can see either. One important factor that may selectively encourage mimicry is the motivation to affiliate. Perhaps we copy what someone else is doing when we want them to like us. Our apparent responsiveness and willingness to do similar things may increase their feelings of closeness (Chartrand & Bargh, 1999). Lakin, Chartrand and Arkin (2008) tested this idea by assessing mimicry following an experience of social exclusion. Participants in their study played a simulated game of 'catch' (cyberball) in which each player is represented by an animated character (avatar) appearing on the computer screen. During the game, the three other supposed players threw the ball to each other but not to the participant's own avatar, inducing an unpleasant reaction similar to that experienced in more realistic exclusion situations (e.g., Williams, 2009).

In Lakin and colleagues' first study, cyberball exclusion increased participants' subsequent mimicry of a female confederate who moved her foot while they conversed. The results of a second study suggested that this mimicry was selective. Female participants who had been excluded by female cyberball players mimicked the female confederate more whereas female participants who had been excluded by male cyberball players failed to show the same effect. Lakin and colleagues concluded that participants were specifically motivated to repair their sense of belonging to the group that had previously excluded them. Another possibility is that the original exclusion situation produced stronger affiliative needs when the other players were in-group members (see Chapter 7). In other words, it may be easier to deal with exclusion by other people who belong to a different social category (e.g., males rather than other females).

Precisely why do affiliative motives increase mimicry? One possibility is that the effect again depends on increased interpersonal attention. For example, participants in Lakin and colleagues' study may have spent longer looking in the direction of the female confederate because they wanted to check for responses to their friendly overtures, or more generally saw her as a target for affiliative attempts. In this case, affiliation does not directly motivate mimicry, but rather creates one of the conditions for its occurrence.

However, a study by Leighton and colleagues (2010) specifically ruled out this alternative explanation by using a task that required continuous attention to the model across all affiliation conditions. Participants were asked either to open or close their hands as quickly as possible after being shown a photographic prompt that showed another person performing either the same movement or the opposite one. Thus, 'compatible' trials asked participants to close their hands when they were presented with a closed-hand prompt and open them when presented with an open-hand prompt. Correspondingly, 'incompatible' trials asked participants to close their hands when presented with an open-hand prompt and open them when presented with a closed-hand prompt. Readiness to mimic was then assessed by comparing reaction times to these compatible and incompatible trials. Relatively faster responses to compatible trials indicates greater mimicry.

Prior to performing the mimicry task, participants in the affiliation condition were asked to unscramble sentences including words relating to affiliation or cooperation. Participants in the control condition instead worked on words unrelated to affiliation. Affiliation-primed participants subsequently responded relatively faster on compatible trials suggesting that they had stronger mimicry tendencies. In other words, it seems that at least some mimicry effects are strengthened when affiliative thoughts are activated even when attention to the target remains constant. Perhaps then, mimicry is part of an attempt to make positive contact with someone else, and to get in sync with them in order to smooth the course of the interaction (e.g., Bernieri et al., 1988; McGrath & Kelly, 1986).

Further support for the interpersonal orientation of mimicry comes from research investigating the precise form in which perceived behaviours get copied during face-to-face conversations. If people automatically did exactly what another person was doing, then one person's movement to the right would be matched by the other person also moving to the right. But when two people are facing each other, that would mean that they moved further apart rather than staying together. If the point is to show the other person that you are oriented to them, then it would be better to mirror their movements by moving to the left. Bavelas, Black, Chovil, Lemery and Mullett (1988) found that mirroring rather than directly mimicking is what people mostly do in face-to-face situations. In other words, they present a bodily stance that the other person can perceive as matching their own stance rather than simply making an identical movement.

Emotional Mimicry

None of the studies considered so far have measured mimicry of movements that might produce emotionally meaningful internal feedback in a primitive emotion-contagion process. What happens then when targets are presented with so-called basic emotion expressions rather than arbitrary body movements? One possibility is that their communicative significance makes them stronger elicitors of matching responses, producing higher rates of mimicry than found in studies of the chameleon effect. Just as we automatically seem to catch other people's yawns (e.g., Provine, 1989), we may also be particularly prone to smile and frown contagion.

However, it is also true that any apparent emotional mimicry is susceptible to a wider range of alternative explanations than mimicry of otherwise arbitrary movements. Identifying genuine cases becomes more problematic when movements already serve social or communicative functions. As argued earlier, if there are other reasons for making a movement, then it is harder to establish that it is prompted directly by another person's corresponding movement. For example, if I smile back at you, this may well be a polite or spontaneous acknowledgement of your greeting rather than a mimicked response. If I pull a scowling 'angry' face in response to your 'anger' expression, I might simply be showing that I am angry about you getting angry with me. Your emotion-related behaviour is meaningful to me, and mine conveys meaning back to you. Thus, I may be responding to the perceived meaning of your behaviour in an emotionally meaningful way rather than simply matching your movements. Despite these interpretational challenges, a number of researchers have specifically assessed mimicry of emotion-related facial expressions in both infants and adults.

Field and colleagues (1982) used live models to present three different 'basic emotion expressions' associated with happiness, sadness and surprise to babies who were less than two days old. Observers positioned behind the models tried to work out which expression was being modelled simply on the basis of the infants' reactions (without being able to see the model's face). They were correct in over three quarters of trials for 'surprise' expressions and over half of trials for the other two presented expressions. Further, the babies' faces were relatively more likely to show certain key facial movements corresponding to each modelled expression during its presentation.

Does this demonstrate an early case of direct emotional mimicry? Possibly. However, it is also conceivable that babies' orientations to the adult model changed in response to what the adult seemed to be doing, bringing about approximately matching facial responses as a result of processes other than imitation. For example, let's assume minimally that babies are predisposed to perceive smiles as invitations to interact (e.g., Fridlund, 1994) or more generally as pleasant stimuli (e.g., Russell, 1997). Apparently mimicked smiles may then reflect either increased affiliation towards the model or increased pleasure in response to a pleasant stimulus. It is also possible that the more pronounced facial distortion in the so-called surprise expression directly affected babies' informational intake causing them to make a wide-eyed response. Or it may simply have been a more arousing stimulus configuration (e.g., Jones, 1996).

Similar interpretational issues apply to the supposed contagious qualities of infant crying. Although one baby's crying often does make other nearby babies cry too (e.g., Simner, 1971), whether this is based on direct mimicry is less clear. Alternative explanations for the matched behaviour are also possible in this case. First, infant crying is pitched and modulated in such a way that it creates a distressing stimulus that may directly elicit crying from other infants (Thompson, 1987). Second, crying serves as a request for adult attention, so other babies may join in to compete with each other for this desired resource (Holodynski & Friedlmeier, 2006). Neither of these processes involves a direct tendency to copy someone else's emotional expression.

Do adults automatically mimic facial expressions? Their movements certainly often match those of other adults in some respects. And as with mimicry of bodily movements, evidence suggests that the social context plays an important moderating role. For example, effects tend to be stronger and more consistent when the source is an in-group member (Bourgeois & Hess, 2008; and see Chapter 7), or when the target's goal is to communicate togetherness. Bavelas, Black, Lemery and Mullett (1986) showed that participants timed their mimicked winces of pain so that the person to whom they were communicating an empathic orientation would see them (see Chapter 3). In other words, their matching facial displays seemed to be intended to establish connections with other people rather than being automatic responses.

Hess and Fischer (2013) specifically distinguished emotional mimicry on the basis that the mimicked movements carry meaningful information relating to the source's appraisals of what is happening. Like Bavelas and colleagues, they argue that emotional mimicry serves to communicate solidarity. This implies that the phenomenon depends on the relative degree of alignment between the source's and target's perspectives. Only when their orientations are close enough to calibrate will their expressions converge. And because the aim is to communicate meaning rather than simply match a physical movement, the target's response need not involve an identical configuration to the source's original expression. Anything that sends back a congruent emotional message serves the same function.

Evidence suggesting that emotional mimicry is based on meaning rather than direct copying comes from a number of sources. Halberstadt, Winkielmann, Niedenthal and Dalle (2009) showed participants a series of morphed faces that mixed together smiling and scowling configurations in equal proportions, thereby producing an ambiguous expression. During phase 1 of the study, these blended expressions were presented in association with either the word 'happy' or the word 'angry' to encourage either of these particular emotional interpretations. In phase 2, the same facial stimuli were presented in the absence of any disambiguating emotion word. Measurement of facial muscle activity revealed that there was significantly greater tension in the brow-lowering muscle (corrugator) during exposure to faces that had been associated with the 'angry' label at phase 1. Thus, participants showed a key component of a scowling configuration in reaction to a stimulus face that they perceived as angry, even when its configural features also indicated smiling. This suggests that mimicry depended on participants' interpretations of the face's emotional meaning rather than its actual physical properties.

A similar meaning-driven effect was found by Tamietto and colleagues (2009). These investigators presented two clinical patients with pretested pictures of bodily postures intended to convey either happiness or fear. Happy body postures induced greater activity in participants' zygomatic cheek-raising muscle and lower activity in participants' corrugator brow-lowering muscle than fearful body postures. As in Halberstadt and colleagues' study, participants seemed to be matching an implied emotion rather than the presented stimuli themselves.

Tamietto and colleagues' findings help to rule out some possible alternative interpretations because their two participants suffered from a neurological condition that prevented them from consciously registering the stimuli that were presented (blindsight). People with this disorder are able to respond to visual stimuli that they are unaware of having seen (e.g., by pointing in their direction). In the study, participants still showed facial muscle movements corresponding to emotional meaning of the bodily stimuli even when the pictures were presented in locations affected by blindsight symptoms. In other words, the meaning-matching process evidently did not depend on explicit inferences about what the body movements might mean because participants did not consciously register the movements in the first place.

These and other cases of so-called emotional mimicry (Hess & Fischer, 2013) are still susceptible to alternative explanations. For example, tension in the corrugator muscle need not reflect mimicked fear or anger or even general emotional unpleasantness. Instead it may reflect the effortful perception of a stimulus with uncertain meaning or one that the perceiver is not sure that they have detected. Tension in the zygomatic muscle may be part of an interpersonal acknowledgement or a communication of reciprocated happiness. Either of these muscles may be pulled, either deliberately or spontaneously, for reasons other than mimicry.

Leaving aside questions about underlying processes, available findings generally suggest that adults sometimes produce facial movements corresponding to the emotional meaning of another person's movements. However, this kind of 'emotional mimicry' (Hess & Fischer, 2013) bears little resemblance to the automatic mimicry originally postulated by Lipps (1907). Instead of assisting interpretation of another person's expressions, it seems to depend on interpreting the expression's meaning in the first place. And instead of coordinating the source and target's perspectives, it works better when their perspectives are already coordinated (e.g., Bavelas et al., 1986; Bourgeois & Hess, 2008).

Could this kind of process provide a first step towards emotion contagion as implied by Hatfield and colleagues or empathy as originally implied by Lipps? According to Hess and Fischer's (2013) analysis, the priority of emotional meaning and motives to maintain or establish contact means that any emotional influence process is well underway before mimicry takes place, leaving less additional work for mimicry to do. If targets have already registered the meaning of the source's presented expression before mimicking it, why would they need mimicry to interpret its emotional meaning? And any subsequent emotion contagion would already factor in the perceived significance of the expression too.

However, the causal priority of perceived emotional meaning may depend on the meaningfulness of the stimuli that are presented. The interpersonal process may operate differently when the source's movements do not conform to any clearly recognisable emotional pattern. For example, Niedenthal and colleagues (2017) argue that facial simulation of subtle or ambiguous expressions assists in the decoding process, thus preceding the perception of emotional meaning. In this case, the target's mimicry movements may contribute to their perception of emotion rather than depend on it, much in the same way that Lipps originally implied. Thus, mimicry may still play some small role in certain kinds of empathy or contagion.

Facial Feedback

Even if mimicry is not direct or consistent enough to fully explain the kind of automatic contagion involved in Hatfield and colleagues' (1994) primitive emotion-contagion process, it is still possible that some forms of mimicked response provide the kinds of interoceptive feedback that could potentially contribute to matching emotions. In this section, we therefore turn to evidence for this second stage of contagion.

Processes

As we saw in Chapter 1, generalised autonomic arousal is not capable of generating the distinctive qualities of contrasting emotional experiences. But what about feedback from facial movements? In principle, it seems conceivable that patterned expressive movements might produce sufficiently differentiated internal signals to specify discrete emotions.

Hatfield and colleagues (1994) distinguished three possible mechanisms that may underlie facial feedback effects. First, the neural signals that initially activate facial muscular movements may also generate corresponding feelings. Thus, the brain tells both body and mind to produce parallel responses that match the other person's emotion. In this case, mimicry seems to be a mere side effect of the contagion process rather than an explanation for it. If the brain already knows what emotional responses to output, what else can facial feedback add to the process?

Hatfield and colleagues' second proposed mechanism is based on inference. The idea is that people may work out the nature of their emotional state on the basis of the information provided by their own facial expression (e.g., 'I'm smiling, therefore I must be happy': Laird, 1974). The main issue facing such an account is how it produces an emotion rather than simply a conclusion about emotion (e.g., Frijda, 1986; Parkinson, 1995). Inferring that you are feeling something is not the same as actually feeling it. Of course, thinking you are feeling something may then lead you to interpret things in ways that actually end up making you emotional. You may for example, test the conclusion that you are happy by doing things that you do when you are happy, and these things in turn may make you happier. However, that indirect process does not provide a viable explanation for immediate and direct contagion effects. In any case, the inferential basis of the process already stops it counting as contagion according to the formulation presented earlier.

The third kind of feedback effect is more direct and depends only on registering the pattern of bodily change as an emotional experience. According to James (1898) and Laird and Bresler (1992), emotional experience simply *is* the perception that your body is reacting in a certain way: nothing further needs adding. If true, this might provide a viable mechanism for the second part of the primitive emotion-contagion process.

Evidence

Does the available evidence support a facial feedback effect that might account for the specific quality of experienced emotion? This question breaks down into two issues (see also McIntosh, 1996). First, do facial movements contain information that is sufficiently emotion-specific to produce discrete emotional experiences? Second, do discrete emotional experiences actually depend on making these movements?

Chapter 2 discussed the first of these issues. A key conclusion was that faces can have different meanings depending on social and cultural context. Although participants from Western societies consistently attribute specific emotional meanings to a small number of facial poses, this does not seem to reflect direct innate connections between basic emotions and distinctive expressions. Further, people often show different expressions or no expression at all when experiencing any single emotion. These facts make it implausible that humans use internally registered information from their own faces to determine what emotion they are experiencing, or that the principal mechanism for producing emotional experience is facial feedback. If faces don't contain fully diagnostic information in the first place, what guarantees that they produce the right emotions?

Perhaps, however, faces can produce emotion-specific information under those particular circumstances when they happen to match some internally specified representation. In this case, it's still worth asking the second question: do faces actually produce the feedback effects implied by the primitive emotional contagion model?

Studies of facial feedback date back to the 1950s. Pasquarelli and Bull (1951) used hypnosis to 'lock' participants' bodies and faces into configurations thought to be characteristic of different emotions. While still under hypnosis, participants were then asked to generate emotions that did not correspond to these adopted postures. Participants who were able to maintain their posture following this second instruction reported being unable to experience the requested emotion. Participants who were able to experience the requested emotion reported being unable to keep their bodies in the originally instructed positions. The researchers concluded that emotions are directly embodied in physically instantiated forms of attitude including facial expression and that stopping the attitude also stops the emotion. In other words, only the appropriate posture seemed compatible with the experience of the associated emotion.

Pasquarelli and Bull's (1951) use of hypnotic suggestion may have made participants especially responsive to experimenters' subtle communications. Participants may have recognised the intended emotional implications of their postures and got the message that the corresponding emotion was not supposed to be consistent with it. Even if the effects were genuine, they show at best that internal feedback can block emotion and not that it can produce it.

Laird (1974) was the first researcher to test the facial feedback hypothesis directly. He informed participants that their muscle activity would be recorded using facial electrodes. While attaching the electrodes, the experimenter touched muscles on the participant's face individually and told the participant to relax or tighten them one by one. This process continued until the face was configured surreptitiously into either a smile or frown. Participants were then presented with slides depicting Ku Klux Klan members (negative condition) and children playing (positive condition). After each slide, participants rated how elated they felt, supposedly so that the experimenter could check for any extraneous emotional influence on facial muscle activity.

Reported elation was significantly higher in the smiling condition, suggesting that the adopted facial expression tended to produce a corresponding emotion. However, this supposed feedback effect accounted for much less variance in elation ratings than the presented slides, which were not rated as strong emotional stimuli in any case. In other words, the facial position did not generate a full-blown emotional experience but instead slightly changed its degree of pleasantness.

Laird took great care to disguise the nature of the manipulated expression to avert the possibility that participants recognised explicitly that they were smiling or frowning. If they had realised that the experimenter was trying to create a specific emotional expression, then this would have given them strong clues about the study's hypothesis (like in Pasquarelli & Bull's study). Knowing the hypothesis often leads participants to adjust their behaviour in ways that support it (responding to the experiment's 'demand characteristics', Orne, 1962). So the danger in Laird's study was that participants would second-guess what the experimenter was trying to do and respond accordingly. For example, they may have thought to themselves: 'The experimenter is trying to make me smile, and asking me how happy I feel. Perhaps the point is to see if smiling makes me experience happy emotions. Maybe I should report more happiness'. Despite his attempts to conceal the hypothesis, Laird had to exclude seven of his forty-five participants who mentioned in post-experimental interviews that they had noticed they were smiling or guessed that there might be a connection between the facial manipulation and the rating procedure.

One of these excluded participants explained how his emotions were affected by the facial manipulation as follows:

> When my jaw was clenched and my brows down I tried not to be angry but it just fit the position.. . . I found my thoughts wandering to things that made me angry which is sort of silly I guess. I knew I was in an experiment and knew I had no reason to feel that way, but I just lost control. (Laird, 1974, p. 480)

Laird argued that a similar but less explicit process also applied to those participants who were apparently unaware of the hypothesis. In his view, they perceived themselves as experiencing emotion on the basis of information registered unconsciously from their faces. However, even setting aside demand characteristics, a range of other factors may have contributed to the small effect reported in this study. For example, it may just have been more comfortable for participants to hold their face in a smiling position during the procedure. The evidence only showed an effect on how positive participants felt, and not on the specific quality of emotional experience, so one or both of the facial positions may simply have made participants feel a little better or a little worse.

Tourangeau and Ellsworth (1979) tested whether two emotions that are both negative (fear and sadness) could be induced using facial manipulation. Participants' faces were subtly manipulated to produce either a gasping, wide-eyed 'fear' configuration or a pouting 'sad' configuration (ostensibly to improve electrode placement as in Laird's earlier study). Having adopted the appropriate facial position, participants watched films showing frightening, sad or neutral scenes.

Watching the contrasting films made predictable differences to participants' reported emotional experience, but the manipulated expressions made no difference at all. In other words, holding a sad face did not make participants sadder about the sad movie or any other movie, and holding a fear face did not make participants more fearful either. In fact, the only reported significant effect was that autonomic activity was lower in a control condition where faces were free to move than in any of the conditions where participants had to hold their face in a fixed position. In other words, the effort involved in controlling facial movement apparently increased arousal levels.

Tourangeau and Ellsworth's study was vociferously criticised by supporters of the facial feedback hypothesis. Notably, Tomkins (1981) argued that the problem with their facial manipulation was that participants had to hold a static expression while the films were shown, meaning that internally perceived signals did not correspond to changes in the emotional content of what participants were viewing. For example, the fear film showed graphic portrayals of industrial accidents including one in which a worker sliced off his fingers in a circular saw. However, participants in the fear expression condition maintained the same gasping face throughout this episode with no change at the key moment of inadvertent amputation or elsewhere. This meant that any facial feedback could not easily be perceived as part of an emotional reaction to the unfolding chain of events. More generally, Tomkins proposed that facial expressions have distinctive dynamic patterns involving their speed of onset and offset (see Chapter 3). Unless facial feedback accurately simulates these temporal dynamics, it cannot produce emotion.

The problem with Tomkins' reformulation of the facial feedback hypothesis is that it is very difficult to test (see Ellsworth & Tourangeau, 1981). If the only way of getting feedback effects is to provide realistic expressions that move in the right way and at the right speed, then there are severe challenges in inducing them experimentally. Obviously, the only way of achieving wholly authentic facial responses is to present genuinely involving emotional stimuli, but then how can we tell whether facial feedback has any separate effect on what people are feeling? If the face is reacting to something emotionally provocative then that something is already driving any emotional reaction.

Nevertheless, Ellsworth and Tourangeau (1981) point out that their data did provide some evidence that resists Tomkins' alternative interpretation. If emotional effects depend on genuine facial expressions, then participants in the control condition whose faces were free to move throughout the procedure should have shown stronger reactions to the films than those in any of the manipulated face conditions. They did not. Unlike in Pasquarelli and Bull's (1951) earlier hypnosis-based study, adopting a conflicting facial position failed to prevent the occurrence of the expected emotional response.

Nevertheless, other issues of interpretation arise from the direct facial manipulations used by Tourangeau and Ellsworth (and Laird before them). Touching participants' faces, telling them to move muscles, and attaching surface electrodes may make them unusually sensitive to what their faces are doing (cf. Leventhal & Mace, 1970), and risks revealing the experimenter's intentions. Many participants probably considered the possibility that they had been made to smile, grimace or frown, and this may have affected how they rated their emotions (even when they did not mention this in post-experimental interviews). One of the most famous tests of the facial feedback hypothesis used a clever experimental procedure that effectively prevented people from realising that specific facial positions were being manipulated at all.

Strack, Martin and Stepper (1988) told participants that their study was about the ability to perform physical tasks without using the parts of the body typically used for these tasks, as injured or disabled people often manage to do. One of the experimental tasks involved writing down ratings of humorous slides with the pen held in the mouth. Crucially, some participants were asked to use their teeth to grip the pen, while others had to use their lips. Using teeth encourages the face to adopt a configuration that resembles a smile, whereas using lips prevents smiling (see Figure 4.2). However, it is unlikely that participants were aware of these expressive consequences while trying to perform the demanding experimental tasks. In study 1, participants using their teeth to hold the pen rated the slides as slightly funnier than participants who used their lips. In study 2, participants using their teeth rated themselves as slightly more amused, but did not rate the slides as funnier. The amusement effect in study 2 was only significant when using an unusually non-conservative statistical criterion.

Strack and colleagues' findings suggest that either holding the pen between the teeth increased positive feelings or holding the pen between the lips decreased positive feelings (or both). However, the inconsistency in results across studies and the small effect size should have raised more concerns about reliability of the findings than it did at the time. Subsequent studies using comparable conditions have failed to produce identical results (e.g., Andreasson & Dimberg, 2008; Soussignan, 2002). Further a systematic attempt to replicate the original study in seventeen different laboratories produced consistently non-significant results

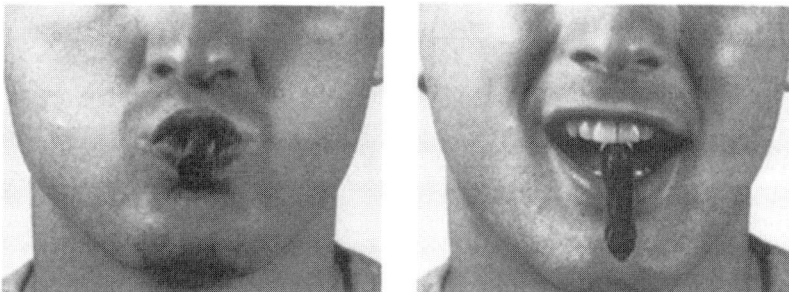

Figure 4.2 Strack, Martin and Stepper's (1988) pen-holding manipulation of facial position

(Wagenmakers et al., 2016). In short, what once seemed the most convincing evidence for facial feedback effects now seems rather less conclusive.

However, constraining facial movements using the pen-holding procedure or other methods may still affect the way that people respond to other facial stimuli. Ito and colleagues (2006) showed that pen-holding affected implicitly but not explicitly expressed attitudes. Research by Niedenthal and colleagues (2017, reviewed in Chapter 2) suggests that wearing a rugby mouth shield may sometimes undermine emotion detection from facial expressions. Perhaps then it is more difficult to relate to other faces' perspectives when facial movements are constrained in certain ways. However, this does not constitute a facial feedback effect in the usual sense.

The growing popularity of Botox injection as a cosmetic procedure in the 1990s provided another way of testing facial feedback effects. Botox smooths out wrinkles by paralyzing facial muscles, meaning that those taking this treatment get less facial feedback than those who do not. Does this also reduce their experience of emotion? A study by Finzi and Wasserman (2006) showed that nine out of ten patients suffering from clinical depression recovered within two months after their faces were injected with Botox. However, we cannot be sure how many participants would have recovered spontaneously without the administration of the injection since there was no control group.

Finzi and Rosenthal (2014) added a control condition where participants received a placebo injection. The Botox-injected group showed greater improvement in their depressive symptoms on all measures. However, it remains unclear whether this difference depended on facial feedback or on the cosmetic changes to appearance that followed Botox treatment. Perhaps participants got more positive interpersonal feedback or otherwise felt better about themselves now that their faces were less wrinkled. The assessing clinicians may also have been influenced by the visible symptoms of the intervention. In short, we cannot be sure whether any effect depended on the Botox-induced reduction in facial feedback rather than other direct or indirect consequences of receiving the injection.

Davis, Senghas, Brandt and Ochsner (2010) assessed Botox-injected and control participants' emotional responses more directly. Participants believed that they had volunteered for a study assessing effects of anaesthesia during medical treatments and that they were in the control condition. They were offered a free cosmetic treatment as a reward for taking part and opted either to receive Botox injections to their brows and eye corners, or injections of a cosmetic filler called Restylane to the folds below their nose.

Participants rated their emotional reactions to disgusting and humorous video clips both before the treatment and two weeks later after the

Botox had taken effect. There were no significant differences between before and after ratings for the Botox group. However, comparisons with the Restylane group revealed an effect on ratings of a series of mildly pleasant video clips that had originally been included as filler stimuli. Botox-injected participants gave these videos less positive ratings at the two-week follow-up.

Davis and colleagues' results provide at best limited support for the facial feedback hypothesis. They seem to indicate that weak positive reactions may be reduced by reducing facial feedback, but this interpretation should be treated with caution for at least four reasons. First, we again do not know whether the effect depended specifically on facial feedback or other consequences of Botox injection on participants' lives in the two weeks between the two testing sessions. Second, the comparison with the control group is problematic because participants were not randomly allocated to the two conditions. It may be that participants who specifically opted for Botox had particular characteristics that affected the change in their response. Third, the change in emotion ratings in the Botox group was very small (around half a scale point on a nine-point scale). Fourth, the difference between Botox and Restylane participants mainly related to ratings collected at the initial testing session before the injections had been administered. Botox participants rated mildly positive clips as slightly more positive than Restylane participants at this time point. By the time the Botox had taken effect two weeks later, the two groups' ratings were actually very similar. Thus, participants who hoped to receive Botox as their free treatment may have felt more excited prior to treatment, and their excitement may have affected their response to otherwise unexciting videos. Contrary to the facial feedback hypothesis, there was no effect on reactions to the more strongly emotional video clips.

It is difficult to draw firm conclusions from the diverse literature on facial feedback effects. This may reflect the fact that any significant differences may depend on a variety of different processes that may or may not include feedback. However, a few clear messages emerge. First, when there are significant effects of facial feedback manipulations, they are always small. Second, they mostly relate to the pleasantness of emotional experience rather than its specific quality. Facial feedback can at best leave participants feeling better or worse but rarely if ever, angry rather than afraid, or proud rather than relieved.

Finally, these small effects on positivity are all susceptible to explanations that do not depend on assuming that interoceptive feedback affects emotion. In the case of direct manipulations of facial position, participants are likely to become more aware of their faces and may conclude that the experimenter wants to test the effects of expression on emotion.

These studies therefore always carry the risk of demand characteristics. In the case of indirect manipulations, including Botox injections, any effect may in fact depend on the method used to change facial response rather than facial response itself. For example, Botox not only removes facial feedback but also induces specific appearance changes that may affect emotions in a number of ways. The only method that seems to avoid these problems involves a disguised but still direct manipulation. However, the weak effect found in the study that pioneered this method (Strack, Martin & Stepper, 1988) has not been replicated despite repeated attempts. In short, the jury may still be out, but it would be surprising if they ultimately ruled that the evidence was strong enough to justify the specific verdict defended by advocates of facial feedback theory.

The Mimicry-Feedback Process

I have argued that the two sequential mechanisms of the primitive emotional contagion model are incapable of explaining either strong or consistent emotional influence. Mimicry is not an instinctive and automatic process that guarantees facial matching under all circumstances, but instead relates to communicative goals that already imply an emotional orientation to the other person. Emotional mimicry depends on emotional meaning rather than producing it, leaving little further work for facial feedback to do in those cases when mimicry does occur. In any case, facial feedback does not produce specific information about emotional quality, and its potential effects on emotional valence, intensity and arousal are too small and unreliable to underlie anything but the mildest and least focused forms of emotional convergence.

A few studies have tested more directly whether emotion convergence actually depends on the processes implied by the primitive emotional contagion model. For example, Hess and Blairy (2001) measured participants' facial muscular activity and self-reported emotion while they decoded emotion from video-clips of facial reactions during an emotional imagery procedure. Participants' facial muscle activity at least partly matched the stimulus faces for three of the four sampled emotions (anger, sadness and happiness, but not disgust). Further, participants' emotional states tended to move closer to the source's emotion, suggesting a small degree of convergence. However, the mimicry effect did not mediate this convergence for any of the measured emotions. Indeed, muscle movements that do not feature in scowling 'anger' faces positively predicted the extent of self-reported anger, whereas muscle movements involved in scowling showed no significant association with self-reported anger. Other studies too have failed to find evidence for mimicry as a mediator of apparently contagious effects (e.g., Blairy, Herrera & Hess, 1999; Gump & Kulik, 1997).

In short, the primitive emotional contagion process running from mimicry through feedback to matching emotion is too weak, disjointed, and unreliable to do the job it was intended to do. It seems highly unlikely that any meaningful emotional convergence results from copying someone's facial expression and then internally registering its emotional implications. So where does this leave the phenomenon of emotional contagion more generally? Is it still possible that a source's emotion produces convergent effects on a target's emotion without factoring in object-directedness and without presenting an emotional stimulus in its own right? The next section considers this possibility.

Entrainment and Synchrony

Alongside mimicry, Hatfield and colleagues (1994) also discussed behavioural synchronisation as a possible source of the internal feedback signals that feature in the primitive emotion-contagion process. Synchronisation sometimes involves the direct copying of another person's movements implied by mimicry, but not always. Its defining characteristic is that the temporal patterns of two or more individuals' movements become aligned with each other. In its simplest form, this may reflect a kind of automatic entrainment analogous to what happens when two adjacent swinging pendulums tend to come into phase with each other, or a person's body clock gradually gets into tune with a different time zone as they register the ecological or cultural zeitgebers manifested in different patterns of light and dark, imposed meal times or the more general activity patterns of people around them. The endogenous rhythms of unfolding behaviours may also adjust to those of other people on tighter time-scales producing coordination over the course of microseconds rather than days or months (e.g., Henrique, 2010; McGrath & Kelly, 1986).

The temporal patterning of infant behaviour partly depends on this kind of developing entrainment process. From an early age, babies are attentive to the dynamic contingencies between their actions and other people's responses to them (e.g., Gergely & Watson, 1996; Murray & Trevarthen, 1985; Tronick, 1989). They are well equipped to coordinate their activities with those of interaction partners, and may even actively impose their own rhythms and changing tempos on their caregivers, directing and orchestrating the dynamic organisation of their interactions (e.g., Kokkinaki et al., 2017; Trevarthen, 1993).

Caregivers also play an active role in the process of temporal coordination (e.g., Beebe et al., 1982). For example, they may explicitly draw an infant's attention to the temporal contours of jointly experienced emotional events using patterned vocal intonation and facial movement (Stern et al., 1985). For example, when a toddler struggles to get a geometrically shaped object through an appropriately shaped hole in a frame, the pitch of the caregiver's voice may gradually increase until it reaches its peak with a sigh or 'Aaah!' sound when the shape finally slots through.

Around the same stage of development, children become increasingly fascinated with songs and rhythmic verses that are associated with patterned movements. Reciting 'This little piggy went to market' while holding each of the child's toes in succession also facilitates engagement with the clear contours of shared growing excitement and anticipation that achieve resolution with tickling and intensive eye contact (Stern, 1999). In these interactions, children learn to attend to the relation between their own emotions and those of others by calibrating them with clearly structured events in the shared environment (Holodynski & Friedlmeier, 2006).

Interactions between adults also often involve mutual entrainment of movements including emotion-related displays and expressions. When people achieve smooth coordination with their conversation partner, this often produces a feeling of rapport (e.g., Bernieri et al., 1994) that may be jointly sensed by both parties. The resulting perception of interpersonal closeness may help to create some of the conditions for socially attuned emotions including normative and group-based emotions (see Chapter 7).

So synchronisation processes are clearly relevant to the emotions experienced by both infants and adults. But does entrainment play a more specific role in emotional contagion? One possibility is that some dynamic profiles of behaviour are specifically associated with distinctive emotional responses (e.g., Keltner & Cordaro, 2017) so that interpersonal entrainment leads to their direct transmission. However, the context-dependence of object-directed emotional activity makes it unlikely that its temporal contours are consistent enough to provide diagnostic internal feedback about categorical emotional qualities. Instead, it may be that the tempo or smoothness of entrained reactions contribute to less specific aspects of emotional experience (e.g., Beebe et al., 1982). For example, it seems plausible that interacting with an anxious person leads to higher levels of arousal and alertness partly because we adjust ourselves to the vigilant jerky movements they present. Correspondingly, slow and evenly paced movements or speech pattern can have a calming or even soporific effect. In both cases, the key question is whether the temporally driven effects depend on behavioural synchronisation or instead reflect direct reactions to the patterning of the presented stimuli (see Bernardi, Bellemare-Pepin & Peretz, 2017).

Relation Alignment

Contagion effects are supposedly independent of the object orientation of the source's emotion and involve direct interpersonal transfer of affective content to the target. By contrast, the interpersonal effects considered in the following sections depend crucially on what the source's emotion is about, or on what the target perceives it to be about. Factoring in object-directedness expands the range of possible interpersonal effects because the source's emotion can direct the target's attention or shape their orientation to a wide range of social or non-social objects in the environment and the relations between them, including relations between the source and target themselves. The most obvious examples happen when both people are focused on the same object and their orientations to that object converge. But people approaching the same object from different angles may also arrive at divergent orientations, and a person's orientation to one object may affect another person's orientation to the first person's orientation or even to a different object entirely. In the following sections, we will start with the most straightforward cases of object-directed emotional influence before extending the discussion to more complex examples of interpersonal calibration and miscalibration.

Social Appraisal

Appraisal theory proposes that emotions depend on how an individual perceives, evaluates and interprets what is happening (e.g., Lazarus, 1991; and see Chapter 1). For example, when you detect something blocking your progress, you become angry and motivated to push against that thing. Campos and Stenberg (1981) distinguished between this kind of individual appraisal and the 'social appraisal of how another individual is reacting to the event' (p. 275). The social appraisal account of emotional influence subsequently developed by Manstead and Fischer (2001) suggests that other people's emotional reactions can guide your own perceptions, evaluations and interpretations (see also Parkinson, 1996).

Sorce and colleagues' (1985) social referencing study provides a good example of this process (see Chapter 1). Here, the mother's wide-eyed gasping 'fear' face discouraged the toddler from venturing out across the visual cliff. In other words, the toddler's behaviour towards an emotional object apparently factored in their caregiver's apparent orientation. At some level, the toddler seemed to work out that the cliff was dangerous on the basis of their mother's emotional reaction. Because the mother apparently appraised the cliff as threatening, the toddler started to see it as more threatening too. Social appraisal thus provides a theoretical account of how one person's emotion might influence someone else. This account applies specifically to contexts where both parties orient to a person, object or event in the shared environment. The outcome is often that their respective orientations towards that object become more closely aligned.

Precisely what happens during social appraisal? Is a single process involved? Or does social appraisal, like appraisal more generally (Leventhal & Scherer, 1987), involve a wide range of interchangeable or interacting processes? The model's key claim is that individuals appraise both events and other people's reactions to those events, and that both kinds of appraisal can contribute to experienced emotions. But how exactly do people appraise other people's reactions and how do the outcomes of that appraisal in turn affect emotion?

Part of the answer may be that other people's reactions provide additional information about what is happening that is processed alongside other non-social information to determine the emotional response. For example, the mother's fear face helps to clarify the relational meaning of an otherwise ambiguous situation for the toddler in the social referencing situation, pushing the toddler's own appraisal towards a threatening interpretation. However, this still leaves open the question of what information is extracted by the toddler from the mother's facial movement and how it then comes to change their appraisal of the visual cliff. Clearly, this could be achieved by a variety of mechanisms, including basic perceptual and associative processes, implicit or explicit categorisation, conceptual inference or deliberative reasoning. Like appraisal theory more generally, social appraisal theory often seems content to specify the explanatory construct at a functional rather than procedural level (e.g., Lazarus, 1991a; see also Leventhal & Scherer, 1987; Parkinson & Manstead, 1992; and Chapter 1). According to this inclusive formulation, social appraisal is whatever process mediates between social information and those emotional outcomes that relate to the perceived meaning of what is happening. Without additional specification, then, we have an account that identifies a type of influence without explaining why it happens.

The alternative is to set out what kinds of process social appraisal might involve in more detail. To count as appraisal, social appraisal clearly needs to involve extracting meaning from information of some kind. To count as social, this information must involve other people. Putting this together, social appraisal involves responding to information about other people's reactions rather than responding more directly to these reactions. So the first question is what kinds of information are driving the process. What is the active informational ingredient of the source's emotion that ultimately brings about its effects on the target's emotion? The most obvious answer is that it is emotional information, and specifically categorical information indicating that the person is experiencing a particular kind of emotion. If we take this as the starting point of the social appraisal process, how exactly might that process unfold?

Reverse Engineering

Hareli and Hess (2010) provide an answer with their 'reverse engineering' model (see also Elfenbein's, 2007 compatible account of 'backtracking'). According to this model, the target works backwards from the source's apparent emotion to make an inference about what appraisal must have caused it. For example, if I notice that you are angry, I use my knowledge about the usual causes of anger to conclude that you are directing blame externally (Weiner, Russell & Lerman, 1979; see Hareli, 2014). This carries implications about the object of your emotion, namely that something potentially blameworthy must have happened. After considering these implications, my interpretation of the situation may change, and my changed interpretation may lead to behavioural and emotional consequences.

Reverse engineering thus implies that the target uses information about the nature of the emotion that the source is experiencing to draw conclusions about the source's appraisal, which then lead to consequences for the target's own appraisal and emotion (see Figure 4.3). The emotion exerts its interpersonal effect by providing information that needs to be decoded and interpreted prior to any reaction. The process may run explicitly with each stage of reasoning conducted at a conscious level. Or it may have become automatic because of prior learned associations between emotions and appraisals. In either case, emotion categorisation and the application of emotion knowledge are necessary preconditions for subsequent inferences about appraisal.

A number of studies have demonstrated that reverse engineering provides a viable explanation of effects of information about a source's emotion on targets' judgements about objects and events. Van Doorn, van Kleef and van der Pligt (2015) assessed the effects of information about a source's emotion on interpretation of ambiguous situations. Participants imagined that their friend was either angry or regretful about a recently experienced

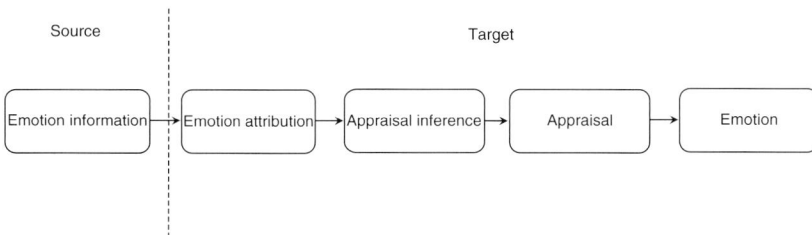

Source | Target

Emotion information → Emotion attribution → Appraisal inference → Appraisal → Emotion

Figure 4.3 The reverse-engineering process of social appraisal (based on Hareli & Hess, 2010)

event. For example, they read that their friend was becoming increasingly emotional when talking about their recent car accident. Anger information led participants to believe that someone else was responsible for what had happened while regret led them to believe that the outcome was their friend's own responsibility. In other words, participants based their conclusions on the appraisal implications of the described emotions in line with the reverse engineering account.

Hess and Hareli (2018; and see Chapter 3) assessed the effects of facially conveyed emotional information on appraisals of less ambiguous objects and situations. The investigators presented photographs of facial configurations associated with emotions alongside photographs of emotional scenes that normally induced disgust, pride, fear or happiness. For example, a smiling face was presented next to a picture of flies crawling over a cake (disgust) or a picture of hands holding a trophy (pride). Participants were told that the face showed the person's reaction to the simultaneously presented object or situation even though the usual emotional interpretations of the face and scene did not match. The key question concerns how the emotional information provided by faces affects appraisal of simultaneously presented objects with different standard emotional interpretations. Hess and Hareli found that participants adjusted their appraisals of the objects to bring them more into line with the emotional implications of the faces. In other words, a nose-scrunching 'disgust' face tended to reduce the appraised pleasantness of associated happy and proud scenes and a gasping 'fear' face tended to increase appraisals of their suddenness compared to other faces.

Although these studies show that reverse engineering can influence judgements and appraisals of objects, these are non-emotional rather than emotional effects. Do participants' emotional reactions to objects also change in response to interpersonally induced changes in appraisal? Fischer, Rotteveel, Evers and Manstead (2004) asked undergraduate participants to imagine that an instructor gave them a poor grade for a piece of work, and that other students had reacted either with anger or sadness to a similar outcome. Participants reported greater anger when told that other students were angry. However, there was no corresponding effect on appraisals of instructor-directed blame, making it unlikely that emotional convergence depended on reverse-engineered appraisals. Instead, other students' presented emotional reactions may have simply established an emotional norm that participants tended to follow (see Chapter 7). Perhaps, then, emotional effects of reverse-engineered appraisals only happen when targets are more directly engaged with the object of the source's emotion (as we shall discuss).

Implicit Social Appraisal

In Hess and Hareli's (2018) study, targets' appraisals of visually presented objects depended on simultaneously presented photographs of a source's facially expressed emotion when the experimenter told participants explicitly that the expression was caused by the object. Other studies have established connections between emotion information and simultaneous objects using less explicit methods.

Bayliss and colleagues (2007) presented participants with a series of pictures of thirty-six different household objects alongside animated nose-scrunching 'disgust' faces or smiling 'happy' faces. Participants' initial task was to classify the objects as either 'kitchen' items (e.g., saucepan, kettle) or 'garage' items (e.g., pliers, screwdriver). As the expression developed, the stimulus face's eyes turned either towards or away from the picture next to it, giving the impression that it was responding either to the depicted object or to something else offscreen.

Participants were asked to rate how much they liked each of the objects. It turned out that objects associated with 'disgust' expressions were liked significantly less than those associated with smiles, but only when the source's eyes were directed towards them rather than away. In other words, it seems that participants only factored in the emotional implications of the presented facial stimulus when it seemed to be specifically directed at the object. This process therefore seems to depend on some form of social appraisal. However, participants subsequently claimed that their ratings were based on their perceptions of how useful or how well designed the objects seemed to be rather than the associated expressions, suggesting that they were unaware of the faces' influence on their judgements. Indeed, the experimental instructions and the nature of the central task encouraged them to focus on the objects and ignore the faces. Bayliss and colleagues therefore concluded that social-appraisal effects may operate implicitly rather than as a consequence of explicit inference.

But do Bayliss and colleagues' findings necessarily depend on social appraisal at all? As in previous gaze-cuing studies, participants classified objects more quickly when the stimulus face's eyes directed their attention towards the place where they appeared on the screen. Perhaps then the initial increase in attention towards gaze-cued objects made association with the prior facial emotion cue stronger or more likely. Correspondingly, diverted stimulus eyes directed attention away from the objects and may have thereby reduced the chances of associative learning. If so, it may be that gaze-cuing coupled with evaluative conditioning (e.g., Hofmann et al., 2010) can explain the apparent social appraisal effects on judgements on the general pleasantness of stimuli. In that case, this would not be an example of implicit social appraisal but the co-occurrence of two processes that have already been shown to operate at an implicit level.

Mumenthaler and Sander (2012; 2015) extended Bayliss and colleagues' methodology by using a wider range of facial stimuli thus permitting comparisons along dimensions other than general pleasantness. The non-social household stimuli that were the objects of judgement in the earlier study were replaced by animated faces showing configurations that matched or differed from the other simultaneously presented faces (see Figure 4.4). Facially conveyed emotion information was intended to affect perception of the emotional content of these stimulus faces (rather than evaluations of non-facial objects as in Bayliss and colleagues' earlier study).

In Mumenthaler and Sander's 2012 study (also discussed in Chapter 3), a peripheral face showed a dynamic 'emotion expression' as its gaze turned towards or away from a centrally presented face. Perceptions of the central face's emotion were influenced relatively more by the peripheral face's expression when its gaze turned toward that central face (as in Bayliss and colleagues' earlier object-directed effect). For example, a peripheral 'angry' face turning its gaze toward a centrally presented 'fear' face increased perceptions of fear in the central face, probably because fear is a more likely reaction from someone at whom anger is

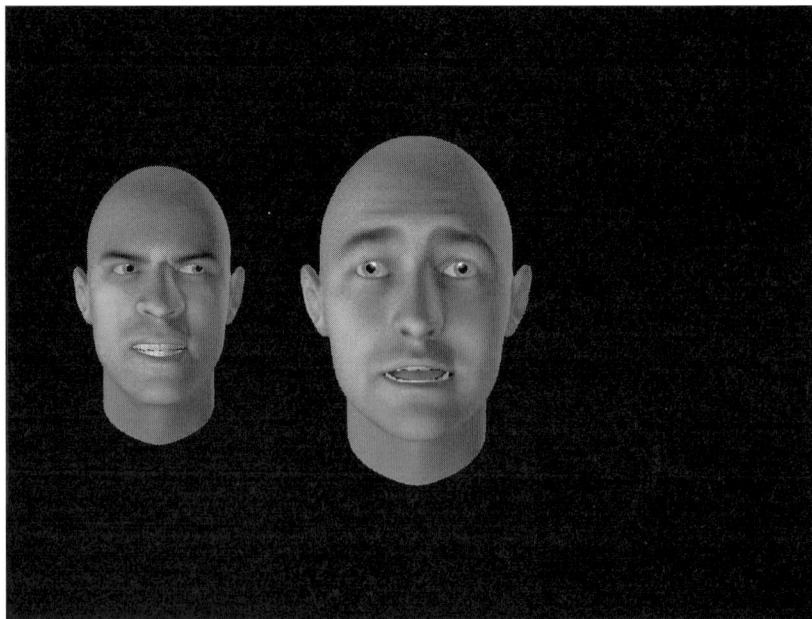

Figure 4.4 Facial judgement depends on gaze direction of peripheral face (Mumenthaler & Sander, 2012)

directed. Mumenthaler and Sander (2015) found comparable effects even when the peripheral anger face was presented subliminally and subsequently masked. As in Bayliss and colleagues' earlier study, the conclusion seems to be that some form of social appraisal can operate without any explicit inferential process.

However, other factors may again have contributed to the reported effects. For example, the peripheral faces may have attracted different levels of attention depending on the nature of the emotion they conveyed. Previous studies have shown that 'anger' faces 'pop out' from the crowd when presented against a background of non-angry faces in certain contexts (e.g., Hansen & Hansen, 1988). Similarly, the peripheral scowling face used in Mumenthaler and Sander's studies may have differed in its relative salience when the central face showed different emotions. Gaze direction is also more easily detectable when eyes are wider (e.g., Lee et al., 2013), potentially making its cuing effects relatively stronger in the peripheral fear condition. Gaze cues may in turn have affected perceptions of the emotion conveyed by peripheral faces. For example, scowling faces looking towards the central face may have seemed angrier than those looking in another direction (e.g., Adams & Kleck, 2003; 2005; and see Chapter 3), partly accounting for their stronger influence on emotion perception. Some or all of these lower-level effects may have interacted and combined to produce the reported findings, without the need for any integrated implicit social appraisal process. Future studies therefore need to disentangle the various possible contributory factors before definitive conclusions are possible.

Dyadic Contact and Interaction

Few social appraisal studies involve actual interactions between people. The source's emotion is usually presented in words, or as a still picture, video clip or animated simulation of facial activity. Further, the situation provoking the source's emotion is typically depicted in a photograph or vignette describing some imagined point in the past with no bearing on anything currently happening outside the laboratory. These methodological factors specifically encourage participants to adopt a detached perspective and to treat the source's emotion presentations as inferential information rather than engaging with them more directly. Do similar processes also operate in genuine interpersonal exchanges? Or do different forms of relation alignment then come into play?

Unlike social appraisal experiments, social referencing studies often involve more or less direct contact between source and target of emotional influence. They consistently show that toddlers' behaviour towards ambiguous objects is shaped by caregivers' emotion communication and its implications for appraisals of those objects. For example, toddlers respond to a mother's gasping 'fear' faces in ways that might reflect appraisals of greater levels of threat (Sorce et al., 1985). Although it seems unlikely that one-year-olds engage in explicit reverse engineering based on detected emotion information, some precursor of the inferential process may already be operating even at this early age.

Schachter's (1959) affiliation research suggests that adults, like toddlers, are motivated to seek out emotional information from others when confronting unfamiliar situations. In one of his studies, female undergraduate students who expected to receive painful electric shocks specifically preferred to wait with other participants who were about to perform the same task rather than with those allocated to a different non-painful one. A key motivation seemed to be social comparison with someone facing a similar fate. Participants apparently wanted to calibrate their emotional appraisals of what was about to happen with other participants' appraisals in order to prepare themselves for the experience. This raises the question of how the interpersonal calibration process subsequently unfolds.

A famous study by Latané and Darley (1968) showed how this kind of social comparison can affect people's orientations to an ambiguous emotional object in accordance with social referencing principles. The researchers' particular interest was in how quickly people intervene in an apparent emergency situation, and whether this depends on the presence of other people. While participants filled out preliminary questionnaires, simulated smoke began to enter the waiting room through an air vent, suggesting that there was a fire somewhere in the building. Seventy-five per cent of participants who were alone in the room went to report this incident within three and a half minutes. By contrast, only 38 per cent of groups of three participants waiting together included anyone who left the room within the full six-minute observation period.

Latané and Darley (1968) explained this effect in terms of pluralistic ignorance. They argued that participants were reluctant to show any sign of panic in front of strangers and therefore adopted an initially calm composure when the smoke first appeared. The inadvertent consequence of concealing anxiety was to convey to each other that the situation was actually not that worrying after all. In other words, participants' apparent unconcern signalled an unrealistically unthreatening appraisal of what was happening. In support of this account, participants were even less likely to report the incident when waiting with two confederates posing as participants who paid little attention to the fake smoke and affected a nonchalant demeanour as the room filled with fumes.

To what extent did Latané and Darley's findings depend on reverse-engineered appraisals? Although participants were clearly affected by other people's emotional expressions, it is not clear whether this resulted from their inferences about the proper interpretation of the situation. Latané and Darley themselves alluded to comparable processes that might operate during 'contagion of panic' (1968, p. 217) suggesting more direct forms of emotional influence. Alternatively, unresponsive targets may simply have been more inhibited when confederates or other participants seemed unflappable. They may not have wanted to be seen as making a fuss, or they may simply have been trying to conform to the norm established by the apparent unconcern of those around them (see Chapter 7). Without direct measures of appraisal-relevant variables, no firm conclusions are possible.

Parkinson, Phiri and Simons (2012) adapted the social referencing methods used in developmental psychology to assess more directly whether adults as well as toddlers arrive at convergent emotional orientations as a consequence of social appraisal. Rather than approaching a visual cliff edge, targets (players) pumped up simulated balloons presented on a computer screen and tried to avoid passing the point where they would burst. In this Balloon Analogue Risk Task (BART: Lejuez et al., 2002), more points are earned the more the balloon is inflated, but all points are lost if the balloon bursts. How big it gets before bursting varies unpredictably from one trial to the next so that players never know exactly how far they can safely go.

The source of emotional influence in this study was one of the target's friends who arrived at the laboratory with them. During the BART procedure, this 'observer's' facial reaction to the balloon inflating was displayed to the player across a two-way video link. Both participants in each pair were told that points earned during the task would be converted to cash that would be shared between them. In order to manipulate emotion communication, observers were covertly instructed either to express anxiety as the balloon inflated or to suppress any expression of anxiety. The prediction was that targets would appraise additional pumping as more risky when the source expressed more anxiety, and that this would increase their reluctance to inflate balloons to their maximum possible size. This predicted effect on risk-taking was confirmed. Players pumped their balloons less and burst them less often when the source was instructed to express rather than suppress anxiety. However, there was no clear evidence that these effects were mediated either by the target's or the source's reported risk appraisals. Controlling for these measures did not remove the significant effect of the expression manipulation on inflation of the balloon, suggesting that effects did not depend on explicit inferences about the meaning of the source's emotion expressions.

Parkinson and Simons (2009) provided further evidence for appraisal-independent emotional convergence using non-experimental methods.

Participants completed electronic questionnaires on hand-held computers as soon as possible after they made any decision that involved other people. The questionnaires included ratings of anxiety and excitement and of risk-related appraisals at the point where the decision was first considered and after the final selection of decision options had been made. Participants also asked the other person involved in the decision (source) to independently make their own ratings of anxiety and excitement. The findings showed that targets' perceptions of the source's anxiety affected their risk-related appraisals. Further, these effects partially mediated emotional convergence effects. However, the source's emotion also significantly influenced the target's emotion even after controlling for measured appraisals, and even after controlling for the source's perception of the target's emotion. In other words, interpersonal emotion convergence was not fully explained by the target's explicit inferences about the implications of the source's emotion, even in a situation where participants were motivated to think carefully about the consequences of what they were about to do.

Bruder, Dosmukhambetova, Nerb and Manstead (2012) systematically manipulated dyadic contact between friends or strangers while they watched movie clips intended to produce amusement, sadness or fear. In the visual contact condition, each participant could see a real-time video-feed of their co-participant's facial responses. In the no contact condition, co-participants watched the clips in separate rooms. Co-participants' self-reports of emotion converged only for the amusing and frightening films in the visual contact condition. In the case of the amusing film, this effect was only found when participants were friends and not when they were strangers. In other words, interpersonal emotional influence seemed to depend on visual interaction between participants and the nature of their relationship. However, none of the reported effects on emotion depended on measured appraisals, which showed no evidence of interpersonal convergence.

The studies reviewed in this section show that interactive contact between people can result in convergence of their emotional orientations towards objects and events. However, these interpersonal effects on emotion are not always accompanied by corresponding effects on explicitly reported appraisal, and even when they are, the effects on appraisal do not seem to mediate the effects on emotion as the reverse-engineering account would predict. The implication is that interpersonal influence in these contexts depends either on implicit social appraisal processes or other forms of relation alignment.

Why does interpersonal interactivity make a difference to emotional influence? At one level, the continuing proximity of another person may produce stronger social pressure to adjust your orientation to theirs (see

Chapter 6). In other words, the key social appraisals may concern norma-tive rather than informational features of the situation. However, a more important consideration is the possibility of active interpersonal influ-ence and regulation (see Chapters 5 and 6). For example, toddlers con-fronting the visual cliff in Sorce and colleagues' (1985) study did not simply register information from the mother's face, but actively sought clarification of the emotional object by directing enquiring glances. Correspondingly, mothers did not simply display a spontaneous facial response but actively attuned their facial communication to the toddlers' apparent interpersonal attention, and explicitly regulated their gaze pat-terns to indicate that the visual cliff was the object they were commu-nicating about. Schachter's (1959) study of affiliation also showed that targets of emotional influence are active information-seekers, and Latané and Darley's (1968) study of social inhibition suggested that sources of emotional influence are active regulators of their emotional communica-tion. When these interpersonal communicative and regulatory processes come together in a real-time interaction, any emotional outcomes may be co-constructed rather than individually determined. Neither party's per-sonal inferences can wholly explain how the influence process unfolds.

Components and Cues

Most social appraisal studies present participants with preselected facial or textual stimuli intended to convey discrete emotional meanings such as anger, fear or sadness. Manipulations are checked by asking participants to confirm that they have attributed the intended emotion to the source. Thus, the research implicitly assumes that interpersonal effects depend on the target categorising the source's emotion. No influence process operating prior to, or independent of, emotion categorisation can be investigated using this methodology. However, isn't it possible that some aspects of a source's emotion might also nudge interpersonal responses without the target working out what emotion the source is experiencing?

Social referencing studies usually put targets in more direct contact with the source's emotion presentation. However, the source is still often instructed to present a categorical emotion to the target. For example, the mothers taking part in Sorce and colleagues' (1985) visual cliff study were specifically trained to display gasping expressions intended to convey fear. Even studies involving unmanipulated dyadic interaction usually channel the source's emotional communication by presenting stimuli designed to produce categorical emotions (e.g., Bruder et al., 2012). Again, these procedures make it more likely that targets respond to the categorical emotional meaning that the investigators have tried to create.

When emotions emerge as multimodal object-directed orientations rather than prepackaged messages, emotion categorisation may play a less central role in mediating their interpersonal effects. Targets may selectively pick up on specific aspects or components of the overall constellation of signals and movements presented by the source. Their responses to these orientation cues need not depend on their emotional implications or any inference about associated appraisals.

For example, Lee and colleagues (2013) showed that participants were better able to detect gaze direction from schematic pictures of eyes taken from a gasping 'fear' face than from pictures of either 'neutral' or 'disgusted' eyes. The main reason is that widened 'fearful' eyes make the sclera's position and orientation more visible. Inversion of these eye stimuli reduced participants' perceptions of their emotionality but did not interfere with detection of gaze direction. In other words, targets tracked gaze more accurately from a source's widened eyes, independent of their perceived fearfulness. Widened eyes also improved discrimination of peripheral stimuli in locations where their gaze was directed (Lee et al., 2013). They served as social cues that pointed out places where action might be happening (Fernández-Dols, 2017). In other words, a subcomponent of an emotion-related facial configuration induced interpersonal attention-orienting effects that did not depend on targets attributing a categorical emotion to the source.

In more realistic situations, dynamic patterns of eye gaze are attuned in real time to unfolding situations that include the target's responses to them. This may facilitate more articulated interpersonal effects. If the source's widened eyes direct the target's attention to emotionally relevant aspects of an object or event, they may also bring additional consequences for appraisal further downstream. Indeed, the perceived relationship between the source's orientation movements and the event towards which they are oriented often helps to specify the emotional significance of those movements (e.g., Adams & Kleck, 2005; Aviezer et al., 2008; Sander et al., 2007; and see Chapter 3).

In addition to gaze cues, other aspects of the source's emotional orientation may also lead targets to adjust their own orientations correspondingly. For example, dynamically articulated movements might entrain the movements of other people so that they attain a common rhythm and tempo (e.g., McGrath & Kelly, 1986; and see previous discussion). Thus, sources engaged in smooth or jerky transactions with environmental objects may tend to solicit correspondingly relaxed or agitated movements from co-actors or interactants. Combining direction of attention with entrainment of movement may facilitate mutual alignment of emotion-related orientations towards objects. Further informational contributions from interpersonal displays and signals may or may not help to consolidate a more articulated emotional experience involving patterned appraisals. In principle, at least, it seems possible that social appraisal processes can consolidate from combined lower-level adjustments, and that information transfer need not be the main driving force behind any resulting interpersonal influence.

One possible implication is that social appraisal, like non-social appraisal (see Chapter 1), often emerges over time from cumulative adjustments in relational activity. In the case of social appraisal, the perceptual and inferential processes are often distributed between different people who register different aspects of what is happening and provide cues to each other about their emergent emotional meaning (Parkinson, 1996; 2001a). The individuals involved do not need to take time out from this activity in order to perform separate private calculations.

Do the kinds of interpersonal calibration implied by dynamic gaze-tracking and mutual adjustment of bodily posture and movement still count as social appraisal processes? The source does not explicitly provide appraisal information and the target makes no inferences about appraisal. Any consequences for the target's interpretation and evaluation of objects or events happens further downstream. The more direct effects operate on the target's embodied relation to the object of the source's emotion, and are manifested implicitly in this changed relational orientation rather than explicitly registered. For all these reasons, these forms of relation alignment seem to stretch our usual understanding of what social appraisal involves.

Summary

In this section, I have argued that the methodologies typically used to assess social appraisal and other forms of object-directed emotional influence prioritise inferential processes that factor in categorical emotional meanings. The fact that categorical emotion information can induce reverse-engineering processes when conditions are right does not tell us what happens when other kinds of emotion-related information are presented in different conditions. No doubt, many of emotion's interpersonal effects outside the laboratory also operate on the basis of inferential processes that are activated by emotion categorisation. The problem is that we cannot yet be sure exactly how many. Future research needs to explore the circumstances under which other kinds of emotional influence take priority.

Conflicting Orientations

Most studies of social appraisal focus on situations where sources and targets approach the same object or event from broadly equivalent or compatible perspectives. The source's emotion is usually about something that might help or hinder the target's goals in a similar way to their own or that is not directly relevant to the target's concerns. The target's appraisal of this object is sufficiently malleable to permit social influence and the source's apparent emotion provides reliable and trustworthy information about the correct or appropriate attitude to adopt. Under these circumstances, as we have seen, appraisals and emotions often converge. Thus, I often end up sharing your apparent positive attitude towards a cake I will only ever see in a picture or one that we are about to eat together. But what happens if I suspect you of having poisoned my slice? What if I know that you are a fan of slapstick comedy and intend to throw the cake at me instead of letting me eat it? Does suspending the default assumption that our perspectives are mutually compatible make a difference to how your emotions affect me? The present section addresses this question.

Inferring Appraisals and Motives

In directly competitive situations such as zero-sum games, benefits experienced by sources imply costs to targets and vice versa. Thus, the source's positive appraisal of an ambiguous event may make the target appraise it more negatively, producing emotional divergence rather than convergence. However, the contingency between sources' and targets' incurred rewards and costs is usually less direct and predictable than this. Targets are often unsure whether sources are about to make a competitive move against them and what its precise consequences might be. Under these circumstances, the source's emotion may provide valuable information about their orientation to what is happening, allowing the target to make any necessary or appropriate adjustments to their own future behaviour. Thus, targets may try to work out how the source is appraising emotionally relevant events rather than how the event itself should be appraised. According to Hareli and Hess's reverse-engineering account (see Figure 4.3), such a process requires fewer inferential steps than the kinds of social appraisal considered so far. The target only needs to draw a single conclusion about the appraisals associated with the perceived emotion.

A good example of a situation where people may either compete or cooperate is the prisoner's dilemma game. The idea behind prisoner's dilemma is that a police officer separately interrogates two suspects who were involved in the same crime. If both refuse to confess and there is no other evidence against them, they can both go free. However, if one confesses and the other does not, the confessing prisoner gets the benefit of having come clean at the expense of the other prisoner whose guilt only becomes apparent because the other prisoner has confessed.

In the economic game based on this scenario, either player can accrue the maximum level of personal benefits (points or cash) by choosing to betray the other player (defect), but only if that other player chooses not to betray them (cooperate). If both players defect, outcomes are worst for both players. If both cooperate, their joint benefits are maximised, but each individually earns less than if they had defected and the other cooperated. The general point is that players' personal interest and shared interest are put into conflict. For this reason, prisoner's dilemma is an example of a 'mixed motive' game, where both cooperation and competition are rewarded under certain circumstances.

In such a situation, deciding whether to cooperate or defect depends crucially on your perception of what the other person is likely to do. If they have cooperated in previous games, this might lead you to expect future cooperation too. But another important clue is provided by how they react emotionally to what happens in the game. This can tell you how they are appraising the outcomes of their cooperation or defection, and whether or not they were trying to achieve those outcomes.

To test these ideas, de Melo and colleagues (2014) assessed the inter-personal effects of information about a player's emotional reactions to events in a twenty-five-round prisoner's dilemma game. Participants played against a computer-animated male avatar (virtual agent), which was programmed to display different dynamic facial movements in response to specified game outcomes. In the 'expressively cooperative' condition, the virtual agent smiled after mutual cooperation and showed a face conveying regret after defecting at the participant's expense. In the 'expressively competitive' condition, the agent displayed the opposite pattern of reactions, expressing regret after mutual cooperation, but smiling after defecting. In other words, the agent's apparent emotions were linked to the outcomes of each round and conveyed his appraisals of those outcomes. For example, regret in response to mutual cooperation implied that the agent blamed himself for having failed to exploit the participant's cooperation. Such an appraisal pattern directly implies that mutual cooperation was not his desired outcome, making future coopera-tion less likely.

Participants ended up cooperating more with the expressively coop-erative agent even though he smiled and displayed regret just as often as the expressively competitive agent across trials. In other words, the interpersonal effects of the source's manipulated emotions depended on the events to which they were oriented. Regret about mutual cooperation and regret about defecting conveyed different messages about the source's appraisals and motives.

In a follow-up study, de Melo and colleagues asked participants to rate their impressions of the agent's appraisals immediately before deciding whether or not to cooperate. As predicted, regret expressions led to greater impressions of the agent's self-blame for defecting, and smiles led to greater impressions that the outcome was motivationally congruent for the agent. Further, these appraisal judgements mediated effects of the agent's emotion expressions on participants' reported intentions to cooperate, consistent with an inferential reverse-engineering process. The motivational congruence indicated by smiling informed the target that the source wanted to produce the outcome, making it seem more likely that they would defect on future trials.

In a further study, the researchers manipulated the other player's verbal communications about appraisals instead of their facial movements. Participants were asked to imagine that they had just found out the outcome of a round of the game, and that the other player had typed a message conveying his appraisal of what had happened using a computer chat system. For example, instead of showing a regret face, the other player wrote: 'I do not like this outcome and I blame myself for it', thus indicating motivational incongruence and self-blame. This appraisal message had similar effects to the facial display of regret, again suggesting that the manipulated faces had affected participants' cooperation levels by communicating appraisals. However, this finding also raises issues about the active ingredient of the earlier facial manipulation. Perhaps participants directly extracted information about appraisal and orientation from the presented facial and gaze cues instead of making inferences on the basis of emotion categorisations in terms of happiness or regret (e.g., Sander et al., 2007; Scherer et al., 2018).

Uncertainty about whether other people will cooperate is also common in interpersonal negotiation situations. Here too, someone else's apparent emotional reaction to events can provide useful information about their motives and likely moves. A systematic program of research by van Kleef and colleagues has focused specifically on these interpersonal effects of emotion in bargaining tasks (see van Kleef, 2016, for a review). In one study, participants took the role of a supplier selling a consignment of mobile phones and had to negotiate as good an outcome as possible with a buyer whose offers were communicated remotely by computer (van Kleef, de Dreu & Manstead, 2004). Participants were told that they would receive information about the buyer's intentions in the form of their typed comments during the bargaining task. In fact, all of these comments were preprogrammed by the experimenters. The presented text messages either indicated that the buyer was angry or happy about the participant's most recent offer. For example, after round 1, their comment was either 'This offer makes me really angry' or 'I am happy with this offer'.

Participants perceived happy buyers as more willing to accept low offers than angry buyers and made smaller concessions to them. The level of these concessions depended on their perceptions of buyers' willingness to accept low offers, again supporting an inferential process such as reverse engineering. In other words, participants deduced that the angry buyer appraised offers as unfair and therefore concluded that only a higher offer would be acceptable to them.

Additional studies by the same research team provided more direct evidence for the operation of explicit inference (van Kleef, de Dreu & Manstead, 2004b). When participants felt under time pressure during the negotiation or were more motivated to reach quick conclusions, the differences between emotion conditions disappeared, suggesting that targets need to allocate cognitive resources to processing the emotional information provided by sources before that information can affect negotiation behaviour.

Reciprocal and Complementary Emotional Outcomes

The previous section reviewed evidence that targets' decisions about whether to compete or cooperate with a source partly depend on appraisal-related implications of the source's emotions. But are targets' emotions similarly affected? Does emotional influence in these contexts depend on inferential processes too?

Although targets conceded more to angry targets in van Kleef and colleagues' (2004a, 2004b) bargaining studies, they also reported higher levels of anger themselves, suggesting an inclination to oppose the source rather than concede to them (see also Friedman et al., 2004). In other words, the reported behavioural effects did not seem to depend upon, or directly relate to, the emotional effects. The investigators concluded that the interpersonal effects on targets' concession were mediated by inferences about the source's limits (as discussed) whereas the interpersonal effects on targets' emotions were mediated by non-inferential affective processes such as contagion (see van Kleef, 2016).

Anger's interpersonal effect in this study clearly did not involve direct calibration of source's and target's orientations. The target's inference that the source appraised the offer as unfair did not make the target see it as unfair too, making them feel convergent anger. However, it remains possible that the target became angry about the antagonistic position that the source was taking: they may have been angry with the source for remaining unsatisfied with their offer. This would mean that the active ingredient of influence still involved the source's object-directed emotion orientation, but that the target was orienting to a different object (e.g., the source's resistance to their offer rather than the offer itself). This kind of reciprocation process seems a more likely explanation of the reported emotion convergence than contagion. Indeed, it is hard to imagine how a target might catch the undirected experiential qualities of an emotion that was only presented remotely in purely textual form.

Why did the target's anger fail to reduce their level of concession to the source? One possibility is that participants refrained from acting on their anger because their own outcomes in the negotiation depended on the source's next move. In other words, they did not want to risk making the source even more angry and uncooperative by making an unacceptable offer. According to this account, the behavioural effect depended on the source's capacity to retaliate. To test this idea, Lelieveld and colleagues (2012) assessed whether the source's power affected target's emotional responses to their anger using a modified version of the ultimatum game. The ultimatum game involves one person suggesting a distribution of resources to another person (recipient) who can either accept or reject it without any further negotiation. In Lelieveld and colleagues' study, the participant was the person making the offer, which was delivered remotely by computer to a supposed recipient. In the high-power condition, the usual rules of the ultimatum game applied and rejection of the offer by the recipient meant that neither party received any resources. In the low-power condition, choosing to reject the offer only allowed the recipient to reduce allocated resources by 10 per cent. Participants were told that the recipient was either angry or disappointed about their initial offer. The recipient's anger increased participants' own anger across both levels of the power manipulation, but in the high-power condition it also increased their levels of fear and led them to make more favourable final offers. Thus, the effect on anger again did not match the effect on concessions, but the effect on fear did.

Why did the high-power source's anger induce fear in targets? Participants probably concluded that angry sources were inclined to reject their offer in both low-power and high-power conditions. However, if the high-power source rejected the offer, they would incur greater costs because all the allocated resources would be lost (rather than only 10 per cent). Thus, inferring that the source appraised the offer as unfair would imply more serious negative consequences in the high-power condition, making the target more fearful and less willing to make an unfavourable offer.

Anger implies externally directed blame and antagonistic action tendencies (e.g., Frijda, 1986). A source's expressed anger thus leads targets to anticipate negative outcomes that will affect them personally. Someone who is angry can potentially make you suffer. By contrast, communication of self-focused rather than other-focused emotions may make targets more concerned about how outcomes may affect the source rather than themselves. Indeed, when sources reacted to the initial offer with disappointment in Lelieveld and colleagues' (2012) study, participants tended to respond with guilt rather than anger or fear. This kind of empathic complementary response seems to depend on at least two factors. First, effects are stronger when the target believes that the source sees them as responsible for the outcome. Thus, Lelieveld and colleagues (2011) found that the source's statement that they were disappointed with the target induced greater guilt than their message that they were disappointed with the offer. Second, effects are weaker when the target approaches the interaction from a competitive perspective. For example, Lelieveld and colleagues (2013) found that disappointment communicated by a student from a different university made targets feel less guilty than disappointment communicated by a student from their own university.

Like disappointment, communicated sadness can also lead targets to feel bad about the target's experienced outcomes. Sinaceur and colleagues (2015) asked pairs of participants to conduct face-to-face negotiations. One participant from each pair was given specific advance training in how to negotiate effectively. This training encouraged them either to maintain emotional neutrality or to express sadness. Targets reported greater other-directed concern, compassion and empathy towards sad sources and made greater concessions to them, but only in conditions which encouraged them to care about the source's outcomes. For example, these effects operated when targets perceived the source as having low power, anticipated interacting with the source in future or perceived the relationship as a collaborative one.

Fear in response to a source's anger, guilt in response to a source's disappointment and compassion in response to a source's sadness are all complementary emotional reactions. They involve acceding to the relational agenda communicated by the source's emotions. By contrast, reciprocated anger is an example of a conflicting emotion, implying a clash between the respective orientations of the two parties. Emotional complementarity is a relatively less likely outcome when sources and targets are in direct competition with one another (e.g., in zero-sum games). However, costs and benefits in most bargaining tasks depend instead on balancing cooperative and competitive decisions. Under these circumstances, targets seem to experience complementary emotions to the extent that the source's personal orientation matters to them too (Wondra & Ellsworth, 2015), either because the source has direct control over their own outcomes (e.g., Lelieveld et al., 2012) or because they care about how the source feels for less practical reasons (e.g., Sinaceur et al., 2015). In face-to-face interactions, sources present emotion dynamically and in attunement to whatever else is happening. These facts may increase the consequentiality of the emotion more directly, thus producing complementary interpersonal responses that depend less on the target's inferential processes (as we shall see).

Interpersonal Meta-Emotion

Complementary emotions do not depend on calibrating interpersonal orientations towards a common object. The source may be disappointed about the outcome delivered by the target, but the target's guilt is about the outcome's effect on the source rather than the outcome itself. It seems therefore that targets' inferences about sources' appraisals can provoke emotional responses not only to the object of the source's emotion but also to the source's relation to that object. Thus, other-focused targets in Sinaceur and colleagues' (2015) study felt sorry for sources whose sadness indicated that outcomes fell short of their expectations. Their compassion was not about the outcomes themselves but the fact that those outcomes were disappointing for the source.

These relational implications of inferred appraisals sometimes lead to interpersonal meta-emotions (Elfenbein, 2014; Parkinson & Simons, 2012). In these cases, the target is oriented to the source's emotional orientation to events and experiences an emotion that takes the source's emotion as its object. Any appraisal focuses on the target's emotional response rather than what the target is responding to. For example, participants in Lelieveld and colleagues' (2012) study may have felt guilty about the source's disappointment and not just about the fact that the outcome failed to meet their expectations. Other examples of complementary meta-emotions include being afraid of someone else's anger (e.g., Lelieveld et al., 2012) or envious of their pride.

Some empathically motivated interpersonal meta-emotions may match the emotions they are about instead of merely complementing them. For example, I may be worried that you seem to be struggling to cope, or more abstractly that you are worried. This is different from worrying about whatever you are worried about, although both kinds of worry often get mixed up with each other (Parkinson & Simons, 2012). I can also clearly feel sad that you are sad or happy that you are happy.

Conflicting interpersonal meta-emotions are also possible. I may be unhappy that you are happy (*glückschmerz*: e.g., Hoogland et al., 2015; Smith, 2013) if I think your happiness is undeserved, or if our relationship is antagonistic. Correspondingly, *schadenfreude* involves taking pleasure in someone else's misfortune and in some cases may be specifically oriented to the unhappiness arising from that misfortune. Finally, some interpersonal meta-emotions bear no obvious relation to the emotions they are about. Examples include being embarrassed by your anger or anxious about your depressed state.

What makes targets orient to the source's emotion rather than the concern it communicates? One important factor is the target's attribution of the source's emotional response to the source's disposition or personality rather than to the source's current motives or situational factors (see next section). For example, if I suspect that you are prone to uncontrollable anger, my reaction to any impending signs of frustration may focus more on the emotion itself than on what it might otherwise tell me about what is going on or how you are likely to react to it. Similarly, people living with chronically depressed people may react emotionally to signs of depression rather than to what that depression might imply about current life events or failed attempts to cope with them (e.g., Coyne, 1976). Correspondingly, people who believe that they personally have an emotional problem may start to experience *intra*personal meta-emotions about their own emotions, which in turn may encourage others to take a compatible interpersonal orientation. Thus, feeling angry or hopeful about your depression can solicit convergent or divergent emotional responses from the people who are close to you. Further research needs to investigate the processes shaping these outcomes and their potential consequences for well-being and relational functioning.

Perceptions of Source Characteristics

In many interpersonal situations, we are more interested in understanding what another person is like than in making sense of whatever object or event they are orienting to, or how they are orienting to it (e.g., Gilbert & Malone, 1995; Heider, 1958). Although information about their current appraisal of events may tell us how they are likely to behave in the immediate situation, information about their more general dispositions potentially allows us to predict how they are likely to behave over a longer time-scale. Targets may thus use information about a source's expressed emotion to draw conclusions about the source's attitudes, character and personality.

   Gilbert, Pelham and Krull (1988) showed participants a silent video-tape of a female source who appeared anxious while conversing with another student who was out of shot. The topics the students were discussing were shown as subtitles at the bottom of the screen. In the anxious topics condition, these topics provided a potential explanation for the source's apparent anxiety (e.g., they implied that she was discussing her sexual fantasies). In the relaxing topics conditions, the topics were relatively less likely causes of anxiety (e.g., world travel). Participants subsequently judged the interviewee to be a more anxious person in the relaxing topics condition when her reactions did not seem to relate to the topics she was discussing. However, this difference disappeared when participants were instructed to memorise the subtitles while watching the video. Apparently, this competing cognitive rehearsal task stopped targets from factoring in the presented information about the possible object of the source's anxiety (even though this information was exactly what they were trying to process). Gilbert and colleagues concluded that perceivers automatically categorise people as having personal characteristics that correspond to their observed behaviour (including their emotional behaviour). Thus, seeing someone acting anxiously leads you to perceive them as an anxious person prior to any inferential process. Any subsequent correction of this initial conclusion requires additional cognitive resources.

In Gilbert and colleagues' study, participants were trying to work out what kind of person the source might be. Krull (1993) showed that asking targets to focus instead on what might have made her anxious produced different results. Under these circumstances, imposing an additional cognitive load reduced rather than increased the extent to which the source was perceived as an anxious person. In other words, automatic categorisation of the situation can sometimes take priority over effortful dispositional inference rather than the other way round. Thus, the target's task-related goals determine whether the source's emotion provides inferential information about that source's personal characteristics or automatically cues an associated person category. These goals depend not only on task instructions but also on whether the situation is competitive or cooperative. Targets may be more focused on the source when the source's next move may incur personal costs for the target, and more focused on the object of the source's emotion when both parties are approaching it from the same angle and with compatible motives.

In Gilbert and colleagues' research, the source's dynamic nonverbal displays provided targets with direct evidence of her anxiety. When targets learn about the source's emotion less directly, more explicit inferences about personality become more likely (e.g., Freeman & Ambady, 2011), even when targets are focused on understanding the person. Hareli and Hess (2010) investigated whether written information about a source's emotion led to reverse-engineered dispositional inferences. In their study, participants imagined that they were evaluating a candidate for employment after reviewing their account of being blamed for failure in a previous job. The key manipulation concerned the candidate's reported emotional reaction to the blame that had been directed at them. When the candidate was angry (rather than calm or sad) about being blamed, participants rated their personality as more dominant and less warm. This effect on personality judgement was mediated by inferences about the candidate's appraisals. For example, participants perceived angry candidates as appraising the event as more urgent, and their inferences about urgency in turn led them to conclude that the candidate was a more dominant person.

Addressing Targets

The research reviewed in this chapter suggests that many interpersonal effects of a source's emotion depend on what that emotion is about and whether it is specifically about the target (e.g., Lelieveld et al., 2011; Steinel et al., 2008). However, an equally important but under-investigated consideration concerns how the source's emotion communication is delivered and who the addressee might be. For example, it seems likely that emotion has a more powerful influence when it is addressed directly at the target of influence. Getting angry with you when you are right in front of me is usually a more effective means of intimidation than merely asking someone else to let you know about my anger.

In most interpersonal bargaining studies, sources are ostensibly unaware that their emotion statements are even being passed on to targets (e.g., Lelieveld et al., 2011). One exception is a study by van Kleef and colleagues (2004a), which included a condition where sources supposedly knew that their written emotion reports would be communicated to participants. Targets reported greater fear in response to sources' anger in this condition. As implied above, anger represents a greater threat when it is addressed explicitly at the person who presents an obstacle to the angry person's goals. These effects may be stronger still when interpersonal contact is more direct (e.g., Sinaceur et al., 2015).

Evidence reviewed in Chapters 2 and 3 suggested that emotion statements and expressions convey appeals or requests to targets as well as implying appraisals, motives and action tendencies (Scarantino, 2017; Scherer & Grandjean, 2008). By showing you my emotional response to what you are doing, I can clearly convey whether I want you to keep doing it, stop doing it or do something else. Thus, anger communication may serve as a request for you to back down or change your ways as well as a communication about blame. Whether you conform to this implied request depends not only on how favourably you might be disposed to me, but also on how concerned you are about how I might react if you fail to comply.

In directly interactive situations, then, responses to a source's target-directed emotions rarely depend solely on inferential processes. Much of the pressure to respond to the emotional orientation comes from the personally directed force of the source's action readiness, and not simply on interpreting that readiness as an indication of emotion. I feel it when you are angry with me (de Rivera & Grinkis, 1986; and see Chapter 1). It makes me want to accede to your demands and respond directly to the interpersonal affordances created by your orientation to me (e.g., Adams, Albohn & Kveraga, 2017). More generally, when a source's emotion is oriented to the target, it pushes or pulls the target's own orientation in particular directions. It encourages certain kinds of emotional reply and discourages others. Many of these effects directly reflect the functional properties of interpersonal emotions (see Chapter 6).

Conclusions

Other people are affected by your emotions in a variety of ways. They may come to think differently about you or the situation you are facing and adjust their behaviour accordingly. They may experience matching, convergent or divergent emotions, which may or may not be about the same thing as your emotions, and may concern your orientation to that thing, or you as the kind of person who adopts that kind of orientation.

These diverse effects depend on equally diverse processes, many of which depend on where the source's emotion is directed, and how it is communicated to the target. When two people are focused on the same object in a non-competitive situation, their orientations often align. They may start to appraise things more similarly and respond with more similar emotions and actions. This convergence may depend on inferences informed by prior knowledge of how emotions work or on less explicit processes of mutual adjustment. Even uncategorised emotions can direct other people's attention, activity and action.

Inferential and non-inferential processes also operate when sources and targets have competing orientations and goals. Under these circumstances, targets often orient to the source's appraisal of the emotion's object rather than the object itself. They may try to work out who they are dealing with or respond more automatically to their opponent's embodied orientation when contact is more direct or when matters are otherwise more urgent and compelling.

Even in potentially competitive situations, targets are unlikely to be wholly insensitive to source's concerns. They may be concerned about the source's emotional reaction or what it tells them about the source's personality. Empathic as well as oppositional orientations are possible.

As we have seen, studies of emotion's effects understandably focus on processes activated by a pre-existing emotion, and pay less attention to how that emotion itself might be interpersonally attuned and responsive in the first place. By design, emotional influence typically flows from source to target with little or no possibility of interpersonal interactivity or feedback. Outside laboratory settings, however, sources are often oriented precisely to the effects their emotions are having on targets. The concern that originally motivated their emotion makes a difference to how their orientations adjust to targets' own developing responses.

This means that we cannot fully understand how emotions exert inter-personal effects without considering their prior social-regulatory functions and how these functions are achieved in practice. The next chapter therefore addresses how people use their emotions to regulate other people's emotions.

CHAPTER 5

Regulating Emotions

People often regulate their emotions when attempting to influence other people. For example, I may try to maintain calm about what is happening to avoid making you worried, or work up my anger or disappointment to make you worry more. In both cases, regulation of my emotion serves to regulate your emotions. This chapter focuses on both intrapersonal and interpersonal emotion regulation and their intended and actual consequences. When two people try to regulate each other's emotions at the same time, their emotions may converge or diverge, producing increasingly compatible orientations or escalating clashes of perspective. In some case of mutual regulation, interactants may successfully achieve regulatory effects that neither individual could have achieved separately.

Cheer up. It's not the end of the world. Count your blessings and count yourself lucky. These are just some of the many things we say to each other to ease the pain of disaster or disappointment. Indeed, we often seem to be just as concerned with making other people feel better as with improving our own feelings.

Everyone likes being happy. Most of the time, we like others to be happy too. Being around happy people can make us happier as well, so we have another reason for wanting them to get happy. And our happy reaction to their happiness may make them happier still. By this logic, it starts to seem surprising that all of us don't end up in a perpetual state of escalating ecstasy. But life inevitably gets in the way. Things go wrong as well as right. And we can't always make ourselves or others happy about that.

And sometimes we prefer to curb enthusiasm or contain excitement. We try to damp down pleasure rather than work it up to avoid the risks of subsequent disappointment or peaking too soon. We may feel that our friends are underestimating risks or failing to detect someone's malicious intent. So we try to get them more anxious or angry instead of calmer. And when it comes to our enemies, we sometimes prefer them to feel bad regardless.

Interpersonal emotion regulation covers all the things we do to change other people's emotions for better or worse. Some of these regulatory

194

activities involve the strategic use of emotional communication. People know that their emotions influence other people's emotions and exploit this knowledge to achieve desired interpersonal effects. I may work up my anger in order to make you feel more guilty or feign enthusiasm to get you more excited. This chapter focuses on episodes where a source regulates their own emotion in order to regulate a target's emotion in this and other ways.

Intrapersonal Emotion Regulation

Before discussing how we use our emotions to influence other people's emotions, we need to understand how we regulate our own emotions in the first place. The first thing to note is that nobody has total control of their personal experiences. Events affect us in ways that can be surprising and overwhelming. Even when fully prepared for what happens, our reactions may still catch us by surprise, knocking us for six or lifting us to greater heights than we had imagined. We may be unable to stop thinking about something we'd prefer to forget or find our attention inexorably drawn to a person or object we are trying hard to keep out of our life or our mind.

Our bodies may also react in ways we don't want them to. We may stumble over words, shake when trying to hold firm or shed embarrassing tears. Hearts may pound, guts wrench and mouths dry. Sometimes when we are emotional, all of our thinking and energy is focused on the thing we are emotional about, and we have neither the time nor capacity to do anything other than respond to it directly. In the grip of an emotion, it often seems inconceivable that we could choose to stop it happening, let alone experience something different.

Despite the involuntary character of some aspects of emotional response, people have the capacity to moderate many of their causes and effects. We can take deep breaths to reduce our arousal or grit our teeth to hold back a laugh or smile. We can look away from something that excites, upsets or disgusts us. We can think about something else or try not to think about anything at all. Some of these strategies directly target the emotion itself and some are focused on its causes or effects.

Classifying Regulation Strategies

A first step toward understanding emotion regulation is to distinguish the various activities we perform to change what we are feeling or expressing. A number of theorists have proposed classification systems that allow us to navigate the evident diversity of our regulation attempts.

Probably the most influential formulation was developed by Gross (e.g., 1998a; 2015). His starting assumption was that emotional episodes unfold in a series of stages, beginning with an eliciting event, followed by its appraisal, which then leads to emotional responses such as facial expressions and autonomic changes (Figure 5.1). Regulation attempts can thus be distinguished according to the stage of the emotion process that they target. Antecedent-focused regulation is either directed at the event prompting emotion or the person's attention to, and appraisal of, those events, whereas response-focused regulation is directed at emotion's symptoms and consequences (Gross, 1998a).

For example, if we want to avoid getting angry about an acquaintance's irritating behaviour, one thing we might do is to simply stay away from any places where we are likely to come across them, meaning that the emotion-eliciting situation does not happen in the first place (situation selection: Gross, 1998a, or niche-picking: Campos et al., 1994). If we find ourselves in our acquaintance's company despite our best efforts, we might attempt to change the emotion-inducing situation by introducing them to someone else so that we don't have to deal with them personally (situation modification). Another possibility is to focus on something that takes our mind off whatever our acquaintance is saying or doing during the conversation (attention deployment). We might also try to change our interpretation or appraisal of their behaviour in order to make it seem interesting or amusing rather than irritating (cognitive change). Or we might target our own reactions by attempting to relax our muscles or suppress any overt expression of irritation (response modulation).

According to Gross, which strategy we deploy depends not only on the nature of the emotional episode and the options available to us but also on dispositional preferences for different kinds of regulation. For example, there are documented individual differences in people's propensities

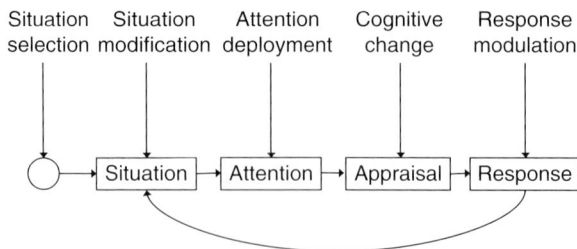

Figure 5.1 Gross's (1998a) process model of emotion regulation specifying five different targets of regulation attempts (reproduced with permission from the American Psychological Association)

to use reappraisal and expressive suppression as regulation strategies (Gross & John, 2003). These different regulatory styles may also be associated with differences in relative success in achieving emotion-regulation goals (e.g., Gross, 1998b).

Emotional episodes may not always unfold in the sequence implied by Gross's process model. For example, some so-called 'responses' may actually precede or overlap with the developing appraisals rather than being caused by them. However, the proposed distinctions between different forms of regulation are still useful because they allow researchers to focus on different kinds of regulation strategy that address different aspects of emotion, and to assess their personal and interpersonal consequences.

Regulation strategies may also be distinguished on the basis of other factors (e.g., Koole, 2009; Larsen, 2000; Thayer, Newman & McClain, 1994). Instead of focusing on what stage of the emotion process is targeted, Parkinson and Totterdell (1999) uncovered distinctions based on the modality and function of strategies. Based on a cluster analysis of 162 self-reported regulation strategies, strategies were classified into those that involved doing something (behavioural strategies, e.g., hugging, drinking, screaming) and those that mainly involved thinking or attentional activity (cognitive strategies, e.g., problem-solving, planning, meditating and fantasising). A further distinction depended on whether strategies directly addressed the emotion or what it was about (engagement strategies, e.g., thinking rationally about a problem, trying to understand feelings, asking for advice or reassurance) or diverted attention or action away from it (diversion strategies, e.g., distraction, withdrawal, running away).

Webb, Miles and Sheeran (2012) combined similar distinctions with Gross's (1998a) stage-based classification. For example, they distinguished between forms of antecedent-based attentional deployment that involve either concentrating on the emotion or emotion-inducing event (attentional engagement) or on distraction (attentional diversion); different forms of attentional diversion that use positive or neutral stimuli for distraction purposes (Parkinson & Totterdell, 1999); and different forms of reappraisal that focus on changing appraisals of the situation, perspectives on the situation (e.g., Kross & Ayduk, 2011) or emotional responses to the situation.

It is possible to make even more fine-grained distinctions between forms of reappraisal based on which appraisal dimensions are the specific targets of regulation. For example, attempts to reduce displeasure by convincing yourself that what is happening is unimportant are generally oriented to appraisals of motivational relevance and can potentially be used across a wide range of emotions. By contrast, attempts to convince yourself that you are not really to blame for a misdemeanour target the specific appraisal of self-accountability and are likely to be applied selectively to self-conscious emotions such as guilt.

Strategy Effectiveness

Which of the different kinds of emotion regulation identified by researchers work best? One way of assessing their relative effectiveness is by checking how successfully they influence the emotions at which they are targeted. Based on a series of studies, Gross and colleagues (e.g., Gross, 1998b) concluded that reappraisal results in greater emotional change than response modulation, and that expressive suppression in particular carries social (e.g., Butler et al., 2003) and physiological (e.g., Gross & Levenson, 1993) costs. Webb and colleagues' (2012) subsequent meta-analysis similarly found that reappraisal tended to be more effective than either response modulation or attentional redeployment (see also Augustine & Hemenover, 2009). However, these general trends disguised differences between subsets of strategies within the broader categories. For example, reappraisal of the emotional response using strategies such as acceptance of bad feelings or thinking of them as understandable reactions to the situation produced less emotional change than either reappraising the situation or taking a different perspective toward it. Similarly, distraction proved to be a more effective form of attentional redeployment than concentration.

If concentration and acceptance are relatively ineffective ways of changing emotions, why do people continue to use them? One answer is that their primary aim may not be an immediate improvement in affective state. For example, it is commonly believed that it is better to confront issues rather than avoid them (e.g., Hayes et al., 1996). Even if this makes you feel worse in the short term, any success in making the issue go away brings longer-term advantages. Similarly, some affect-improving strategies carry negative implications for more general mental health (Aldao, Nolen-Hoeksema & Schweizer, 2010). For example, avoidance of objects that make you afraid can stop you learning how to cope with or confront those objects, thus exacerbating any initial phobia (e.g., Mowrer, 1947).

Another possible reason for using strategies that don't *always* achieve intended emotional changes is that they *sometimes* do. Indeed, the same strategy often appears to have different effects in different studies (e.g., Bush et al., 1989; Gross & Levenson, 1993; Zuckerman et al., 1981). Many theorists have concluded that the effectiveness of different kinds of strategy depends on the context in which it is deployed, meaning that no single technique for regulating emotion is consistently effective under all circumstances (Aldao, 2013; Dunn et al., 2009; Nolen-Hoeksema, Wisco & Lyubomirsky, 2008; Parkinson & Totterdell, 1997).

If the effects of emotion regulation are variable and context-dependent, then being good at regulation is not about consistently using certain strategies instead of others. Indeed, Bonanno and Burton (2013) argue that effective emotion regulation depends on having a wide repertoire of strategies at your disposal and the flexibility and ability to tailor and adjust strategy deployment to meet the changing requirements of the prevailing situation. It may also mean weighing up the costs and benefits of short- and long-term effects (e.g., Doré, Silvers & Ochsner, 2016) to achieve deferred gratification rather than trying fruitlessly to have your cake and eat it.

Regulatory Direction and Trajectory

Early emotion-regulation research mainly focused on strategies for reducing negative emotions or maintaining or intensifying positive ones. However, there are also circumstances when people try to do the opposite and make themselves feel worse rather than better. Parrott (1993) provides several examples of this kind of pleasure-reducing regulation, including cases where people feel they should suffer for the sake of spiritual betterment. Indeed, research suggests that people sometimes actively seek to expose themselves to pain because they believe they deserve punishment for prior transgressions (the so-called Dobby effect, inspired by the self-flagellating elf from the Harry Potter books: Nelissen & Zeelenberg, 2009). Diary research suggests that pleasure-reducing regulation is less common than pleasure-increasing regulation in everyday life, but that participants report regulating emotions in both directions in certain circumstances (e.g., Gross, Richards & John, 2006; Kampfe & Mitte, 2009). In other words, people usually try to be happier, but not always.

In addition to the direction of travel on the dimension of pleasure, we can characterise regulation on the basis of the starting point on that dimension. It makes a difference where the regulator sets off as well as where they want to get to. Thus, pleasure-increasing regulation may involve intensifying a pre-existing positive emotion (up-regulation of pleasure) or alleviating a pre-existing negative one (down-regulation of displeasure). Correspondingly, pleasure-reducing regulation may involve damping down positive emotion (down-regulation of pleasure) or increasing negative emotion (up-regulation of displeasure).

Sometimes, people may also try to replace one kind of unpleasant or pleasant emotion with another. For example, to stop yourself feeling depressed about a knockback, you may attempt to work up your anger in order to mount a spirited protest. To deal with your admiration for a close friend's success, you may encourage yourself to experience pride about your own role in making it happen. Such episodes sometimes involve two separate processes in which one emotion is down-regulated and another is up-regulated. However, it is also possible that people attempt to transform their appraisal of events or orientation to them more directly. We therefore need to characterise the associated regulation attempt in terms of the trajectory from the initial emotion to the intended one.

These cases of emotional replacement suggest that pleasure is not the only important dimension to consider when attempting to understand emotion regulation. Indeed, many regulation attempts target levels of arousal instead. For example, Lane and colleagues (2011) presented evidence that sportspeople often try to get themselves into an angry frame of mind before an event, partly because they believe that this energises them for the impending contest. However, there may also be more specific characteristics of an angry orientation that make it particularly suitable for certain competitive contexts (Tamir, Mitchell & Gross, 2008). For example, anger tends to be associated with feelings of power (e.g., Roseman, 1984) and action tendencies that push against external resistance (e.g., Frijda, 1986). On an interpersonal level, anger may also carry the advantage of diminishing any residual sympathy for potential losers. Thus, people may try to get themselves into particular emotional states not only because of their arousal or pleasure-related qualities, but because they prepare them to pursue more specific relational agendas.

Hedonic and Instrumental Motives

Pleasure-increasing regulation is easy to understand. Self-evidently, feeling good is rewarding and therefore provides an obvious motivation for thought and action. But why would anyone want to make themselves experience less pleasure? As we have seen, one answer is that feeling worse in the short-term may lead to longer-term benefits for well-being. This explains why we sometimes resist the temptation of a second biscuit or push ourselves past the edge of discomfort during an exercise session. We all know that some of the things that make us feel better are bad for us and some of the things that make us feel worse are good for us.

We have also seen that some unpleasant emotions such as anger may have intrinsic characteristics that bring practical advantages for performance. Some theorists even believe that the feeling of unpleasantness itself can be useful in certain circumstances. For example, Schwarz and Bless (1991) argued that negative affective states encourage an analytic, detail-focused style of information processing whereas positive affective states encourage looser, more heuristic processing, and broaden the available range of thoughts and behaviours (e.g., Fredrickson, 2001), thus facilitating creativity (e.g., Isen, Daubman & Nowicki, 1987). Based on this idea, people might wish to make themselves experience less rather than more pleasure in order to undertake work that requires care and attention to detail (Cohen & Andrade, 2004; Parrott, 1993). Correspondingly, they might choose to cultivate pleasant emotions not only because they feel good but also because they assist with certain kinds of task involving the need for unfocused, lateral or original thinking.

However, more recent research suggests that the effects of pleasant and unpleasant emotions on thinking styles are not consistent across contexts (e.g., Huntsinger & Ray, 2016). Huntsinger, Isbell and Clore (2014) argue that negative emotion presents a stop signal indicating that whatever is currently happening is problematic, whereas positive emotion presents a go signal indicating that current activities should continue. In this view, negative emotions only activate analytic thinking when participants are currently engaged in heuristic thinking. Correspondingly, pleasant emotions only maintain or enhance heuristic thinking when participants are already in an heuristic mode. In either case, the pleasantness of the emotion simply indicates whether the current thinking style should cease or persist. Whether practically oriented emotion-regulation attempts follow the logic of this more context-dependent model is a question that awaits further research.

Tamir (2009) distinguishes between hedonically motivated emotion regulation that is intended simply to increase pleasure for its own sake and instrumental emotion regulation that is designed to fulfil practical goals other than increasing immediate pleasure (see also Tamir, Ford & Gilliam, 2013). Tamir (2016) further distinguished four different forms of instrumental regulation focused on facilitating task-related behaviour (performance motives), boosting your sense of mastery or competence (eudaimonic motives), understanding yourself or the world (epistemic motives) and changing your relations with other people (social motives). The next section focuses specifically on socially motivated emotion regulation.

Socially Motivated Regulation

People often attempt to regulate their emotions for social reasons. We may work up our happiness and enthusiasm in order to seem more likeable, or tone down our delight after victory because we do not want to be seen as gloating in front of a vanquished opponent. We may attempt to follow the display or feeling rules associated with specific social situations such as weddings and funerals (Hochschild, 1979). And more generally, we may tailor our emotional conduct and experience so that it more closely matches the norms and rules prevalent in our group or society (e.g., Tsai, Knutson & Fung, 2006). On average, participants in a diary study by Kalokerinos, Tamir and Kuppens (2017) reported having social motives for regulating their emotions in relation to over 12 per cent of the recorded negative events. This proportion would probably have been higher still if the investigators had sampled positive as well as negative experiences.

Many instances of socially motivated emotion regulation involve damping down emotions that may be perceived negatively by others. Trying to stop laughing in sober situations such as formal ceremonies or meetings is a common experience for many of us. Caring professionals need to avoid showing shock or disgust when confronted with patients or clients with gory injuries or who have lost control of bodily functions. Actors need to hold back stage fright to make their performance more convincing to the audience, and boxers need to suppress fear to avoid undermining their attempts to intimidate opponents. Teachers sometimes need to contain their anger when young pupils are unruly or disruptive.

In many of these cases, people down-regulate their emotions partly because their work role demands it, illustrating a process known as emotional labour (Hochschild, 1983; and see Chapter 8). Employees sometimes merely suppress their outward displays of emotion while continuing to experience the socially proscribed emotion (surface acting: Hochschild, 1983). At other times, they fully engage with the emotional role demanded of them, immersing themselves completely in an institutionally dictated emotional orientation to social events (deep acting). For example, a flight attendant interviewed by Hochschild explained how she dealt with an obnoxious passenger in the following terms: 'I try to remember if he's drinking too much, he's probably scared of flying. I think to myself, "He's like a little child." Really, that's what he is. And when I see him that way, I don't get mad that he's yelling at me. He's like a child yelling at me then' (p. 55). This form of reappraisal of social relations brings potential benefits during the immediate interaction but may have more damaging consequences for the emotional labourer in the longer term if it leads to habitual acceptance of abuse and exploitation (see Chapter 8).

Emotions may be up-regulated as well as down-regulated for social purposes. Research reviewed in Chapter 4 has shown how emotions affect other people's responses in negotiation contexts. For example, negotiators who express anger often receive greater concessions from others because they are perceived as having higher limits (e.g., van Kleef et al., 2004b) and being tougher (Sinaceur &

Tiedens, 2006). Awareness of the effectiveness of angry negotiation styles may therefore encourage negotiators to make themselves angrier. Indeed, research participants instructed to up-regulate their expression of anger achieved better outcomes when negotiating with someone who had relatively low levels of power (Sinaceur & Tiedens, 2006). Similarly, bill collectors report using anger as a means of intimidating recalcitrant debtors (e.g., Sutton, 1991). Tamir, Mitchell and Gross (2008) also provide experimental evidence that people spontaneously choose to make themselves angrier by listening to anger-inducing music or recalling angry incidents in advance of a quasi-social confrontational task (playing the *Soldier of Fortune* video game).

Other unpleasant emotions can also bring benefits in certain kinds of social interaction. Sinaceur and colleagues (2015) found that participants who up-regulated their sadness received better outcomes when negotiating with someone who cared about their situation. Hackenbracht and Tamir (2010) further showed that participants preferred to appear and feel sadder in order to get someone's help in averting a potential loss.

The idea that sadness functions to solicit help from others and that anger serves to intimidate them echoes Fridlund's (1994) behavioural ecology approach to facial displays (see Chapter 3). According to Fridlund, the pouting face often associated with sadness is intended to recruit caring responses in appropriate circumstances whereas the scowling 'anger' face threatens attack. How then do the social motives conveyed by facial activity relate to the social motives encouraging emotion regulation? One possible answer is that emotion regulation involves a relatively more explicit form of social influence that exploits preexisting implicit interpersonal effects of emotion expression and motive communication. Displaying a threat face does not require us to think ahead about how it might affect our antagonist whereas working up our anger often involves factoring in anticipated consequences (e.g., Tamir et al., 2008). However, this distinction starts to break down if we propose that emotion regulation itself can also operate implicitly (Gyurak, Gross & Etkin, 2011). Indeed, Braunstein, Gross and Ochsner (2017) argue not only that emotion-regulation goals can be activated unconsciously (e.g., by priming) but also that the processes that regulate emotion in response to these goals may operate below the level of awareness (e.g., as a result of implicit affective learning). Perhaps then explicit emotion regulation is simply a special case of the more general relation-aligning functions of emotional orientations. I will revisit this issue later in the chapter when considering the regulatory functions of regulated emotions.

Interpersonal Emotion Regulation

Some forms of socially motivated emotion regulation specifically target other people's emotions. It may serve our purposes to get someone else into a particular emotional state by directing emotion at them. For example, Sinaceur and colleagues' (2015) research showed that negotiators who up-regulated expressions of sadness solicited greater empathy and compassion and that those emotional responses led to more favourable negotiation outcomes. Thus, people might choose to up-regulate an emotion to induce a complementary emotion in another person, in anticipation of the practical or social benefits that the induced emotion might encourage.

Of course, we do not need to regulate our own emotions in order to regulate someone else's. We can also perform non-emotional actions that change their feelings and orientations. Niven, Totterdell and Holman (2009) extended the methodology used by Parkinson and Totterdell (1999) to classify the range of interpersonal rather than intrapersonal regulation strategies. Questionnaires and diaries were used to collect participants' reports of trying to make someone else's emotions more or less pleasant, or more or less intense, yielding a set of 378 distinct strategies for interpersonal emotion regulation. These strategies were then sorted into categories by a different set of participants and the results were subjected to hierarchical cluster analysis (see Chapter 2).

The two-cluster solution derived from this analysis distinguished strategies that were intended to increase the pleasantness of the target's emotion from those intended to reduce pleasantness. For example, interpersonal pleasure-increasing ('affect-improving') strategies included 'making time for the target' and 'buying the target a drink', whereas interpersonal pleasure-reducing ('affect-worsening') strategies included 'being unfriendly toward the target' and 'giving the target the 'silent treatment'. Given that it is difficult to change someone else's emotions simply by engaging in private mental activity, it is perhaps unsurprising that Niven and colleagues found no evidence for Parkinson and Totterdell's earlier distinction between cognitive and behavioural strategies in the interpersonal domain. However, both pleasure-increasing and pleasure-reducing categories included subcategories corresponding to engagement (e.g., 'giving the target advice' and 'challenging the target's behaviour' respectively). Diversion-related subcategories of interpersonal distraction (e.g., 'arranging a social activity for the target') and the use of humour ('acting silly to make the target laugh') also featured among the pleasure-increasing 'acceptance' strategies.

Hedonic and Instrumental Motives

Like intrapersonal regulation, interpersonal regulation is not always intended to increase immediate pleasure. Although we often experience satisfaction when we make our allies feel good or our enemies feel bad, we may also have other instrumental reasons for trying to influence their emotions.

Netzer, van Kleef and Tamir (2015) adapted Tamir and colleagues' (2008) experimental procedures to assess whether instrumental considerations motivate interpersonal emotion regulation. Participants were told that another participant was about to play a computer game that involved shooting virtual antagonists (*Soldier of Fortune*), and that this other participant's performance would determine participants' own monetary rewards. In the partnership condition, participants believed that they would earn more if the player's score was higher. In the rivalry condition, they believed that they would earn more if the player's score was lower. Participants chose to present the game to the player as more aggressive and to select anger-inducing music for them to hear before the game in the partnership condition. These choices depended on participants' expectation that anger would improve the player's performance. In other words, participants opted to encourage more unpleasant emotions in allies rather than rivals, because they believed that this would maximise their personal benefits.

In Netzer and colleagues' (2015) studies, participants did not actually meet the person whose emotions they were trying to regulate and were unable to observe any unpleasant consequences that person might have experienced. Do people also try to make their friends and allies feel worse when directly interacting with them? Or does seeing them suffer moderate regulatory choices? Face-to-face encounters allow interactants to adjust their real-time regulation on the basis of its observed interpersonal effects. If I see you getting upset about a story I am telling, I can always tone it down to make it more palatable. Or I might choose to play up or exaggerate its more gruesome elements for dramatic or comic effect. Exploring how these processes might play out in directly interactive settings is an important task for future research (see Parkinson, Niven & Simons, 2016).

Using Your Emotions to Regulate Other People's Emotions

Netzer and colleagues' (2015) research permitted participants to influence another person's emotions remotely based on cold rational considerations. However, many of the things we want other people to feel more or less emotional about are things that affect us emotionally too. We want others to share our enthusiasm for a recent TV program, film or book, or to respond with appropriate guilt and contrition for the offensive thing they have just said to us. In these cases, we may work up or tone down our own emotion precisely to induce a desired emotional response from someone else.

Only a subset of the strategies reported by participants in Niven and colleagues' (2009) classification study explicitly mentioned regulating one's own emotions in order to regulate the emotions experienced by the other person. In particular, some of the reported rejection-related strategies used for interpersonal affect worsening involved expressing annoyance or pride (e.g., 'acting annoyed toward the target' and 'bragging to the target about how good you are'), and some of the reported acceptance-related strategies used for interpersonal affect improvement involved conveying love or amusement (e.g., 'making the target feel special and cared about' and 'acting silly to make the target laugh'). However, many other varieties of emotion also have established effects on other people's emotions (see Chapter 4), thus offering the opportunity for their use in interpersonal emotion regulation. Indeed, practically any kind of emotion can influence another person's orientation to its object, and practically any interpersonal emotion can induce complementary emotions in the person at whom it is directed. People may therefore regulate a wide variety of their own emotions in order to exploit the possibilities presented by these two kinds of emotional influence.

Manipulating Social Appraisal

Political speakers who want their audience to experience anger about the misbehaviour of opponents or other kinds of injustice not only tailor their presentation of the facts but also express anger themselves. A detached and neutrally presented report of an objectionable event may lead people to believe that there is little to get upset about. By contrast, escalation of appropriately expressed righteous indignation sets the tone for outraged responses. Sometimes we need to make ourselves emotional about something in order to make other people get emotional too.

These rhetorical uses of emotion exploit the principles of social referencing. Just as a mother's smile encourages a toddler to feel secure about crossing a potentially threatening precipice (Sorce et al., 1985), an orator's apparent annoyance indicates that people ought to feel aggrieved about whatever they are talking about. Someone on the opposing side of the debate might then attempt to defuse the tension by presenting their otherwise offensive conduct as simply expedient. In either case, communication targets arrive at their orientation towards a potentially emotional object on the basis of the source's apparent emotion. In other words, the source's intrapersonal emotion regulation regulates the target's emotion as the result of a social appraisal process (see Chapter 4).

People also use emotions to negotiate with others about their orientations to emotional objects in less formal settings and using less contrived tactics. Parkinson, Simons and Niven (2016) explored the regulation of worry in conversations between heterosexual romantic partners, focusing in particular on one partner's responses to the other partner's expression of problem-related anxiety (see Parkinson & Simons, 2012). Participants were video-recorded while discussing concerns that affected them both. Immediately after the discussion, they reviewed the videotape and gave continuous ratings of their own and their partner's level of worry using a mouse-controlled slider scale. They also rated the extent to which they had wanted their partner to feel less worried (interpersonal worry-reduction motives) and the extent to which they had tried to be calm in order to reduce their partner's worry (interpersonal calming).

Female partners' interpersonal calming attempts depended on the extent to which their male partners expressed worry. Indeed, female partners' motives to make their partner feel calmer responded in real time to changes in their male partners' worry levels. The corresponding effects were not significant for male partners' interpersonal regulation attempts.

One possible reason for this apparent gender difference arises from the fact that there are two possible interpretations of the motives behind interpersonal worry expression. Expressing worry to your partner may be part of an attempt to solicit reassurance and emotional support. In this case, interpersonal calming is the desired and appropriate responses. However, people may also present worry to their partners in order to draw their attention to something potentially threatening on the horizon (interpersonal alerting). In this case, the desired and appropriate interpersonal response is to express more worry rather than less. In other words, interpersonal alerting is a pleasure-reducing interpersonal regulation strategy implemented for the purpose of redirecting or intensifying the other person's focus on a potential cause for concern. Ultimately, the instrumental motive behind interpersonal alerting may be to recruit an ally who can help address the problem, but in the short term the goal is to get the other person to take that problem more seriously than they currently seem to be doing.

Female partners consistently rated themselves as using interpersonal calming less and interpersonal alerting more than male partners in Parkinson and colleagues' research. Further partners' perceptions of each other's habitual use of interpersonal calming and alerting showed a similar pattern, suggesting that male partners also perceive female partners as more likely to use interpersonal alerting strategies. If male partners interpret a greater proportion of their female partners' worry expressions as attempts to make them more worried, then this helps explain why they are less likely to use interpersonal calming in response.

Interpersonal calming is likely to backfire when your partner's expressed worry is itself part of an interpersonal alerting attempt. If they are up-regulating their worry in order to get you to take a threat more seriously, then any apparent reduction in your worry suggests that their regulatory attempt is not succeeding. Their response therefore may be to work up their worry even more. In response, you may redouble your attempt to show calm in order to reduce their apparently increasing worry. It is easy to see how interactions following this pattern might produce an escalating spiral of mismatched interpersonal emotions and mistargeted emotion regulation.

Parkinson and colleagues (2016) found some evidence for this kind of interpersonal process. Female partners reporting higher levels of inter-personal alerting tended to have partners who reported being more inclined to use reappraisal to regulate their emotions (Gross & John, 2003). In other words, women apparently used alerting more often on partners who tend to minimise the seriousness of potential threats. The corresponding effect was non-significant for male partners, suggesting that women may be more sensitive to their partners' use of reappraisal and thus more likely to respond by trying to counteract its effects.

Of course, interpersonal emotion regulation also carries consequences for the regulatory response of the person whose emotions are being regulated. People may respond to interpersonal regulation attempts by trying to regulate the other person's emotions too. In face-to-face inter-actions, the result is that partners often adjust their emotions in real time to each other's emotions, meaning that mutual regulation attempts lead to stable patterns of matching or complementary emotions. I only try to convince you how worrying things really are when your orientation to what is happening is clearly discrepant from my own. More commonly, partners in close relationships instead start out with broadly aligned or complementary orientations to commonly experienced events that con-verge still further as a consequence of continuous reciprocal influence. Instead of back-and-forth interpersonal regulation, this socially distributed process involves co-regulation, where interactants are commonly involved in shaping a shared emotional stance (e.g., Butler & Randall, 2013).

Regulating Target-Directed Emotions

In Parkinson and colleagues' (2016) research, participants' worries were directed at concerns that were shared or sharable by both partners. Interpersonal regulation served the purpose of aligning emotional orientations towards a common object or event. Do similar regulatory processes also operate when the targeted emotion is instead directed at the person doing the regulation? For example, I may want you to feel less angry with me rather than less angry with someone else. In order to achieve this, I may need to work up complementary emotions such as guilt or sympathy instead of simply down-regulating my own anger.

Biglan and colleagues (1985) compared problem-solving interactions of couples experiencing different levels of marital distress. Their specific focus was on behavioural sequences in which one partner's emotion-related behaviour affected the other partner's immediate response. In distressed couples, wives presented relatively fewer depressive symptoms in the moments immediately following their husband's aggressive behaviour, suggesting that husbands of depressed wives might use anger to regulate their wives' depression in real time (coercion). However, husbands were also relatively less aggressive immediately after their wives' presentation of depressive symptoms, suggesting that wives' presentation of depressed emotion may have regulated the anger that was being directed at them (appeasement).

Nelson and Beach (1990) showed similar anger-reducing effects of presented depression among couples in early but not later stages of marital discord, suggesting that partners may stop responding positively to expressed depression when compassion fatigue sets in (e.g., Coyne, 1976) and interpersonal demands start to seem overtaxing and burdensome (Johnson & Jacob, 2000). Although this research supports the idea that emotions such as depression may serve interpersonal regulatory functions by reducing target-directed anger under certain specific circumstances (see Chapter 6), the reported effects may not depend on spouses' active up-regulation of depression. Simply being depressed may solicit comforting or appeasement behaviour from partners, regardless of how the depression arose in the first place.

However, Overall and colleagues (2014) presented clearer evidence that relationship partners up-regulate negative emotion expressions in order to induce more sympathetic responses from their partners. Their research focused in particular on the interpersonal effects of an anxious attachment style (e.g., Bowlby, 1973), which involves chronic fear of rejection by other people, and acute sensitivity to cues indicating the possibility of abandonment. Anxiously attached individuals tend to respond to threats to their close relationships by actively seeking support and reassurance from the other party. Overall and colleagues (2014) induced relationship threat by asking couples to discuss how each partner wanted the other partner to improve. Independent judges then coded the video-recorded interactions for indications that participants were trying to make their partners feel guilty (e.g., Vangelisti, Daly & Rudnick, 1991), by exaggerating their expressions of feeling hurt (e.g., pouting or sulking, emphasising how their partner's behaviour was affecting them negatively or reminding partners of their relational obligations).

Anxiously attached participants reported greater hurt feelings, and their hurt feelings were more strongly associated with attempts to up-regulate their partner's guilt (as observed on the videotapes). Partners responded to up-regulated hurt expressions by becoming more guilty as intended. In other words, partners who felt threatened by implied criticism made themselves appear more hurt in order to make their partners feel more guilty. Partners' successfully induced guilt in turn provided reassurance that they cared about the relationship, thus reducing the hurt partner's anxiety about rejection. However, the immediate emotional benefits of this interpersonal up-regulation of guilt were offset by a reduction in the partner's perceptions of relationship quality. Feeling bad about something your partner accuses you of making them feel also seems to make you feel worse about your relationship with them more generally.

A further downside to directly soliciting a partner's guilt is that any reassurance is evidently produced in response to a specific request rather than spontaneously, thus undermining its relational value. One possible response to any associated doubts about the authenticity of the partner's guilty response is to express greater hurt in order to seek further reassurance. Ultimately, this escalated solicitation of guilt may discourage partners from providing continuing support (cf. Coyne, 1976).

Apart from the studies described so far, very little research has directly addressed people's attempts to regulate emotions that are directed at them. One possible reason for this omission is that responses to self-directed emotions often seem more like direct emotional reactions than interpersonal regulatory attempts. Your anger may directly make me feel angry rather than encouraging me to work up my anger to discourage you from continuing with yours. Or your hurt feelings or expressed disappointment may directly make me feel guilty rather than encouraging me to work up my guilt in order to reassure you. As we shall see in Chapter 6, even these more direct 'reactions' may serve the function of regulating someone else's emotions. However, it is less clear that they are planned strategically in order to solicit those interpersonal effects. Distinctions between different kinds and levels of regulatory process will be considered further in the concluding section of this chapter.

Using Other People to Regulate Your Own Emotions

Our discussion of interpersonal emotion regulation has focused on how people regulate other people's emotions ('extrinsic' emotion regulation in

Gross's, 2015 terms). However, another 'intrinsic' (or self-directed) form of emotion regulation is also interpersonal because it involves using other people to regulate our own emotions (Zaki & Williams, 2013). For example, we might seek social support in the form of advice or reassurance when we are feeling anxious or distressed. If our support-seeking attempt is successful, we may end up feeling less anxious or distressed as a consequence.

Clearly, intrinsic and extrinsic interpersonal emotion regulation are not mutually exclusive. Indeed, Overall and colleagues' (2014) study (see previous section) showed how anxiously attached people try to solicit reassurance from their relationship partners about the security of their relationship by encouraging those partners to experience guilt. In this case, extrinsic interpersonal emotion up-regulation of partner's guilt serves the purpose of intrinsically down-regulating our own anxiety. It is also possible that regulation of other people's emotion can serve the function of up-regulating our own unpleasant emotions. For instance, if a boxer wants to work up anger in preparation for a fight, they might first try to provoke their opponent into getting angry with them.

These examples also raise the possibility that intrinsic interpersonal regulation can bolster or reinforce the intended effects of extrinsic interpersonal regulation. If a boxer uses anger to provoke an opponent, then that opponent's angry response in turn serves as a provocation that helps the first boxer up-regulate their own anger. Similarly, an anxiously attached person's tentative presentation of hurt feelings may start to induce their partner's guilt, which then provides interpersonal feedback that facilitates the anxious person's adoption of a hurt role in the relationship. In real-time interactions between people, one person's presentation and regulation of emotion may be sustained and encouraged by the ongoing emotional feedback provided by the other person. Indeed, what starts out as a strategically regulated emotion may start to seem more spontaneous as it develops in coordination with the other's reciprocal emotion presentation. Another boxer's angry reaction to our deliberate provocation may make us genuinely angry. A similar phenomenon happens in everyday situations when we need to raise our voice to make ourselves heard by others. If they interpret our shouting as anger directed at them, their angry response may make us angry too.

Conversely, intrinsic interpersonal regulation may produce interpersonal consequences that work against its intended effects, rather than bolstering them. For example, people may share their worries with friends or partners in order to receive worry-alleviating reassurance (Parkinson & Simons, 2012; Parkinson, Simons & Niven, 2016), but their partners may respond by getting more worried themselves. The outcome may be an episode of co-rumination with each person's worry feeding off the other's (e.g., Rose, 2002; Rose, Carlson & Waller, 2007).

In both intrinsic and extrinsic interpersonal emotion regulation, individuals actively seek to influence other people's behaviour. However, the conduct or presence of other people can also regulate our emotions without any active solicitation from us, just as our conduct or presence can regulate their emotions without us intending it. For example, we may feel less anxious about an interview because there are other people around or because those other people engage us in distracting conversation even when they have no specific desire to provide comfort. Or we may do things that provoke another person's desired anxious state fortuitously rather than by either their or our design.

All of these alternative scenarios seem to involve regulatory activity, begging the question of which constitute bona fide examples of interpersonal emotion regulation. Should we reserve the concept for cases where one person actively and consciously targets someone's emotions with the goal of influencing them (e.g., Niven, 2017)? Or do other more implicit interpersonal moves and adjustments that result in emotional changes also count (e.g., Gross, 2015)? Should it be called interpersonal emotion regulation when we use other people to regulate our own emotions (intrinsic interpersonal regulation: Zaki & Williams, 2013) or should we restrict the phenomenon to regulation of other people's emotion? There is no right answer to these stipulative questions, but the current terminological confusion can bring misleading consequences. In my view, the clearest and most central cases of interpersonal emotion regulation happen when we make strategic attempts to change someone else's emotion (see also Niven, 2017). However, as we have seen, intrapersonal and interpersonal forms of regulation often become intertwined in everyday situations, and explicit interpersonal influence can shade into implicit processes. This means that boundaries of the phenomenon are likely to remain fuzzy and tentative when applied in practice.

Emotions as Regulated and Regulatory

People are clearly aware of many of the effects that their emotions can have on other people. They have plenty of experience observing the reactions of the targets of their anger, or of those who provide sympathy or comfort when they are sad. Even the slowest learner soon picks up on the resulting opportunities for interpersonal manipulation. Indeed, advice about using emotions for the purposes of persuasion dates back at least to the time of the ancient Greeks (Aristotle, tr. 1991) and probably much earlier.

It is also clear that many aspects of emotional conduct are susceptible to either direct or indirect control. We know that we can get ourselves either more or less involved in what is happening around us. We are skilled at regulating our attention and can look away or cover our ears when necessary. We can engage or become detached. We can choose to take deep breaths or voluntarily relax or contract muscles in our bodies. We can raise or lower our voices. We can bite our lips or turn their corners up or down. We can stare intently at someone. We can decide to say something nasty or kind, loving or hateful. We can work ourselves up or down.

Putting together our capacities for emotional control with the opportunities they present for influencing other people makes the prevalence of interpersonal emotion regulation unsurprising. From an early age, children's emotion expressions are attuned to the availability of potential responders. They start to cry after a fall only when it is clear that their carers can see or hear them (e.g., Fridlund, 1994). They cry louder when other crying children are competing for attention (Holodynski & Friedlmeier, 2006).

On the basis of these observations, it starts to seem possible that any or all of the documented interpersonal effects of infants', children's and adults' emotion depend on regulation, that emotions are relational actions oriented to anticipated interpersonal responses rather than simply reactive passions. In that case, there is no need to distinguish emotion regulation from the regulatory effects of getting emotional. If the emotional process itself is regulatory, then a less complicated one-factor model seems possible (Campos, Frankel & Camras, 2004). Perhaps emotion is always intrinsically attuned to the possibilities of influence. Where then does emotion end and regulation begin?

Emotion regulation is usually taken to imply that some first-order emotional process is subjected to a second-order control process (Gross, 2015). This model fits well with the age-old Western idea that unruly passions need to be tamed by cultivated reason (see Kappas, 2011). The natural and automatic emotional response is thus subjected to rational attempts to bring it into line (Lutz, 1988). If emotions are reactive mental states then they are easily detached from the rational and instrumental mechanism that seeks to exert top-down influence over them. However, if emotions themselves are already forms of relational activity or action readiness modes, distinguishing them from putatively separate regulatory processes is more problematic.

Some cases of apparent emotion regulation may involve conflict between two emotions rather than the operation of two different kinds of process (Campos et al., 2004). For example, I may start to feel guilty about being angry with you, and the interpersonal repair processes associated with this guilt may help to counteract the interpersonal antagonistic processes associated with my anger. In this case, the two competing processes operate at the same level and involve similar mechanisms. There is no need to hypothesise any higher-level regulatory system.

However, as Tamir's (2009; 2016) research suggests, people also regulate emotions for non-emotional reasons (see also Niven, 2016). An emotion's goals may conflict with longer-term instrumental concerns, including the desire to experience emotions at some point in the future. Thus, the tension driving emotion regulation is not always between two emotionally driven processes that are equally regulatory. Sometimes, someone whose advice you have learned to follow just tells you to contain your excitement or tone down your anger. Sometimes we follow emotional norms established by our culture (Tsai, Knutson & Fung, 2006) or organisational training (Hochschild, 1983) by working on our feelings or expressions (e.g., Hochschild, 1979). And sometimes adopting a specific emotional demeanour is part of a career plan or identity project unlikely to reach fruition any time soon. So emotions are both regulatory and regulated. And sometimes, but not always, their regulation is achieved by regulatory emotions. The next chapter focuses on these regulatory functions more directly.

CHAPTER 6

Social Functions

A central function of many emotions is to influence other people. Indeed, people often engage in emotion regulation precisely to modify or extend the interpersonal regulatory functions that emotions already serve. This chapter focuses on these regulatory functions, and on how emotions acquire them in the first place. According to social functional theories, emotions play a role in achieving interpersonal goals relating to affiliation, interpersonal distance, dominance or appeasement. Supporting this account, many socially oriented emotions are directly attuned to their actual and anticipated interpersonal consequences. Emotions not only communicate appraisals and relational orientations, but also provide more direct incentives and disincentives that motivate other people's responses or prompt their cessation. Emotion components such as facial and bodily movements serve social functions too, either by communicating information, or by cuing adjustments in attention and action more directly. Although natural selection contributes to the development of many of these functions, emotions only consolidate into integrated strategies of social influence over the course of socialisation and enculturation.

What's the point of emotions? Sometimes it seems that they just get in the way of what we are trying to do. The jitters of social anxiety may mess up the good impression we want to present, making us even more concerned about what other people will think. Excitement about winning can take our focus off performing well enough to achieve victory. Jealousy can push away the lover we were struggling to hold on to. Perhaps, then, attaining our goals requires us to contain or expunge our emotions, and to regulate them for instrumental purposes whenever possible.

Despite their potentially disruptive effects, most psychologists believe that emotions serve important functions, and yield important benefits. Just because emotions can interfere with some kinds of activity, that doesn't mean that they don't also fulfil other kinds of purpose. Our social anxiety may disrupt smooth performance but still solicit sympathy, help and concessions. Excitement may be distracting but serves to motivate and energise us and the people around us, providing a reminder of why we are all working towards the same goal. Insecurities conveyed by jealousy may provoke our partner's annoyance but still remind them how strongly we are bonded together. So, emotions that hinder some goals can also help with others when the circumstances are right. The fact that they don't always achieve their purpose doesn't mean that they don't have a purpose in the first place.

As the above examples suggest, many of the functions served by emotions relate to their effects on someone else. In this chapter, I will explore the idea that many emotions facilitate the alignment and configuration of relations between people and coordinate their respective orientations to environmental objects and events. Indeed, they may be designed precisely for these purposes.

Functions

What does it mean to say that emotions serve functions? The key idea is that emotions assist in the operation of a wider system of activity that gives them their purpose and operating characteristics (e.g., Keltner & Haidt, 1999). Emotions are part of something bigger and help that bigger something to work properly. In the case of interpersonal functions, the bigger thing that emotions are a part of is the network of relationships between people, which in turn is located within the wider context of groups and societies. Emotions can help to stabilise or modify interpersonal relationships often supporting broader collective or cultural norms. According to many social functional theorists, the ultimate purpose of this functional relation alignment is to increase the chances of survival, reproduction, or promote inclusive fitness.

Evolutionary theorists argue that emotions must have served some function at some point in natural history or else they would not have been built into the human mental system. Their functions may or may not be as relevant for contemporary humans as they once were for our ancestors (e.g., Tooby & Cosmides, 1990). Correspondingly, cultural theorists argue that emotions have taken their particular form partly because they help or once helped people to operate in specific societies (Lutz & Abu-Lughod, 1990). These approaches are not mutually incompatible. It may be evolutionarily advantageous to promote societal functioning, and it may be culturally functional to accommodate biologically functional capacities. Nature and nurture aren't necessarily in competition with one another. In this section, I consider some of the practical and social functions that might account for us having certain kinds of emotions as human beings and as members of a given society.

Practical Functions

The most common functional explanations for emotions focus on their direct relevance for physical survival. Because our ancestors were more likely to survive if they were equipped with emotions that helped them exploit practical opportunities and avoid practical problems, genes producing those emotions have passed down the generations. According to this account, emotions are evolutionary strategies for dealing with life-preserving and life-threatening situations, and their most direct function is to facilitate practically helpful behaviours in relevant contexts. For example, fear may prepare your muscles and metabolism for running away from dangerous predators, and anger may get the body ready to physically attack or confront antagonists who might otherwise inflict potentially lethal injuries.

However, specific behaviours are unlikely to be practically advantageous across all contexts in which any emotion occurs (see Chapter 1). For example, running away may sometimes increase the chances of survival but it is not usually the most adaptive response to a dangerous predator that can run faster than a human. Similarly, fighting antagonists who are evidently stronger than us may be counterproductive. However, it remains possible that natural selection still favoured both kinds of response because they generally increased the probability of survival and reproduction, even if they sometimes went wrong.

Some appraisal theorists argue that emotions derive their adaptive benefits from the delimited flexibility of their behavioural implications (e.g., Smith & Ellsworth, 1987). They are designed to operate when a rapid but not entirely predetermined response is needed. On the one hand, these situations provide too little time or opportunity for exhaustive consideration of all possible behavioural alternatives on the basis of explicit and systematic reasoning. On the other hand, their variable and changing functional requirements cannot be met by any fixed action pattern or reflexive adjustment. Thus, emotions prepare the mind and body to perform certain actions without dictating the precise behaviours used to perform those actions across all contexts. They are off-the-peg heuristics rather than bespoke strategies or one-size-fits-all algorithms.

There are alternative variants of this delimited flexibility account. The first argues that the behavioural response stays fixed but there is flexibility in whether or not it is executed. According to this view, emotions are decoupled reflexes (e.g., Scherer, 1984; 2001), which prepare the body for a specific response but do not elicit that response directly, leaving scope to hold back from acting when further deliberation is required. Thus, fear gets the individual ready to run away in case running away is urgently necessary, but doesn't automatically make the individual actually run.

The second account of flexibility suggests that the behavioural response itself has flexible characteristics. For example, Frijda (1986) argues that emotions involve general action readiness modes rather than specific behavioural tendencies. From this perspective, appraisal detects a concern that needs attention without preparing any specific behavioural response to it. Emotions therefore activate and prioritise goals (e.g., Oatley & Johnson-Laird, 1987) and encourage certain behavioural trajectories without specifying lower-level bodily movements.

A third possibility is that emotions allow flexibility at both the input and output end of the process (Smith & Ellsworth, 1987). Both appraisal and action readiness would then be quicker and dirtier than in carefully deliberated decision-making but still slower and cleaner than reflexive elicitation of fixed action patterns. In any case, the shared functionalist claim of most appraisal theories is that emotions get us ready to deal more efficiently with problems, challenges or threats without unduly restricting our capacity to adjust to the specific event that is unfolding.

Some of the practical concerns that emotions address involve other people. For example, fear may sometimes help us escape from social rather than purely physical threats and anger may ready us to fight against a human being rather than an inanimate object. In these cases, practical functions are also social functions. However, emotions can also influence other people in ways that are not as immediately or obviously practically functional. The next section focuses on these less directly practical social functions.

Social Functions

In order to operate in human society, individuals have to coordinate their actions with those of the other people around them. They may require help in performing an action or need to stop someone else hindering its performance. It may be necessary to establish alliances or create social boundaries (Fischer & Manstead, 2016). Emotions play a role in many of these social functions, by drawing other people's attention towards or away from relevant concerns and directly or indirectly regulating their behaviour.

Emotion's most widely discussed social functions arise from its practically relevant relational implications. Adopting an emotional orientation to events not only prepares you to deal with them on a practical level, but also displays your stance to other people, bringing potential effects on their behaviour. For example, Darwin (1998) discussed how dogs stand tall and make themselves look large and menacing when confronting potential antagonists. This posture not only serves the practical function of preparing an attack, but also serves the communicative function of showing the other dog that direct confrontation is imminent. Indeed, part of the point of adopting the menacing stance may be precisely to convey this warning. As a consequence, the other dog may adjust their own stance by being less confrontational. Both dogs may ultimately back down instead of fighting and thereby live to fight another day.

Submissive rather than dominance displays can serve corresponding communicative functions. Adopting a self-protective fearful orientation not only shows potential antagonists that you do not present a threat but may also recruit assistance from stronger allies. Indeed, when small children first confront a threatening situation, their bodies are not sufficiently developed or coordinated to permit effective fight or flight. Any practically adaptive functions of their movements and cries therefore depend on the responses they solicit from caregivers. In other words, early fear reactions may increase the chances of survival by encouraging adults to engage in protective responses rather than by preparing infants to physically escape under their own steam. Similarly, Bowlby (1973) argued that the function of infant distress following separation from a caregiver is to keep that caregiver close.

These examples suggest that practical and social functions often overlap and intertwine. Sometimes practically oriented responses serve the secondary function of influencing others and sometimes socially oriented responses serve indirect practical functions. To the extent that emotions promote the integrity or future viability of the group or society more generally (e.g., Keltner & Haidt, 1999; and see Chapter 7), they will also indirectly produce practically beneficial consequences, because being part of an integrated collective itself increases the chances of gene transmission.

Reproductive and Inclusive Fitness

Many evolutionary theorists explain socially functional emotions by reference to their implications for reproductive and inclusive fitness in addition to direct survival (e.g., Tooby & Cosmides, 2008). Gene transmission depends on producing offspring and promoting their potential for subsequent reproduction (reproductive fitness). Family members other than direct offspring also share a proportion of your genes so their survival and reproductive success is also a relevant consideration (inclusive fitness). Emotions can motivate social behaviours that either directly support these tasks or communicate the capacity to promote them to others (Keltner, Haidt & Shiota, 2006). For example, jealousy may encourage actions that directly maintain a monogamous sexual relationship or signal attachment and commitment to partners, while warning off potential rivals. Both kinds of effect potentially protect parental investment in progeny and maintain access to future procreative possibilities (Buss & Schmidt, 1993).

Evidence for these accounts usually depends on demonstrating that emotions are sensitive to predicted factors relating to reproductive or inclusive fitness. For example, Shackelford, Buss and Bennett (2002) argue that heterosexual men are relatively more jealous than women about sexual infidelity because of its implications for paternity of offspring, and the potential costs of their sustained parental investment in children who may have different biological fathers. Because women can be confident that their children share their own genes, they should be relatively more concerned about their male partners' 'emotional infidelity' which implies a loss of commitment to future investment in the relationship and less contribution to child-rearing. The US students questioned about scenarios in which a romantic partner engaged in either sexual or emotional infidelity broadly showed these predicted gender differences. Male students tended to report that they would be relatively more distressed and find it more difficult to forgive their partner if they found out that they had performed sexual acts with someone else than if they had formed a deep romantic relationship with that other person. Female students tended to show the opposite pattern of preferences.

Real-world relationships rarely offer such a clear binary choice between alternative forms of romantic betrayal. Both are clearly upsetting for most people regardless of their gender or sexuality, especially when they go together (as they often do). When asked to make a hypothetical judgement, the fact that women in contemporary Western society focus more on 'emotional' considerations seems hardly surprising given prevalent sex roles and stereotypes. Any reported gender differences could just as easily reflect malleable cultural roles and norms as fixed outcomes of prior evolutionary pressures.

More generally, many evolutionary explanations run the risk of presupposing that whatever social arrangements currently prevail consolidated only because they promote gene survival. Correspondingly, emotions that support or promote those arrangements are seen as serving the adaptive purpose of sustaining them. In other words, things are as they should be and our emotions help to keep them that way. But natural and cultural ecologies differ across times and places, and the capacity of humans to adjust to local circumstances may be precisely what has helped them to reproduce, support kin and survive. Later in the chapter, we will consider ways in which emotions can serve cultural as well as biological functions.

Interpersonally Attuned Emotions

Finding conclusive evidence for or against claims that emotions evolved over the course of natural history is difficult. We cannot directly track the development of emotions and its sensitivity to changing ecological pressures, partly because most of the action took place so long ago, and partly because phylogenetic processes operate over such extended time-scales. Fossil records tell us relatively little about the evolution of psychologically functional capacities and historical records are usually too sparse to provide clear proof or disproof. Comparative analysis of other primates can provide clues about certain functional behaviours but direct homologues are rare. Some of the things that human beings can do are distinctively human.

Partly for these reasons, functionally inclined psychologists usually make do with more local and targeted hypothesis testing. Instead of assessing whether emotion serves or once served broad functions at a general level, they make more specific predictions about the factors shaping the operation of particular emotions in more immediate contexts.

The fact that emotions often have useful interpersonal effects (see Chapter 4) already raises the possibility that some of these effects reflect their social functions. For example, if anger can enhance success in competitive tasks (e.g., van Kleef et al., 2004a), then the point of getting angry may be precisely to communicate toughness in order to facilitate competitive success (e.g., Sell, Tooby & Cosmides, 2009). However, showing that an emotion brings a particular interpersonal effect is not enough to prove its social functionality because many effects may be secondary, peripheral or fortuitous. For example, I may find it amusing that you are so anxious about some trivial impending event, but it would usually be a mistake to conclude that the point of your anxiety was to solicit my amusement in the first place. In order to demonstrate functionality, we need to establish that the emotion is more directly attuned to its actual or anticipated consequences.

Central heating serves the function of keeping your home warm by switching on when the temperature falls below the thermostat's set point and switching off as soon as it reaches it. You can check whether your heating system is working properly by observing its response to changes in temperature. Similarly, you can assess the social functionality of an emotion by testing whether it is put into action by an event relevant to a social goal or concern, and whether it adjusts in direct response to factors relevant to progress in addressing that concern. For example, fear might be activated in situations requiring practical or emotional support from other people, and might persist and intensify until that support is forthcoming, but then cease as soon as the support has been successfully solicited. If so, it makes sense to say that fear has the function of soliciting social support because it responds to the developing need for social support and continues only until that need is fulfilled. This specific example suggests a general research strategy for demonstrating that any emotion serves a particular function. Investigators should attempt to establish that its onset, escalation and termination are attuned to progress in dealing with the predicted functional concern. In practice, most studies focus only on some parts of the functional sequence of events. However, convergent findings about social causes, moderators and effects of emotions still allow us to draw tentative conclusions about functionality. In the following sections, I consider illustrative examples of emotions to which social functions have been attributed, and evaluate evidence for their functional operation.

Embarrassment

Embarrassment presents an initial puzzle for social functionalists, because being embarrassed often gets in the way of creating the impression of being calm and in control in front of other people. What then might the positive social consequences of embarrassment be? A popular answer is that it serves to mitigate the negative impression that might otherwise result from a gaffe or faux pas, or more generally from the failure to execute action according to social rules of conduct. Getting things wrong in this way already makes people think worse of you. Acting as if nothing had happened may be a bad move under these circumstances. That would suggest either that you don't care about the usual etiquette or are unaware of it. If instead you acknowledge the inadequacies of your performance, and show that you would prefer others not to focus attention on them, this demonstrates your sensitivity to social norms and commitment to adhere to them better in future. In support of this account, Semin and Manstead (1982) found that judgements of people who had committed social gaffes were more positive if they expressed embarrassment than if they did not (see also de Jong, 1999).

Do the apparent reparatory effects of embarrassment reflect the emotion's intrinsic social functions? If mitigating negative social impressions is the central point of getting embarrassed, we would expect embarrassment to be expressed until the target of the communication gets the message, but not afterwards. Leary, Landel and Patton (1996) tested this prediction. Participants in their experiment were first asked to make a recording of their personal rendition of the schmaltzy song 'Feelings' thus raising their concerns about negative social evaluation. Some participants were then provided with an opportunity to communicate their embarrassment to the experimenter while others were not. In the social communication condition, participants were asked to rate their emotional response privately, before the experimenter returned to the room, picked up the questionnaire, and nodded to show that he had registered the information it contained. Participants who received this interpersonal feedback ended up less embarrassed than those whose questionnaires the experimenter had not looked at and those who had not made any emotional ratings in the first place. In other words, embarrassment reduced when participants found out that the witness to their imperfect performance was aware that they were embarrassed. This suggests that embarrassment is attuned to the influence it has on other people, supporting a social-functional account. More specifically, many theorists argue that the central function of embarrassment is to regulate social impressions that might otherwise be under threat, making the emotion a form of appeasement behaviour (Keltner & Buswell, 1997).

In Leary and colleagues' study, participants communicated their embarrassment by making ratings on a questionnaire. Its interpersonal effects depended on an encapsulated emotional meaning represented in words. However, social functions may also be served by the nonverbal cues, signals and movements often seen in embarrassing situations. Keltner (1995) argues that embarrassment typically involves reddening of the face, diversion of gaze and lowering of the head. This pattern of movements directly conveys a desire to be removed from other people's evaluative gaze, and other people often seem to pick up this message and react by looking away (e.g., Leary et al., 1992). In other words, embarrassment displays may function to deflect social attention prior to any mitigation of negative evaluations from others. Based on evidence such as this, some theorists argue that the minimal condition for embarrassment is not a social gaffe but rather the unwanted social attention that such a gaffe might produce (e.g., Halberstadt & Green, 1993; Leary et al., 1992). This would help to explain why people often feel embarrassed when they have done nothing wrong (e.g., Miller, 1992; 2004; Sabini et al., 2000). For example, receiving an award in public can sometimes be as embarrassing as tripping over on the dance floor.

A study by Reddy (2000) found that even two-month-old infants consistently show facial and attentional activity similar to adult embarrassment displays (Keltner, 1995) after engaging in sustained eye contact with someone else (see Figure 6.1). Their reactions involved turning their head away from the other person while beginning to smile. Sometimes, they also moved their arms to cover their faces. Adults viewing these 'coy smiles' on videotape interpreted them as indications of embarrassment, bashfulness or coyness (Draghi-Lorenz, Reddy & Morris, 2005). Of course, this does not mean that the babies actually felt embarrassed in the same way that an adult might do. And even if they did, they were clearly not aware that what they were experiencing was 'embarrassment' at this stage of development. However, the fact that nonverbal signals associated with the adult version of this emotion are produced in response to social attention at such an early age suggests that at least some of the associated social functions can operate without any articulated apprehension of their relational implications. Infants can show adults that interpersonal attention should be moderated long before they work out what the emotional meaning of their attention-deflecting display might be. It seems likely that some of the functions served by adult embarrassment displays also depend on similar dynamics of interpersonal adjustment and are achieved by means other than explicit emotion communication.

Anger

Another emotion that is oriented to intended interpersonal consequences is anger. Although some forms of anger may directly prepare the body for physical confrontation, their main point may still be to display a threat rather than actually go through with the dangerous business of fighting. More generally, anger positions the other person as infringing on our literal or metaphorical territory and directs blame at them. The implication is that negative consequences will follow if they do not back down or otherwise correct their problematic behaviour (Keltner, Haidt & Shiota, 2006).

Research on bargaining shows that anger can serve as an intimidation strategy that induces fear in its target (e.g., van Kleef et al., 2004a). Indeed, some theorists argue that the emotion's primary function is to attain advantage in competitive encounters by displaying strength and dominance (e.g., Sell et al., 2009). Interpersonally induced fear thus motivates the target to engage in corrective responses that address the object of the source's anger. When anger is directed at someone's ongoing behaviour, it is intended to make that other person stop what they are doing (e.g., Fischer & Roseman, 2007). When anger concerns someone's prior behaviour, it is intended to solicit some form of reparation. In both cases, anger presentation may be designed to solicit regret or guilt from the other person in addition to any fear response.

If soliciting apology and recompense is one of the social functions of anger, the emotion should intensify until the perpetrator responds with

Figure 6.1 Infants showing 'coy smiles' (Reddy, 2000, reproduced with permission from Wiley/Blackwell)

the required response. In face-to-face settings, people are usually attuned to any signs of irritation and respond quickly as soon as they begin to notice them. Any appeasing response is then rapidly picked up by the irritated person whose irritation will consequently reduce. However, if the perpetrator is slow to detect our growing anger, or if we are slow to detect their apology when it does arrive, then anger may continue to escalate until both messages are successfully transmitted and received. Such a situation might happen when channels of remote communication are disrupted due to an erratic internet connection, or limited bandwidth (Parkinson & Lea, 2011). Similarly, the subtleties and nuances of a message can sometimes get lost in translation when using text-based forms of communication that lack the usual nonverbal backchannels (e.g., Kiesler, Siegel & McGuire, 1984). In the absence of direct interpersonal contact, readers do not always pick up on writers' intended tone of voice or style of delivery. For example, recipients of politely worded emailed requests do not always appreciate the level of their urgency.

Another context in which anger communication and acknowledgement often get disrupted is behind the wheel of an automobile. When another driver cuts in on you forcing you to slam on your brakes, a fixed stare, murmured swear word or clenched fist are often insufficient to get them to register your disapproval. They are not close enough to see or hear you even if they happen to be looking in your direction in the first place. And if they realise their mistake, the usual appeasing gestures are unlikely to get back to you easily or immediately either. If you want a visible and unambiguous apology, you need to make it absolutely clear that you are angry in a way that will penetrate the shell of your car and cross the distance between the two vehicles. This might be achieved by accelerating until you are very close behind and flashing your lights and honking your horn. If you are lucky, the other driver may raise a hand that can be seen through the car window or flick on their hazard lights in acknowledgement. More likely, they will wonder why you are driving so aggressively and dangerously, and want you to apologise to them for that. If so, there is the danger of a vicious circle in which your increasing anger provokes increasing counter anger in an escalating spiral ending in reciprocated road rage.

Some evidence for this kind of interpersonal process comes from a study comparing people's recollections of recent incidents of anger on and off the road (Parkinson, 2001b). In both kinds of incident, participants reported that they wanted the other person to know that they were angry and to apologise for what they had done. However, in cases of anger while driving, they reported that the other person was significantly slower to detect their anger. Further, the reported intensity of their anger was positively correlated with how long the other person took to detect it.

Barriers to interpersonal communication are clearly not the only reason why people seem more anger-prone while driving. On the road, someone else's misbehaviour can have fatal consequences. The stakes are already high. Further, some drivers may pay less attention to the usual social norms when they feel protected and anonymous within their vehicles. The fact that behaviour on the roads may be worse and more dangerous than elsewhere in itself provides fuel for intensified anger. But the inadequacy of the usual forms of anger communication when shielded from others by glass and steel may also be a factor that contributes to road rage. If making another person back off or back down is the social function of anger, then the emotion is likely to persist and intensify until it gets through any barriers impeding its interpersonal transmission.

Guilt

If anger functions to solicit a target's guilt by directing other-blame at them, guilt may serve the corresponding function of appeasing the source's anger or disapproval by acknowledging that blame. If so, the self-accountability appraisals associated with guilt (e.g., Smith & Lazarus, 1991; and see Chapter 1) may be associated with taking on the interpersonal role of a culpable transgressor and communicating your blameworthiness to the victim. In short, becoming guilty may convey a commitment to make up for perceived wrongdoing (Keltner, Haidt & Shiota, 2006).

Evidence for the interpersonal orientation of guilt comes from studies that assess its social consequences. For example, O'Malley and Greenberg (1983) showed that participants imposed relatively smaller fines on defendants who expressed remorse in an imagined legal trial. In their view, perpetrators' guilt served as a form of downpayment towards recompensing the victim for the harm they had experienced. More generally, guilt is associated with a readiness to repair an interpersonal relationship and make amends to the other person (e.g., Frijda, Kuipers & ter Schure, 1989). Indeed, a number of studies have shown that people are inclined to apologise when they feel guilty (e.g., Baumeister, Stillwell & Heatherton, 1995; Howell, Turowski & Buro, 2012). Guilt also seems to be attuned to its relation-repairing effects, and to be sustained until these effects are achieved. For example, guilt tends to dissipate once people are able to apologise to the victim of their transgression but persist if apology is not an immediate option (e.g., Shore, Katic & Parkinson, under review).

If the point of guilt is to repair the relationship with a person who feels offended (Baumeister, Stillwell & Heatherton, 1994), then perhaps the sense that the other person is blaming you is what provokes the emotion rather than any internally directed self-blame. Although perceiving self-directed blame is usually associated with genuinely feeling blameworthy, sometimes people close to you blame you for things that you know you haven't done. A common response on such occasions may be to express anger or dismay that they could think to accuse you of such a thing. However, it is possible to feel guilty too, especially if you empathise with the victim's situation (e.g., Lelieveld et al., 2012) and can understand why they might have reached the wrong conclusion.

Experiences of this kind do not match the prototypical representation of guilt episodes and often seem aberrant or irrational. This makes them difficult to investigate using self-report methods. Participants may be unsure whether they truly qualify as instances of 'guilt' or may be reluctant to acknowledge their occurrence because they seem unreasonable or unsuitable for presentation in a scientific context. They may not come to mind easily when asked to think of a clear example of the emotion. However, many of these reporting biases can be reversed in studies that explicitly ask participants for their unreasonable as well as reasonable guilt memories (Parkinson, 1999) or for prospective and retrospective reports of being blamed without justification (e.g., Parkinson & Illingworth, 2009). Under these circumstances, a notable minority of participants report feeling guilty without appraising themselves as personally accountable for whatever has happened, mainly in situations where someone close blamed them for something that was not actually their fault. For example, one participant wrote that: 'My friend had a go at me over something she accused me of telling someone else that should have remained confidential. I hadn't said anything'. Another participant reported feeling blamed without self-blame in response to a sibling's irrational anger: 'My brother has schizophrenia. I found out about ten months ago. I feel a lot of guilt, not really blame but guilty feelings towards the whole thing because I am OK. When he snaps at me I feel I have done something, even though I know that of course no one is to blame'. In both cases, the participants said that they felt guilty despite not being or feeling responsible for the event for which they were being blamed.

Being unfairly accused of a transgression may be a relatively rare antecedent of guilt, because the target of blame is likely to focus on the unfairness of the accusation in addition to its implicit interpersonal demand to put things right. Perhaps partly for this reason, guilt may be a more common response when someone close to you expresses hurt feelings (Overall et al., 2014; and see Chapter 5), sadness (Hackenbracht & Tamir, 2010; and see Chapter 5; Sinaceur et al., 2015; and see Chapter 4) or disappointment (Lelieveld et al., 2013; and see Chapter 4) about what has happened. These emotional orientations draw attention to negative consequences for the suffering person rather than the other person's role in bringing about those consequences. For this reason, they may be less likely to solicit defensive interpersonal reactions and more likely to evoke sympathy and attempts to resolve relational issues.

Some of the reports of guilt in response to feeling blamed provided by Parkinson and Illingworth's (2009) participants seemed to depend on this less direct invocation of personal responsibility. For example, one such incident was described in the following terms: 'My brother confessed to me how he felt our parents were more proud of me than him ... He felt very upset and bad about his own recent failings – being kicked out of Uni. I had never been aware he felt that way' (p. 1605).

The commonly reported phenomenon of survivor guilt (e.g., Hutson, Hall & Pack, 2015; Niederland, 1961) may depend on similar processes. It is certainly possible that escaping a plane crash or collapsing building may lead to thoughts about inequities in fulfilling the right to survive, musings about what made you deserve to continue living rather than others and so on. However, it is also true that actual or imagined conversations with bereaved relatives may make you realise that they are wondering why it is you rather than their loved one who made it through. Perhaps the sense that you are indirectly associated with their suffering is what brings on the guilt.

Taken together, these observations suggest that guilt can be driven by relational concerns and oriented to addressing these concerns rather than depending on any purely personal appraisal process. The sense of being blamed or otherwise associated with someone else's suffering provides an interpersonal incentive for putting things right.

Contempt and Moral Disgust

According to Rozin and colleagues (1999), contempt is a reaction to moral transgressions in the realm of community rather than those in the realms of autonomy or divinity, which produce anger and disgust respectively. In other words, we feel contempt towards people who fail to fulfil obligations and duties associated with their social role or position in society (and not towards those who threaten our individual rights or sense of purity). From this perspective, the social function of the emotion may be to disassociate ourselves from people who threaten to disrupt social relations.

Rather than restricting contempt to a specific moral domain, Fischer and Roseman (2007) argue that the emotion is experienced when there is little prospect of bringing a target back into line after any kind of transgression. By contrast, anger serves the purpose of regulating a target's behaviour when regulation seems possible. Consistent with this account,

Fischer and Roseman found that anger was reported more often following transgressions by friends whereas contempt was reported more commonly following transgressions by strangers, and that this difference depended on participants' perception that they had the capacity to change the transgressor's behaviour. In other words, people tend to believe that they have greater influence on their friends than on strangers and this makes them relatively less likely to feel contempt towards their friends.

Another reason why strangers were more likely to solicit contempt was that their behaviour was more commonly seen as reflecting their personal characteristics, rather than being a temporary aberration prompted by current circumstances. This finding too supports the interpersonal controllability account because misbehaviour stemming from a deep individual flaw is not something that anger can possibly influence. A more successful strategy involves having nothing further to do with the perpetrator and treating them with contempt.

Along similar lines, Hutcherson and Gross (2011) propose that contempt functions as a social avoidance response directed at people whose lack of competence presents a potential threat to the effective performance of collaborative tasks. Incompetence is unlikely to be corrected in the short term so interpersonal dissociation is likely to be preferable to the potentially costly active response associated with anger. Hutcherson and Gross (2011) specifically distinguish contempt from moral disgust, arguing that the latter emotion is attuned to someone else's negative intentions rather than their lack of competence. Moral disgust also encourages more active exclusion or social rejection than contempt.

Both social avoidance and active rejection are capable of inducing interpersonal effects that help the corresponding emotions to perform their intended functions. A target who accepts the source's contemptuous or disgusted appraisal of their character is likely to experience complementary shame or humiliation (e.g., Mann et al., 2016) with the associated desire to withdraw from the relationship. Thus, one of the interpersonal functions of these other-directed emotions may be to achieve social exclusion (Fischer & Giner-Sorolla, 2016) or separation. Emotional blame about a transgression that is perceived either as controllable (Fischer & Roseman, 2007) or as an imminent threat to the self (Hutcherson & Gross, 2011) may take the form of anger and serve to encourage the target to experience guilt and engage in interpersonal repair. By contrast, emotional disapproval of a transgression that is perceived as reflecting the target's internally driven and consistent response tendency may take the form of contempt or disgust and serve to encourage the target to feel ashamed and avoid future contact.

Regulatory Function

Although an emotion's attunement to consequences provides evidence of functionality, it does not prove that the emotion itself is intrinsically functional. Instead, the emotional person may be engaging in functionally oriented emotion regulation. For example, participants in Leary and colleagues' (1996) study may have been up-regulating their embarrassment with the purpose of conveying an identity-protecting message to the experimenter. Similarly, drivers in Parkinson's (2001b) study may have been strategically escalating their anger presentation to get the transgressor to notice them and make an appropriate response. If so, it might be argued that it is not emotions that are directly functional but rather people's successful attempts to control them.

One reason for taking such a position is the common belief that emotions are simply reactive states which are triggered by prior events rather than oriented to anticipated consequences (see Chapter 5). Conditions that just come over us passively and uncontrollably don't seem to be capable of actively achieving strategic and directed effects on what is happening. From this angle, making emotions work for you requires a separate control process that puts the raw material of our passion to the service of our intentions (Kappas, 2011). However, if emotions are modes of relational activity serving a motivational agenda, their capacity to operate directly on the practical and social environment to which they are oriented seems less puzzling. From this perspective, emotions need no supplementary control system to regulate the people, objects and events at which they are oriented.

Is it possible to draw a clear line between these regulatory and regulation-based accounts? As we saw in Chapter 5, some theorists argue that regulation always implies an explicit attempt to change what you are feeling or showing based on a conscious intention to bring about an anticipated consequence (e.g., Niven, 2016). According to this view, evidence of lack of forethought would support a more directly functional explanation of consequence-attuned emotions. But what about cases where people have learned to use their emotions to exert interpersonal effects as a result of implicit processes? They might know *how* to influence other people emotionally without knowing *that* they are doing so. For similar reasons, several theorists argue that emotion regulation can operate below the level of explicit awareness (e.g., Braunstein et al., 2017; Gyurak et al., 2011). In this case, is there any hard and fast criterion that could distinguish between an interpersonally oriented functional emotion and an automatic goal-driven attempt to upregulate that emotion? For example, how could we tell the difference between strategic anger worked up by unconsciously reappraising events to seem more blameworthy, and interpersonally functional anger activated by an implicit other-blame appraisal? Given that emotional responses to developing social situations usually involve a continuous process of reappraisal in any case (e.g., Lazarus, 1991; Scherer, 2001), self-regulation may already be built into the emotion process (Kappas, 2011).

Perhaps then regulation simply extends the regulatory functions that emotions already have (see Chapter 5). Upregulating an emotion that achieves directly functional effects on others is simply an elaboration of that emotion's more intrinsic regulatory properties. But then where do emotions get their regulatory power in the first place? If emotions are prepackaged biological solutions to survival- or reproduction-related challenges, then humans may have evolved to produce them when confronted with functional concerns and to respond to other people's expression of them by meeting their functional demands. In other words, we might start life with basic emotion programs that output interpersonally functional response syndromes that automatically solicit co-evolved counter-reactions from caregivers and others. Regulatory competence would then develop as a function of experiencing the prior interpersonal effects of these preprogrammed emotions.

However, it seems more likely that emotions consolidate over the courses of social development in attunement to the social feedback that caregiver and others provide (Parkinson, Fischer & Manstead, 2005; and see Chapter 3). From this perspective, people develop emotions as implicit social influence strategies before learning to deploy more explicit resources to regulate them. If so, the boundary between early-emerging emotional functions and subsequent forms of emotion regulation is necessarily a fuzzy one. This does not mean that emotion regulation cannot also operate as an independent process when people try to counteract the more intrinsic effects of their emotions. It simply means that consequence-attuned emotions always involve regulatory processes at some level (e.g., Campos et al., 2004; Kappas, 2011; and see Chapter 5).

Facial Displays

Most theorists attribute functions to discrete integrated emotions such as embarrassment, anger or contempt rather than their separable subprocesses. Thus, emotions are assumed to serve their purposes because of their overall structure and meaning (e.g., as captured by a core relational theme: Smith & Lazarus, 1993). For example, anger serves to intimidate an opponent by virtue of being a coordinated set of responses that prepares the body and mind for attack and conveys this preparation to the person at whom it is directed. Correspondingly, fear serves to facilitate escape by increasing vigilance to potential threats and informing potential allies of this threat (or signalling submissiveness to any potential antagonist). In both cases, a patterned set of cognitive, physiological and behavioural changes provides an organised and coherent strategy for achieving a functional outcome.

However, as we saw in Chapter 4, many of emotion's interpersonal effects may operate in a more piece-meal manner without any need for top-down integration. For example, patterns of eye movement permit the pickup of functionally relevant visual information and signal to others where potentially significant events might be occurring (e.g., Parkinson, 2017) regardless of whether they are associated with a specific emotion. Further, a fixed stare shows the person at whom it is directed that they are the object of the source's attention and potential action. It can then serve as part of an interpersonal threat or challenge when combined with other facial movements. Similarly, pushing against an object is easily readable by others as an effortful attempt to displace it. Perhaps then, emotion's functionality partly depends on the separable functional effects of these lower-level facial and bodily processes.

The strongest and most consistent evidence that emotion components serve interpersonal functions relates to facial activity. Indeed, some of the interpersonal functions usually attributed to fully articulated emotions may be achieved purely by making a certain kind of facial movement. And the functional effects of that movement need not depend on any transmitted emotional meaning (Fridlund, 1994).

The interpersonal orientation of many facial movements is supported by evidence of their selective attunement to potential addressees (e.g., Kraut & Johnston, 1979; and see Chapter 3). Research into audience effects strongly suggests that the extent of facial activity depends on who else is around to pick up the signal (see Parkinson, 2005). The presence of an audience does not always intensify display, but amenable audiences with compatible motives usually do. Even implicit audiences can affect facial activity (Fridlund, 2001). Indeed, imagining an idealised addressee may elicit stronger facial displays than interacting directly with an unsympathetic audience. For example, we may show more pouting, help-seeking faces when we are on our own and thinking of parents or intimates than when telling a stranger how we feel face-to-face (e.g., Jakobs et al., 2001).

More direct evidence for the social functionality of facial movements may be obtained by following the same strategy used to demonstrate that discrete emotions are socially functional. In particular, researchers need to show that facial activity is attuned to the responses of the person at whom it is directed. For example, if a facial display appears when there is a direct possibility of communication and disappears when the message has been conveyed or when the addressee becomes unavailable, then this supports its socially functional orientation.

Research conducted by Bavelas and colleagues (1986) supports the first part of this prediction. Participants witnessed a staged accident in which a heavy TV monitor dropped onto the experimenter's already bandaged fingers. In one condition, the experimenter was directly facing the participant, allowing eye contact. In the other condition, the experimenter was positioned at right angles to the participant and turned away soon after the apparent injury. Participants in the eye-contact condition winced empathically in a way that capitalised on the interpersonal visibility of their display. In other words, their winces tended to increase in intensity up to the moment when they met the experimenter's gaze directly. In the condition without eye contact, wincing was either absent or died away when participants became aware that the experimenter was not looking in their direction. In short, participants' facial activity was precisely timed to take advantage of the responsiveness of the other person, thus demonstrating its interpersonal orientation.

Not all of the interpersonal functions served by facial movements depend on conveying specific emotional meanings (e.g., Crivelli & Fridlund, 2018). For example, differently configured smiles seem to serve distinctive functions regardless of whether they are directly related to happiness or other affective states. According to Martin, Rychlowska, Wood and Niedenthal's (2017) classification, affiliative smiles are characterised by upturned corners of lips that are pressed together, but do not include the eye-crinkling component of supposedly joyful Duchenne smiles. They are sometimes interpreted as 'polite' or even 'false' smiles (e.g., Ekman & Friesen, 1982; Shore & Heerey, 2011), but Martin and colleagues argue that their central function is to signal a willingness to interact accompanied by an absence of social threat. Although affiliative smiles may sometimes be associated with unpleasant-feeling emotions such as embarrassment (e.g., Keltner & Buswell, 1997), they may also be adopted simply for the purpose of facilitating social interaction.

How did facial movements acquire their capacity to exert functional influence on other people? Fridlund (1994) argues that their production and perception co-evolved for adaptive purposes. For example, facial cues associated with readiness to attack such as narrowed eyes and gritted teeth may have become progressively exaggerated over the course of natural selection because they tended to make antagonists back off from physical confrontation, thus increasing the chance that the source's genes are passed to later generations (ritualisation: e.g., Andrew, 1963). However, facial movements only provide an adaptive advantage to the extent that the people at whom they were directed are attuned to their presentation. It doesn't help to narrow your eyes and grit your teeth if no one notices what you are doing. It wouldn't be a display in the first place if it was never registered by anyone else. Thus, evolution of a functional communication system requires progressive perceptual attunement to increasingly ritualised facial displays and vice versa (co-adaptation: e.g., Kölliker, Brodie III & Moore, 2005).

Cultural learning is also capable of yielding comparable functional effects, perhaps even removing the need for any natural selection of ritualised displays (Tomasello & Call, 1997) or corresponding perceptual sensitivities. For example, caregivers implicitly model exaggerated facial movements for infants (Holodynski & Friedlmeier, 2006) and selectively direct their attention to relevant facial displays that are presented by other sources. Over the course of development then, children may become attuned to conventional facial signals and learn how to respond to them in socially functional ways. Effective communicative responses are further consolidated by cumulative practical experience of their unfolding consequences in real-time social interactions. Thus, natural selection, social learning and online adjustment may work together to produce a functionally effective set of facial signals and complementary attunements to those signals (see also Chapter 9).

Communicative Meaning and Force

As we have seen, emotions and emotion components often serve interpersonal functions by communicating appraisals and action tendencies. Anger directs blame at someone else, a fixed stare signals the direction of visual attention and poised tensing muscles indicate the specific behaviour that is being prepared. One way of understanding these processes is to argue that perceivers decode the semantic meaning of the source's expressions and behaviours and draw inferences about how best to respond (e.g., Hareli & Hess, 2010). However, this account does not fully capture the motivating power of emotion communication that is directed specifically at another person. A scowling face does not merely provide information that the source is appraising someone else as blameworthy, it also threatens negative consequences if the target does not respond by changing what they are doing. The emotion communication provides an interpersonal incentive (e.g., Keltner & Haidt, 1999) in the form of a warning or promise and not just a factual message. In other words, people don't usually make cold rational decisions about how they might respond to someone else's emotion. Instead, they are pushed or pulled in particular directions by the force of the other person's relational activity. As de Rivera and Grinkis (1986) put it: 'I may feel the "heat" of *your* anger' (p. 352). To cool things down, I may demonstrate my commitment to make amends by showing complementary guilt.

Conversational Demands

Emotional requests and commitments may be conveyed in words as well as by facial displays and bodily movements. Here too language may have pragmatic force as well as semantic meaning (see Chapter 2). Saying that I blame you or that I am angry with you may well activate representations of prototypic representations of blame or anger which allow you to predict what I might do and how best to react. However, an angry speech act also invokes norms and prescriptions about what kinds of reply are socially acceptable.

One way of understanding how verbal communications encourage rather than compel specific interpersonal responses draws on the idea of preference structures developed in the field of conversation analysis (e.g., Levinson, 1983). According to this account, speech acts are generally organised in two-part call-response sequences known as 'adjacency pairs' (Sacks, 1992). The first part serves to restrict the range of permissible responses that should be produced by the addressee in the second part. Thus, the appropriate response to a question is an answer, and the alternative relevant responses to an expressed judgement are agreement and disagreement.

When several possible responses to the first part of an adjacency pair are equally relevant, one of them is usually more normatively appropriate than others. For example, if I invite you to come to my party, accepting the invitation is the 'preferred' response (Pomerantz, 1984), meaning that an accepting reply can be delivered immediately and without equivocation. However, if you are unable or unwilling to accept, declining the invitation requires more conversational work (i.e., it is the 'dispreferred' option). Instead of responding immediately, you may pause, thereby signalling potential trouble and at the same time providing me with an opportunity to release you from any implied obligation to accept. Or you may present an elaborate excuse, apology or counter-offer. Just saying 'no' without marking your failure to cooperate with my expressed wishes would be neither polite (e.g., Brown & Levinson, 1987) nor felicitous (e.g., Austin, 1962).

When the first part of an adjacency pair presents the speaker's judgement, the preferred second part involves agreeing with that judgement (Levinson, 1983). Similarly, the preferred response to the appraisal communication conveyed by an emotional statement should endorse the communicated appraisal. Thus, if you say that you blame me for something I have done or that you are angry about it, my path of least interpersonal resistance is to acknowledge that I am to blame. Any attempt to counter or deflect your blame would be an appropriate but dispreferred option requiring further elaboration and effort on my part. In other words, the socially prescribed reply to an angry claim about my blame-worthiness is to apologise or communicate that I am feeling suitably guilty. Thus, a target-directed emotion communication tends to encourage a complementary emotional response.

The appraisals that are presented by emotional speech acts need not relate directly to the addressee. For example, you may instead tell me that you are angry about something that someone else has done. In these cases, the statement carries similar pragmatic force to a caregiver's directed facial display in a social referencing experiment. It encourages the target to align their orientation towards the emotion's object with the stance that is being taken by the source. Thus, communicated anger about a third party normatively constitutes an appeal for emotional corroboration either in the form of explicit agreement that the party acted illegitimately or shared anger about their conduct. In other words, an object-directed emotion communication tends to encourage a convergent emotional response from the addressee.

Clearly, appraising is not the only speech act that can be performed by emotion-related utterances (see Chapter 2). Words representing emotions can also convey threats, make commitments, request help and repair relationships. In all of these cases, engaging with the conversation commits you to a restricted range of possible responses, some of which involve less reparatory work than others. There are normative constraints on how people are supposed to be affected by other people's emotion communications.

Emotional Inflection

Even when speech acts involve no direct communication of emotion, delivering them in an emotional way may still support their conversational functions. For example, speakers are normatively entitled to repeat a delivered question persistently until an answer is provided. In many cases, a questioner may also reinforce the moral obligation to respond appropriately by increasing the levels of emphasis and clarity with which the message is delivered (e.g., 'Didn't you hear what I just said?'). This escalation of pragmatic pressure may additionally involve intensified presentation of any associated emotional incentives, conveyed by changes in the volume, tone and rhythm of the speaker's voice. The dangers of non-compliance are signalled by the speaker's evident readiness to take further action if necessary. The channels combine to convey the speaker's insistence that the topic of conversation is something that should be relevant to the addressee (e.g., Sperber & Wilson, 1986). The resulting interpersonal dynamics are analogous to those that characterise nonverbal interchanges where people cannot easily pick up each other's orientational cues. For example, similar processes seem to operate when a driver attempts to direct anger at another driver whose attention is focused elsewhere (Parkinson, 2001b).

Correspondingly, hearers may deliver emotion-related signals in order to sidestep any normative demand for a relevant response. They may storm out of the room (e.g., Evaldsson & Melander, 2017) or break down in tears (e.g., Hepburn & Potter, 2012; and see Chapter 2). In each case, the relational agenda is suspended, and the co-regulated rhythms of mutually entrained interaction are temporarily disrupted. Thus, emotion communication not only involves conforming to implicit conversational conventions but also unsettling those conventions when they become difficult to sustain. Indeed, most societies develop standardised functional procedures to deal with recurrent situations where the normal guidelines for social interactions need to be put on hold, and many of these procedures involve the deployment of emotional language and paralanguage (e.g., Averill, 1980).

The material presented in this section generally supports the argument that pragmatic emotion communication serves the function of social influence. Speakers persist with first-part requests until relevant responses are received, much like angry and embarrassed people maintain their emotion presentations until they get across to their targets or audiences. Correspondingly, the fact that addressees need to take special measures to avoid the normative requirements of speakers' conversational moves confirms that they are sensitive to the functional pragmatic demands being made on them. Finally, the ability to use nonverbal and verbal signals to suspend the usual conversational obligations clearly serves its own cultural functions.

Cultural Functions

Most theories explain the social functions of emotions in evolutionary terms (e.g., Fischer & Manstead, 2008; Keltner & Haidt, 1999). In their view, natural selection led humans to acquire emotions that served to promote survival, reproduction and inclusive fitness. However, gene transmission may also be served by providing cultural resources that permit the acquisition of socially functional emotions during a person's individual development. Indeed, the cultural variability of emotion syndromes (e.g., Parkinson, Fischer & Manstead, 2005; and see Chapters 2 and 3) suggests that inheriting environmental openness might be the best way of ensuring that socialised emotions are tailored to their specific ecological niches. Perhaps we inherit only the capacity and raw materials needed to develop culturally appropriate emotions (e.g., Parkinson, 2012).

One of the few writers to focus on the cultural factors that shape emotional function is Averill (e.g., 1980). His social constructionist theory not only addresses specific emotions, such as anger (Averill, 1982), love (Averill, 1985; Averill & Boothroyd, 1977), hope (Averill, Catlin & Chon, 1990) and grief (Averill & Nunley, 1988), but also provides a set of general principles explaining why societies provide us with emotions in the first place. From Averill's perspective, emotions are transitory social roles enacted when cultural norms come into conflict with each other. The function of emotions is to patch over tensions between competing pre-scriptions for behaviour. For example, Anglo-American societies socialise their members both to uphold justice and to avoid intentionally harming other people. In situations when someone else has committed a serious misdemeanour that affects you personally, you are therefore placed in a normative dilemma. If you simply let it pass, you have flouted the justice-upholding norm in a situation where it is most directly relevant to your own concerns. However, if you explicitly try to punish the other person, you have failed to follow the pacifistic norm.

Averill (1982) argues that cultural evolution has provided a strategy for finessing this problem. A third set of norms prescribing the performance of the angry role is designed specifically to escape the competing demands of retribution and pacifism. By getting angry, you can threaten retribution without taking the responsibility for the flouting of pacifistic norms otherwise implied by this action. Because your conduct is per-ceived both by you and the other person as performed out of anger rather than being premeditated, you need not take full responsibility for its consequences.

Over cultural history, the angry role has developed to meet the norma-tive requirements of situations such as this; conforming to its prescrip-tions allows people to be perceived as unhappily angry rather than maliciously aggressive. I shout at you because my socialised desire for fairness means that I cannot let what you did stand unopposed, but my shouting is *angry* shouting because to attack you deliberately would be unacceptable in my society.

Averill's theory implies that emotions may bring short-term positive advantage at the expense of more negative longer-term societal out-comes. They shore up calcified prescriptions or practices that are mutually contradictory when exposing their tensions might bring more productive consequences in the distant future. For example, the historic development of the ideal of romantic love may have helped insulate a specific relational context from surrounding institutional arrangements that otherwise attach little value to self-expression of any kind (Averill & Boothroyd, 1977). People came to believe that they could only practise their authentic individuality in private with a single other person, and

that the identity they adopted in more public spheres of life was fundamentally detached and alienated. Arguably, a more radical means of
reconfiguring relational possibilities might have yielded less regressive
societal consequences. More generally, culturally functional emotions are
not usually conducive to social progress or political change. They encourage a mystificatory false consciousness that conceals the true ideological
purpose of our actions and prevents us from questioning the current
status quo (e.g., Lukács, 1971).

Conclusions

Emotions serve social functions by aligning relations between people or
reconfiguring their respective orientations to objects and events. Indeed,
many social emotions are specifically attuned to their effects on other
people, coming into play when particular interpersonal concerns become
apparent, intensifying if interpersonal feedback suggests that those concerns have not been addressed and terminating once their interpersonal
purpose is fulfilled.

Emotions achieve their interpersonal functions by communicating
appraisals and indicating action tendencies to other people, affording
complementary responses from them, and providing direct incentives that encourage cessation or continuation of their actions
(Keltner & Haidt, 1999). All three of these alternative operations
can be performed by separable emotion components such as facial
or postural movements rather than fully coordinated emotional
response patterns. Correspondingly, emotional speech acts can influence other people either because of their semantic content or pragmatic force.

Although emotion's social functionality depends on resources
acquired by natural selection, these resources only come together during
cultural socialisation as children learn how their movements and attentional adjustments bring consistent and meaningful effects on caregivers
and others. This also means that humans can acquire culturally and
historically specific forms of emotional orientation and communication
that fit with the normative ideals and prevalent practices of their local
cultural and historical context.

Adopting a social functional perspective does not imply that emotions
always produce beneficial social consequences (e.g., Parrott, 2001). After
all, tactics and strategies that work most of the time also sometimes fail,
and those that solve immediate problems occasionally cause more lasting
damage. In some cases, emotions or their components may even be
dysfunctional byproducts of other functional activities. Or they may
once have served purposes that long since ceased to apply (Darwin,

1872). However, emotions continue to adjust and adapt to the natural and cultural environments in which they operate. Historical forms such as accidie and melancholy (Harré & Finlay-Jones, 1986) may become increasingly irrelevant to contemporary concerns and fall into disuse while new relational positions such as transphobia and technostress emerge and develop to meet changing subcultural or societal needs. Humans find alternative ways of communicating and enacting relational orientations as words, tools and technologies develop. Not everything works immediately or under all circumstances and progress can be erratic or misdirected, but we continue to learn, develop and adjust. Many of the emotions we enact or improvise end up affecting other people just as they were supposed to do.

CHAPTER 7

Groups, Teams and Crowds

Emotions not only affect other people individually but also help to form and consolidate wider social alliances or divisions. This chapter focuses on emotion's effects and functions in group life and on how interpersonal processes might scale up to produce collective outcomes. Ingroup members' emotions signal their shared or distinct social identities and communicate relevant group norms, as well as aligning intragroup relations more directly. Mutual entrainment of movements may be facilitated by temporally structured interaction rituals, and joint participation in collective action can reinforce a sense of efficacy and shared purpose. Emotions not only align relations within groups but also between them. Like interpersonally targeted emotions, intergroup emotions are often attuned to actual or anticipated responses from their targets and respond directly to emotional feedback from the outgroups at which they are directed. Many theorists explain these social-functional outcomes by reference to single-minded processes of self-categorisation and group-based appraisal, paying relatively less attention to the relation-aligning consequences of the collective enactment of identities. However, group emotions make most sense when grounded and contextualised in processes of group mobilisation and intergroup exchange.

Have you ever shouted at the TV? Imagine some politician spinning the official line on any current controversy. They try to tell you that things are not what they seem, that the statistics about climate change, economic progress or social inequality are distorted or otherwise misleading, that the government has had to make difficult decisions under challenging circumstances. Or that we're only in this situation because of the mess left by the previous administration. None of it is ever their fault. And according to them, things are nowhere near as bad as they blatantly are.

What's the point of getting angry under these circumstances? How could the message ever get through? The glass separating you is not like a car window that you can wind down so that they feel the force of your rage. The target of your blame is in some secure studio miles away even if the interview is live rather than recorded. It's not like you'll ever meet up face to face.

241

But even in direct interactions, anger is not only about influencing the person you're angry with. It's also about taking a position with respect to whatever they are doing or representing, emphasising its offensive quality. And often other people are around to see how much you care about it. Anger can align you against another person or group, but it can also align you with people who are inclined to share your orientation.

Some of us let off steam about things we see or read even when we are on our own. But even then, we probably have half a mind to share our feelings with whoever might happen along. It certainly feels validating and empowering if someone else gets angry about the issue too. And even in a solitary situation, our anger may involve the sense of being part of a wider community of like-minded, right-thinking people united by a shared sense of indignation, all lined up in opposition to anyone who dares resist our unanimous stance out of stupidity, malice or bare-faced self-interest. Together, we feel ready to do what it takes to make a difference, by engaging in contestation or more direct forms of action.

It's tempting to believe that some media-savvy politicians have started to do or say outrageous things precisely to provoke angry reactions from viewers like you and me. The collective ire they encourage among certain sectors of the electorate helps them define and reinforce social boundaries. It permits their misguided allies to identify their own distinctive position in direct contrast to ours. And it gives them warrant to get righteously angry in return, spitting bile under the pretence of telling it how it is. And so the collective finger-pointing escalates. Next come the sticks, stones and ballistic missiles. There are no winners when the politics of hate take hold.

As all of these examples suggest, emotions operate in a wider sphere of social relations than time-limited one-to-one interactions. Their effects and functions spill out into collective intergroup and political life. This chapter addresses these more inclusive social arenas starting from the bottom up.

Social Identification

At one level, a group is simply a collection of people. Thus, the human race, the population of China, a football squad, the people attending a meeting and a nuclear family all constitute groups of one kind or another. Obviously, there are differences in how emotions operate in each of these groups. But are there also common principles? Are the features that make any group a group important considerations in understanding emotions and their social influence?

In social psychology, the most influential approach to groups is based on Tajfel and Turner's (1979) social identity theory and its direct descendants, most notably Turner and colleagues' (1987) self-categorisation theory. The central assumption of these theories is that seeing yourself as a member of a group changes your perceptions of other members of the same group (ingroup members) and of people belonging to different groups (outgroup members). Group members start to perceive other ingroup members as more similar to them and outgroup members as more different (outgroup distinctiveness) but more similar to one another (outgroup homogeneity, e.g., Jones, Wood & Quattrone, 1981).

Some of these effects are thought to be direct consequences of mere categorisation (e.g., Tajfel & Wilkes, 1963). They are analogous to shifts in perception of colour when green transitions to blue. Chromatic stimuli with small differences in electromagnetic wavelength are seen as more different when they span the boundary between distinct regions of the spectrum than when they are both on the same side of that boundary (e.g., Bornstein, Kessen & Weiskopf, 1976). Similarly, someone may be perceived as more different from you when you categorise them as belonging to a different group (e.g., Taylor et al., 1978), and someone may be perceived as more similar when they share your social identity.

In addition to social perception, self-categorisation also biases judgement and behaviour so that the ingroup is treated more positively and the outgroup more negatively. Group members want to see their own group as distinctive from, and superior to, other groups on identity-related dimensions, and make decisions that support this positive distinctiveness. For example, classic studies using the 'minimal group paradigm' (Tajfel et al., 1971) demonstrate that simply being assigned to an ad hoc group based on arbitrary criteria (such as supposed preference for art by Klee or Kandinsky) leads participants to allocate resources more to their own group than an outgroup even when this leads to lower overall ingroup benefit (e.g., Billig & Tajfel, 1973).

Perceptions of ingroup and outgroup members' emotions can differ too. Ingroup bias already implies that outgroup members should be seen as having less positively valued emotions than ingroup members. However, some researchers argue that the devaluation of outgroup emotions is sometimes more than merely a matter of degree. According to this infrahumanisation hypothesis, distinctively human emotions are often reserved solely for the ingroup. By contrast, members of certain outgroups are perceived as capable of experiencing only 'basic' emotions that are shared by both humans and animals (e.g., Leyens et al., 2000; 2001).

Our perceptions of outgroup capacities and characteristics also carry implications for the way we interpret and respond to their behaviour. If we anticipate less sophisticated emotional reactions, then we are likely to present our own relational orientation in different and potentially more antagonistic ways (Parkinson, Fischer & Manstead, 2005). For example, we may use aggression to provoke fear instead of trying to encourage outgroup members to accept their collective guilt and engage in reparation. Outgroup bias might thus produce an escalating spiral of reciprocal hostility. However, infrahumanisation is certainly not an automatic or inevitable consequence of outgroup bias. For example, men usually do not deny women's capacities to experience non-basic emotions even in explicitly gender-related contexts (e.g., Viki & Abrams, 2003).

Although social identity approaches emphasise the importance of collective aspects of social life (e.g., Turner & Oakes, 1986), their explanations of group effects mainly rely on processes operating at the level of individual cognition (e.g., Jahoda, 1989; Tetlock, 1986). The focus is on how people perceive and categorise themselves and other people in terms of group allegiances rather than the actual relations between groups and their members, making it seem as if groups are mainly inside people's heads rather than outside in the dynamic social world. Indeed, self-categorisation theory implies that a group can be brought into existence simply by changing people's perceptions of their similarities with other people.

Such an approach makes the world of groups a shifting and indeterminate realm. There are always a range of identities available for anyone to adopt. At any particular time, I may be thinking of myself as a human, an Englishman, someone over six feet tall, a Manchester United supporter, an Oxford University professor or someone queuing for stamps at the post office. Or I may consider myself to be uncertain about my identity as masculine or androgynous, heterosexual, middle class, middle-aged or none of the above. When any of these possible social selves becomes salient, it changes the way I relate to others who share or do not share my current self-categorisation. And all this may happen independent of any structural relations with or against other people and groups depending on social inequality, access to resources, or physical location within the environment.

One advantage of this proposed flexibility is that it makes it easy to manipulate group membership in experimental studies. Indeed, one reason for the continuing popularity of the self-categorisation approach is that it fits well with standard social psychological paradigms. However, as we shall see, researchers are increasingly testing the limits of these paradigms by exploring how groups operate in the hurly burly of real-time contact and conflict outside the laboratory.

Group-Based Appraisal

If social identity changes perceptions and judgements about people and events, it should also affect emotion-related appraisals. Appraisal theories argue that emotions depend on perceiving what is happening as relevant to personal concerns (e.g., Lazarus, 1991a; and see Chapter 1). Unless what is happening makes a difference to what we want for ourselves, there is nothing to get emotional about. However, we clearly have a personal stake in other people's lives, so emotions do not always need to depend on direct self-relevance.

Groups of other people matter to us too. We care about whether the team or political party we support wins, loses or otherwise prospers or suffers, and our emotions respond accordingly. According to Eliot Smith's (1993) influential account of group emotions, this happens because their successes and failures are relevant to a currently salient social identity. We appraise things as congruent or incongruent with the goals of the groups we identify with, and this leads to group-based emotional responses (Smith, Seger & Mackie, 2007).

Supporting this account, several studies have shown that group members respond emotionally to events that affect other members of their group, even when those events do not affect them personally in any direct way. For example, Yzerbyt and colleagues (2003) presented Belgian students with a concocted news report implying that another Belgian university was planning to deliver advanced teaching purely in the English language. Participants who were encouraged to see themselves as part of the national student population (and who identified more strongly with this generic student identity) reported being more angry and more inclined to intervene than those who were encouraged to see themselves as students of their own particular university. In other words, emotional reactions to events affecting other people depended on the relative salience of a shared social identity.

Kuppens and colleagues (2013) collected more direct evidence about group-based appraisals by asking participants to list their thoughts about identity-relevant issues. Making the social identity of 'student' salient again tended to increase anger about the imposition of the English language for advanced teaching (at least among participants who believed that the proposed change was a bad thing). Further, this effect depended on participants' thoughts about student-related concerns.

Instead of targeting identity salience, Doosje and colleagues' (1998) experimental study of group-based guilt manipulated perceptions of personal and ingroup responsibility for an intergroup transgression. Participants were presented with bogus information about the degree of outgroup bias shown by themselves and by other members of their group. Group-based guilt was significantly lower when participants believed that neither they nor their group had been biased than when they believed that their group had been biased, but that they personally had not been. In other words, guilt seems to be a possible reaction to misbehaviour committed by other members of your ingroup even when you are not personally responsible. Doosje and colleagues argue that similar principles apply to a nation's collective guilt about crimes committed by previous generations (e.g., German guilt about Nazi atrocities, or British guilt about colonial exploitation: see also Branscombe & Doosje, 2004).

Group-Based Emotions

The findings presented so far show that closer identification with a particular group tends to make people more emotional about events that are relevant to that group's concerns. Analogous effects also seem to apply when people feel closer to other people for reasons other than shared group membership. As parents, we often feel angry about things that happen to our children or guilty about things our children have done. Similarly, we don't like it when our friends suffer or when they do things we don't personally approve of. It can even be embarrassing to watch the protagonist of a movie caught in an awkward social situation. Standard appraisal theory can deal with all these examples of vicarious or empathic emotion simply by acknowledging that many of people's goals and concerns relate to other people (e.g., Wondra & Ellsworth, 2015). The extent to which someone else matters to us for whatever reason determines the motivational relevance of their experienced outcomes and our emotional response to those outcomes.

Is there any need for a separate kind of appraisal that applies specifically when people are close to us because of their shared group membership? Does it make a real difference when events are relevant to social identity rather than personal identity, even if the self whose concerns are being appraised is a relational self in the first place (Andersen & Chen, 2002)? A number of theorists have answered both of these questions in the affirmative (e.g., Kuppens et al., 2013). Indeed, it is often argued not only that group-based appraisals operate according to different principles but also that the group-based emotions they produce are qualitatively different from individual or interpersonal emotions.

Smith, Seger and Mackie (2007) specifically distinguished group emotions from individual emotions based on their role in regulating group-related behaviour as well as their association with group identification. In their study, participants were asked to rate how strongly they experienced various emotions when thinking of themselves as an individual and as a member of various groups based on nationality, university membership and political affiliation. Different profiles of emotion were reported for these different contexts, suggesting that emotions experienced when a social identity is salient may be distinct from those experienced when operating individually. However, different emotion profiles were also reported for each of the sampled social identities suggesting that it may be the specific relational context that is important rather than the fact that a group context was specified more generally. Presumably, people would also be likely to report different emotion profiles when at work or at home, and when performing a number of different individual activities such as eating, sleeping, or driving. So what makes the group dimension special?

One answer concerns the degree to which group-based emotions are shared across group members. In Smith, Seger and Mackie's study, there was greater cross-participant similarity between the emotion profiles relating to social identities than between those reported for individual experiences. Further, the extent to which participants identified with the relevant social identity determined how similar their emotion profile was to profiles reported by other group members. In other words, group members seem to respond similarly to group-relevant events especially when they identify strongly with their group. This may mean that they are more susceptible to a genuinely collective emotional experience when in direct contact with one another. From a relation-alignment perspective, emotions arising in group contexts reflect alliances and antipathies operating at a wider scale than applies to interpersonal interactions. As we shall see, this can certainly make a difference to how emotional episodes play out, and how imagined and actual responses from other people shape their progress. However, that does not necessarily mean that we require different theoretical principles to make sense of them.

Smith and colleagues' (2007) methods specifically encouraged participants to make clear distinctions between individual and group emotions. However, such a stark contrast rarely applies in everyday life (de Rivera, 2014). When people think about their emotions in less rarefied contexts, they hardly ever restrict themselves to purely individual experiences. Emotions relating to family members, lovers, friends and enemies are likely to feature heavily. The question therefore arises of how these relational emotions might fit into the individual–group dichotomy.

Asking people to report emotions they experience when thinking of themselves as individuals is problematic not only because emotions rarely, if ever, occur outside of any relational context, but also because people don't usually explicitly consider their personal identity before experiencing an individual emotion. Mostly they just react directly to the concern that has arisen. Smith and colleagues' instructions therefore cue people to unrepresentative instances of individual emotion that specifically depend on a sense of personal idiosyncrasy or identity salience. This makes it less surprising that their profiles tend to be distinctive and idiosyncratic too.

Intragroup Interaction

Investigating groups purely on the basis of a person's individual social identification has obvious limits. If thinking of yourself as a group member in private can affect your emotions, what happens when you actually come into contact with other members of your group who also think of themselves in similar ways? Does direct engagement with unfolding group interactions supplant, intensify or otherwise transform the emotional effects of social identification?

All of the forms of interpersonal emotional influence considered in Chapter 4 potentially extend into group contexts. The emotional reactions of other ingroup members can guide appraisals of what is happening, entrain embodied orientations or activate regulatory norms. What difference does being part of a shared group make to these processes? As the number of influence agents increases, interpersonal effects might well get stronger, especially when those agents all share a common perspective and purpose with the target of influence. But does this produce a qualitative or merely quantitative difference?

Social theorists have debated the concept of a 'group mind' for more than a century (e.g., Durkheim, 1893). Discussions revolve around whether it makes sense to talk about a collective mentality that operates at a deeper, wider or higher level than individual thought and interpersonal dialogue. If so, what would that mean for collective emotionality? Does the fact that more than two people share similar evaluative orientations to the same thing at the same time transform what is happening at the emotional level? Do the outcomes require different explanatory principles?

Social identification itself cannot provide a sufficient basis for any qualitative shift from personal to collective processes for the two reasons considered earlier. First, adopting a social identity is a private cognitive change carrying only indirect implications for group life. Second, the self is a fundamentally relational entity in the first place making any transition to a group-based identity seem less dramatic and extreme anyway (de Rivera, 2014; Swann et al., 2012).

What then makes group-based emotional influence different from other forms of interpersonal influence? One possibility is that the social exchanges taking place in group contexts have a different character to those that occur in purely dyadic situations. Members of groups who interact with one another often influence more than one other person at a time, and the other people they influence exert reciprocal influence in return. A situation of emotional resonance (e.g., Durkheim, 1912) may thus develop when multi-directional emotional influence bounces back and forth around the group, yielding collective outcomes that are greater than the sum of their individual and interpersonal parts.

Group-Based Social Appraisal

As we have seen, group-based appraisal involves assessing the relevance of events for a salient social identity. For example, thinking of yourself as a student makes student-related concerns more motivationally relevant and emotionally charged (Yzerbyt et al., 2003). In group-based *social* appraisal, knowing how other group members react to events affects your own appraisal and emotional reaction. Their emotional response tells you how the group appraises whatever is happening, instead of you working it out purely by yourself. In other words, the effect depends on observed reactions of other group members rather than your own private registration of group relevance.

This form of emotional influence need not involve direct interaction between group members. You may find out by other means what other members of your group think and feel. For example, a group leader's mission statement may be circulated by email or as a web-based announcement and still set the emotional tone for followers. Similarly, indirect communications from other ingroup members without any special hierarchical position or status can also reduce intergroup prejudice. For example, simply being told that a member of your group is friends with an outgroup member can increase your own positive feelings towards the outgroup to which they belong (e.g., Wright et al., 1997). However, such an effect may be more compelling and powerful when you are directly exposed to the ingroup member's behaviour and can observe their unfolding emotional reactions during the encounter (e.g., van der Schalk et al., 2015). In other words, perhaps vicarious intergroup contact is more powerful than indirect, non-visual contact.

Only a few studies have assessed the prejudice-reducing effects of vicarious contact. Mazziotta, Mumendey and Wright (2011) found that German students who watched videos of another German student having a friendly conversation with a Chinese student subsequently felt warmer towards Chinese people (see also Ioannou, Al-Ramiah & Hewstone, 2017). The effect was mediated by participants' increased feelings of self-efficacy about intergroup interaction. Mazziotta and colleagues concluded that observing someone similar to the self successfully dealing with a potentially difficult social situation showed participants how they might be able to do the same thing themselves. In other words, vicarious learning explained the findings. However, group-based social appraisal might also have been a contributory factor. Just as a toddler finds out that a visual cliff is safe by observing the caregiver's happy demeanour (Sorce et al., 1985), participants in Mazziotta and colleagues' study apparently inferred that Chinese people were less threatening after watching an ingroup member's relaxed conversation.

What happens when the ingroup's appraisals are communicated by more than one other group member? What if they can interact freely instead of being observed remotely, thus allowing reciprocal operation of social appraisal processes? Kuppens and colleagues (2013) presented Belgian participants with a bogus news story suggesting that the sister of the late Belgian singer-songwriter Jacques Brel had decided to donate his belongings to a museum in France rather than Belgium. Subsequent group discussion of this issue led to more indignation than did discussion of differences between traditional and contemporary French chanson. Further, group differences in indignation depended on the opinions participants reported expressing during the discussion. Participants who made negative comments that referred to national concerns tended to report greater indignation and anger. In a related study by Yzerbyt, Kuppens and Mathieu (2016), self-reported appraisals of fairness specifically mediated the emotional effects of discussion. In other words, a process of group-based social appraisal apparently intensified emotional responses towards a group-relevant issue.

Analogous effects also occur in studies of group polarisation (Moscovici & Zavalloni, 1969), where attitudes and opinions tend to become more extreme following discussion with like-minded people. For example, when people are favourably disposed to taking an action that is potentially costly, talking about it together can make that decision more likely (the so-called 'risky shift': Stoner, 1961; see Wallach, Kogan & Bem, 1962). Thus, gamblers in Blascovich, Ginsburg and Howe's (1975) study bet more of their own money on a blackjack game when playing with other gamblers than when playing alone.

Three broad explanations have been proposed for group polarisation. The first depends on participants pooling a range of alternative arguments for the view that they all hold. The chances are that another member of your group will provide you with new reasons for holding your own opinion, thereby strengthening it (e.g., persuasive arguments theory: Lamm & Myers, 1978). Even repetition of the same argument may increase its apparent effects (Brauer & Judd, 1996). However, group polarisation also occurs when participants are simply told of other people's initial positions without knowing what their reasons for taking those positions might be (e.g., Myers, Bach & Schreiber, 1974), so factors other than repetition and argument strength must also play a role.

The second explanation depends on the motivation to see yourself as better than other people (self-enhancement: Sedikides & Strube, 1997). Finding out that other people share similar opinions leads you to doubt your own positive distinctiveness and makes you want to move further in the direction that you value. In other words, polarisation results from a process of interpersonal comparison in which people ramp up the intensity of their views so that they stand out from others (Sanders & Baron, 1977).

The third explanation argues that group-based social comparisons are also involved in polarisation effects (e.g., Turner, 1991). The expressed opinions of ingroup members provide information about the group's norms as well as about your own position in relation to those norms (referent informational influence). Not only do you want to be a better representative of your group than other ingroup members, but also you want your group to have a distinctive position in relation to rival groups (Brewer, 1991). To emphasise your own position as a prototypical member of a distinctive group, you shift your view so that it is more extreme than the apparent consensus (Turner, Wetherell & Hogg, 1989). If all group members adjust their positions for similar reasons, then the group prototype may continue to shift, and continue to induce further adjustments.

Positive group distinctiveness should only motivate attitude change for participants who identify with the group (Turner, 1991). Several studies support this prediction. For example, Mackie and Cooper (1984) found that participants who had listened to a tape-recorded discussion shifted their own attitudes towards the group norm when they believed that they were about to join the group of discussants, but not when they believed they were about to compete with the group. Similarly, Mackie (1986) found that polarisation only occurred when participants were encouraged to focus on group performance rather than individual performance. In other words, having a shared and salient social identity seems to be a necessary condition for group polarisation effects.

The same processes that contribute to group polarisation of attitudes probably also play a role in producing polarised appraisals and emotions. Analogous to the effects of argument strength, other people's apparent emotional orientations can draw our attention to previously unregistered aspects of objects or events, potentially intensifying our emotional reactions. For example, other fans' shouts and disapproving stares directed at the player of an opposing football team whose foul against your team's star striker remained undetected by the referee may lead you to reappraise what happened yourself. Perhaps you started out being unsure about whether the challenge was unfair or malicious but other supporters' reactions changed your perspective. In situations such as this, other group members' orientations not only affect your appraisals of what is happening but also the value that you attach to taking a particular relational stance. You may end up expressing even stronger disapproval because you want to be closer to the ingroup norm and further away from the outgroup position (referent informational influence).

The studies reviewed so far suggest that other group members' expressed appraisals and emotions provide information and incentives for bringing your own emotions into line with group norms. In most cases, the experimenters specifically established a shared identity by manipulating a group-relevant topic of discussion or an explicit inter-group context. But perhaps shared emotions can themselves provide a basis for a common social identification in contexts where the bound-aries between groups are less obvious. For example, we may be unsure about another person's political allegiance until we see how they react emotionally to public pronouncements by spokespeople from rival parties.

Livingstone and colleagues (2016) manipulated information about the emotions expressed by other students in response to a supposed proposal to toughen the marking of university assignments and exams as a way of dealing with the problem of grade inflation. Angrier participants were more likely to see themselves as sharing a social identity with other participants who appeared to be similarly angry about this proposal. They were also more inclined to select those participants as work-mates on a subsequent task. These effects of 'emotional fit' (Livingstone et al., 2011) did not simply depend on shared attitudes because other partici-pants who were presented as equally disapproving but not similarly angry were selected as work-mates relatively less often. Thus, observed emotions provide social information that helps us to define group boundaries (Oakes, 1987), leading to alignment with some people and against others.

Livingstone and colleagues' findings suggest that group-based social appraisal need not begin with a shared self-categorisation. Instead, peo-ple arrive at convergent orientations as a result of negotiation with other potential group members. Mutual influence may develop in parallel with a growing sense of identification, with both processes reciprocally influ-encing one another. Porat and colleagues (2015) presented data addition-ally suggesting that people may explicitly up-regulate group-endorsed emotions in order to feel more strongly that they belong with the group. In their research, the measured or manipulated need to belong to the Israeli national group predicted the extent to which participants reported wanting to feel sadness on Memorial Day. Whether such intragroup instrumental emotion regulation was intended to enhance an internal sense of identification or to demonstrate public conformity to group norms is difficult to determine. However, in either case, the intragroup functions of shared emotions seem to be explicitly recognised by group members, who may exploit them for their own and the group's advantage even when that makes them feel worse in the short term.

Intragroup Contagion

Group-based social appraisal involves alignment of group members' orientations towards group-relevant objects and events, leading to emotional convergence. The idea of intragroup contagion (like emotion contagion more generally: see Chapter 4) is that emotions spread more directly between people who are together, regardless of where those emotions are directed. For contagion to occur, it should not matter whether group members' emotions are focused on common concerns. Simply being with other people who are happy should make you feel happier too. Intragroup affective transfer of this kind may be mediated by processes of behavioural mimicry (e.g., Chartrand & Bargh, 1999), embodied simulation of other group members' emotions (e.g., Niedenthal et al., 2010) or entrainment of bodily movements (e.g., McGrath & Kelly, 1986) operating during periods of close contact between people.

Perhaps the clearest evidence for multi-person affective transfer of this kind was provided by Barsade (2002). In her study, participants played the role of managers who each made their case for awarding a bonus to a specific nominated employee during a simulated team meeting. Unbeknownst to participants, the first person to take their turn in the discussion was a male drama student serving as a confederate of the experimenter. This confederate adopted one of four emotional styles involving pleasant or unpleasant affect combined with either high or low energy. For example, in high-energy conditions, the confederate made frequent eye contact, spoke with a strong voice and sat straight in his chair, and in pleasure conditions, he smiled frequently. Participants' self-reported and video-coded affective state improved most in conditions where the confederate presented pleasant affect (regardless of the manipulated level of energy). In other words, the valence of participants' emotional reactions tended to converge with the confederate's expressed affect over the course of the discussion. Participants' task performance was also superior in this pleasure condition.

What process accounts for these findings? Primitive emotion contagion might be one alternative. However, it is also possible that the confederate's initial presentation set the general affective tone for subsequent presentations and discussion. Participants may simply have followed the confederate's lead and therefore approached the task from either a positive or negative perspective. Arguably, then, the confederate may simply have established an affective norm to which participants subsequently oriented (Barsade & Gibson, 1998; Delvaux, Vanbeselaere & Mesquita, 2015). If so, the results are analogous to those obtained in studies demonstrating that a leader's affective style impacts on group affect and performance (e.g., Sy, Côté & Saavedra, 2005; van Kleef et al.,

2010; and see Chapter 8). Alternatively, exposure to a smiling and apparently happy confederate may simply have created a more pleasant experience for participants.

There are also questions about whether Barsade's reported effects genuinely arose from group processes rather than interpersonal ones. The findings do not tell us whether the confederate's nonverbal behaviour produced a cascade of reciprocal ripples or merely a parallel set of effects that operated independently on each of the other individuals in the group. Although the group's affect changed in the direction of the confederate's expressed affect by the end of the discussion, no evidence was provided about how group members influenced each other's affect over the course of the interaction. In order to address this limitation, it is necessary to track processes of emotional convergence at multiple time points (e.g., Delvaux et al., 2015).

Several other studies have also shown that the affective states of people working as teams are often interlinked (e.g., Bartel & Saavedra, 2000; George, 1990; Totterdell, 2000; Totterdell et al., 1998). For example, Totterdell (2000) found that players on the same professional cricket team tended to share similar levels of happiness at different stages of a four-day match. The aggregated affective state of the team at each time point predicted individual players' affect, which in turn affected performance in the game. Team members who reported higher levels of susceptibility to emotion contagion (Hatfield et al., 1994) were affected relatively more by other players' affective states, supporting the operation of direct affect transfer. Further, affective similarity between players on each team could not be fully explained either by commonly experienced hassles or levels of playing performance during the match, suggesting that contact with other team members rather than convergent processes of social appraisal led to the reported emotional influence.

Although Totterdell's study provides a compelling example of emotional convergence when team members work together over extended periods, the realistic setting did not permit manipulation or control of all potentially influential variables. This means that the findings cannot prove that other unmeasured aspects of team functioning such as team coordination or collective flow (e.g., Csíkszentmihályi, 1990; Páez et al., 2015) did not lead to the convergence in happiness and the effects on performance.

Another common limitation of studies of shared group affect (like studies of emotion contagion more generally: see Chapter 4) arises from their focus on general pleasure or displeasure rather than specific pleasant or unpleasant emotions (Barsade & Gibson, 2012). Arguably, the intragroup transfer of more focused relational orientations necessarily requires more than simple contagion. A few studies have assessed how specific emotions might spread through groups. For example, Duffy and Shaw (2000) aggregated ratings of envy directed at other team members by students working together on extended projects and found that group scores predicted the degree of social loafing. More envious teams tended to have members who spent more time letting others do the work. However, the investigators did not control for individual-level effects of envy, again making it uncertain whether this reported effect reflected genuinely group-based processes.

Emotion Norms

Delvaux, Vanbeselaere and Mesquita (2015) conducted a more rigorous longitudinal study of specific emotions experienced by student work groups preparing an assessed assignment during a full university semester. Participants completed online questionnaires on four separate occasions marked by key points in the progress of their joint projects. These questionnaires included ratings of the intensity of anger and gratitude towards other members of the group during the periods of collaboration. Delvaux and colleagues also assessed emotion norms by asking participants how desirable and appropriate it had been to experience anger and gratitude while working with other group members.

Team members' levels of anger and gratitude converged to produce greater intragroup emotional similarity as the project reached completion. Further, the anger and gratitude experienced by the group as a whole at each time point predicted group members' individual levels of each of these emotions at the subsequent time point (even after controlling for the previous individual-level score), suggesting that participants were influenced by their earlier sense of how the group generally felt about what was happening. Correspondingly, individual-level emotion influenced subsequent group-level emotion. This pattern of findings is consistent with the proposal that group members' emotions influence each other, but again provides no direct evidence for the operation of contagion. Instead, it seems possible that angry group members simply provoked angry reactions from other group members whereas grateful group members tended to solicit reciprocated gratitude.

Delvaux and colleagues also showed that emotion norms contributed to their reported effects. Beliefs that anger and gratitude were desirable and appropriate predicted reported levels of these emotions at the next time-point, suggesting that participants regulated their emotions to match perceived norms. These norms in turn seemed to depend on the emotions experienced at the previous time-point, suggesting that group members learn which emotions are appropriate by observing other group members' responses. However, anger, gratitude and their perceived

desirability and appropriateness probably also depended on how collaborative work on the project was progressing. Participants probably got
more angry and felt that it was more desirable to be angry when other
team members were not pulling their weight or when their contributions
to the project were of low quality. Correspondingly, the experience and
perceived appropriateness of gratitude may well have reflected positive
input from other group members. If unmeasured processes relating to
collaboration and work progress drove both emotions and emotion
norms, it is hard to estimate the more direct relations between these
factors. In all likelihood, emotional orientations to progress became
more aligned over the course of group interactions producing emergent
norms about their appropriateness. However, the extent to which these
processes operated independently of what was happening at a more
practical level cannot easily be determined from the reported data.

Anger and gratitude directly contrast along dimensions of valence and
interpersonal appraisal. This means that any factor affecting either emotion is likely to have an opposite effect on the other. Consequently, some
of the apparently emotion-specific effects reported in Delvaux and colleagues' (2015) study may in fact have depended on general levels of
pleasure or positive interpersonal attitudes. Delvaux, Meeussen and
Mesquita (2016) dealt with this problem in two subsequent studies that
assessed two different forms of the same pleasant emotion, pride, specifically pride about the self and pride about the work group to which the
student belonged. If emotion convergence depends on primitive contagion, then pride's group-relevance should not make a difference.
However, if group members use emotions to calibrate their orientations
to group-relevant objects and events, then only levels of group-related
pride should converge over time. Supporting the latter explanation,
Delvaux and colleagues (2016) obtained convergent effects for group-
pride but not self-pride similar to those found for anger and gratitude
in the earlier study. Study 2 also showed that higher-status group members exerted greater emotional influence than lower-status group members, consistent with the idea that they play more of a role in setting
emotion norms for group-relevant emotions. As in the earlier study, the
unmeasured relationship between group pride and project progress
raises some interpretational issues, but the cross-lagged emotion-
specific effects still seem promising.

Beyond Contagion

None of the research showing that affect and emotions can spread within
groups specifically supports a contagion-based account. Although some
studies show that affect sharing is not fully explained by common

exposure to emotion-relevant events (e.g., Totterdell, 2000), they still provide no positive evidence that effects are mediated by mimicry or mutual entrainment. Investigators rarely assess alternative mediators such as emergent emotion norms which play a demonstrable role when appropriate measures are included (Delvaux et al., 2015). Further, the fact that effects only apply to group-relevant emotions suggests that it may be shared orientation to events rather than shared undirected affect that is driving convergence (Delvaux et al., 2016). Rather than primitive emotion contagion, an implicit form of collective relation alignment, analogous to more explicit group-based social appraisal, may be the most important underlying process.

Some studies suggest that group members' facial movements tend to converge in a similar way to their more general emotional orientations. For example, Bourgeois and Hess (2008) found that participants selectively mimicked ingroup but not outgroup facial activity associated with negative emotions. By adopting a similar expression to someone else, the mimicker conveys empathy or solidarity with them (e.g., Bavelas et al., 1986; Hess & Fischer, 2013, and see Chapter 4), which may be counterproductive in intergroup contexts when antagonistic displays may lead to retaliation. In intragroup contexts, by contrast, mutual mimicry may help to establish a shared relational orientation which produces emotional convergence without the need for any contagion-related internal feedback process.

Entrainment and Temporal Coordination

When people are close to one another in a shared space, they are often acutely sensitive to the movements and expressions of the other people around them. These nonverbal signals enable them to coordinate their activities over time. The resulting interpersonal entrainment processes (e.g., McGrath & Kelly, 1986; and see Chapter 4) may spread beyond dyads to get the wider group into sync. Local adjustments of the pace and temporal patterning of practical and communicative activities become more widely distributed as near neighbours mutually influence one another in succession. The dynamic structure of group behaviour may therefore consolidate over time partly as the result of bottom-up interpersonal processes. The resulting sense of moving as one may then add an implicit sense of unity that facilitates shared emotionality as well as collective action.

A number of studies have shown that getting people to do things in synchrony with one another increases cooperation, solidarity and mutual liking (e.g., Anshel & Kipper, 1988; Wiltermuth & Heath, 2009). For example, Reddish, Fischer and Bulbulia (2013) asked small groups of participants to perform repeated actions such as moving their legs and arms up and down in time to a metronome beat played over headphones. For some groups, the rhythm was synchronised across participants thus producing simultaneous movements. For other groups, each participant moved to a different beat. Participants in the synchronous condition perceived their group as more unified and shared more money with other members in a subsequent cooperation task. These effects were stronger still when participants were explicitly instructed to get into sync with each other. In other words, deliberately trying to act together induces unity more powerfully than simply finding out that your actions are coordinated with those of other people. Reddish and colleagues concluded that part of the solidarity-inducing effect of moving together depends on a sense of shared intentionality (e.g., Tomasello & Carpenter, 2007), and that the growing sense of achieving a collective goal reinforces feelings of satisfaction with the group. The group becomes an entity that actively affords participation thus adding a sense of flow to collective action (Csíkszentmihályi, 1990; Páez et al., 2015). Relatedly, the imposed collective goal meant that participants needed to make reciprocal adjustments to each other's movements with entrainment processes operating equally in both directions (*symmetrical* entrainment, e.g., Clayton, Sager & Will, 2004). Indeed, every person not only needed to attend explicitly to the people around them but also had to provide overt cues that served to help those people pick up the rhythm. By contrast, participants in the metronome-paced synchronous condition individually adjusted their own behaviour directly to a fixed pattern delivered non-socially. Asymmetrical entrainment of this latter kind is likely to provide a relatively less effective means of generating solidarity between people.

According to Durkheim (1912), a high-intensity emotional state of collective effervescence is an automatic consequence of symmetrical entrainment when large groups get together. As he argued, 'The very act of congregating is an exceptionally powerful stimulant. Once the individuals are gathered together, a sort of electricity is generated from their closeness and quickly launches them to an extraordinary height of exaltation. Every emotion expressed resonates without interference' (p. 217). In other words, attunement to other group members' responses may make people particularly susceptible to a form of contagious emotional influence.

Durkheimian effervescence may be specifically facilitated and reinforced by structured activities that impose a rhythm and tempo on group members' activities (i.e., zeitgebers). Repeated patterns of movement provide a common focus and make it easier for people to join in with whatever others are doing. A clear and simple example is provided by the 'muscular bonding' achieved by military personnel marching in time and in a common direction (McNeill, 1995, p. 2). Other more articulated communal activities also encourage temporal coordination of physical activity (e.g., Henriques, 2010), thus reinforcing the sense of being and working together (the 'corporeal experience of solidarity': Collins, 2004, p. 48). Collins (2014) argues that these 'interaction rituals' can serve the function of helping people to share their emotions. Shared emotions then intensify as a result of reciprocal social feedback, and are transformed by the resulting sense of intersubjective empowerment (see Figure 7.1).

Mutually matched activities carry a particular emotional resonance when they are materially effective or meaningfully expressive. Partly for this reason, much of the research into the effects of moving together has focused on dancing (e.g., Hagen & Bryant, 2003; Reddish, Fischer & Bulbulia, 2013; Tarr, Launay & Dunbar, 2016) or singing (e.g., Clift & Hancox, 2001; Pearce, Launay & Dunbar, 2015). In both cases, movements often represent feelings and ideas that potentially resonate with shared concerns. In singing, the topic is also conveyed in words that are carried by voices whose perceptible qualities directly reflect the movements that participants are currently making. Choirs can pick up these meanings and movements even without physically touching each other.

Heider and Warner (2010) specifically investigated devotional four-part harmony singing following the 'Sacred Harp' tradition in the southern United States, which brings together people with disparate social identities and produces a new sense of community. Singing sessions create a collective experience by virtue of mutual embodied intragroup influence, carried by the shared focus on the sound and the sacred symbolic text it animates. Trebles, altos, tenors and basses face each other on separate crowded benches arranged in a 'hollow square', their voices reverberating in time with the rhythm. Heider and Warner report that participants experience intense emotions during their singing sessions, often turning to face their neighbours while delivering particularly

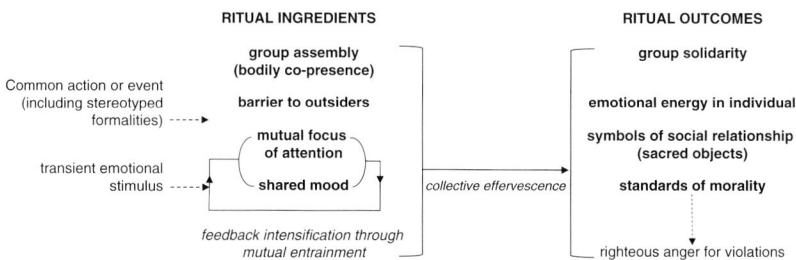

Figure 7.1 Collins' (2004) interaction ritual model

relished lines of lyrics. Performances usually conclude with hugging and effusive good will.

As well as expressing communal religious fervour, coordinated singing can also channel common identification with a country or its representatives. Slater, Haslam and Steffens (2018) assessed effects of the collective expression of 'passion' during the team singing of national anthems before football matches in the 2016 UEFA European Championship. Before the games, players in each team stood in a line, often with arms around each other's shoulders, and sang along while their country's anthem was played on the PA system. Slater and colleagues argued that the passion with which team members sing in these contexts reflects their solidarity and commitment to the shared aims associated with their country's fate in the tournament. It also communicates this common sense of purpose to other team members, the fans in the stadium and the opposing team who may be intimidated by any apparent show of strength. Thus, more passionate singing should be associated with better outcomes in the match that follows.

For the study, independent coders rated the strength of passion of each team's singing using broadcast TV footage, based on vocal volume, facial expressions indicating focus and physical closeness between players. Slater and colleagues found that higher passion scores were associated with conceding fewer goals in the subsequent game, and with winning games during the knockout phase of the tournament. Apparently, then, team members can get in tune with each other's emotional commitment and sense of determination during collective singing. Active regulated involvement in this kind of structured joint activity may serve the functions of establishing and communicating solidarity and empowerment.

Losing Yourself in the Crowd

If the reciprocal influences operating between members of small groups makes emotions more likely to spread, what happens as these groups get larger? As emotions bounce back and forth between ever-increasing numbers of individuals, does that ultimately produce a resonance catastrophe, where the idea of emotional distinctiveness and separation gets lost in the crowd?

The idea of a group mind acquired its most sinister overtones in early accounts of mob psychology. Thinkers such as Gustave Le Bon (1895) argued that crowds encourage a feeling of anonymity (cf. Zimbardo, 1969) and give people a sense of power derived from the force of numbers. Their capacity for critical reasoning diminishes, and suggestibility and susceptibility to contagious processes both correspondingly increase. Socialised inhibitions on irrational and uncivilised instincts are lifted, and the released feelings and impulses spread rapidly between people, with potentially escalating destructive consequences.

According to Reicher (e.g., 1987), this depiction of large groups as unregulated, unruly and chaotic is a caricature. People don't lose their identity and self-control in the crowd, getting caught up in whatever passing whim or desire happens to take hold. Instead, their focus shifts from personal to group-related concerns, to which they respond in an organised and purposive manner. They are guided by a shared social identity with its associated practices and norms.

For example, massed football fans may have a reputation for undirected hooliganism, but in fact their sporadic aggressive acts are typically oriented to specific actions undertaken by outgroups or other agencies that are perceived as illegitimate from the ingroup's perspective (e.g., Stott, Hutchison & Drury, 2001; Stott et al., 2007). Stott and colleagues (2001) conducted an ethnographic investigation focusing on public disturbances before the 1998 FIFA World Cup first-round match between England and Tunisia in Marseille, France. Travelling England supporters viewed the aggression displayed by fellow fans as incited by the unpoliced provocative behaviour of the Tunisian contingent. For example, one England supporter commented that 'It felt like everybody else was against us. Even the police was against the English. The Tunisians were getting away with murder' (p. 369). According to Stott and colleagues, the perception of provocation changed attitudes towards ingroup aggression directed at the outgroup. Behaviour previously viewed as reflecting the objectionable volatility of a small minority of troublemakers started to seem like legitimate retaliation or self-defence. Thus, the group adjusted, coordinated and mobilised to address the changing demands of a developing intergroup situation, rather than acting on the basis of blind instinct.

How might emotions feature in these intergroup dynamics? Group-based social appraisal provides one mechanism whereby a group's norms can change and adjust over time. Emotional responses to external challenges and threats communicate appraisals to other crowd members. Those close to any action may express irritation, thereby conveying that an outgroup action is illegitimate. Aggressive ingroup responses may start to solicit approval (Mackie, Devos & Smith, 2000; Smith & Kessler, 2004) rather than explicit condemnation. A new context-attuned consensus begins to emerge driven partly by nonverbal negotiations at local levels, and progressively filters outwards.

Regulating Crowd Emotions

Individuals and subgroups may also engage in activities that are specifically intended to regulate the crowd's emotions, thus encouraging or alleviating anger or enthusiasm (Goldenberg et al., 2016). For example, Granström (2011) analysed fans' chants during Swedish ice hockey matches. Some of these chants explicitly induced solidarity between supporters by emphasising common identity or the team's positive qualities. The team was described as 'the best' or its name was repeated, often preceded by 'Come on!' Designated cheerleaders often initiated this kind of chant at specific times when aggressive or hostile noises were developing in other isolated pockets of the crowd, or when fans were becoming disheartened after a setback in the game. Their evident purpose was to shift the emotional tone of the group.

In UK football matches, more informal subgroups of supporters also often orchestrate chants in order to lift spirits or simply to increase levels of shared involvement. There is usually at least one section of any soccer stadium whose occupants take on the task of getting fellow fans to help cheer on the players, often using drums, trumpets or other improvised instruments to establish a rhythm and melody. Even squads battling to avoid relegation are thus regaled with massed voices maintaining that they are 'the finest football team that the world has ever seen'.

Solidarity and good cheer are not always successfully maintained. Even among the gathered supporters of a single football team, there are likely to be contingents with different orientations to what is happening, who may resist rather than accede to any emerging norm or attempt to pull them back onside. More generally, crowds often contain rival factions who distinguish themselves by showing contrasting reactions to events (e.g., Pehrson et al., 2013), at least until some decisive external pressures bring them into line. In most circumstances, people are inclined to identify selectively with others whose emotional stances are already convergent with their own perspective (e.g., Livingstone et al., 2011), but events of compelling collective significance may overcome initial divisions to bring more disparate individuals and subgroups together. Attempts to regulate crowds therefore depend on how well the regulators represent the changing norms of targeted group members.

Shared Engagement

According to social identity theory, group-level phenomena are never an automatic consequence of large numbers of people coming together. Individuals need to share their self-categorisation and sense of common group membership before any collective emotional experience can develop (e.g., Hopkins et al., 2016; Neville & Reicher, 2011). It is not sufficient for each person to identify with the same group independently. Instead, group members need to be with others who they know are also self-identifying in the same way. They need to feel that everyone else around has a common focus, purpose and set of concerns. Being together en masse in the same place facilitates this process in crowd contexts.

Sharing identity with the other people around you also brings more direct emotional consequences (Hopkins et al., 2016; Neville & Reicher, 2011). For example, Dundee United supporters in Neville and Reicher's (2011) study reported how they derived a sense of belonging, acceptance and validation from watching matches together. Novelli and colleagues (2013) even found that identifying with the group increased tolerance for overcrowding at a well-attended music festival and thereby enhanced emotional well-being. Getting close to people who accept you and share your identity can clearly be a pleasant experience. These positive feelings of shared identity are further intensified by other crowd members' notice-ably convergent emotional reactions to group-relevant events (e.g., Livingstone et al., 2011). Hearing the roar of the crowd as your team's striker slips past the final defender and sensing the unanimous excite-ment as they close in on the goal makes the common purpose manifest to everyone present.

Collective Efficacy

A related reason why it can feel good to be part of a crowd is that it facilitates participation in collective action. It is empowering to work together with large numbers of like-minded people. Change seems pos-sible. Results can be achieved. For example, in 1996, 6,000 anti-traffic protestors (supporting the Reclaim the Streets movement) overcame police resistance to occupy part of an elevated section of the M41 motor-way in West London, where they held a party and drilled holes in the asphalt to plant trees. One of the attendees described the celebration in the following terms: 'If you're left completely free to do whatever you want, it doesn't feel as wa-hey! exciting as, as the whole crowd pulling together against some opposition and then achieving what it wants, cos you all feel like this sense of unity, and purpose' (Drury et al., 2005, p. 316). Thus, the pleasing sense of intragroup coordination associated with collective action may be intensified by feelings of shared efficacy when facing external challenges to the attainment of group goals.

Hopkins and colleagues (2016) investigated the experiences of religious pilgrims attending an annual month-long Hindu festival (the Magh Mela) in Allahabad, India. Some of the most devoted attendees (known as *kalpwasis*) stay for the entire period keeping to a rigorous spice-free vegetarian diet and engaging in regular rituals and prayers. Adherence to these restrictive devotional practices is facilitated by close contact with other kalpwasis who prevent distraction and set appropriate examples for each other. Perhaps surprisingly, kalpwasis describe their experience of the Mela as one of sublime bliss (*ananda*). In response to explicit questions asking about the extent to which they felt more happy and fulfilled than they had ever felt in their lives, they pushed the ceiling of the rating scale by scoring an average of 4.79 of 5 (where 5 meant 'completely'). Based on regression analyses, the authors concluded that a sense of shared identity led to simultaneous increases in feelings of being supported by other group members and collective empowerment, both of which contributed to the overall ecstatic experience.

Swann and colleagues (2012) argued that intense physical states of extreme arousal, excitement or suffering intensify the sense of unified agency and animated solidarity induced by collective practices. For example, some initiation rites involve psychoactive drugs, serious danger or physical damage to the body (Whitehouse, 1996). Konvalinka and colleagues (2011) investigated a fire-walking ritual taking place at summer solstice in a small Spanish village. During this ritual, participants first dance around the dying flames as loud music plays and the crowd cheers them on. A trumpet then signals each person's turn to walk barefoot across glowing embers that can reach a surface temperature of 677 degrees Celsius.

For Konvalinka and colleagues' study, both fire-walkers and spectators wore compression belts that monitored their pulse throughout the ritual. Spectators' heart rates were relatively slower but showed similar dynamic patterns of change to those of the fire-walkers themselves, consistent with a process of affective synchronisation (see also Xygalatas et al., 2011). Evidence from another study suggests that increases in physiological arousal experienced during a similar ritual are accompanied by high levels of self-reported happiness when the fire-walking finishes (Fischer et al., 2014). Apparently, then, fire-walkers can serve as conduits for a form of collective emotional heat.

According to Swann and colleagues (2012), participation in this kind of intensive collective practice not only produces stronger cognitive identification but also leads to a more visceral fusion of identity where personal agency is experienced as expressing the collective will of the group. The identity fusion construct is operationalised using a pictorial self-report item where the self is represented by a circle that may overlap to different degrees with a larger circle representing the group (Swann et al., 2009). A state of maximal fusion positions the self-circle at the centre of the group-circle so that the collective entirely encloses the self, which nevertheless maintains its integrity as part of the group (see Figure 7.2). Corresponding verbal self-report items include 'I am one with my group' and 'my group is me'.

Swann and colleagues argue that identity fusion is distinct from social identification because social identity does not replace personal identity.

Self	Group	Self	Group	Self	Group	Self	Group	Self	Group
A		**B**		**C**		**D**		**E**	

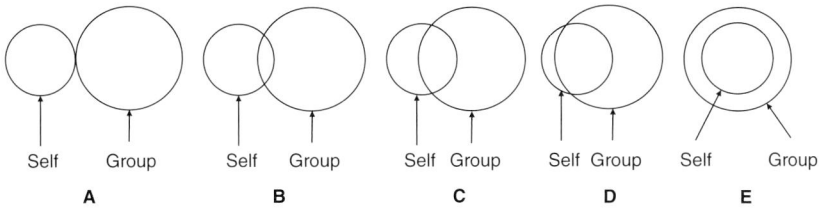

Figure 7.2 Operationalising identity fusion (Swann et al., 2009, reproduced with permission from the American Psychological Association)

Instead, identity-fused participants see their personal identity as expressing the identity of the group. If so, identity fusion may also transform the experience of group-based emotions so that individual selves channel the affect and energy of the group members around them.

Research reviewed in this section shows that shared participation in collective activities and a sense of shared identification both contribute to the development of mass emotions. However, these effects are also reinforced by less articulated bottom-up processes of interpersonal entrainment, which in turn are facilitated by particular kinds of temporally structured rituals, especially those involving extreme experiences. According to Páez and colleagues (2015), sharing mutually attuned emotions can intensify identification with your group, thus producing a positive feedback loop potentially leading to further emotional escalation (see also Collins, 2004). If this developing intragroup process centres on events that already carry intense emotional power, effects are likely to be even stronger.

Intergroup Relations

Group-based social appraisal and intragroup attunement extend the inferential and non-inferential processes of interpersonal emotional influence considered in Chapter 4 to larger collectives whose social practices and arrangements may facilitate (or constrain) their operation. Like in dyads, emotion convergence in groups depends on compatibility between the orientations of sources and targets (e.g., shared social identity or common goals and concerns) and serves broadly affiliative functions (Fischer & Manstead, 2016, and see Chapter 6).

But what happens when emotions are directed at outgroups or their members? In these cases, the function might be social distinction or distancing rather than affiliation, leading to emotional conflict or divergence instead of convergence. We may feel hostile towards members of competing groups and they may respond by becoming afraid, guilty or reciprocally angry in return (cf. Weisbuch & Ambady, 2008). More generally, the same kinds of emotional dialogue and reciprocal influence that operate in interactions between individuals may also operate when different groups come into contact.

As we have seen, group-based emotions depend on identifying with or acting alongside members of a group or collective. They can take a range of possible objects that relate to the shared concerns of the group. Intergroup emotions are a specific form of group-based emotions distinguished by the fact that they are oriented to objects or events that also concern another group (e.g., Iyer & Leach, 2008; Parkinson, Manstead & Fischer, 2005). For example, they may be directed specifically at the other group itself, as in the case of intergroup hate or admiration, or they may relate to something that the other group has done, such as an act of aggression or apology. Alternatively, they may be about events or circumstances that affect the ingroup in different ways from the outgroup, as in the case of national sympathy following a natural disaster in a foreign country, or intergroup envy when a local economic slump selectively impacts the ingroup but not the outgroup. In the following sections, I separately consider these two kinds of intergroup emotion.

Outgroup-Directed Intergroup Emotions

The stereotype content model developed by Fiske, Cuddy and Glick (2002) proposes that emotional orientations to outgroups depend on the ingroup's stereotypic perceptions of their characteristic levels of warmth and competence. These perceptions in turn depend on the nature of intergroup relations, with warmth reflecting cooperation rather than competition between groups and competence reflecting the outgroup's relative power or status compared to the ingroup. Fiske and colleagues' model represents an advance on previous unidimensional accounts of prejudice that focus only on the negativity of outgroup attitudes. It allows the possibility of having stereotypes with mixed evaluative content by feeling warm towards an outgroup perceived as incompetent (intergroup pity) or cold towards an outgroup perceived as competent (intergroup envy). When warmth and competence evaluations align rather than conflict, emotional reactions are less equivocally positive or negative. Thus, outgroups perceived as low in both warmth and competence elicit ingroup contempt, whereas outgroups perceived as high in both warmth and competence elicit admiration.

Although the stereotype content model mainly focuses on fixed perceptions of stable outgroup characteristics, changes in intergroup relations may also alter intergroup orientations over time. Previously competitive groups may start to cooperate, thus increasing perceptions of their warmth, and previously high-status outgroups may lose resources or capacities, thus decreasing perceptions of their competence. As history unfolds, intergroup admiration or envy may correspondingly transition to pity or contempt. Indeed, a functionalist rather than reactive perspective allows us to see each of these emotions as a motivator of action that is intended to realign intergroup relations. For example, envy about another country's superior effectiveness may encourage citizens to support policies that might increase their own country's relative power or status.

Do the dimensions of warmth and competence exhaust the possible distinctions between outgroup-directed emotions? And correspondingly, are any important socially directed group emotions excluded from the stereotype content model? Perhaps the most obvious omission concerns emotions relating to direct ingroup threat (Parkinson, Fischer & Manstead, 2005). Uncertainty about effective coping when faced with the particular forms of power-based 'competition' involved in ingroup-directed aggression or collective victimisation (e.g., Noor et al., 2017) may provoke intergroup anxiety and fear rather than envy. Reactions such as this therefore seem to depend on more than perceptions of low outgroup warmth and high outgroup competence. Indeed, Alexander, Brewer and Herrmann (1999) argue that outgroup power and status need to be considered separately rather than being collapsed into a single competence dimension. Thus, thinking of another group as having the capacity to affect ingroup outcomes directly (power) may bring different emotional consequences from believing that they have a positive reputation or high levels of credibility (status: Brewer & Alexander, 2002). Even finer distinctions between emotionally relevant outgroup characteristics may depend on their particular historical relations with the ingroup and their specific goals and concerns in present circumstances (e.g., Dijker, 1987).

Alexander and colleagues (1999) argue that one of the functions of outgroup images is to justify existing structural relations between groups with different levels of status, power and competitive intentions. For example, two groups that are roughly equal in power and cultural status may be in direct competition for resources. This state of affairs encourages each group to engage in actions that conflict with the other group's goals. Representation of the outgroup as an enemy helps to rationalise and excuse this hostile orientation. Similarly, if the outgroup is relatively lower in power, the ingroup may take advantage of their capacity to exploit them. Under such circumstances, representing the outgroup as dependent and in need of paternalistic care helps the ingroup to avert any imperialistic implications that their exploitation might otherwise carry. More generally, outgroup perceptions depend on ideological processes that distort rather than merely reflect prevailing intergroup relations. Outgroup-directed emotions may therefore help to sustain justificatory ideologies among ingroup members, and to defend the ingroup's position when confronted by critical audiences (including external agencies and the outgroup itself).

Outgroup images carry further implications for ingroup perceptions of outgroup emotions (cf. Leyens et al., 2000), which may also contribute to ingroup emotional responses. For example, an outgroup represented as dependent may be perceived as susceptible to help-seeking or attachment-related emotions, thus evoking ingroup care, pity or condescension. By contrast, a high-competence, low-warmth outgroup may be seen as proud, contemptuous or simply uncaring and thus solicit complementary ingroup emotions other than just envy.

Rodriguez Mosquera, Kahn and Selya (2017) showed that American Muslims' perception that other Americans perceived them as 'frightening' predicted their anger about the unfairness of that stereotype. This angry response potentially reinforces non-Muslim Americans' perception of Muslims as frightening, thereby producing a self-fulfilling prophesy (Snyder & Swann, 1978). In addition, characterising Muslims as fear-inducing serves to justify repressive action, which in turn exacerbates intergroup conflict (cf. McNeill, Pehrson & Stevenson, 2017). Thus, intergroup emotions may depend on actual and imagined dialogues between groups based on accurate or biased perceptions of their respective emotional propensities.

Event-Directed Intergroup Emotions

Some intergroup emotions are oriented to temporally localised group-related events rather than stable outgroup characteristics or structural intergroup relations. These events include actions or omissions by either group, or externally imposed changes of circumstance that affect each group in different ways. Emotional responses to these events depend on similar processes to those considered in the earlier, more general, discussion of group-based emotions. For example, salient social identities attach emotional significance to identity-relevant events including those that also concern the outgroup (group-based appraisal; e.g., Doosje et al., 1998). Further, group members may adjust their emotional orientations towards outgroup-relevant events to match those of other ingroup members (group-based social appraisal: e.g., Kuppens et al., 2013) or engage in forms of collective mutual adjustment (e.g., Totterdell, 2000). In these cases, the actual, perceived and anticipated responses of the outgroup may also contribute to the development and diffusion of emotions among ingroup members. Assuming that group-based emotions, like interpersonally directed emotions, serve social functions, they should be similarly attuned to their intended consequences. When these consequences involve the outgroup, then the outgroup's corresponding orientation often makes a difference to how ingroup emotions are enacted, mobilised and regulated.

According to self-categorisation theory (e.g., Turner et al., 1989), social identification enhances members' need to distinguish their own group from other groups. Indeed, group attitudes not only become polarised by aligning with convergent ingroup positions (e.g., Moscovici & Zavalloni, 1969), but also as a counter-reaction to the contrasting positions of outgroup members. For example, Hogg, Turner and Davidson (1990) showed that ingroup members urge greater caution when they believe that an outgroup prefers a more risky course of action, but favour increased risk when they believe that an outgroup prefers to be cautious. Thus, disagreement with outgroups can polarise perspectives, with obvious (but as yet under-investigated) consequences for emotions and emotion-related norms.

Competition and Conflict

Some of the most obvious examples of intergroup emotion happen when groups are in direct competition with each other. In these cases, outcomes that advance ingroup goals tend to block outgroup goals and vice versa. Thus, group members tend to be unhappy about their ingroup's competitive failures and about competing outgroups' successes, and happy about their ingroup's successes and about competing outgroups' failures.

These patterns of reaction may even extend to situations where the ingroup and outgroup are not in direct competition with each other. For example, group members may gloat about a victory simply because it implies that their ingroup is currently experiencing relatively more success than a comparable outgroup. Correspondingly, several studies have shown that ingroups may relish outgroup defeats that are inflicted by agencies unrelated to themselves (intergroup schadenfreude). For example, Leach, Spears, Branscombe and Doosje (2003) investigated Dutch participants' reactions to the elimination of the Germany team in the quarter finals of the 1998 FIFA World Cup tournament. Germany is one of the Netherlands' main historical rivals in soccer, with a superior record of success in international competitions. Indeed, the Netherlands team had already been eliminated by Brazil at an earlier stage of the 1998 World Cup. Leach and colleagues reminded some participants of the Netherlands' historically weak performance levels and of their recent elimination from the present World Cup. Participants who focused on these status threats (and were generally interested in football) reported higher levels of schadenfreude in response to Germany's defeat, suggesting that the emotional reaction was driven by reputational concerns.

In a similar subsequent study, Leach and Spears (2009) also found that intergroup schadenfreude was associated with more positive evaluation of the ingroup, consistent with the idea that the emotion serves the function of improving feelings about belonging to a previously threatened group (see also Yam & Parkinson, under review). Parallel functions have also been attributed to interpersonal schadenfreude which can serve to repair individual self-esteem following a relational setback (e.g., van Dijk et al., 2011).

When stakes are higher, more direct confrontations between groups often involve mutual hostility and escalating violence (e.g., Halperin, 2016). When two competing groups have incompatible perspectives and interests, intergroup anger cannot easily serve the function of changing the outgroup's behaviour (e.g., Fischer & Roseman, 2007), and may therefore be intensified in renewed influence attempts. Each group may be angry not only about the event as seen from the ingroup's perspective but also about the fact that the other group's reaction is so hostile (intergroup meta-emotion). Dealing with an angry opponent introduces an additional level of conflict and the possibility of more negative future consequences if the outgroup's anger translates into direct intergroup aggression. A shared sense of illegitimacy and unfairness consolidates in each group, exacerbating intergroup antagonisms even further. At some point, mutual antipathy may harden into a fixed emotional attitude of contempt, serving a persistent intergroup distancing function (Fischer & Manstead, 2016).

Reconciliation

Intergroup hostility does not always persist and crystallise. Under many circumstances, groups try to find ways of working together or at least coexisting without conflict. Intergroup reconciliation often provides an attractive alternative to escalating antagonism. Nadler and Shnabel (2015) argue that transgressors and victims have different needs that need to be addressed in any restorative intergroup exchange. For example, if the ingroup has deprived an outgroup of resources or restricted their movements or range of action, then any corrective action needs to address the resulting threat to the outgroup's sense of agency. Thus, the ingroup's collective apology may involve showing appropriate respect for the outgroup's position, acknowledging the harm that has been done, and committing to corrective action. However, the outgroup's response also needs to address the transgressing ingroup's own needs by demonstrating appropriate forgiveness. This allows ingroup members to maintain a sense of their own group's moral status and warmth. The apology–forgiveness cycle implied by Nadler and Shnabel's needs-based model of intergroup reconciliation has obvious parallels with the interpersonal processes of accusation and appeasement discussed in Chapter 6. Intergroup anger may be similarly designed to solicit apology or recompense by inducing guilt in its target.

Consistent with this social functional account, intergroup anger is usually motivated by specific actions of an outgroup that are appraised as illegitimate and as conflicting with ingroup goals (e.g., Iyer & Leach, 2008; Leach et al., 2006; Stott et al., 2001). Correspondingly, it encourages support for ingroup action targeting the outgroup's conduct, including demands for compensation (Iyer, Schmader & Lickel, 2007) and apology. In other words, the ingroup's anger serves the function of soliciting restorative outgroup responses. Indeed, group members seem to be aware of the potential strategic advantages of communicating outgroup-directed hostility and may explicitly work up their anger in order to solicit desired intergroup consequences (Porat, Halperin & Tamir, 2016).

De Vos and colleagues (2013) argue that the communicative function of intergroup anger is to change the outgroup's behaviour in ways that maintain rather than disrupt intergroup relations. However, the simultaneous experience of intergroup contempt may undermine anger's conciliatory functions by communicating social rejection (Fischer & Roseman, 2007). Consistent with this account, Dutch students who read about a German student's anger about hostile intergroup behaviour felt more empathy towards the German outgroup and were less inclined to act in negative ways towards them. However, these positive effects disappeared when participants either believed that the outgroup member's anger was mixed with contempt or adopted an ingroup perspective instead of seeing things from the angry student's point of view. These findings suggest that anger may convey relationship-repairing signals that lead to reconciliation rather than antagonism, at least when ingroup and outgroup orientations are potentially compatible (e.g., when a shared overarching social identity is available).

The causes and effects of intergroup guilt are broadly complementary with those of intergroup anger. In particular, group members feel guilty when the ingroup has transgressed against an outgroup and their guilt motivates reconciliation with, and reparation towards, that outgroup. For example, Doosje and colleagues (1998) asked participants from the Netherlands to read a historical account of their nation's historical exploitation and oppression of Indonesian people. In one experimental condition, information about Dutch colonists' positive contributions to Indonesian infrastructure and legal procedures was also included, thus introducing ambiguity to participants' appraisals of the implications for national identity. In this ambiguous condition, participants who identified more strongly with their Dutch nationality reported relatively less group-based guilt and were less willing to support international reparation, probably because they were more motivated to selectively interpret the materials in ways that maintained their group's reputation (e.g., Branscombe & Miron, 2004). For example, highly identified participants may have attributed any negative intergroup consequences of their country's past behaviour to individuals or factions who were unrepresentative of the group as a whole (Hornsey, Okimoto & Wenzel, 2017). In other experimental conditions, participants read only unambiguous positive or negative information about their nation's colonial past. Group-based guilt and support for intergroup reparation were significantly higher in the negative condition and the effect on reparation was mediated by guilt. In other words, collective guilt can motivate attempts to restore relations with the victims of ingroup transgressions.

How do victim outgroups respond to transgressing ingroups' guilt? Wohl and colleagues (2013) found that intergroup transgressions were more likely to be forgiven when associated apologies were perceived as genuine expressions of remorse (see also Berndsen, Hornsey & Wohl, 2015). It therefore seems that group-based guilt serves to repair intergroup relations following ingroup misdemeanours in ways that parallel the interpersonal effects of individual guilt (e.g., Baumeister et al., 1994, and see Chapter 6).

Dialogue

As with interpersonal emotions, the social functionality of intergroup emotions is best demonstrated by showing that they adjust online to the changing responses of their targets (see Chapter 6). If outgroup-directed emotions escalate until the ingroup receives feedback of their intended effects on outgroup behaviour and then decrease in intensity, this suggests that they are functionally oriented to their intergroup consequences. However, very few of the relevant studies directly put members of different groups into contact with one another in ways that would permit this kind of test (Nadler & Shnabel, 2015), focusing instead on more remote perceptions of the other group's characteristics, orientations or intentions or on reactions to recalled or imagined intergroup encounters (e.g., Shnabel et al., 2009; Tabri, Wohl & Caouette, 2018). Indeed, it is practically impossible to recreate the kinds of intergroup interchange that operate in real-world sports events (e.g., Stott et al., 2001), political protests (e.g., Neville & Reicher, 2011) or violent conflicts (e.g., Gausel et al., 2018) within the constraints of a laboratory context.

However, some experiments do involve interactions between individual representatives of different groups. For example, Greek Cypriot participants in Ioannou and colleagues' (2017) study either had a face-to-face conversation with a Turkish Cypriot student (serving as the experimenter's confederate) or observed this conversation remotely while it was happening. The outgroup confederate's presentation of affiliative affect served the function of alleviating ingroup members' intergroup anxiety even when intergroup contact was vicarious rather than direct. Similar experimental procedures might usefully be adapted to investigate the intergroup dynamics of emotional accusation and restitution.

Taking a step in this direction, Shore and colleagues (2019) assessed how remotely delivered emotional communications impact on intergroup behaviour following an ingroup member's failure to reciprocate a trusting move from the outgroup. Scores on a pretest ostensibly divided participants into two separate minimal groups and participants then observed representatives from each of these groups play a trust game with each other using computer-mediated communication. An outgroup representative took the role of investor and transferred seven out of their group's ten points to the ingroup, which was then multiplied by a factor of three to give the ingroup twenty-one points in addition to their original allocation of ten points. Participants then observed a representative of their ingroup returning zero points, thus breaching the outgroup's trust. In response to this outcome, the supposed outgroup representative sent back a text message expressing either anger or disappointment. Participants then themselves took the role of investor in a second trust game and decided how many points to transfer to the outgroup.

Outgroup anger communication led to relatively higher allocation of resources to the outgroup in this second trust game, and the effect was mediated by participants' self-reports of diminished pride. In other words, participants presented with an angry outgroup reaction to an ingroup breach of trust felt less proud about the consequent increase in their own group's resources, and consequently returned more of these resources in a subsequent intergroup transaction. Thus, outgroup anger communicated an appraisal that prior ingroup behaviour was illegitimate, thereby serving the intergroup function of encouraging a change in future transactions.

These results are clearly consistent with a social-functional account of intergroup anger, which shaped intergroup responses by communicating the outgroup's appraisal of the ingroup's actions. However, because the only contact between the members of the two groups involved an exchange of successive text-based messages, the investigators were unable to assess the real-time attunement of intergroup emotions to their intended outgroup addressees more directly. Future research should therefore explore similar intergroup emotional dialogues and negotiations in more realistic and dynamic settings.

Conclusions

In this chapter, we have seen how emotions may spread and converge among people who are together in a common space, working on a common task or identifying with a common group. Their shared emotions in turn may help to consolidate or reinforce shared social identity. The resulting reciprocal validation of perspectives and sense of collective empowerment can transform experiences during group-related events (Neville & Reicher, 2011). Thus, affiliative intragroup emotions colour group members' emotional perceptions of whatever is happening. More generally, intragroup emotions serve the function of building and maintaining relations between ingroup members, and negotiating common orientations to identity-relevant objects, including the establishment or adjustment of group norms (e.g., Stott et al., 2001).

Collective practices such as interaction rituals may also contribute to the consolidation and intensification of group emotions by providing a common rhythm and tempo to shared activities, and facilitating the mutual entrainment of emotion-related nonverbal signals and movements. When collective rituals also carry symbolic significance and involve extreme experiences, the resulting shared emotions may become especially intense and involving.

In intergroup contexts, the perceived emotions of outgroup members may either lead to the polarisation and consolidation of divergent ingroup perspectives or prompt conciliatory emotional moves. Ingroup members present intergroup emotions in order to influence the orientations and actions of outgroups, and outgroup members may adjust their own emotional orientations accordingly. Given congenial circumstances, these intergroup processes may lead to appeasement, forgiveness and peaceful coexistence rather than exacerbation of tension and conflict. Indeed, group members may be oriented to these possible outcomes when regulating their experience and expression of intergroup emotions (e.g., Goldenberg et al., 2016; Porat et al., 2016). Thus, group emotions serve comparable functions to interpersonal emotions and can be used for similar purposes when group members try to align and realign intragroup or intergroup relations.

CHAPTER 8

Working with Emotions

Emotional influence not only depends on a person's group member-ship, but also on their particular position within the group's structured interpersonal relations. When the group is part of a wider organisa-tion, additional regulatory regimes may constrain or afford particular forms of emotional conduct. This chapter focuses on how work roles shape emotion communication and regulation. Team leaders' emo-tions can set the emotional tone for work-groups, encouraging soli-darity and common purpose. In the service sector, clients and customers impose different kinds of emotional demand on employees. Workers whose jobs involve interacting with consumers present the company's outward face, and are encouraged to regulate their emo-tional presentations accordingly (emotional labour). Caring profes-sionals need to manage the potential personal costs of empathising with clients undergoing potentially devastating life changes. In all of these cases, employees' emotions influence and are influenced by the people they deal with in their working lives.

The classic sitcom, *Fawlty Towers*, features a hotel proprietor who is consistently rude and hostile to his guests, and by turns incompetent and tyrannical in dealings with his long-suffering staff. His snobbery and prejudice lead him to fawn over those he sees as social superiors but show unconcealed contempt for the supposed riff raff. If it weren't for his lapses into exaggerated obsequiousness, his abrasive manner might at least have the virtue of authenticity. But that's little consolation for the victims of his bile.

Those of you not old enough to have lived through the 1970s may fail to recognise the grain of truth in John Cleese's portrayal of Basil Fawlty. Unlike its distant descendant, *The Office*, the series made little attempt at documentary-style realism, but its observations still carry a historical, even nostalgic, resonance. Back then, it was not unusual to be ignored or actively abused by service personnel, at least in the UK. Indeed, British tourists returning from the States often regaled anyone prepared to listen with tales of their friendly and congenial reception – how everyone from counter staff to bus drivers welcomed them with metaphorically open arms. And soon they started to demand more from the folks back home.

This cultural dynamic is nicely illustrated by the American guest at Fawlty Towers insistently demanding a Waldorf salad after kitchen hours are officially over. The message was clear. The psychological distance between a jumped-up boarding house in Torquay run by 'the British Tourist Board's answer to Donald Duck' and the Marriotts, Hiltons and Astorias of the USA was another gulf of Atlantic proportions.

Now things are different even in Europe. It started with simple competition for increasingly discerning customers, including American tourists. Hotel, restaurant and supermarket chains began to train their employees in presenting the required impression. Smiling soon became obligatory. Discourtesy of any kind was beyond the pale. Then came the mobile apps, the Trip Advisor rankings, the Facebook likes and dislikes. It became common to be asked by your barista or pension advisor to leave an online review rather than scribble some perfunctory comments in the dog-eared visitor book. If you wouldn't mind. If it's not too much trouble. If you really are happy with our service today.

Notwithstanding the demands of social media and other forms of electronic monitoring, rules and norms for presenting emotions in economic transactions have clearly evolved. What may have once been implicit and unregulated now involves codes and procedures, monitoring and evaluation. In March 2018, British journalists took evident relish in recounting the story of a waiter who was sacked from a restaurant in Vancouver, Canada, for alleged discourtesy to his colleagues. Contesting his dismissal in a complaint filed with British Columbia's human rights tribunal, the plaintiff, Guillaume Rey, argued that he was not being rude, he was just French, and French culture 'tends to be more direct and expressive'. Tribunal member Devyn Cousineau was quick to state her reservations about the strength of the plaintiff's arguments. She wrote that 'Mr Rey will have to explain what it is about his French heritage that would result in behaviour that people misinterpret as a violation of workplace standards of acceptable conduct' (*The Guardian*, 26/3/2018). I like to imagine that Monsieur Rey's presentation to the court will draw on the scathing depiction of North American society offered by his fellow countryman and cultural critic, Jean Baudrillard (1988):

> Smile if you have nothing to say. Most of all, do not hide the fact you have nothing to say nor your total indifference to others. Let this emptiness, this profound indifference shine out spontaneously in your smile. *Give* your emptiness and indifference to others, light up your face with the zero degree of joy and pleasure, smile, smile, smile.
>
> (p. 34, emphasis in original)

In 2009, the Keikyu Corporation, a railway operator in Japan, installed Omron 'Smile Scan' consoles at fifteen of its stations and one of its training centres (Negishi, 2012). Platform staff were expected to check their facial expression when they arrived for work by posing for the machines. Smile Scan provided smile quality scores ranging from 0 to 100 and gave instructions about how to improve the current rating ('lift your cheeks' and 'narrow your eyes'). Employees were also encouraged to carry around a photograph of their highest-rated smile throughout their shift for future reference. As yet, companies haven't started to use similar software as part of their staff appraisal regimes, but perhaps that's only a matter of time. At least outside France.

Codes of interpersonal and institutional contact clearly continue to differ across societies and subcultures. And the application of these codes also depends on who you are and where you stand in relation to other people. However, the general lesson is that the way we relate to one another emotionally not only depends on our socialisation and group membership but also our more specific relative positions in articulated organisations, the modes of interaction that are available to us.

In particular, service personnel are encouraged to follow specific norms and prescriptions regarding emotional conduct and to regulate their emotion and its expression accordingly. Correspondingly, leadership carries the additional responsibility of setting the affective tone or emotional climate of the organisation more generally. In both respects, Basil Fawlty fell far short of any known standards then or now. Even in little England just before punk attitudes took hold, his leadership and emotional labour pushed the limits of social tolerance. And it seems unlikely that he'd be on the shortlist for any kind of service job in Canada, Japan or anywhere else.

This chapter is about how emotional influence and emotional regulation depend on people's organisational and institutional roles and positions, and on the power at their disposal. How can a leader's emotional communications affect the motivation and behaviour of employees? How does adopting different kinds of emotional orientation affect the reactions of customers and clients, and how do those reactions in turn affect service providers and other professionals whose business is to deal with other people, both at a practical and emotional level? The following sections consider theory and research addressing these questions.

Leadership and Power

The capacity to influence other people's emotions is not evenly distributed among members of any group or organisation. So why do certain individuals come to be more influential than others? Does their emotional power depend simply on their individual characteristics or prior resources, or are social and organisational processes also at work?

It is tempting to view power as a personal quality that some individuals have and others do not. Consistent with this intuitive account, there do seem to be certain skills, personality dispositions and physical features that tend to increase the probability of attaining or maintaining power (e.g., Chaiken, 1979; Judge & Bono, 2000; Judge, Piccolo & Kosalka, 2009; Vergauwe et al., 2018). Typically, however, these personal factors only facilitate social influence in specific institutional, cultural and practical contexts (e.g., De Hoogh, Den Hartog & Koopman, 2005; Waldman et al., 2001). Their usefulness depends crucially on how potential followers are inclined to respond to their specific application (e.g., Baker, 2007; Howell & Shamir, 2005). In other words, power is a relational rather than individual phenomenon (Conger & Kanungo, 1987; Keltner et al., 2008). It depends on the social positions that people occupy as much as their personal characteristics, reflecting the unequal distribution of various forms of advantage and disadvantage. Powerful people are generally people with greater access to resources that can influence other people's actions and emotions. And they may lose that access if institutional arrangements change. At any time, their power may confront various kinds of individual or collective resistance.

The resources available to powerful people can take a variety of forms. A physically powerful person can literally push you into a corner. Someone with a loaded gun or full wallet can provide less direct incentives or disincentives. A congenial individual is fun to be around, and able to recruit allies who can provide various kinds of additional resources. Someone can become powerful simply because others like what they say or how they say it. Or they can use their contacts or access to media outlets to make their message heard.

Some kinds of power depend on the organisation's assignment of a powerful position to an individual, irrespective of any other resources they might be able to access. When groups perform practical tasks, orchestration and calibration of their individual actions often requires an articulated division of labour. Some people or groups of people are likely to be involved in directing the activities of other people or groups of people. In other words, different members of most organisations have different rights and responsibilities, and differences in their consensually acknowledged capacity to exert social influence.

In many cases, the power associated with specific local resources ultimately extends into other domains. For example, someone who is widely admired may be given a leadership role that in turn provides access to other means of exerting power. Correspondingly, someone with access to any kind of non-social resource may be able to use that resource to encourage other people to like them or at least to pretend that they do. However, power does not inevitably seep out into neighbouring spheres of influence. It may stay contained in separate silos. Specific forms of power may remain restricted to specific kinds of situation.

The interpersonal effects of a powerful person's emotions also seem to depend on the particular resources at their disposal. Someone threatening you with a gun can induce fear or defiance but does not usually inspire your admiration or love. Someone providing effective emotional support is rarely the object of contempt. However, there are also some general principles underlying the operation of emotional power across these contrasting cases. Regardless of their power base, relatively more powerful people have a bigger impact on other people's outcomes, and can exert greater control over interpersonal rewards and punishment than less powerful people. The following sections address both general and context-specific explanations for power's tendency to increase the extent of emotional influence.

Consequentiality

Having more power means being able to exert more influence on what happens. In other words, the things that more powerful people do, including the emotions they communicate, tend to have a greater impact on other people's outcomes. Because other people's emotions depend on the outcomes they experience, this means that more powerful people's emotions often have more influence on other people's emotions too (e.g., Anderson, Keltner & John, 2003).

The consequentiality of powerful people's emotions makes those emotions salient and motivationally relevant to other people (e.g., Keltner et al., 2008; van Kleef et al., 2008). Their interpersonal impact is greatest when they are specifically directed at their target and are about something directly relevant to that person's concerns. For example, a leader's love, gratitude and respect lead us to expect that they will influence events in our favour whereas their hate, anger and contempt make our prospects seem worse. In each of these cases, the emotion conveys information about the powerful person's specific positive or negative intentions towards us. Because the person is powerful, we also know that they have the capacity to follow through on those intentions and that following through is likely to change our lives in some way.

In other words, power can underwrite and emphasise the messages that emotions convey to other people. Emotional promises and threats are usually more effective when the person presenting them has the capacity to back them up. For example, Lelieveld and colleagues (2012; and see Chapter 4) showed that anger elicited more fear and yielded more concessions during bargaining when communicated by a more powerful source (see also Overbeck, Neale & Govan, 2010). Correspondingly, having relatively lower power than another person makes us more likely to concede to their demands (e.g., van Kleef et al., 2006).

However, many of these effects are context-sensitive. Power only directly underwrites emotional communications that relate to its specific sphere of influence. Although we may sometimes cooperate with a powerful person's emotional intentions simply because we know that they are generally powerful, more usually we are sensitive to the extent to which they have the resources to act on the specific intentions communicated by the emotion that they present. For example, if we are negotiating with an angry person whose power provides them with alternative options for attaining the resources we are offering even if they abandon their negotiation with us, we are more likely to concede to their demands (e.g., van Kleef et al., 2006). However, we may be less willing to make similar concessions if the other negotiator's power instead relates to their popularity with people we have never met. By extension, different kinds of power potentiate the effects of different emotions in different contexts. Future research therefore needs to focus on the specific conditions underlying the impact of more localised forms of emotional power.

Strategic Uses of Power

The fact that powerful people's emotions make more of a difference to our lives means that they can use their emotions more effectively when trying to influence us. They may strategically work up or play down their verbal and nonverbal presentation of emotion in order to achieve desired interpersonal effects. For example, a transformational leader may seek to generate enthusiasm in a work team by delivering an optimistic speech presenting an inspiring vision of the company's mission in an excited manner (Bass & Riggio, 2006; Bono & Ilies, 2006). Or an authoritarian boss may angrily threaten wage cuts in an attempt to increase productivity. In both cases, the powerful person regulates their emotional communication strategically in order to produce emotional effects on others who are less powerful. Intrapersonal emotion management thus serves the purpose of interpersonal regulation (e.g., Little, Gooty & Wiliams, 2016; and see Chapter 6).

The general principles explaining the potency of leaders' emotional influence attempts are the same as those addressed in the previous section. A powerful person's interpersonal or intragroup emotion regulation is more likely to be successful because their emotions carry more serious implications for others. However, again, the impact of their emotions also depends on their relevance to the specific resources to which they have access. Leaders who overextend themselves by trying to regulate followers' behaviour in areas outside their usual sphere of influence require higher levels of social capital to achieve success.

One way in which this kind of social capital may be acquired is by aligning with valued positions within your network. Powerful people may have more pervasive influence when they are able to present themselves as a central representative of their group or organisation, or when they express emotions that engender a stronger sense of identification with that broader collective (e.g., Hogg & van Knippenberg, 2003). These possibilities are addressed in the following section.

Referent Emotional Influence

In Chapter 7, we saw how group identification can change a person's responses to ingroup and outgroup members and to events that are relevant to group concerns. These effects are facilitated by a variety of factors including common participation in coordinated and practically effective activities and a sense of shared group allegiance in situations where group members are in each other's physical presence. In this section, I consider the possibility that powerful individuals such as group leaders can exploit these factors by putting themselves in a position that maximises their intragroup emotional influence.

Self-categorisation theory differentiates between relatively more or less central ingroup members in terms of their relative prototypicality (e.g., Turner et al., 1989), defined as the extent to which members possess the valued characteristics of the group (i.e., those characteristics that allow positive differentiation from other groups). Just as a prototypical exemplar of the semantic category of 'fish' carries all the distinctive features that make a fish seem most identifiably fish-like and maximally dissimilar from un-fish-like things (see Chapter 2), a prototypical group member embodies the defining qualities that make a group different from other groups in ways that suggest superiority on the dimensions that matter to its members.

Group polarisation effects (see Chapter 7) suggest that ingroup members adjust their orientations to bring themselves closer to perceived group norms (e.g., Turner et al., 1989) and to prototypical group members who best represent and exemplify those norms. In other words, prototypicality is associated with greater social influence on other ingroup members (e.g., Hains, Hogg & Duck, 1997). If a more prototypical group member is angry or enthusiastic about something, then other group members are relatively more likely to get angry or enthusiastic about it too.

The social influence exerted by prototypical members is not only likely to be stronger, but also affects a greater number of people. Prototypicality is related to how widely a group member's attitudes and values are shared with other group members. Sharing attitudes and values in turn increases interpersonal attraction and affiliation (e.g., Byrne, 1961). Thus, more prototypical group members are likely to come into contact with larger numbers of ingroup members, who are also more motivated to share their orientations. In other words, member prototypicality is usually associated with network centrality (how widely connected group members are with other group members: e.g., Wölfer, Faber & Hewstone, 2015), which has been shown to facilitate intragroup influence (e.g., Kameda, Ohtsubo & Takezawa, 1997; Venkataramani, Green & Schleicher, 2010).

Taken together, these considerations also make it more likely that prototypical group members get nominated and selected for leadership positions, which may further increase their capacity for influence (e.g., Hogg & van Knippenberg, 2003). The process of socialisation into the leadership role may then induce changes in values and attitudes that bring them even closer to the group's prototype. Correspondingly, transformational leaders may try to bring group members' values and attitudes more into line with their own (Hogg, 2001). In either case, the leader's prototypicality is likely to increase. Finally, to the extent that leaders are seen as representing the group or organisation, other members' perceptions of their prototypicality are likely to increase too.

Because leaders are perceived as prototypical group members for all of these reasons, their appraisals of group-relevant events tend to carry more weight in determining the emotional reactions of other group members (e.g., Fransen et al., 2016). This means that leaders often exert emotional influence on followers by a process of group-based social appraisal (e.g., Kuppens et al., 2013; Yzerbyt et al., 2016; and see Chapter 7). For example, witnessing a leader's anger about a challenge facing the organisation tends to make the rest of the group angry too. However, the motivation to be closer to the group prototype does not always produce emotional convergence. If your leader or any other prototypical group member is angry with you, the desire to protect your social identity may encourage you to change your emotion and behaviour in ways that allay their anger.

Leaders are also able to exploit their relational position strategically in order to influence other group members' emotions according to these principles. Expressing emotional solidarity and common purpose not only makes a leader seem more prototypical but also increases followers' levels of social identification with the group making them more amenable to emotional influence. In other words, access to certain socially attuned rhetorical strategies may allow an individual to use their emotions to bring other group members into line before attempting to exert other forms of social and emotional influence.

This section has argued that one way in which people may become powerful is by increasing other people's perceptions of their prototypicality and taking advantage of the influence that prototypicality confers (e.g., Fransen et al., 2016). Thus, a career politician may affiliate with a particular party because the diversified attitudes and opinions of its membership leave a power vacuum somewhere in the middle ground where a clear prototypical position (or third way) can be staked out. To achieve wide influence, it is not necessary to get everyone to agree with you. Mapping out a central territory that broadly overlaps with the disparate positions of the majority is often enough to create or reinforce a sense of shared identity. An alternative is to focus on a clearly defined subgroup whose views can be more clearly characterised and consolidated, then try to bring others on-side. In either case, getting into a prototypical group position can add clout to your attempts to exert emotional influence.

Temporal Coordination

Solidarity may be encouraged not only by communicating identity-concordant appraisals, but also by entraining temporally structured bodily movements. Chapter 7 discussed how synchronised action can contribute to emotional effervescence and the shared sense of togetherness. Just as an externally imposed rhythm can help people get in tune with one another, leaders can also set the pace and pattern of temporally structured group activities.

When group activities require precise coordination, maximising the effectiveness of performance often specifically requires a designated individual to serve as a human zeitgeber. For example, eight-person rowing crews need to keep their strokes precisely in time with each other at different stages of a race as the currents and eddies change. They may all be in the same boat, but that boat gets pushed and pulled by the surrounding river and the demands of the contest. Similarly, members of the string section of an orchestra have their sheet music to guide their performance and can pick up cues from other musicians nearby, but also need to calibrate timings, harmonies and shifts of emphasis across greater social distances to make the piece work effectively and with appropriate artistry. In both these instances, rhythm, pace and effort are choreographed by a specific person who takes a directing role, namely the cox in the case of the rowing crew and the conductor in the case of the orchestra.

Both coxes and conductors are typically positioned so that they directly face other group members. Coxes pull faces, shout instructions and make encouraging comments to the crew. But their emotional influence is not entirely carried by the meaning of their nonverbal or verbal communication. Entraining urgency or enthusiasm in the rhythm of the strokes also plays a role. The tempo and dynamics of voice and facial expression contributes to the coordination of the team's practically and emotionally oriented movements. The shared rhythm not only increases the sense of solidarity but also provides a perceptible and physical manifestation of the team's emerging emotional attitude. The cox's specific relational and physical position contributes to their capacity to generate a shared sense of contained excitement as the race reaches a possible victorious conclusion, or to rechannel anxiety or anger into increased positive effort (e.g., Pescosolido, 2002, on the comparable role of the crew captain).

Unlike coxes, orchestra conductors cannot bark instructions at musicians because that would detract from shared appreciation of the music. Instead, they make highly structured visible movements including facial expressions to keep performance on course and modulate its dynamic qualities as necessary. Their baton not only specifies the targets of any implied instruction but also makes the spatial and dynamic qualities of their gestural communication more easily detectable. One of the points of the collective work is to generate an affecting performance. Conductors therefore use movements of their face, body and baton to clarify and shift the emotional emphasis in the different stages of the symphony or concerto. Their capacity to influence the emotions of musicians and audience again partly depends on the specific forms of temporally articulated and physically embodied influence that their organisational position confers. Here as in other leadership contexts, it therefore seems possible to mobilise groups emotionally by getting them into sync with each other and by directing the dynamic qualities of their orchestrated performance.

In some cases, the ability to establish, modulate and maintain intragroup rhythms of activity derives from power that is based on leader prototypicality or access to practical resources. In other cases, it simply reflects a person's allocated position in the group, and the fact that their movements and directions are a central focus of other members' attention while they are occupying that position. In either case, the coordinating role also confers a form of emotional power.

Limits of Power

By definition, having power in a certain emotional domain means being able to exert influence within that domain. Thus, knowing which of your buttons to press and having the ability to press them allows me to upregulate your anger. Power in any particular domain can often seep out into other domains too. For example, making you angry in front of our boss may make me seem relatively more calm and competent by comparison, thus increasing my potential for social influence more generally. Based on examples such as this, it might start to seem that even domain-specific power carries its own momentum and inevitably extends into ever-wider spheres of influence. Fortunately, however, there are often obstacles that stop power from running its implacable course. Resources may be redistributed or taken away. Other people may acquire new resources that trump those of previously powerful individuals. All of these factors set limits on the exertion of power by anyone who currently has it.

Leaders' awareness that power may decay or be snatched away may lead them to moderate its exertion in anticipation of future retaliation by others who may acquire power at some future point. Correspondingly, the possibility of gaining power may encourage relatively less powerful people to defy emotional demands delivered by powerful people whose influential positions seem unstable or difficult to sustain. Taken together, these social dynamics suggest that people whose power is insecure need to monitor the motives and behaviour of subordinates in order to detect potential threats to their currently powerful position (Keltner, Gruenfeld & Anderson, 2003). In particular, they may become sensitive to hostile intentions conveyed by subordinate anger (Stamkou et al., 2016). Thus, there may be exceptions to the general rule that powerful people's emotions carry more weight. If power is built on unsteady foundations, then the anger of the previously powerless may sometimes have the capacity to unsettle things to a relatively greater extent.

Stamkou and colleagues' (2016) study obtained direct evidence for this kind of effect. Members of each pair of participants were assigned with separate roles that they were told would permit one of them (the leader) to control the outcomes experienced by the other (the subordinate). Participants then completed a task that ostensibly assessed their suitability for leadership roles (Lammers et al., 2008). Bogus feedback about performance on this task then indicated that the participant allocated the role of leader was either relatively ill-suited or well-suited for leadership. Both participants in each pair were thus led to believe that the leader's power was either legitimate or illegitimate. Leaders with illegitimate power were quicker to detect and better at identifying facial indications of anger in subsequent tasks. In other words, these participants became relatively more attuned to emotions indicating that their power needed defending. Stamkou and colleagues also found that subordinates who perceived the leader's power as illegitimate were better at identifying fear, suggesting that they became attuned to possible opportunities for exploiting the illegitimate leader's weaknesses.

The emotion-detection tasks used in Stamkou and colleagues' research involved making judgements about the facial expressions of people who had no direct role in participants' leader–subordinate relations. The findings therefore suggest that the effects of illegitimate power on emotional attunement extend beyond the immediate context in which that power is exercised. Future research should assess whether similar processes can also operate in more context-sensitive and dynamically modulated ways during ongoing struggles for power.

Emotionally Effective Leadership

Gone are the days when organisational theorists argued that leaders need to stay calm and level-headed when performing the rational business of management (e.g., Blackmore & Sachs, 1998; Weber, 1924). It is now commonplace to emphasise the advantages of engaging emotionally with employees (Brotheridge & Lee, 2008) and their problems (Dogan & Vecchio, 2001), eradicating or quarantining toxic emotions (Frost, 2003), creating a positive affective climate (Dasborough et al., 2009; Humphrey, Burch & Adams, 2016; Sy & Choi, 2013) and, more generally, 'leading with emotional labour' (Griffith et al., 2015; Humphrey, Pollack & Hawver, 2008; Sy, Horton & Riggio, 2018). The literature on these topics already risks becoming unmanageably unruly and diverse. Are there any bottom lines?

Unsurprisingly, leaders with positive moods (Sy et al., 2005) or expressing positive emotions (Bono & Ilies, 2006) tend to induce more positive feelings in their subordinates or work teams, and are generally liked by them more (e.g., Newcombe & Ashkanasy, 2002). Positive, high-arousal emotions such as enthusiasm and excitement may produce even better impressions (e.g., Connelly & Ruark, 2010), partly because they can give followers the impression of a charismatic leadership style (Damen, van Knippenberg & van Knippenberg, 2008).

Negative emotions too can have positive effects on productivity (Sy et al., 2005), especially when used by leaders with a transformational rather than transactional leadership style (e.g., Connelly & Ruark, 2010). However, effects can differ for different negative emotions expressed by different leaders. For example, male leaders' anger sometimes leads to greater perceptions of effectiveness than their sadness, but this difference may be reversed for female leaders' anger and sadness (Lewis, 2000), probably because of gender stereotypes concerning powerful emotions (e.g., Fischer & Evers, 2011; Hess, Adams & Kleck, 2005). A further complication is that female leaders' sadness is evaluated more negatively when it is perceived as relating to the leader's dispositions and thus implying a sense of powerlessness (Schaubroeck & Shao, 2012). Clearly, no specific kind of leader emotion produces consistently positive effects under all circumstances and for all kinds of leader. Further, few of the studies include comparison conditions that would allow us to determine whether the emotions of non-leaders would bring similar interpersonal effects (e.g., Barsade, 2002: and see Chapter 7).

Mostly, leaders' emotions and emotion management strategies bring interpersonal and intragroup effects in the ways that have been discussed earlier in this book (see Chapters 4, 5 and 7). They provide information about the leader's motives and orientation to the situation (social appraisal), direct employees' attention and action towards particular objects and events in the work environment (relation alignment), incentivise or disincentivise different kinds of behaviour (social reinforcement) and influence group norms and attitudes (group-based social appraisal and referent emotional influence). Above, I suggested that many of these processes carry more weight when a leader is able to exert power in domains relevant to the concerns of the emotion in question. A boss's anger about an employee's work performance is likely to be more impactful than the anger of a passing stranger because the boss has the capacity to impose direct punishments to back up that anger, including potentially terminating employment. In addition, leaders who are prototypical group members (or who make themselves seem prototypical) gain additional social capital that further facilitates the effects of their emotions.

The consequentiality associated with domain-relevant power also carries implications for a leader's selection of interpersonal emotion-regulation strategies. There is no single kind of strategy that always works best either for leaders or anyone else. As ever, the key is to be flexible and appropriately sensitive to the context (e.g., Bonanno & Burton, 2013; and see Chapter 5). However, power permits leaders to be generally more successful in regulation attempts directed at employees whose outcomes they can influence, especially when the emotions themselves are power-related (e.g., anger: see Tiedens, 2001). However, the downside is that employees may come to see leaders' emotions as consistently strategic and even start to discount some of their implications (e.g., Kim et al., 2017).

In sum, leaders' emotions mostly seem to work in similar ways to the emotions of non-leaders, but influence a wider range of people and impact on those people to a greater extent. However, the exertion of the emotional power conferred by leadership is context-specific, impermanent and susceptible to various forms of individual and collective resistance from those on which it is imposed. The balance of emotional power gets even more complicated when employees also have to deal with people outside the organisation.

External Relations

In previous sections, we considered how a person's organisational posi-tion changes the ways in which their emotions affect other members of the same organisation. The present section turns to the outward face of organisational emotions. Two interrelated topics have attracted the most research attention in this area. The first focuses on ways in which service workers manage their emotions when dealing with customers. The second relates to caring professionals' regulation of emotional invol-vement with clients or patients in therapeutic encounters. In both cases, the norms, practices and regulatory regimes associated with an occupa-tional role make a difference to how employees use their emotions to influence the responses of people outside their organisation. The follow-ing sections review each of these topics in turn.

Service Encounters

Emotional labour (Hochschild, 1983) involves regulating emotions in the service of organisational rather than personal or relational goals. It hap-pens most commonly when public-facing employees are expected to deal with clients or customers in ways that present their employers in a positive light. In order to produce the required interpersonal response, employees have to work on their emotions, by suppressing irritation, forcing smiles and otherwise orienting to the emotional needs of the people they are paid to keep happy.

The psychological study of emotional labour has its roots in microso-ciological studies of 'the presentation of self in everyday life' by Goffman (1959) and others. However, the book that is mainly responsible for kickstarting the systematic program of research on this topic is *The Managed Heart* by Arlie Hochschild (1983). Hochschild succeeded in put-ting her intensive examination of interpersonal episodes in the context of a more broadly applicable and psychologically informed theory. Her analysis was influential partly because it captured a previously uncharted but wholly recognisable set of phenomena, and partly because it caught a wave of change in customer-oriented organisational culture.

As post-industrial service economies reached maturity, companies in the late 1970s and early 1980s were trying to outdo each other in manu-facturing saleable client-focused practices. In other words, they were trying to be the precise opposite of *Fawlty Towers*. The goal was to make consumers feel that the company's brand was the one that cared about them the most. Indeed, this was the era when Pacific Southwest Airlines boasted in promotional jingles and TV adverts that their flight attendants' smiles were not 'just painted on' (unlike those adorning the noses of their fleet of aircraft, Hochschild, 1983, p. 4). Correspondingly, company training programmes encouraged cabin crew to go the extra mile, by stretching and pulling not only their facial muscles but also their hearts and minds. Employees were taught to work on their private feelings as well as their public displays of emotion, using techniques akin to Stanislavskian method-acting, thereby projecting an organisationally sanctioned simulation onto the more prosaic reality of their service encounters.

Hochschild (1983) focused in particular on how company prescriptions about appropriate demeanour and conduct were beginning to encroach into the supposedly private territory of emotion. She suggested that personnel who were trained to manufacture authentic but socially prescribed emotions risked losing contact with the underlying power-drenched character of their relations with customers, increasing their willingness to acquiesce to unreasonable and oppressive demands. For her, 'a cost to emotion work' is that 'it affects the degree to which we listen to feeling and sometimes our very capacity to feel' (p. 21). Thus, a female flight attendant encouraged to deal with obnoxious passengers by treating them like valued guests in her own home might lose the ingrained intuitive tools for navigating conflict situations both in and outside the flight cabin. Her innate emotional compass might get pulled away from its natural magnetic pole. More generally, emotional labour may help construct a false consciousness which prioritises what the company requires over what employees might otherwise want and need for their own sake.

Hochschild's (1983) motif of the managed heart reproduces the familiar distinction between the internal and natural core of spontaneous emotional life and the relational forces impinging from outside (cf. Kappas, 2011; and see Chapter 6). But what if hearts already operate in relation to other hearts? What if the underlying conflict is between different levels of social structures and processes, rather than personal and political concerns?

Goffman (1961), whose earlier work provided one of the inspirations for Hochschild's analysis, addressed apparent tensions in role-based conduct not by resorting to notions of a natural asocial self, but by showing how different kinds of relational position sometimes rub against one another or collide: 'When the individual withdraws from a situated self he does not draw into some psychological world that he creates himself but rather acts in the name of some other socially created identity' (p. 107). In other words, 'he frees himself from one group, not to be free, but because there is another hold on him' (p. 123).

Goffman gives the example of a surgeon who refrains from exerting the formal authority permitted by his elevated social position during an operation, affecting self-deprecation or using incongruously casual terminology. These role slippages, he argues, are unlikely to reflect personal dissatisfaction with the prestigious social position of a high-ranked medical practitioner. Instead, they reflect attunement to the task of maintaining smooth relations between members of a team who need to coordinate their responses to achieve a commonly desired outcome. Informality softens the oppressive implications of direct commands or orders, that might otherwise produce interpersonal friction. Thus, the surgeon's interpersonal orientation switches from one set of role-related concerns to another. Similarly, a flight attendant who fails to carry off a convincing display of politeness may be attending to other less troublesome passengers who are equally disturbed by their neighbour's offensive demands. And it's not only clients and customers who define the prevailing interpersonal situation. Emotional labourers may also shift their social register away from the immediate work role and towards their relational position as friends of other cabin crew, representatives of a trade union or members of families with whom they might share experiences at some later stage.

For Hochschild (1983), working on emotion for organisations makes employees lose touch with their authentic personhood. However, Goffman's analysis instead suggests that any alienation may reflect attachment to an alternative social identity rather than the basic demands of an independently constituted self (Parkinson, 1991). There is no need to suppose that things get wholly personal once emotions enter the picture. In Goffman's (1961) terms, such an assumption reflects the 'touching tendency to keep a part of the world safe from sociology' (p. 134), in this case, a heart that continues to beat to its own independent drum, despite the competing rhythms of social activity surrounding it.

Leaving aside the romantic notion of the spontaneously pulsing individual heart, Hochschild's insight was that emotional labour has a previously unanalysed dark side. She gave a voice and vocabulary to less systematic or coordinated concerns previously expressed by service personnel themselves, and thus helped to facilitate their resistance to excessive demands from employers. Cabin staff and their representatives soon intensified their complaints and protests about many of the most restrictive injunctions about their face-to-face dealings with customers, who otherwise might have taken greater advantage of their acquiescence.

Even from the consumer angle, the imposition of a rigorous regime of authentic emotion presentation soon started to change perceptions about what genuineness really involved and whether it was always desirable. Manufacturing a close-to-perfect simulation of stereotypical naturalness sometimes produces more negative reactions than simply attending imperfectly to informal rules of attentiveness and politeness. It's something like the uncanny feeling viewers get when computer-animated movie characters start to look a little too much like human actors (e.g., Mori, 1970, tr. 2012). Improvisation and spontaneity have consequently begun to replace authenticity as the holy grail of customer relations, but even this apparent development brings costs. Most of us would prefer not to get stuck waiting behind someone trying to express their personality by developing a relationship with an over-talkative customer. We're probably not even bothered whether they play nice with us. As noted by a store manager interviewed by Sutton and Rafaeli (1988): 'Customers who are in a long line don't care if we smile or not. They just want us to run like hell' (p. 475).

The historical evolution of organisational training for service work is paralleled by research that has developed or contested many of Hochschild's ideas. In the following sections, I review some of this research and suggest further ways of extending our understanding of emotional labour and its social effects and consequences.

Costs of Service Work

Employees whose jobs involve direct contact with clients or customers have distinctive social identities and role demands. They are part of work groups operating within organisational hierarchies and regimes of power. However, an important part of their role is also to present their company to people outside it, people whose concerns are not always directly compatible with the employing organisation. These competing demands often produce tensions and stresses. For example, a passenger insisting on an immediate refill cannot easily be accommodated when the flight is full and other passengers are equally hungry and thirsty. Despite these common conflictual situations, there may also be times when the dictates of good customer relations are more congruent with satisfying and effective performance of the job. We should not assume that meeting client demands is a painful and damaging chore for everyone under all possible circumstances.

Early research on emotional labour tended to focus purely on the downsides. Starting with Hochschild's (1983) book, a literature rapidly developed that addressed the costs suffered by service employees who try to avoid reciprocating the anger or hostility that customers often direct at them or otherwise make themselves emotionally affable and accessible to the people they have to deal with as part of their jobs. Some of these costs arise from the immediate demands of emotional labour, whereas others reflect longer-term consequences.

Hochschild (1983) attributed many of the immediate costs to emotional dissonance. Festinger's (1957) earlier notion of cognitive dissonance implied that people feel uncomfortable when they simultaneously hold two psychologically incompatible beliefs, and that this motivates them to change one or both of those beliefs (or come up with a third belief that reconciles the other two). For example, thinking about the health consequences of alcohol consumption after your fourth or fifth drink may lead you either to change your mind about the importance of those health consequences or to refrain from joining in the next round. Either of these strategies allows you to bring the dissonant beliefs that you have drunk too much and that drinking is bad for you more closely into line, thus relieving your cognitive discomfort. Correspondingly, emotional dissonance reflects a conflict between different emotional demands. For example, smiling at a customer you'd prefer to punch on the nose requires you to hold back at least one of your emotional orientations to what is happening. This not only involves mental effort but also induces an uncomfortable sense of psychological inconsistency. You may feel like you are presenting emotions that are not wholly your own. Repeated experiences of this kind may in turn lead to deeper and more lasting consequences such as alienation, burnout (Maslach, 1982) or 'going robot'. Forcing yourself to care about customer needs may ultimately drain your capacity to care about much at all.

As noted above, Hochschild's (1983) emphasis on these negative consequences was part of a justified critique of exploitative organisational practices. However, subsequent researchers have pointed out that not all forms of emotional labour produce unremittingly damaging outcomes (e.g., Ashforth & Humphrey, 1993; Rafaeli & Sutton, 1987; Wong, Tschan & Semmer, 2017). Finer distinctions between contexts and processes may allow us to identify more precisely what the positive, neutral and negative active ingredients might be. Costs and benefits likely depend not only on the nature of the specific practices employed during emotional labour but also on the relational contexts in which they are deployed.

Surface-Acting and Deep-Acting

Hochschild (1983) distinguished two techniques that service employees use to manage their emotional performance. Surface acting involves adjusting external demeanour to produce the appearance of the intended emotion and responding to the implicit and explicit display rules (Ekman, 1972; and see Chapter 3) that the organisation enforces. Thus, emotional labourers report that they sometimes 'plaster a false smile' on their face when dealing with customers and try to cover up any outward signs of anxiety or irritation ('put on a brave face' and 'grin and bear it': Parkinson, 1991, pp. 430–1). These attempts to tense or contract certain muscles while holding others immobile produce no direct effects on employees' appraisal of what is happening or what the customer might be doing.

By contrast, deep-acting involves a more active and thorough attempt to manufacture emotional concern for customers' needs and desires. Instead of focusing on appearances, deep actors try to generate the underlying relational orientations that make whatever the customer thinks, feels and does actually matter to them. Instead of merely responding to display rules, deep-acting involves conforming to feeling rules (Hochschild, 1979). As an illustration of how this might be achieved in practice, an experienced flight attendant delivering a training program for *Delta Airlines* told the following anecdote about dealing with an angry passenger (known as an 'irate' in informal company parlance):

> Once I had an irate that was complaining about me, cursing at me, threatening to get my name and report me to the company. I later found out his son had just died. Now when I meet an irate I think of that man. If you think about the other person and why they're so upset, you've taken attention off yourself and your own frustration. And you won't feel so angry. (Hochschild, 1983, p. 25)

From the present relation-alignment perspective, distinguishing so starkly between surface- and deep-acting perpetuates an unhelpful dichotomy between private and public aspects of emotion. It reproduces the idea that the essential characteristics of emotion are hidden inside an individual person rather than manifested in their dynamic dealings with the social environment. For this reason, it may be better to think of surface-acting as an attempt to control the specific aspects of emotional performance that are the most direct objects of customers' attention, such as facial displays and bodily movements. By contrast, deep-acting targets a relatively wider range of emotion-related processes including the attentional activity, appraisals and thoughts that can activate and sustain other components of the emotion syndrome.

Whatever else they might involve, surface-acting and deep-acting clearly require different kinds of emotion regulation (e.g., Grandey, 2000). Surface-acting involves regulating visible signs and symptoms of emotion. For example, service workers may try to conceal their spontaneous facial movements (e.g., by affecting a coughing fit to cover up unwanted laughter or adopting a 'poker face') or feign the expression of an emotion that does not match their current appraisals. In other words, the forms of emotion regulation that are most directly associated with surface-acting include expressive suppression, simulation and masking, all of which count as 'response modulation' in Gross's (1998a) terms.

By contrast, deep-acting seems to be an antecedent- rather than response-focused regulation strategy, typically involving reallocating attention or reappraising the current situation in order to produce intended emotional outcomes. For example, flight attendants trained to imagine that the flight cabin is their living room at home where passengers are welcome visitors (Hochschild, 1983) learn to mentally reconfigure the work situation in ways that set the stage for transformed emotional orientations to what is happening. Correspondingly, emotional labourers who think of customers as helpless children (see Chapter 5) or victims of personal trauma shift to a more empathic, other-focused perspective with associated emotional consequences.

Hochschild (1983) argued that both surface-acting and deep-acting can be damaging to well-being because they encourage employees to distance themselves from their authentic feelings. However, she saw deep-acting as more costly because it penetrates closer to the heart of personal identity. By contrast, Grandey (2000) proposed that surface-acting is relatively more maladaptive because any associated response suppression involves a more effortful and less effective form of emotion regulation than the reappraisal associated with deep-acting (e.g., Butler et al., 2003; Gross & Levenson, 1993; and see Chapter 5).

Consistent with the latter predictions, Brotheridge and Lee (2003) found that participants' scores on a self-report measure of surface-acting reliably predicted their level of emotional exhaustion and depersonalisation, whereas deep-acting scores did not. Results of relevant meta-analyses similarly confirm that surface-acting (but not deep-acting) tends to be associated with negative outcomes such as low job satisfaction and increased stress across a range of studies (Hülsheger & Schewe, 2011; Kammeyer-Mueller et al., 2013; Mesmer-Magnus, DeChurch & Wax, 2012).

However, there are issues with the self-report questionnaires typically used to measure surface-acting in these studies. Items typically assess participants' perception that their work role requires them to put on an act rather than engaging with customers more spontaneously. The resulting scores may therefore depend on participants' sensitivity to any organisational pressures to change their behaviour rather than their actual use of emotion regulation. In this connection, Rafaeli and Sutton (1987) argue that workers who feel that the emotional demands of their employers are legitimate are less likely to suffer negative consequences. They are 'faking in good faith'. By contrast, workers who feel that their employers' emotional demands are illegitimate fake in 'bad faith' and therefore feel worse about their emotional labour. Perhaps then, self-reports of surface-acting partly reflect employees' lack of identification with their customer-oriented work role (Ashforth & Humphrey, 1993; Parkinson, 1991), and the associated sense of alienation from the products of their emotional labour. Dealing with customers may seem more like effortful surface-acting when your feelings about customers (and your job more generally) are already negative.

Consistent with this reasoning, Kammeyer-Mueller and colleagues' meta-analysis (2013) showed that measures of surface-acting were predicted by participants' dispositional tendencies to experience negative emotions and by their perceptions that their jobs involved suppression of bad feelings. However, surface-acting remained a negative predictor of job satisfaction even after controlling for these effects, suggesting that its negative impact does not only depend on workers' feelings that their organisation encourages them to cover up negative emotions for the benefit of customers. Kammeyer-Mueller and colleagues therefore concluded that the experience of surface-acting reminds employees of the distance between their actual feelings and the emotions that the job requires them to express (i.e., emotional dissonance, in Hochschild's, 1983, terms).

Another methodological issue is that most studies rely on aggregate cross-sectional measures that ask participants about their general experiences of emotional labour at a single time-point. This makes it impossible to determine whether surface acting is a cause, correlate or consequence of dissatisfaction with the work situation and customer relations. Although studies using longitudinal (e.g., Hülsheger, Lang & Maier, 2010) or diary methods (e.g., Judge, Woolf & Hurst, 2009; Totterdell & Holman, 2003; Wagner, Barnes & Scott, 2014) often also find worse outcomes for surface-acting than deep-acting, even here some of these effects may depend on factors that prompted the regulation of emotion in the first place. For example, service workers may be more inclined to report pretending to feel something they are not feeling when they have recently been dealing with customers or line managers whose behaviour towards them makes them feel angry or anxious. Indeed, employees report using more surface-acting when customer aggression is more stressful (Grandey, Dickter & Sin, 2004) and when their supervisors are abusive (Carlson et al., 2012). Customer interactions that last for longer periods of time also seem to be associated with a greater demand for emotional labour (Morris & Feldman, 1996). Perhaps then, some of the apparently negative consequences of surface-acting are attributable to the changing work pressures that encourage its use rather than its inherent costliness.

To gain a better understanding of emotional labour, it is important to consider how regulatory attempts adjust dynamically to customer and supervisor demands on a tighter time scale than is usually investigated. For example, employees may intensify their use of surface-acting only during episodes when their expressions fail to solicit the required interpersonal feedback quickly enough. If so, the apparent costs may reflect the continuing use of a strategy which is not successfully producing intended effects during interactions with clients.

Disentangling the relevant unfolding processes in real-world organisational settings is difficult. Even diary studies that collect multiple observations for every work-shift (e.g., Totterdell & Holman, 2003) rarely track
moment-by-moment variations in the implementation of emotional
labour in relation to unfolding affective events (e.g., Beal et al., 2006;
Beal & Trougakos, 2013; Diefendorff & Gosserand, 2003). However,
some studies have used real-time measures to address related issues in
more controlled settings. For example, participants in Gabriel and
Diefendorff's (2015) study took on the role of call-centre employees who
had to assist a student from another university with the task of preparing
a presentation using PowerPoint software. Unbeknownst to participants,
the caller's contributions to the telephone interaction were prerecorded so
that they could be delivered at appropriate moments. His initial remarks
were polite, but he then became increasingly rude before finishing the
interaction in either a polite or rude manner depending on experimental
condition.

When the task was complete, participants listened to an audio recording of the telephone call and made continuous ratings of their own
emotional reactions and of the extent to which they had used surface-
acting and deep-acting as the conversation progressed. Unsurprisingly,
participants reported more positive emotions during periods when the
caller was polite. Further, both caller incivility and self-reported negative
emotion prompted emotional labour in the form of surface- and deep-
acting. These findings support the contention that some of the negative
consequences of emotional labour reported in earlier studies may have
depended on the interpersonal pressures provoking its use.

Interestingly, Gabriel and Diefendorff also found close interrelations
between participants' ratings of their use of surface-acting and deep-
acting over time, suggesting that both forms of emotion regulation may
be deployed simultaneously and that the line between them may sometimes be difficult to draw. Thus, online emotional labour may often
involve a combination of regulation strategies used in tandem (e.g.,
Cossette & Hess, 2015), making it harder to isolate their separate real-
time effects. In retrospective studies, participants' selective recall of these
strategies may make them seem less interdependent than they really are.

Alternative Regulation Strategies

Emotional labour research has started to move away from crude comparisons between surface-acting and deep-acting and to focus instead on
more specific forms of emotion regulation and their effects. Investigators
have increasingly come to realise that surface-acting does not necessarily
equate with expressive suppression, and that deep-acting does not necessarily equate with reappraisal (e.g., Grandey & Melloy, 2017). Finer

distinctions between the different possible regulatory strategies used in different forms of emotional labour permit a more nuanced understanding of their context-sensitive effects.

One issue with previous formulations is that the selective focus on suppressive forms of surface-acting tended to restrict the range of customer interactions that researchers sampled. For example, people might be most inclined to cover up their expressions when they are in situations that are difficult to reappraise in a more positive light, and when the other people around are unlikely to be sympathetic or helpful. In contexts such as this, they may not be able to stop themselves from feeling bad but at least they can conceal their susceptibility from people who might otherwise make things even worse.

Operationalising deep-acting as reappraisal similarly constrained the focus of investigation. Emotional labourers are more likely to reappraise situations that are susceptible to a range of alternative formulations (i.e., those with greater reappraisal affordances, Suri et al., 2018). When there are fewer degrees of cognitive freedom, alternative means of deep-acting such as attention deflection using distraction or other forms of cognitive disengagement may be preferred. Evidence consistent with this reasoning was obtained by Sheppes and colleagues (2011). Their research showed that participants preferred to think of something neutral when confronted by more intense emotional stimuli, but to consider alternative appraisals when emotional stimuli were less powerful. Thus, deep-acting involving reappraisal may seem to have relatively better consequences than surface-acting because of the weaker emotional situations that typically prompt its use in the first place. Indeed, Sheppes, Catran and Meiran (2009) found that reappraisal may be more effortful and difficult to implement when the emotional meaning of a negative stimulus has already consolidated. Similarly, deep-acting may be more costly if the pressing reality of an unpleasant social situation is hard to ignore or reformulate.

Reappraisal itself may also take a variety of forms (see Chapter 5). In early research by Lazarus's research group (e.g., Speisman et al., 1964), participants exposed to upsetting films were instructed to adopt different attitudes involving intellectualisation or denial which differentially affected their emotional reactions (see Chapter 1). The forms of reappraisal deployed during service encounters are more likely to involve different kinds of role-taking or modulating the salience of alternative social identities (as we shall see), but here too different effects may depend on their mode, focus and appropriateness. For example, when a customer complaint inadvertently touches on one of the employee's specific sensitivities, or is potentially interpretable as a deep personal insult, self-distancing (e.g., Kross & Ayduk, 2011) may work better than increasing levels of interpersonal involvement. By contrast, when a customer is making a reasonable demand at the end of a work shift when personal resources are starting to deplete, it may be more effective for an employee to work on their relational orientation more directly by using perspective-taking strategies (Totterdell & Holman, 2003).

More generally, investigating emotional labour as a form of emotion regulation (e.g., Grandey, 2000) implies not only that a wider range of strategies than expressive suppression and reappraisal needs to be considered, but also that their relative effectiveness needs to be evaluated across different possible contexts of use. This more differentiated approach is likely to lead to the conclusion that no single strategy works best under all circumstances (cf. Aldao et al., 2010), and that regulatory effectiveness depends on flexibility and the ability to tailor emotional labour to the specific demands of the current situation (e.g., Cossette & Hess, 2015; and see Chapter 5).

It is also important to acknowledge that not all consequences of emotional labour depend directly on its emotion-regulatory components. Organisationally imposed pressure to work on expressions and feelings may itself impact on well-being and performance, not least because it may lead to a sense of diminished personal control (Hochschild, 1983; Rafaeli & Sutton, 1987). Choosing to adopt a particular interpersonal style because it is consistent with a valued social identity is more likely to bring positive consequences (e.g., Parkinson, 1991; 1995). In other words, the motives shaping regulatory efforts contribute to their outcomes in addition to the processes whereby regulation is achieved (e.g., Niven, 2016; Tamir, 2016).

Collaborative Emotional Labour

Despite their attention to organisational predictors and outcomes, most researchers treat emotional labour as a mainly individual matter. It is the isolated worker who personally manages their emotions and those of their customers and clients. However, most service employees interact with their co-workers before, during or after performing their emotional tasks. This allows them not only to collaborate in performing emotional labour but also to support one another in a process of 'reciprocal emotion management' (Lively, 2000, p. 33). For example, a colleague may stand close by when a customer seems likely to become abusive (cf. Spencer & Rupp, 2009), or more actively offer sympathy and social support (e.g., McGuire, 2007). Further, emotional labourers often work in teams to achieve emotional effects on customers, as illustrated when waiters and waitresses come together to sing 'Happy Birthday' to a diner at a restaurant. Indeed, it may be easier to get involved in the performance when mutual encouragement spreads through a group of people working on a common task (see Chapter 7). As yet, few researchers have directly investigated these interpersonal and intragroup emotional labour processes.

Customers and clients can also help or hinder in the process of delivering emotional labour (Rafaeli & Sutton, 1987). Like co-workers they may sometimes respond to mistreatment of service employees by showing concern or offering help (e.g., Henkel et al., 2017). More generally, cooperative customers may help to sustain and reinforce the definition of the social situation being presented by a service worker by adopting an appropriate complementary role (e.g., Goffman, 1959). Thus, one of the flight attendants interviewed by Hochschild (1983) reported that the passenger's response to surface-acting encouraged a deeper identification with the implied relational orientation: 'If I pretend I'm feeling really up, sometimes I actually get into it. The passenger responds to me as though I were friendly, and then some more of me responds back' (p. 56).

Some authors have argued that examples such as these imply that the usual distinction between surface-acting and deep-acting ignores a third option of expressing genuine customer-directed emotion (e.g., Ashforth & Humphrey, 1993; Cossette & Hess, 2015; Diefendorff, Croyle & Gosserand, 2005). An alternative interpretation is that the rewards of client engagement may sometimes lead employees to embrace the relational orientations associated with their work in a more whole-hearted manner.

Parkinson (1991; 1995) suggested that this is most likely to happen when service jobs permit a greater degree of improvisation, personal discretion and flexibility (e.g., Cossette & Hess, 2015), and when client interactions extend over longer periods of time or are recurrent (e.g., Morris & Feldman, 1996). For example, a physiotherapist, personal trainer or life coach may well develop more deeply involved relationships with clients even when their emotional implications comply with the employing organisation's requirements (e.g., George, 2008). Surface-acting may transition to deep-acting, and deep-acting may reinforce the social identity associated with the satisfying performance of emotional labour. A further relevant consideration is the kind of service that an employee is providing. Thus, delivering promotional offers often encourages deeper role-identification than dealing with customer complaints.

Similar reasoning also suggests that working on identification with your work role may be an effective form of deep-acting in certain organisational contexts. Instead of actively taking the client's perspective, employees may persuade themselves that the company's needs concord with their own and come to see client reactions as emotionally relevant for that reason. Again, such practices are facilitated by collaborative work between employees who work together as coherent teams in the performance of service tasks. For example, waiters and waitresses at a restaurant may cultivate a sense of bonhomie in their interactions with each other as well as with diners. Organisations also have their own stake in encouraging this kind of esprit de corps as evidenced by the various team-building exercises and away-days that are prevalent in contemporary managerial practice. Participation in such events clearly involves similar kinds of emotion regulation to emotional labour. Perhaps, then, the ability to engage enthusiastically with paint-balling or orienteering may turn out to be a transferable skill after all.

Organisations provide practical as well as interpersonal resources to facilitate emotional labour. For example, they may institute promotional campaigns intended mainly to induce goodwill in the target market. If these campaigns are successful, they can also make it easier for employees to manage customers' emotions. In some cases, employees may even play a direct role in delivering prizes or administering loyalty programs, thus permitting an additional means of interpersonal emotion regulation. These examples reinforce the point that emotional labour often involves a reciprocal process operating between service workers and their clients. Making a customer happy may make it easier to behave positively towards them too. Thus, employees may regulate their clients' emotions as an indirect way of regulating their own emotions as well as vice versa. The next section focuses specifically on the impact of emotional labour on its interpersonal targets.

Interpersonal Effects on Customers

The central aim of emotional labour is to influence customers' affective states rather than employees' own well-being. Several studies have directly addressed these interpersonal effects. The most common (and least surprising) finding is that customers generally react more positively to service employees who show happier expressions. For example, Tidd and Lockard (1978) manipulated the intensity of smiles delivered by an experimenter who was working as a cocktail waitress when approaching tables for drink orders. When leaving the cocktail lounge, customers smiled back at the waitress more when she had delivered a higher intensity smile. Male but not female customers also left bigger tips in this high-intensity smile condition. In another study, Pugh (2001) found that bank customers reported more positive feelings and evaluated the service they received more positively after interacting with tellers whose facial expressions indicated higher levels of positive affect. Similarly, Tsai and Huang (2002) showed that customers spent longer in shoe shops when service staff greeted them, smiled and engaged in eye contact when they arrived.

Evidence from these studies confirms that emotional labour often affects customers in the intended way. Although relation-alignment processes such as social appraisal probably contribute to the reported interpersonal effects, few researchers have directly assessed their operation. Indeed, most studies resort to the default explanation of emotional contagion without systematically evaluating possible alternative accounts. Barger and Grandey (2006) tried to provide more direct evidence that contagion is a key factor by showing that customers' reciprocated smiling mediated effects of employees' emotion presentations on judgements of service quality. However, customers may have smiled back at service workers either as a polite acknowledgement or a communication of their own happy response rather than as a consequence of any contagion-related mimicry (e.g., Kim & Yoon, 2012).

A number of studies have assessed whether surface-acting and deep-acting have different interpersonal effects on customers. According to Hochschild (1983), organisations first started to encourage deep-acting in response to a perceived customer demand for authentic emotional engagement. If so, one implication is that customers should react relatively more positively to service workers who use this form of emotional labour. Consistent with this argument, Grandey (2003) found that university administrative assistants' reported use of deep-acting was positively correlated with co-workers' evaluations of the quality of the service they provided, whereas the corresponding correlation was negative for surface-acting. Controlling for the effects of employees' reported job satisfaction did not remove this difference, making it unlikely that prior disaffection with the work role explained the reported relationships between style of emotional labour and service quality.

Groth, Hennig-Thurau and Walsh (2009) collected data from both customers and employees after a wider range of service encounters. Reported deep-acting tended to increase customer evaluations of employees' customer orientation and service quality whereas reported surface-acting had no consistent effects. In a related study, Chi and colleagues (2011) analysed customer feedback on restaurant waiters' service delivery provided on comment cards handed out to diners. Waiters' reported use of deep-acting positively predicted both perceptions that the waiter had exceeded diners' expectation and levels of received tips. By contrast, surface-acting positively predicted level of tips only for waiters scoring relatively higher on a personality measure of extraversion, perhaps because their smiles seemed more reflective of their character and less forced even when they were actually put on.

Stronger conclusions about the causal impact of deep-acting on customer responses require experimental methods. Grandey and colleagues (2005) therefore manipulated an actress's use of different styles of emotional labour to present a positive demeanour in the role of a hotel receptionist. Participants watched the videotape of her deep-acted or surface-acted performance while imagining themselves as the guest with whom she was interacting. Their ratings of satisfaction with the encounter were higher in the deep-acting condition, but only when the receptionist competently performed the tasks of locating their reservation and delivering appropriate information. Rated satisfaction was generally lower across experimental conditions when the receptionist made mistakes entering the guest's name and could not immediately find the reservation because she was looking at the wrong computer screen. These findings suggest that service performance may override effects of emotional labour (e.g., Sutton & Rafaeli, 1988). Alternatively, participants may have simply perceived the receptionist's smiling as relatively less appropriate when the interaction was not proceeding smoothly. Under these circumstances, apologetic displays relating to embarrassment or guilt may have been more welcome.

Hennig-Thurau and colleagues (2006) trained drama students to use deep-acting or surface-acting to convey positive emotions to participants who had been recruited to try out a new personalised service offering advice about renting movies on DVD. The actors were instructed to use Stanislavskian method-acting techniques for the deep-acting condition, and to work on their displays but not their internal feelings in the surface-acting condition. Participants' emotions improved to a greater extent over the course of their interaction with the actor in the deep-acting condition. Improvement in emotions also positively predicted participants' satisfaction with the encounter, which in turn positively predicted their intentions to use the service in future. However, the instruction to express but not feel positive emotion may have made the surface-acting condition relatively more difficult to perform leading to mixed emotional signals. Indeed, actors' levels of smiling were also lower in this condition than in the deep-acting condition.

Despite the specific limitations of the individual studies, the overall pattern of results suggests that employees' deep-acting of positive emotions tends to improve customer satisfaction whereas surface-acting does not usually yield comparable effects. This conclusion is also supported by the results of Hülsheger and Schewe's (2011) meta-analysis which found that deep-acting's positive effects on customer responses tended to parallel its positive effects on employee well-being. This raises the possibility that one of the reasons deep-acting employees feel better is that they are responding to the positive interpersonal feedback that they solicit from customers (as we shall see).

Why does deep-acting enhance customers' responses to service delivery? A number of factors relating to the configuration, timing and context-attunement of deep-acted displays may affect interpersonal perceptions, interpretations and reciprocated behaviour. However, most of the relevant research has focused specifically on customers' perceptions of emotional authenticity. The idea is that successfully implemented deep-acting should lead to genuine expressions of emotion rather than inauthentic simulations, and that customers are sensitive to this difference. For example, deep-acting may be better able to produce Duchenne smiles rather than polite or fake smiles. Although none of the supposed markers of emotional authenticity provide unambiguous evidence about a person's internal state (see Chapter 3), it remains possible that customers' perceptions of authenticity based on these facial cues (or on their dynamic relation to unfolding events) account for their greater levels of satisfaction with emotional labour delivered using deep-acting.

Unfortunately, researchers have often operationalised perceived authenticity by asking participants about the extent of employees' deep-acting rather than about how genuine the presented expressions seem (e.g., Houston, Grandey & Sawyer, 2018). For example, items on a commonly used scale include: 'the employee worked hard to feel the emotions that s/he needed to show to me' (Groth et al., 2009, p. 974). Perversely, this means that questions intended to assess whether respondents perceive expressions as authentically reflecting genuinely felt emotions in fact ask how much effort employees have put into manufacturing them. Indeed, Groth and colleagues originally developed the scale to assess 'emotional labour detection accuracy' rather than emotional authenticity as such, devising their items by rewording self-report items used to assess service workers' deep-acting and surface-acting attempts.

Groth and colleagues' (2009) own study found that effects of deep-acting on perceptions of service employees' customer orientation were stronger when scores on their detection-accuracy measure corresponded to employees' own ratings of the extent to which they had used deep-acting (in other words when customers agreed with employees about their regulation style). As the authors argue, this effect probably reflects customers' recognition of the effort that employees have put into the performance of their service role rather than customer perceptions of emotional authenticity per se. In other words, participants may simply have perceived deep-acted expressions as having been worked on more thoroughly than surface-acted expressions (whose detection was assessed using items describing the employee as 'just pretending'). Perhaps, then, any more positive interpersonal effects of 'perceived authenticity' scores reported in subsequent studies actually depend on customers' recognition of service employees' greater commitment to pleasing them.

Glomb and Tews (2004) developed an alternative measure of emotional authenticity based on employees' self-ratings rather than customers' interpersonal perceptions. Respondents are asked to report how often they express a number of specific pleasant and unpleasant emotions when they really do not feel that way. Using this measure, researchers have shown that higher reported frequencies of genuinely expressed unpleasant emotions tend to be positively related to the employees' levels of emotional exhaustion (e.g., Glomb & Tews, 2004; Medler-Liraz & Seger-Guttmann, 2018). However, none of the relevant studies have yet provided clear evidence of interpersonal effects of employees' authenticity scores on customers' experiences. At any rate, employees' judgements of how accurately they are expressing their emotions are not necessarily reflected in customers' perceptions.

Although most of the studies reviewed in this section suggest that deep-acting generally makes customers feel better about service encounters, not all customers seem to respond equally positively. For example, Houston, Grandey and Sawyer (2018) found that deep-acting improved White US participants' evaluations of service quality but not those of Black participants. The researchers attributed this difference to the fact that Black customers' previous experiences of service delivery had lowered their expectations. The interpersonal effects of surface-acting do not apply universally either. For example, Wang and Groth (2014) showed that covering up negative emotional reactions worsened customer reactions to a lesser extent when customers had a closer relationship with the service provider, and to a greater extent when the provided service was more personalised. Taken together, the findings from these two studies suggest that customer responses are shaped by the different norms about appropriate emotional presentations that apply to different people in different contexts (e.g., Cheshin, Amit & van Kleef, 2018). Future studies also need to address whether any differential interpersonal effects of deep-acting and surface-acting depend on the specific strategies that service workers deploy to regulate their emotions and expressions.

Interpersonal Effects on Service Employees

When the purpose of emotional labour is to improve relations with customers, employees not only need to work up positive emotions or expressions but also to suppress any negative emotional reactions to customers. This is made particularly difficult when those customers behave badly or direct negative emotional communications at service employees. A number of studies have focused on how employees react emotionally when customers get angry or upset with them, thus presenting the converse of the positive interpersonal effects considered in the previous section.

Dealing with customer anger is a central component of some service jobs such as working in complaints departments. Grandey and colleagues (2004) studied call-centre workers at a utility company who had to deal with enquiries about bills. On average, the sampled employees reported experiencing seven events per day when a customer had become 'very angry' and directed verbal aggression at them. Overall, this number constituted approximately 15–20 per cent of the calls that employees had to take. Unsurprisingly, employees reporting higher numbers of angry calls rated their stress and emotional exhaustion as higher and were more likely to be absent from work in subsequent days. More recent diary-based research by Chi, Yang and Lin (2018) suggests that negative effects of unpleasant customer interactions may even spill over into home life. Apparently, employees are not always able to follow company advice of 'Don't TIP' (Don't Take It Personal: Grandey et al., 2004, p. 405).

Sliter and colleagues (2010) presented evidence that effects of customer rudeness on employee well-being partly depend on the associated demands of emotion regulation. Bank tellers experiencing more customer incivility also reported suppressing negative emotions and faking positive emotions to a greater extent. Further, controlling for the effects of customer incivility on emotional labour significantly reduced incivility's effects on both emotional exhaustion and service performance, suggesting that regulation of emotional responses to problem customers is personally costly.

Customers' emotional behaviour towards service employees is not always negative. Indeed, one motive for seeking jobs in the service sector may be to enjoy positive interactions with the people that you deal with. Zimmermann, Dormann and Dollard (2011) showed that customers' levels of positive affect prior to interactions with dealers or mechanics at car dealerships positively predicted these employees' subsequent levels of positive affect. This effect was mediated by employees' rating of how supportive and appreciative customers had been towards them. Holman (2016) also found that positive interactions with customers improved outcomes for employees. In his study, supermarket clerks whose customers smiled, made eye contact and conversed with them suffered less from emotional exhaustion.

Interpersonal Mediators of Intrapersonal Outcomes

So far, we have seen how service employees' emotions and expressions affect customers, and how customers' emotions and expressions affect service employees. In this section, we consider evidence that these two processes work reciprocally and in combination. For example, it seems possible that engaging with customers using deep-acting solicits positive interpersonal feedback that in turn improves employee well-being.

Rafaeli and Sutton (1987) emphasised that emotional labour is an interactive process that depends on how customers respond to workers' regulation strategies. For example, employees may use escalating emotional influence attempts when their target does not respond as intended or they may damp down their regulatory activities when a desired interpersonal response is immediately forthcoming. More generally, the customer's response provides interpersonal feedback concerning the success of interpersonal emotion-regulation attempts in addition to motivating emotion regulation in the first place. Employees communicate emotions that customers reciprocate or fail to reciprocate, and employees in turn respond to customers' reciprocation or failure to reciprocate (and so on). Alternatively, customers present emotional complaints to which service employees respond, and customers in turn react to employees' response and its perceived adequacy. In either case, the interaction process involves one or more interpersonal emotion cycles (Hareli & Rafaeli, 2008). Considering either person's actions or reactions in isolation fails to capture the socially distributed nature of what is happening during the service encounter (see also Côté, 2005).

One implication of this analysis is that the personal costs and benefits of emotional labour experienced by employees may partly depend on how customers respond to its implementation. For example, service personnel are likely to feel better when customers react positively to their interpersonal presentations of emotion. Testing this idea, Kim and Yoon (2012) used similar methods to those used in Barger and Grandey's (2006) earlier study of reciprocated smiling, but assessed employees' affect in addition to customers' affect. Two separate coders assessed the extent to which service personnel and potential buyers in clothing and accessory stores expressed positive affect during interactions that involved advice about selecting particular items for purchase (e.g., 'this new dress fits you very well' and 'this colour would be better for you', p. 1062). Immediately afterwards, both employees and customers were given brief questionnaires including additional ratings of each other's expressions of positive affect during their conversation. As predicted, employees felt happier when customers reciprocated their expressed positive affect. Further, the effect of employees' smiling on their own happiness depended entirely on customers' reciprocated smiling, thus suggesting that interpersonal rather than interoceptive feedback underlay the interpersonal influence process (see Chapter 4).

Emotional interactions between employees and customers may involve vicious as well as virtuous circles (e.g., Groth & Grandey, 2012). Traut-Mattausch and colleagues (2015) argued that service employees often defensively devalue customers when they present complaints. Customers often respond to the communicated devaluation by devaluing the employee in return. Clearly, this relational dynamic has the potential to produce an escalating spiral of mutual contempt. In their studies, Traut-Mattausch and colleagues separately investigated different aspects of this interpersonal process, focusing mainly on individual perceptions rather than interactive behaviour. For example, one of their studies involved mystery callers telephoning the hotline of a German airline with aggressive complaints. These callers tended to rate the airline employee's competence and performance as worse than did callers whose enquiries did not involve complaints, consistent with the devaluation hypothesis. However, it is also possible that employees' attempts to deal with customer anger interfered with the quality of the information they were able to provide, thus producing a more negative impression of their competence. In order to substantiate the proposed vicious cycle of reciprocated devaluation, future studies need to track the interpersonal process throughout its full course taking into account both sides of the dialogue.

Zhan, Wang and Shi (2016) used diary methods to assess employee perceptions of customers' positive and negative emotional behaviour. Employees' self-reported use of surface-acting predicted their perceptions of more negative treatment by customers which in turn predicted reported levels of negative affect and emotional exhaustion. Conversely, deep-acting increased perceptions of positive customer treatment and employee positive affect. Zhan and colleagues' daily diary data allowed them to track changes in the use of emotional labour and subsequent variations in affect over time. However, employees' perceptions of customer mistreatment may have been distorted by their own emotional responses or their attempts to regulate these responses using reappraisal or other means. As the investigators acknowledge, this raises questions about whether similar findings would be obtained using dyadic designs (e.g., Kim & Yoon, 2012) where both parties to service encounters provide their own data. Dyadic diary studies that use more time-intensive or continuous measures (e.g., Gabriel & Diefendorff, 2015) should provide more definitive evidence about the dynamic operation of these relational processes.

Reappraising Emotional Labour

Hochschild's (1983) original formulation of deep-acting was intended to draw attention to exploitative regulatory regimes that intruded into service workers' experiences at a profound level, managing their hearts as well as their limbs, hands or faces. In her view, the imposition of feeling rules carried potential costs over and above those of mere display rules. In particular, employees trained to change their emotional perspective towards customers might lose touch with the concerns underlying their emotions even outside their performance of the prescribed work role. Consequently, their grasp of authentically involving emotional events might also begin to slip in their home lives.

Organisational psychologists have rarely found direct evidence of these supposed costs of deep-acting, and often demonstrated benefits instead. Some of these apparent benefits may reflect investigators' restrictive focus on the use of reappraisal as a means of deep-acting and the limitations resulting from assessing only directly reportable short-term effects. Someone who has worked up identification with their work role in order to see things from the customer's perspective may not be explicitly aware of the effort involved or its impact on alternative future identifications. Arguably, employees who are fully immersed in the Stanislavskian method don't see what they are doing as acting or emotion regulation in any case. In other words, the costs of deep-acting may be difficult to detect using questionnaires, diaries or direct behavioural observation, or otherwise slow to surface.

However, the more obvious interpretation of the available findings is that deep-acting does not always cause lasting or pervasive damage. Rather than shifting the register of emotional labour, it merely exploits a wider range of possibilities for transforming relationships with customers, facilitating the adoption of new kinds of roles and social identities. What makes the consequences of these strategies functional or dysfunctional is not how deeply they intrude into personal consciousness but how they reconfigure the relations between people for better or worse in the specific situations where they are deployed. They are sustained or disrupted by the interpersonal feedback they solicit.

Therapeutic Encounters

Research into emotional labour has mainly addressed costs and benefits of up-regulating positive emotions or down-regulating upsetting reactions to interpersonal mistreatment. However, other kinds of emotional engagement with customers are also possible. Relationships may develop over extended or repeated service encounters that involve less obviously manufactured emotions (e.g., Ashforth & Humphrey, 1993). Indeed, the pleasures of getting to know other people provide one of the key motives for pursuing socially oriented careers. Employees don't need to use either surface- or deep-acting when they already care about their clients, even if their caring depends on identification with a prescribed work role rather than any extra-occupational personal identity. Except for any regulation that might be required to work up this role identification in the first place, the associated emotional performance does not even seem to involve emotional labour as such.

However, there are still potential costs and benefits to these work-related emotions, which may require distinctive kinds of regulation and emotional labour further downstream. In particular, employees who are emotionally engaged with their clients' personal traumas or tragedies may sometimes feel that they need to detach or distance themselves either to protect their well-being or to stay focused on any technical aspects of their work performance. In these cases, their job is not to cover up or reappraise their response to any anger or aggression that customers may direct at them, but instead to regulate their level of empathy and involvement with the other person's anxiety, distress or pain (e.g., Benbassat & Baumal, 2004; Hodges & Biswas-Diener, 2007). They need to decide which parts of the client's life are genuinely their personal business too.

Issues of empathy regulation come to the fore in the caring professions. Although the emotions that doctors, therapists and nurses experience towards or about their clients are not usually seen as institutionally enforced distortions of their spontaneous responses, the energy expended in their enactment and regulation can still take its toll, and adopting effective strategies of emotion management may still make a difference to experienced outcomes. How much and what kind of empathy should carers show towards their clients and patients? It is widely believed that perceived risks of overinvestment need to be balanced against the prospect of becoming uncaring and immune to other people's suffering (e.g., Gleichgerrcht & Decety, 2012). Neither extreme of empathy nor total apathy seems a workable solution. Where should the line be drawn?

Detached Concern
Western caring institutions have traditionally encouraged a professional attitude of 'detached concern' towards clients (Lief & Fox, 1963). In some organisations, training regimes explicitly enforce and foster this perspective. In others, it develops more informally as a result of occupational socialisation. For example, an American medical intern quoted by Daniels (1960) recounted the process whereby emotional investment in patients who are seriously ill can decrease as a function of experience:

> As a student in medical school I tended to become more emotionally identified with the patient, or at least with those who were the loved ones of the patient. I had to learn to restrain myself, to see that this is just another case of something that will go on and on and never end completely as long as there is human life and death.   (p. 260)

For this respondent, managing empathy ultimately came to involve selectively rationing personal engagement and preserving psychological distance:

> [Y]ou know, intellectually, what it must feel like to be facing death or for the loved ones to know this fact, but you don't, except in a few cases, feel the deep sorrow – this you reserve for your own loved ones ... Today, for instance, there was a man admitted with cancer of the larynx. He will never talk again after it is removed. Today and tonight he chatted cheerfully with his family. Tomorrow night, his speech will be gone forever. You can say, 'I am sorry, old chap', or something of that nature, or think the same, but inwardly you cannot become too personally involved.   (p. 260)

Instead of covering up what they 'really feel', medical practitioners such as this intern actively avoid letting themselves feel it in the first place. Their reappraisal strategy is similar to the intellectualisation condition from Speisman and colleagues' (1964) experiment, where participants were instructed to view ritual suffering from a detached anthropological perspective. Unlike service personnel, carers practising detached concern do not work up positive interpersonal emotions, but instead adopt an orientation that allows them to focus on technical rather than interpersonal aspects of what they are doing. This reframing of events (e.g., Gleichgerrcht & Decety, 2012; Hodges & Biswas-Diener, 2007) might be seen as a form of deep-acting, and clearly involves active regulation attempts, at least until automaticity takes over. However, the purpose is not to please or mollify the patient but rather to maintain a certain pattern of relations that are believed to permit effective performance of the task at hand.

For many more recent commentators, detached concern involves striking the wrong balance between impersonality and overinvestment. Indeed, different organisations, societies and historical eras have tipped the scales of empathy either up or down. For example, the ideal of 'whole-person care' in contemporary medical practice implies a greater degree of individual attention and engagement than earlier ideas of detached concern (e.g., Derksen et al., 2016). Many authors explicitly encourage the development of a more empathy-driven approach (e.g., Halpern, 2001). In their view, adopting a matter-of-fact perspective towards events that seriously impact your clients' lives may bring costs not only for their well-being but also for your own ability to understand and respond to their situation. Intellectualisation and detachment may well moderate immediate unpleasant feelings of sympathy and pity, but they also take away some of the sense of engagement and involvement that can sustain motivation. Interpersonal rewards as well as costs lose some of their impact.

However, detached concern often develops not only as an ideological preference, but also as a practical response to job demands. Increasing workloads coupled with protocol-based procedures have led to corresponding reductions in doctors' emotional engagement with patients (e.g., Derksen et al., 2016). Indeed, Butalid, Bensing and Verhaak (2014) coded GP–patient interactions that had been videotaped in the Netherlands between 1977 and 2008 and found that the frequency of statements expressing empathy or offering reassurance reduced significantly following the introduction of clinical guidelines in 1990. Changing the emotional style of caring therefore involves more than revising training procedures. It also requires allocation of resources to permit reconfiguration of work tasks.

Burnout

One of the arguments for cultivating detached concern is that it helps to avoid the risk of burnout, one of the most commonly discussed long-term effects of engaging emotionally with clients or customers. The basic idea is that personal resources for interpersonal investment ultimately become overtaxed and depleted. The internal battery powering empathic responses simply runs flat.

The first academic formulation of burnout is usually attributed to Freudenberger (1974), who used the term to characterise the personal experiences of carers and administrators involved in the free clinic movement, originating in Haight Ashbury in the late 1960s. Freudenberger was a consulting psychiatrist who worked alongside other volunteers at a free clinic in New York's Lower East Side, where many of the clients were homeless people or drug addicts. His insights were based on observations of his colleagues as well as more direct personal experience of the newly labelled condition. Freudenberger's use of the term 'burnout' may have been inspired by its related usage to describe the mental hollowing out that resulted from protracted abuse of illicit drugs (Schaufeli, Leiter & Maslach, 2009). By extension, Freudenberger suggested that energised engagement with emotionally rewarding interpersonal care can ultimately incapacitate the maintenance of that emotional energy. For Freudenberger and many of the theorists who built on his work, 'frustrated idealism was a defining quality of the burnout experience' (Schaufeli et al., 2009, p. 206).

According to Freudenberger, one of the key factors prompting burnout was disillusionment with previously charismatic leaders, when promised progressive results failed to materialise. Disaffection supposedly began to set in roughly a year after a clinic was established, and involved staff members 'bad-rapping' the boss and sharing their negative opinions and emotions leading to 'psychic damage to the whole clinic' (1974, p. 160).

Despite this initial reference to intragroup processes, Freudenberger, like the researchers who followed him, soon turned most of his attention to individual rather than social risk factors and symptoms (see also Freudenberger, 1975).

Ginsburg (1974) developed a parallel formulation of burnout from the perspective of management studies at around the same time. For him, the underlying metaphor was of the company hotshot or rising star in a business career, whose shine and energy ultimately fizzle away when the need to keep on impressing becomes oppressive, and the upward trajectory starts to level off. A similar description of burnout as an individual existential condition was provided more than a decade earlier in Graham Greene's 1961 novel *A Burnt Out Case*. Its central protagonist was a disillusioned architect who no longer found pleasure in his life, work or fame. His attempt to escape a successful career designing award-winning churches takes him by chance to a clinic for lepers deep in the Congo, where he finds parallels between his wasting mental state and the physical mutilations of the patients around him. Psychological flames have somehow consumed his faculty for engagement in a similar manner to the leprosy bacterium's capacity to eat away at the sufferer's nerves, removing sensation. Trying to explain his condition to the local doctor, he writes: 'A vocation is an act of love ... When desire is dead one cannot continue to make love. I've come to the end of desire and to the end of a vocation' (p. 42). However, the doctor's tentative diagnosis is that the debilitating process may not yet have reached its conclusion: 'Perhaps your mutilations haven't gone far enough yet. When a man comes here too late the disease has to burn itself out' (p. 37). Both Ginsburg's and Greene's formulation of burnout bear relations to earlier notions of professional exhaustion (e.g., Veil, 1959; see Thirioux, Birault & Jaafari, 2016), and both suggest that the condition need not be terminal.

The flexibility of the burnout concept, illustrated by these interrelated but different narratives, may be one of the reasons for its continuing popularity. However, the downside is that uncertainties about its core underlying meaning remain (Heinemann & Heinemann, 2017). At any rate, more recent formulations typically acknowledge the multifaceted nature of burnout experiences (but see Kristensen et al., 2005).

The person most centrally responsible for the popularisation of the burnout concept is Christina Maslach (1982), who developed the most commonly used self-report measure of the phenomenon. The Maslach Burnout Inventory (MBI: Maslach & Jackson, 1981) includes three subscales assessing exhaustion (e.g., 'I feel emotionally drained from my work'), cynicism (e.g., 'I feel I treat some recipients as if they were impersonal "objects"') and inefficacy (e.g., disagreement with 'I deal very effectively with the problems of my recipients', pp. 102–3). In other words, burnout is usually operationalised in terms of emotional disengagement, psychological distance and self-depreciation, respectively.

Although the MBI's emotional exhaustion and cynicism scales show moderate positive intercorrelations, inefficacy is only weakly associated with the other two dimensions (Schutte et al., 2000), suggesting that burnout subscales do not necessarily assess a wholly unitary or unified construct (Kristensen et al., 2005). However, scores on all three MBI dimensions tend to be predicted by the frequency and level of client contact in caring jobs (e.g., Maslach & Pines, 1977; Shanafelt et al., 2014), consistent with the argument that each of them indexes negative reactions to engagement with others.

Although burnout applies most directly to occupations that involve interacting with other people, it may also be extended to include engagement with less directly social aspects of jobs (echoing Ginsburg's, 1974, and Greene's, 1961, conceptions). This extended formulation presents problems for the original version of the MBI, whose items mostly focus on working with 'recipients' of emotional care. However, other measures have been developed to deal with the broader remit (Kristensen et al., 2005; Maslach, Jackson & Leiter, 1996). Correspondingly, 'burnout' in common parlance has become a catchall description of a jaded inability to generate enthusiasm in any kind of work task. In people-focused jobs, emotional involvement in clients' problems is said to take its toll on the carer's own emotion over time, partly because of the effort of engagement, leading to an interpersonally withdrawn orientation where involvement is minimised. In other occupations, the disengagement resulting from exhaustion may be intellectual or physical as well as emotional and social (Kristensen et al., 2005).

Despite its scientific, professional and popular currency, the concept of 'burnout' remains controversial (Heinemann & Heinemann, 2017). Some writers argue that the core phenomenon is simply exhaustion, and that conceptually distinct varieties of emotional, physical and cognitive exhaustion are closely intercorrelated making it empirically unnecessary to distinguish them (e.g., Kristensen et al., 2005; Pines & Aronson, 1981; Shirom & Melamed, 2005). According to Kristensen and colleagues, different varieties of burnout achieve their more specific meaning and consequences when individuals attribute their fatigue to different possible life domains, specifically their personal lives, their work or the clients that they have to deal with.

Stamm's (2008) Professional Quality of Life Scale (ProQOL V) focuses specifically on outcomes experienced by professional carers who are directly exposed to the suffering of their clients. In her model, burnout is just one component of compassion fatigue (Figley, 1995; Joinson, 1992), which also includes the other empathy-related dimension of secondary traumatic stress, reflecting the extent to which carers feel suffering following exposure to clients' suffering. ProQOL also separately assesses compassion satisfaction, thereby acknowledging that interpersonal compassionate engagement does not inevitably involve costs to the carers' well-being. This alternative formulation raises questions about exactly how burnout should be located in the panoply of possible costs and benefits of caring, and about its specific relevance to certain kinds of occupational context.

There are also disagreements about the status of burnout as a diagnostic category. Although medical professionals in Sweden and the Netherlands routinely use the concept (see Schaufeli et al., 2009), 'burnout' still does not feature in the American Psychiatric Association's official classification (*DSM-5*; APA, 2013, the Diagnostic and Statistical Manual of Mental Disorders), perhaps because its precise relation to other established clinical syndromes remains unclear. Although researchers have shown that burnout as measured by MBI specifically relates to work contexts, whereas self-report depression scales relate to factors outside work (e.g., Bakker et al., 2000), key aspects of the multifaceted operationalisation of the burnout construct may still boil down to localised learned helplessness attributed to dealing with clients (cf. Kristensen et al., 2005) or secondary traumatic stress disorder (e.g., Figley, 1995).

However, symptom-based formulations such as this encourage individualised therapeutic interventions that divert attention from the institutional practices that help to sustain and reproduce individual carers' potentially maladaptive responses to the demands of caring jobs (e.g., Maslach & Leiter, 1997). For example, Dyrbye and colleagues (2009) showed that medical students' ratings of the quality of their learning environment negatively predicted burnout scores, even after controlling for personal life events (see also van Vendeloo et al., 2018). More objective aspects of the work environment, such as being on hospital rotation and having overnight shifts, also increased reported levels of burnout, suggesting that effects do not depend simply on biased negative perceptions of the work context.

Declining Empathy

Maslach's (1978) early writings conceptualised burnout as a direct self-protective reaction to the personal intrusions presented by client complaints and problems. In other words, she saw the syndrome as constituting an extreme form of the organisationally sanctioned attitude of detached concern. From this angle, burnout develops because clients tend to present issues that are unpleasant and carers are obliged to focus on negative aspects of these issues as part of their work role. The resulting social pressures tend to encourage longer-term psychological disengagement.

Evidence about the more immediate emotional costs of caring interactions comes from research that focuses on one of the most difficult social situations that medical personnel have to confront, namely delivering bad news to patients or their relatives. For example, doctors often face the unenviable task of informing people that they have a life-threatening disease or that life-saving surgery has been unsuccessful. Hulsman and colleagues (2010) asked medical students to engage in two successive interactions with a trained actor taking the role of a patient. In one interaction, the student had to take the patient's history. In the other interaction, the student had to break the news that the patient's blood test revealed an HIV infection. Participants reported higher anxiety and stress and showed signs of greater physiological arousal in the bad news condition. Subsequent studies using similar methods have supported this finding (see Studer, Danuser & Gomez, 2017, for a review).

Van Dulmen and colleagues (2007) assessed the way in which medical students delivered bad news during simulated patient interactions (see also Shaw, Brown & Dunn, 2015). Participants who reported greater levels of anticipatory stress and anxiety gazed at the patient less and expressed less concern during their conversation, supporting the idea that disengagement may be a strategy for dealing with the emotional costs of patient involvement. Reported stress levels following the interaction were also lower when the participant had empathised less with the patient. However, fatigue-related alertness deficits as well as empathy regulation may have contributed to disengagement from the interaction. Indeed, participants with lower pre-interaction heart rate (which is related to attentional activity) also gazed less at clients.

Another stressful aspect of contact with patients is the pain that many doctors have to inflict during medical procedures. Decety, Yang and Chen (2010) found that physicians showed less evidence of differential brain responses than control participants with no medical experience when shown videos of people being pricked with a needle rather than touched with a cotton bud. The investigators concluded that doctors learn to regulate their vicarious stress responses at an early stage of stimulus processing, thus making them less susceptible to empathic suffering.

Do repeated experiences of stressful interactions with patients lead to more lasting effects on empathy as proposed by Maslach's (1978) model? A number of studies have supported such a view. For example, Neumann and colleagues' (2011) literature review concluded that empathy declines were pervasive but particularly pronounced following medical trainees' experience of clinical practice, suggesting that doctors may harden their hearts partly in response to the emotional issues associated with direct interaction with patients.

However, more recent studies have suggested that reduced empathy is not an inevitable consequence of medical experience and training (e.g., Costa, Magalhaes & Costa, 2013). In Mahoney, Sladek and Neild's (2016) study, the only negative change occurred during the first year of studying medicine, and even this decline may have reflected the fact that the earliest wave of data was collected at the students' very first lecture, when heightened excitement coupled with a desire to impress may have artificially boosted reported empathy.

Smith, Norman and Decety (2017) found declines in scores on some dimensions of empathy over the course of medical training but these were offset by increases in perspective-taking and emotion contagion, suggesting a more complex pattern of changes than implied by earlier studies. Using a more direct measure of empathic responses to patient suffering, Gleichgerrcht and Decety (2014) similarly showed that doctors with more years of clinical experience perceived the suffering of a video-taped patient as relatively lower, but did not report feeling reduced vicarious distress.

Many studies of the impact of clinical experience and training on empathy have failed to include suitable control groups. Handford and colleagues (2013) therefore compared the extent that empathy declines with increasing maturity in both medical and non-medical samples. They found that the experience of dealing with patients during medical training may actually reduce the extent of empathy reduction that otherwise occurs as a consequence of life experience. Maturation-dependent empathy declines may thus help to explain the more negative conclusions of other studies lacking appropriate age-matched control groups. Indeed, Gleichgerrcht and Decety (2013) found no effects of length of medical experience on any measured dimension of dispositional empathy after controlling for age and gender. Overall, the mixed findings suggest that differences in institutional socialisation of doctors in different contexts, societies and historical eras may lead to variable effects of medical training and experience on empathy-related consequences (cf. Dyrbye et al., 2009), that only sometimes involve less engagement with patients.

Although medical training and experience do not necessarily diminish the capacity for empathy, practitioners may not always elect to exercise their empathic abilities when dealing with the emotionally affecting problems presented by their patients. Defending their well-being or attempting to maintain a professional demeanour may still lead them to disengage from emotional aspects of stressful interactions. Some of the findings of Gleichgerrcht and Decety's (2014) study are potentially consistent with this interpretation. Participants who scored high on the compassion fatigue dimension of Stamm's (2008) ProQOL scale but low on the compassion satisfaction dimension rated videotaped patients' suffering and their own vicarious response as worse than those whose high compassion fatigue was accompanied by high compassion satisfaction. In other words, unless they experience engagement with suffering patients as rewarding, doctors may react to its emotional demands by minimising the degree of perceived suffering, leading to less personal suffering as a consequence.

Patients' Responses
Withholding empathy may sometimes improve doctors' immediate experience of stressful interactions, but what effect does it have on patients? A number of studies have investigated whether physicians' use of patient-centred communication improves patients' experiences. For example, Schofield and colleagues (2003) asked recently diagnosed patients to recall the specific interaction with medical staff when they had first found out that they had cancer. Patients remembered lower levels of anxiety when doctors had prepared them for the diagnosis and discussed their feelings during the conversation. The presence of relatives or friends that the patient wanted with them during the conversation also reduced anxiety. Although it is possible that patients' emotional responses distorted their perceptions or recollections of what happened during the interaction, or even changed the way that doctors dealt with them in the first place, the results still suggest that medical personnel who adopt different communication styles when delivering bad news may solicit different emotional reactions.

Suchman and colleagues (1997) intensively analysed the verbal content of doctor–patient interactions across a wider variety of situations, and noted that doctors routinely ignored or avoided patients' apparent invitations to offer empathy. For example, in the following extract (Suchman et al., 1997, p. 680), the physician refrains from engaging with the patient's current life situation (the authors' interpretations are included in squared brackets):

PATIENT: I'm in the process of retiring . . . [empathic opportunity]
PHYSICIAN: You are?
PATIENT: Yeah. I'll be 66 in February, [potential empathic opportunity]
PHYSICIAN: Do you have Medicare? [potential empathic opportunity terminator]

The investigators argue that patients who present empathic opportunities that are not taken up by doctors may consequently intensify their presentation of concerns. Clearly, this may result in the doctor facing a more difficult interpersonal situation than would have arisen had they communicated empathy at an earlier stage.

Gemmiti and colleagues (2017) video-recorded paediatric consultations to assess effects of doctors' communication styles on the responses shown by patients' parents. When doctors displayed more nonverbal cues suggesting interest and concern, parents' cortisol levels increased less during the consultation, suggesting that they found the interaction less stressful. However, interpretational issues again arise because the investigators were unable to control for all factors that might have encouraged doctors to be more empathic or patient-focused in the first place. For example, doctors may have felt less constrained in their interactions when the child's problem was less serious or when their parents already seemed less worried about it. Indeed, any factor that initially increased the potential for parent stress may have influenced doctors' communication styles prior to any impact on outcomes later in the consultation.

Some of these interpretational issues are avoided by studies that manipulate doctors' communication experimentally. A number of studies have presented patients with simulated interactions in which doctors communicate negative prognoses in alternative emotional styles. For example, Zwingmann and colleagues (2017) compared participants' responses to clinicians who presented a diagnosis of cancer using either low or enhanced patient-centred communication (see also Fogarty et al., 1999). When asked to take the perspective of the patient in the presented video of this interaction, participants who themselves had been diagnosed with cancer reported higher levels of anxiety following the delivery of the diagnosis, but the increase was greater in the low patient-centred communication condition. Future research needs to establish whether the specifically empathic aspects of this communication style were the active ingredients in producing this reported effect.

If patients respond to doctors' unempathic communication with increased stress and anxiety (e.g., del Piccolo & Finset, 2018), and doctors respond to stressful interactions by withholding empathy (van Dulmen et al., 2007), there is an obvious risk of these effects mutually reinforcing one another in a positive feedback loop. Doctors may disengage more in response to the increased anxiety that their disengagement provokes in patients (e.g., Kafetsios et al., 2016). More research needs to address how intrapersonal effects of doctors' empathy withdrawal are mediated by their interpersonal effects on patients (see Côté, 2005, and the previous section for discussion of similar issues relating to service encounters). It is also important to note that not all patients want their carers to be empathic across all circumstances. Sometimes, concerns may be presented as a request for reassurance that things are not so bad and a matter-of-fact response may then be more effective (Parkinson & Simons, 2012). Projecting an air of calmness and mastery can serve its purposes in alleviating patient distress too.

Guidelines for Empathy
Many of the studies investigating interpersonal effects of doctors' communication styles are motivated by the laudable aim of developing recommendations about the best practices for minimising patient distress. Two of the most commonly used sets of guidelines are SPIKES (Baile et al., 2000) and NURSE (Pollak et al., 2007). The E in the SPIKES acronym specifies step 5 of the communication task as 'addressing the patient's EMOTIONS with empathic responses' (Baile et al., 2000, p. 306). NURSE encourages empathy across more of the constituent letters of the mnemonic, with N standing for Naming patient's emotion, U for Understanding and E for Exploring by encouraging patients to elaborate on their emotions. More recently, the EMPATHY tool (Riess & Kraft-Todd, 2014) has been proposed as a way of focusing doctors' attention on nonverbal as well as verbal aspects of patient's responses. E means establishing Eye contact, M, P and A mean attending to facial Muscle movements, Posture and Affect respectively, and so on.

Despite the consistent demands for enhanced empathy, its maximisation does not necessarily lead to optimal outcomes (e.g., Tully et al., 2016). It remains unclear whether doctors should be empathic in the same way or at similar levels regardless of the patients' changing emotional orientations to what is happening. For example, co-rumination about bad news may exacerbate negative reactions in both parties (Rose et al., 2007). More generally, some authors have questioned whether prescriptive guidelines for empathic communication are helpful and suggested that more flexible strategies are better suited for accommodating to the wide range of contexts that medical personnel may face (e.g., Eggly et al., 2006).

Korsvold and colleagues (2016) provide examples of different ways in which doctors respond to the different emotions presented by adolescents receiving a cancer diagnosis in the presence of their parents. In one of the two reported cases, a teenage male patient with a sarcoma makes sarcastic comments and swears at the doctor, who attempts to close down the emotional aspects of his presentation. In the other, a pregnant female patient suffering from leukaemia expresses helplessness and distress and receives a more comforting and directly sympathetic response from her doctor. Of course, it would be premature to conclude that patients who encourage the interpersonal approach solicit different interpersonal responses to those who push other people away merely on the basis of these isolated examples. However, the general point that no one-size-fits-all approach works across the board still stands. Indeed, findings from studies that only sample interactions involving the delivery of bad news may underestimate the variability of relevant processes and effects. When a broader range of consultations is considered, doctors' interpersonal behaviours seem to have even less consistent effects on patients' stress-related autonomic responses (del Piccolo & Finset, 2018) and the quality of patient care (Boerebach et al., 2014). Medical personnel may face a wide variety of patients with different cultural backgrounds (e.g., Schouten & Meeuwesen, 2006), different coping styles and different problems that are presented in different institutional and interpersonal settings. Finding ways of adjusting their communication accordingly can be difficult.

Even if appropriately flexible and context-sensitive guidelines could be provided, there is no realistic prospect of doctors and patients staying permanently happy about each other's behaviour in all circumstances. The life-affecting challenges confronted by both parties are bound to get in the way of completely smooth relations in at least some situations. Nevertheless, improving relational responses to specific recurrent problems remains a practicable goal for more focused research.

Emotional Labour in Different Contexts

How do the different organisational demands placed on service workers and caring professionals affect the kinds of emotional labour they each perform? The first difference concerns empathic engagement and perspective taking. Service workers may actively align themselves with customers' orientations to events in order to up-regulate their level of interpersonal concern and positive attitudes. By contrast, carers may actively avoid empathising with patients in order to protect themselves from the costs of overwhelming compassion or maintain focus on the technical aspects of their job. Thus, both kinds of employee reappraise the social situation in order to regulate their emotions, but in the case of carers, empathy towards clients is relatively more likely to be reduced than enhanced.

Another important difference concerns the relative power and status of employees and their clients. Employees who are engaged in service encounters often occupy lower rungs of the organisational hierarchy and are obliged by their superiors to defer to paying customers. By contrast, many professional carers have greater power and status than most of their patients, and even those who do not can often make decisions about patient well-being without protracted negotiation, giving them at minimum a form of localised institutional power. Patients are aware of the practical and social costs of thwarting the caring activities of medical personnel or otherwise undermining their professionalism, and often regulate their own emotional presentations accordingly.

These interpersonal imbalances mean that caring professionals and service workers orient to the targets of their emotion presentations in subtly different ways, and targets' interpersonal responses bring different kinds of reciprocal effect. For example, carers experience emotional costs when patients suffer precisely because those patients are dependent on their care. Although service workers may also care about their customers' suffering, they are relatively more attuned to their anger and irritation because of the negative consequences associated with the expression of these emotions by powerful people (e.g., van Kleef & Côté, 2007).

However, these power and status differentials are neither fixed nor inevitable. Procedures for formal complaints are increasingly available to patients as well as service receivers. Risks of litigation and negative publicity continue to rise. And in some sectors of private medicine, transactions between doctors and patients have already started to seem more like service encounters. Patients who pay high fees demand the kinds of attention that those fees imply. They expect their hospitals to operate like five-star hotels. Caring then becomes a commodity just like the smiles delivered by flight attendants, baristas or receptionists. And commodification not only changes the modes of empathy regulation that caring professionals deploy but also introduces new forms of service-oriented emotional labour. None of this means that economic exchanges necessarily undermine or otherwise distort the intrinsic value that doctors and nurses derive from their work. However, it seems clear that carers consequently confront a wider range of stressors and need to extend the range of their regulatory competences in order to deal with them.

To develop a fuller understanding of emotional labour and management, we need to explore the full variety of possible ways of regulating relational orientations to customers before, during and after service encounters, including those targeting attention, appraisal and behaviour in different ways. Many of these strategies may involve recruitment of assistance from co-workers or supervisors, and may be enacted in teams rather than individually. Individuals, dyads or groups may also deploy various tools and shared practices to help them with the task of interpersonal regulation. For example, different communication technologies may be exploited to selectively restrict or facilitate access to different channels of emotional information. Any of these techniques may succeed or fail and bring positive or negative consequences for the people using them depending on how they are enacted and the contexts in which they are deployed.

CHAPTER 9

Reorientation

This concluding chapter summarises ideas and evidence presented earlier in the book and sets out the general principles of a relation-alignment approach to emotional influence. I develop the argument that emotions are embodied orientations to objects, events or people that converge or conflict with other people's orientations, rather than internal mental states that only make indirect contact with the social world. Their effects and functions depend crucially on the dynamic interpersonal, intergroup, organisational and societal systems within which they operate. Emotion's range of social influence extends cumulatively over the course of socialisation, as caregivers deliver culturally informed responses to children's increasingly articulated orientations. The capacity to use words and faces in symbolically mediated pragmatic communications ultimately permits conventionalised forms of social influence that are less constrained by immediately pressing situational concerns, facilitating more strategic forms of interpersonal regulation. However, even fully socialised adults remain susceptible to less explicit forms of emotional influence, and do not necessarily register the meaning of the emotional operations shaping their own dynamic responses. Thus, our emotions affect other people in a variety of ways, none of which depend directly on the mediated transmission of private meanings. People learn to keep their emotional inclinations to themselves only after becoming sensitive to their prior social effects.

Why is studying emotions so challenging? A biological specimen can be dissected to determine its structure and constitution. Tissue samples can be sliced, mounted onto glass slides, and examined under a microscope. We can observe how they operate in situ as well as in vitro. We can expose them to different forces, chemicals and conditions to determine how they are predisposed to respond. So why don't similar strategies work for emotions?

Even an internal organ functions differently when operating as part of a wider system, when its dynamic connections with other parts of the body and the wider world are engaged. Hearts swell and beat in time with the changing rhythms of circulatory processes, the intake of air through the lungs and coordinating activity in the brain. And these internal operations respond in real time to the changing demands of the external environment and the people in it. Metabolic responses that seem simple and unitary in fact achieve coherence from their contextualisation in more articulated relational structures. Perhaps, then, similar principles apply in the case of emotions too.

In this book, I have argued that we can't get to the heart of an emotion either by breaking it down into components or by seeing it as an intact entity abstracted from the arenas in which it is designed to function. Attending to emotion's dynamic operation in practical and social contexts provides a clearer and more productive understanding.

By contrast, most psychological theories continue to assume that emotions are primarily internal states or processes. Explaining emotion's effects in the social world then requires some medium of expression. What emotion does to other people is always indirect, partial and potentially inauthentic. What gets to the surface is not the same as what is at the heart.

I have argued that this approach gets things inside out. To get to the core of emotion, we don't need to peel away outer layers (Averill & Nunley, 1992), but instead work from their intricate dynamic operation as situated activities. Emotions start out as relational processes that are distributed between people orienting dynamically to each other and to objects and events in the shared environment. Much of how they work is there for all to see, if we look carefully enough.

In this final chapter, I set out the principles of this outside-in relation-alignment approach and review the variety of ways in which emotions affect the people at whom they are directed. To set the stage for this integrative analysis, it's worth reviewing some of the key conclusions reached in earlier chapters of the book.

Making Emotions Emotional

When formulating his pioneering theory, William James's central aim was to move beyond mere classification of emotions as intact mental objects and get to the processes that explained their nature and variety. For him, earlier descriptive accounts provided at best a naïve local geology of the internal world obsessed by the trivialities and minutiae of representation: 'I should as lief read verbal descriptions of the shapes of the rocks on a New Hampshire farm as toil through them again' (James, 1898, p. 448). As an alternative, James sought to identify the generative processes that produced emotional experience ('the goose that lays the golden eggs', 1898, p. 448). According to his theory, these processes involved direct perception of the distinctive bodily changes triggered by emotionally relevant events. Confronting a wild bear in the woods automatically produced a coherent pattern of physiological responses that were registered as fear.

James's ideas paved the way for constructionist approaches to emotion (Barrett, 2017). For example, Schachter (1964) argued that emotional state depended not on interoceptive signals alone, but on how those signals related to interpretations of the current situation. Felt arousal in response to the appearance of a wild bear might be perceived as excitement rather than fear when on a hunting expedition. Instead of directly detecting internal emotion-defining information, individuals needed to make sense of how their bodies were reacting to what was going on outside.

Taking this approach several steps further, Barrett (2017) argued that emotional experience is constituted by a process of embodied simulation, involving selection of the best-fitting multimodal memory trace and its application to the current person–environment transaction. Emotion becomes emotion as the consequence of an active process of adjusting predictions about what is about to happen based on context-attuned emotion representations.

Schachter and Barrett both correctly rejected the idea that emotions are indissoluble wholes. They sought to identify processes that come together to generate emotional phenomena rather than simply character-ise what their essential nature might already be. However, like James before them, they continued to assume that emotions are located primar-ily inside individual bodies and brains.

In Chapter 1, I argued that emotion's distinctive qualities depend more directly on their operation across the boundaries between people and their responsive practical and social environments (de Rivera & Grinkis, 1986). Emotions are dynamic and distributed processes of relational activity (Frijda, 1986) and not simply internal events. Abstracting any momentary mental state from these processes risks missing their orienta-tional aspects, the fact that the emotional person is poised on the brink of acting. We cannot fully understand the charge, force and colour of what is happening by freeze-framing the action in mid-flow.

From this relation-alignment perspective, the process that we call 'anger' is neither the perception of a pattern of internal bodily signals, nor the integration of those signals with situational information. It is not even the attempt to simulate what may be about to happen. Instead it is part of an ongoing transaction with a meaningful world of social, institu-tional and material forces, an effort to push aside something blocking the trajectory of our current action, using whatever means are currently at our disposal.

When emotions are directed at other people or when they recruit other people in object-oriented activities, the actual and anticipated orienta-tions and activities of those people also form part of the emotional process. Our relational stances and operations are co-constructed dyna-mically from interpersonal, intragroup and intergroup interactions.

Getting Across from Heart to Heart

If emotions were private, how would they surface in the public world? Most researchers assume that internal emotional meanings find expression in words or nonverbal signals that allow their communication to other people. They claim that emotions are associated with specific names and distinctive facial movements that can reveal what the individual is feeling. However, the indirectness of the communication process makes it susceptible to manipulation and distortion.

Instead of focusing on how precisely or accurately words or faces reflect an individually localised emotion process, the present approach addresses their role in processes of relation alignment. The question is not whether verbal concepts and nonverbal expressions correspond to specific emotions, but rather how they serve to influence other people as part of a more inclusive emotional process. What then do speech acts and facial movements actually do, and how does what they do relate to emotions?

Verbal Language

Nouns such as 'anger', 'fear' and 'joy' sound like names for mental states, and adjectives such as 'angry', 'fearful' and 'joyful' seem to be descriptions of people having those mental states. Similarly, adverbs such as 'angrily', 'fearfully' and 'joyfully' apparently characterise how someone having the mental states performs an action or otherwise responds to what is happening. The semantics of all these words seem straightforward. They capture a common-sense cultural theory of how emotions work.

Verbs representing emotions are less common and more complicated. You can 'love', 'hate', 'envy' or 'resent' someone. You can 'regret' what you have done or 'fear' that things may not turn out well. However, the subject of most other English-language emotion verbs is not the person having the emotion but the person or event that is causing it. Someone or something can 'anger', 'embarrass' or 'disgust' you, but when it is you doing the angering, embarrassing or disgusting, the words don't refer to your own emotions but those of the person you are affecting. And many emotion words simply don't have a single-word English verb form at all. It is not possible to 'joy', 'pride', 'jealousy' or 'contempt' anyone or anything. In most cases, the grammar stops us from thinking of emotions as things that we do rather than things that happen to us.

Most psychological studies of emotion concepts focus on the meaning of nouns (see Chapter 2). When comparing and classifying these words in explicit terms, participants do not draw clear boundaries around the associated categories. No precise set of features seems to define either individual emotion names such as 'anger' (Russell & Fehr, 1994) or the more general concept of 'emotion' (Fehr & Russell, 1984). The words don't pick out clearly specifiable objects in the psychological world. Instead, emotion concepts may be represented in the form of scripts setting out the sequence of events that unfolds in a prototypical instance of the relevant emotional episode (e.g., Kovecses, 1990; Russell & Fehr, 1994; Shaver et al., 1987), or as populations of context-dependent perceptual simulations (e.g., Barrett, 2017). In neither case does the emotion name itself tell us exactly what a person is experiencing or expressing, how they are appraising what is happening or what they are about to do.

We can get a fuller understanding of emotional language by investigating how it works in practice outside the rarefied context of any constrained laboratory task intended to dissect purely semantic meaning. Instead of simply describing someone's internal state, emotion words used in the wild mostly serve to defend positions, allocate blame, make promises or threaten negative consequences (e.g., Edwards, 1999). Saying that I am angry may be a warning of what might happen if you continue to act in the way you are acting. From this perspective, talking emotionally is not a way of indirectly indicating the nature of a private experience but instead a more direct means of aligning relations between people. Emotion words thus link up with and extend the other functional aspects of the overall pattern of activity. Any consistency in their meanings reflects the relational agendas that are supported by their usage.

Nonverbal Communication

Parallel arguments can be made about the functions of facial activity and postural movements in relation to emotion. Researchers have often focused on the emotional meanings that perceivers attach to facial configurations that have been preselected precisely because they typify a specific emotion concept. But even in constrained judgement tasks, the meaning attributed to these facial stimuli partly depends on what questions are asked and what response alternatives are provided. And when faces are attached to bodies or associated with situational information, their meaning is further transformed. In fully realistic contexts, facial activity serves its functions in dynamic attunement to ongoing events and the responsive behaviour of other people.

As with emotion words, a fuller understanding of how facial movements operate requires attention to their deployment in unfolding interpersonal interactions. Rather than expressing something inside, nonverbal changes often reflect direct adjustments to what is happening or signal future trajectories of action (see Parkinson, 2017). They can

reward or punish and make promises and threats just like verbal statements. The use of facial movements as cultural symbols representing
emotion scripts or embodied experiences is secondary to these more
immediate functions.

Investigating Interpersonal Effects

Research into emotion's interpersonal effects often makes similar common-sense assumptions about the ability of words and faces to convey
specific emotional meanings. Experimental procedures allow investigators to select and present facial and verbal stimuli that convey clear
appraisals to targeted participants in a manufactured laboratory context.
Any resulting influence depends on the cultural concepts that the
manipulated verbal and nonverbal signals are designed to activate.

Even researchers postulating more directly contagious processes
assume that any interpersonal effects are mediated by targets internally
registering the emotion category that their mimicked nonverbal
responses represent. I smile in response to your smile and implicitly
recognise my own smile as an indication of happiness. In other words,
researchers of all stripes see the apprehension of emotional meaning as
a central or necessary part of emotional influence even when interactants
have already made interpersonal adjustments to each other's emotional
orientations prior to any process of categorisation.

This emphasis on inferred appraisals or activated emotion concepts
restricts our understanding of the interpersonal effects of emotion. In
most experimental studies, the investigated influence process begins
with the arrival of information that already encapsulates a discrete emotional meaning. Outside the laboratory, any production of categorical
information about emotion only consolidates after interpersonal calibration and regulated communication have started. Researchers need to
devote more attention to the socially attuned processes that shape the
source's presentation of emotional information in the first place.

For example, it seems unlikely that toddlers participating in social
referencing studies first work out that their mother is afraid, conclude
that she appraises the visual cliff as dangerous, then infer that it may
represent a threat to them too, before finally deciding not to risk crossing
onto the glass. Instead, they are already oriented to the visual cliff as
a potential barrier, and already oriented to their mother at the other side.
Their orientations then adjust to mother's changing stance towards the
precipice as they tentatively move towards it. They register her widening
eyes and gasping mouth in relation to what is happening and what they
are doing. At some point in this process, a specific emotional meaning
may emerge, but it consolidates from online negotiation and other

processes of distributed cognition operating between mother and child, not on the basis of either party's private sense-making. Thus, targets as well as sources play active roles in emotional influence processes. Emotion communications are tactical moves that are oriented to other people's moves rather than simply sources of information for inferential processing.

Regulation and Regulatory Function

In some cases, a source's presentation of emotion may be part of a strategic attempt to convey emotional information or to influence the target's behaviour more directly. For example, you may want me to see that my actions are making you angry so that I stop doing what I am doing, or you may simulate anger just to make me feel bad. In other words, people exploit their knowledge about how emotions can affect other people in order to exert social influence.

Does regulation make a difference to the process of emotional influence? According to inferential accounts, once an emotion is communicated, its categorical meaning remains the same regardless of whether it is regulated or unregulated. However, emotion regulation that is implemented specifically for the purpose of social influence is also likely to be attuned and responsive to any interpersonal feedback about its effectiveness. In other words, regulators may strategically adjust their emotions online to ensure that they bring about their intended interpersonal consequences. For example, if your initial display of irritation does not stop me doing whatever you want me to stop doing, you may deploy additional tactics to get me to notice your reaction and take it more seriously (e.g., Parkinson, 2001b).

Along similar lines, caregivers in social referencing situations use directed patterns of gaze to indicate clearly that their communicated fear concerns a particular object in the environment. Alternated attempts to establish eye contact with the toddler further convey that the caregiver's object-oriented gaze carries implications that they should also attend to. In other words, the source's communication is specifically designed to influence the target's understanding of what is happening (Clément & Dukes, 2017). In order to achieve this ostensive and didactic purpose, the source needs to attend to how the target responds and make any necessary adjustments to their delivery of relevant information.

The strategic considerations motivating interpersonally attuned emotion communication may also come into play when neither party is explicitly trying to work up or tone down their emotions. According to many social functional accounts, the purpose of certain emotions is precisely to influence other people in the first place. Thus, anger may already be a means of changing other people's unwanted behaviour with a built-in sensitivity to interpersonal feedback regarding its success in achieving this purpose. Distinguishing emotion regulation from regulatory emotion is difficult both in theory and practice (e.g., Kappas, 2011). However, it seems clear that emotions can have interpersonally attuned interpersonal effects even when the source has no explicit intention to bring these effects about. Perhaps then, strategic regulation of emotion for the purposes of social influence is simply an extension of a less articulated process of relation alignment.

Functional Origins

Most functional accounts assume that emotions are innate strategies that have evolved over the course of natural selection to deal with adaptive challenges and opportunities. However, functionality may also be an outcome of cultural evolution, life-time socialisation or the changing forces and pressures of a situation that is unfolding in the present moment. Specification of these other emotion-shaping processes leaves less work for hard-wiring to do (e.g., Lewis & Liu, 2011). Indeed, natural selection may depend mainly on providing the resources and conditions for the operation of emotion-producing developmental systems that are suitably responsive to changing environmental needs (Parkinson, 2012).

The ecosystem to which humans adapt is itself partly a cultural product. Societies manufacture material structures that facilitate the reproduction of certain kinds of social relations and power arrangements (Parkinson, Fischer & Manstead, 2005). The tools and practices that people develop within their specific relational niches partly depend on their innate tendencies to seek out pre-specified rewards and avoid pre-specified costs, but the overriding principle shaping cultural evolution is the fundamental human capacity to be flexible and open to possibilities (Schwartz, 1974). All that we need to inherit from our ancestors, then, are the basic resources that set the conditions for developing more or less coherent modes of emotional activity as we interact with a world that is (to some extent) already socially constructed (e.g., Camras, 1992).

Beyond Interpersonal Relations

The functional agendas shaping emotion presentation and regulation rarely reflect purely individual or interpersonal motives. Emotions also further the causes of the groups and organisations to which those individuals belong. Indeed, interpersonal negotiations are shaped by the pre-existing allegiances and antipathies that each agent brings to the immediate situation, and by the broader social structures that determine possible outcomes.

Interactions often involve more than two people at any given time in any case. The direct intervention of other ingroup or outgroup members or representatives of institutional authority may modify or complicate the interpersonal process either by provoking direct individual responses or by changing the ways in which individuals deal with one another.

Two topics have dominated research into these kinds of multi-person emotional influence. The first concerns how an individual's self-categorisation as a group member affects their responses to other people's emotions. The second focuses on the intrapersonal and inter-personal effects of organisational pressures to regulate emotions and expressions.

Collective Relation Alignment

Shared social identity usually leads to greater convergence of interpersonal emotions. One reason is that people attend more to other people's orientations when they are likely to be compatible with their own. In addition, ingroup members' apparent perspectives on events provide useful information about normative appraisals of relevant objects and events, especially those relating to ingroup and outgroup members. They tell us not only how things are but also how favourably we ought to be disposed towards them.

Motivational factors also play a role in intragroup emotional conver-gence. For example, the desire to maintain ingroup approval encourages conformity to the emotional orientations displayed by other group mem-bers and divergence from the emotional orientations displayed by mem-bers of competing outgroups. Correspondingly, registering a match or mismatch with other people's emotional orientations allows people to recognise their shared or contrasting group memberships (e.g., Livingstone et al., 2011).

Other effects of group emotions depend on implicit processes of reciprocal adjustment rather than explicit registration of normative information or capitulation to perceived social pressure. Indeed, one factor that contributes to the perception of shared group membership and mutually emotional orientation is the sense of being coordinated with the other people around you, attending to the same things in the same ways at the same time. Some collective practices seem to have developed specifically to encourage these kinds of dynamic intragroup attunement (e.g., Collins, 2004).

Further fuel for group emotions comes from the sense of empowerment associated with collective activity with a common purpose. The potential for effective implementation of social change engendered by working together as a group means that people may be more influenced by other people's outcome-oriented emotions in intragroup contexts than in interpersonal settings. Emotions related to striving are also likely to spread more easily when group members are pulling together to achieve collective aims.

Work-Role Demands

When social arrangements involve intragroup or institutional hierarchies and power differentials, the incentives to bring emotions into line are often more compelling. There may be sanctions against displaying or enacting forms of emotion that deviate from prevalent prescriptions and norms. These social pressures assume special prominence when subordinates need to present the public face of a commercial organisation in direct interactions with clients or customers. Employees occupying these boundary-spanning roles are often encouraged to work on their emotions as well as the technical aspects of their jobs (e.g., Hochschild, 1983).

Research into emotional labour has focused separately on its consequences for employee well-being and for customer satisfaction, but rarely addresses interrelations between these intrapersonal and interpersonal effects. A fuller understanding of the phenomenon requires greater attention to reciprocal relational processes. For example, service workers who engage more with customers' needs and desires may solicit more positive interpersonal feedback, which in turn sustains and deepens their emotional engagement. Interactions with colleagues and supervisors can also help to create a collaborative spirit of mutually reinforcing encouragement. Some forms of emotional labour are only implemented successfully with collective will and effort.

When these socially distributed processes take hold, the line between strategic regulation and unselfconscious enactment of socially functional emotions again starts to blur. Workers can only become alienated from their 'true' emotions if we assume that those emotions reside in a private and insulated location that is detached from the hurly burly of social interaction. Instead, any experienced conflict may reflect the competing demands of simultaneously activated social identities or role positions. It can be uncomfortable when different potential addressees pull you in different directions.

A different set of tensions characterise work roles in the caring professions. Doctors, nurses and therapists need to steer a course between engaging empathically with clients' problems and distributing their energy and time resources across a variety of other social and technical aspects of their jobs. In some circumstances, projecting an air of mastery and competence may be a more effective strategy than engaging directly with a patient's pain and anxiety.

Stress, burnout and alienation are clearly serious problems in service and caring occupations. However, treating them as primarily personal issues that require individually targeted interventions may be insufficient. Although health and occupational psychologists tend to focus on risk factors relating to the deployment of inappropriate emotion-regulation strategies or individual characteristics such as low levels of resilience, institutional interventions are often more effective ways of easing problems that boil down to workload or an unmanageable balance of task demands (e.g., Butalid et al., 2014). Emotional labourers can only work with the materials that are provided.

Relation Alignment

As we have seen throughout this book, our emotions can affect other people in a variety of ways and perform disparate social functions across a range of interpersonal, group-based and institutional contexts. Is there a common thread to their modes of operation? From the present perspective, emotions consistently involve processes of relation alignment, whereby evaluative orientations towards objects or people solicit functionally relevant responses from other people. In some cases, these functional effects are achieved mainly by the dynamic entrainment of bodily movements and the reciprocal coordination of attentional cues. In other cases, orientations are signalled or communicated more explicitly before they affect anyone else. The following sections set out the basic principles behind these practical and communicative processes.

Evaluative Orientations

Any emotional orientation is inherently relational because it depends not only on the individual's own attentional attunement and action readiness but also on wherever their attention and action are directed (e.g., Frijda, 1986). This relationality is social when emotions are either directly oriented at other people or oriented to other people's orientations to social or non-social objects. Even when an emotion's primary object does not directly involve anyone else, its orientation still often relates to someone else's orientation in some way. We can't help considering what other people will think and feel about what we do. Because most non-social objects are first encountered in the context of infant-caregiver interactions, our inclinations to approach or avoid them are socially cultivated and conditioned from the outset. For all these reasons, evaluative orientations to non-social objects are unlikely to operate purely in a private realm. If and when they do, it is not clear that they properly qualify as emotions in any case.

Emotional orientations are necessarily dynamic as well as relational. They adjust to the changing forces presented by the objects, events and people at which they are directed. When people are responding emotionally to another person, that person's ongoing responsivity is an interlocking component of the relation-alignment process. And even emotional objects that are not intrinsically social can still actively facilitate or impede relational agendas. Approach and avoidance movements may need to recalibrate as their target gets closer or further away or obstacles to forward or backward progress need to be shifted or displaced. When we get angry with our computer, it is often because it refuses to let us get on with what we are trying to do.

It is tempting to treat a person's evaluative orientation to something as a mental state or process, involving a cognitive appraisal of whatever is happening (e.g., Lazarus, 1991a). However, the directedness of emotional conduct also implies focused activity of the body and sensory organs (Arnold, 1960). Our limbs and muscles respond to the pulls and pressures exerted by the material and social world. We actively collect or reject different kinds of information about what is going on around us. We take specific stances towards particular aspects of the situation and these stances adjust as the situation changes. We lean towards or away from something, stare at it or look away. We brace ourselves against the shock of contact or huddle up in a protective ball.

When emotions concern recalled, imagined or anticipated situations, their embodied aspects may be less obvious (e.g., Stemmler, 1989). However, we still make physical adjustments as we circle round simulations of how the episode might otherwise turn out. We hold private conversations and rehearse possible ways of coping with things. And we often share our conjectural positions with others in order to recalibrate our perspectives or try out possible ways through (e.g., Rimé, 2009). In all of these cases, the capacity to become emotionally engaged with a virtual situation depends on prior experience of engagement with relational forces and contingencies that are more imminent and directly pressing.

When our orientation is part of a directly engaging interaction with someone else, many of the interpersonal effects emerge from mutual dynamic adjustments in the lines of action that both of us are pursuing. When we are focusing on some non-social event during an interpersonal interaction, our respective orientations may become more or less coordinated as a function of unfolding nonverbal negotiations and recalibrations operating between us. In both cases, our orientational movements and signals may also carry implications that go beyond the immediate situation. Other people respond to the symbolic meanings and anticipated pragmatic consequences of our relational orientations as well as the more direct pressures and affordances that are presented. Someone else may explicitly attempt to regulate our orientation by strategically modifying their own orientation. In the following sections, I consider how these different processes operate and how they might interrelate.

Active Adjustment

At their most basic level, relation-alignment processes involve adjusting dynamic movements to the changing resistances and affordances of the practical and social environment. Think of being backed into a tight corner by someone, bracing yourself against the increasing forward momentum of their body, preparing to push back. Think of how your muscles tense and your limbs lock into place, where you look and what you try to make happen. All of these aspects of your relational orientation reflect moment-by-moment adjustments to the pressures you are confronting. The respective positions of you and your antagonist emerge from the operation of the relational system.

Even this kind of direct physical adjustment is not simply a passive process of succumbing to external forces. Social and non-social objects only present obstacles or opportunities when you are already pursuing a line of action into which they intrude. The evaluative aspects of your orientation always reflect impediments or openings that are presented by the unfolding transaction. In the case of interpersonal interactions, the social-relational process involves convergence, divergence or conflict of behavioural trajectories rather than simply being pushed or pulled in certain directions by someone else.

Cuing

When adjusting their orientations, people respond not only to the immediate relational situation but also to cues about where it is heading. Each person's behavioural trajectory is often directly discernible from patterned shifts of attention and changes in physical stance in relation to events in the shared environment (e.g., Mead, 1934). A deflected glance or tensed set of muscles indicates what someone else is about to do and to what they are about to do it. Responding to these cues, we make anticipatory moves that factor in the apparent direction of other people's behaviour.

Because other people respond to the cues that we deliver, presenting those cues provides an additional means of influencing their behaviour. Staring at something can thus serve the dual functions of collecting information and directing another person's attention to whatever you are staring at. Cuing provides the basis for many of the more articulated communicative effects of emotions. Humans probably have innate capacities that allow them to capitalise on the possibilities it presents.

Signalling

Any cue needs to be picked up by someone else in order to influence their orientation. When two people are directly interacting with each other, their interpersonal attention is already calibrated and each interactant remains sensitive to even subtle shifts in the focus of attention and action. However, at other times, cues need to be specifically emphasised or exaggerated in order to be socially effective. They start to acquire signalling functions that are tied less directly to their practical origins.

For adaptive reasons, human bodies are configured in ways that make many of their orientational movements readily detectable by other humans. Colour contrasts make eye movements highly visible (e.g., Kobayashi & Kohshima, 1997) and eyebrows enhance the salience of eye-widening or eye-narrowing movements (e.g., Godinho, Spikins & O'Higgins, 2018). The directed operation of sensory organs is clearly specified by head turns and facial changes. Hands, arms and vocal systems are also pre-adapted partly to facilitate communication. We are all equipped with the means to attract and redirect other people's attention even when they are not already attuned to what we are doing.

Many of emotion's communicative functions depend on humans' capacity to display perceptible signals of their changing orientations to what is happening. Practical movements with enhanced detectability can be used to influence other people's orientations at greater range and over timescales that extend beyond the immediate situation. A sudden cry alerts others to potential dangers that they had not previously detected. A scowl provides a warning of interpersonal resistance even before interaction begins. In both cases, the display does not simply deliver information about the semantic meaning of the current situation. The signal of danger or obstruction also carries pragmatic force because the signaller's body is evidently prepared to act in the way that their display indicates. Other people who are engaged with the signaller or the signalled concern either need to disengage or to respond with complementary or conflicting orientations of their own.

Emotional Socialisation

In the previous section, I argued that processes of attentional calibration and orientational adjustment provide the basis for more elaborate forms

of emotional influence involving strategic communication and regulation. But how exactly do these more articulated functions develop? The
obvious answer is that human infants start out with a small set of primitive capacities which extend and multiply over the course of development. However, even in early infancy, humans act within relational
systems that already carry more articulated meanings and implications.
Caregivers' contributions to relation-alignment processes immediately
make them more active, functional and significant. Thus, socialisation
involves implicit processes gradually becoming more explicit and strategic as well as progressively higher functions accumulating. The following
sections set out some of the key stages in this developmental sequence
(see also Parkinson, Fischer & Manstead, 2005).

Influencing Caregivers

Caregivers are the most dynamic, salient and important part of a human
infant's environment for much of its early life. Even if babies were not
born with innate sensitivities to certain specific features of social stimuli
(e.g., Nagy & Molnár, 2004), they would quickly learn to orient to those
stimuli and register their qualities, thereby adjusting to the affordances
that social participation provides.

   Caregiver–infant interaction rapidly transforms into a process of negotiation. Infants pull faces and make sounds that call for interpersonal
attention or resist that attention when it becomes overstimulating or
otherwise painful. Caregivers are attuned and responsive to these symptoms of apparent desire or discomfort, and often attend to any associated
needs (e.g., Csibra & Gergely, 2009). Their responsiveness in turn reinforces the infant's presentation of the cues to which they respond. The
forms of learning arising from these interpersonal contingencies supplement any prior phylogenetic ritualisation of patterned displays (Andrew,
1963). Infants' biological capacities to show perceptible signs of their
behavioural trajectories are channelled along lines mapped out by their
changing social environment. These signs quickly become means to different kinds of end.

   Babies clearly do not need to be fully deliberative autonomous
agents to play their part in these socially functional emotion episodes.
At the earliest stages of development, coordination of symptoms,
signals and actions depends on the reciprocal scaffolding provided
by caregivers' online responsivity. For example, consider the coupling
of gaze aversion with coy smiles shown by young infants in Reddy's
(2000) study (see Chapter 3). Two-month-old infants are incapable of
appreciating at an explicit level that turning their head away from
another person communicates their desire to break from interpersonal

engagement. Instead, two separate systems of implicit response just happen to come together. Overstimulation resulting from sustained eye contact needs to be contained, but reduction of that overstimulation reignites the urge to maintain social contact. The delicate balance between these two conflicting impulses produces a patterned display that performs a more articulated function in the context of the ongoing exchange with the caregiver, and the caregiver's dynamically attuned adjustment gives added coherence to what emerges. Correspondingly, infants register the effects of what they are doing on dynamically responsive caregivers and learn to make changes to their orientational movements in order to modulate these social effects. Over time, they learn how to take advantage of these interpersonal contingencies in a more strategic manner.

Calibrating Orientations

Young infants typically orient either to another person or to an object in their non-social environment, but rarely to both at the same time. The growing capacity to attend to relations between a person and something or someone else (e.g., Carpenter, Nagell & Tomasello, 1998) further extends the range of possible social influence. Triadic rather than merely dyadic relations can now be aligned.

Caregivers already play a role in infants' object-directed orientations even before triadic relation alignment fully consolidates. When cooperative adults are around, a child who makes obvious efforts to attain some goal often gets what it wants. Simply stretching an arm towards an object that is out of reach may encourage a nearby parent to bring it close enough to grab. Pushing at some obstruction may result in its removal by a bigger and stronger human. Practical object-directed movements may thus acquire additional signalling functions that factor in caregiver's responses (e.g., Vygotsky, 1978). However, at early stages of development, infants stay focused primarily on the object itself and simply adjust their orientation in ways that happen to recruit helpful input from other people. This kind of spontaneous signalling only starts to become more strategic and deliberate when the child registers the dependence of expected outcomes on caregiver responses. Indeed, a parent may playfully withhold the object that an infant is reaching for, thus emphasising the potential discrepancy between relational orientations towards objects in the shared environment (e.g., Hobson, 2002).

Social referencing studies demonstrate that toddlers are sensitive to adults' emotional orientations to toys, visual cliffs and other salient objects within their field of vision by the end of the first year of their lives (see Chapter 4). Their back-and-forth switching of visual attention from object to reference person (referential looking: Russell, Bard & Adamson, 1997) serves the dual functions of collecting relational information and soliciting interpersonal guidance about the appropriate stance to adopt. By this stage, children are clearly able to actively adjust their orientations to objects and events so that they are better calibrated with those of significant others.

Toddlers also learn that bringing someone else's orientation into line with their own is not always straightforward and often requires additional effort and emphasis. Their attempts at interpersonal regulation start to involve more explicit object-related communications that factor in the possibility of interpersonal resistance. Thus, adopting a specific stance towards what is happening acquires the strategic function of redirecting another person's attention and action, thus reconfiguring both parties' respective relations towards objects in the shared environment.

Explicit Communication

The meaningful interpersonal consequences of children's changing relational orientations provide the basis for their developing capacity to use their movements in symbolic ways. They begin to appreciate that the sounds they make and the faces they pull lead to significant and consistent effects. The time horizon of their anticipations gradually extends beyond the immediate situation. They learn to orient to perspectives other than their own even when no one else is physically present.

In social referencing situations, toddlers are already responsive to another person's directed orientation to an object, and already attuned to any discrepancy with their own orientation. However, interpersonal calibration still depends on shared attention to an object in the immediate physical environment. The child looks at the object and then at the adult. The adult looks at the object and then at the child. The coordinated gaze patterns of both parties directly specify the topic of the implicit conversation.

Learning to use their displays and gestures symbolically allows children to refer to objects that are out of sight and out of reach, thus extending the range and scope of interpersonal influence. Things that happened in the past or might happen in the future can be referenced in addition to those happening right now. Communicating your relational orientation to an anticipated event already provides a means of regulating other people's orientations to that event. The development of more strategic control over the various means of communication additionally allows their online adjustment to meet the specific needs of any particular addressee.

The patterns of interaction that emerge when signalling and explicit representational capacities consolidate differ in important respects from the intersubjective forms of infant-caregiver interaction that operate at earlier stages of development. The interpersonal pressures exerted by the communicated relational orientations are less direct. For example, when infants turn their heads away and show coy smiles during infancy, this brings immediate consequences for the nature of the intersubjective contact between mutually engaged parties. By contrast, an older child who displays comparable signs of 'embarrassment' or explicitly states that they are feeling embarrassed merely presents a possible behavioural trajectory that broadly encourages a compatible interpersonal response. The motive for acceding to this kind of symbolically communicated emotional request still relates to relationship maintenance. However, it is easier for addressees to disengage or actively resist the presented relational agenda. As we shall see, the normative considerations that shape the range of possible responses to any facially or verbally delivered emotional communication partly depend on the specific cultural implications of the expressions and words that it contains.

Cultural Articulation

The world that first confronts human infants is principally a world of social relations. Newborns need to be equipped with capacities that allow them to adjust to, and operate within, such a world. Correspondingly, caregivers need to be attuned and responsive to infants' capacities to relate to them (e.g., Csibra & Gergely, 2009). The practical environment also presents consistent opportunities and obstacles to which relational activities must accommodate. All of these considerations impose a consistent structure on the developmental process.

However, there are also important variations in societal arrangements, relational practices, and practical contingencies across different cultural contexts. Human infants need to be flexible enough to exploit the specific possibilities that are locally available to them. Indeed, adaptability is often a more efficient way of dealing with changing or unpredictable challenges than pre-adaptation. Perhaps then human beings have acquired genetic predispositions designed to facilitate openness to experience.

Humans stay in direct contact with caregivers for a more extended period of their early development than any other terrestrial animal, allowing greater scope for adaptive enculturation. Infants' enhanced interpersonal attunement allows them to take full advantage of the opportunities for social learning that caregivers are predisposed to provide. Cultural socialisation thus operates within a partly inherited developmental system (e.g., Oyama, 1985). In the following sections, I consider some of the ways that cultural factors influence and redirect the process of emotional socialisation and the different patterns of emotional relations that they produce.

Tacit Cultural Functions

Because caregivers' communication, regulation and behaviour are shaped by their prior experience and cultural learning, the interpersonal feedback that infants receive is already infused with norms, knowledge and beliefs. For example, parents in different societies may view a baby's frustrated struggle against external resistance (e.g., Camras et al., 1992) either as a legitimate demand for freedom and independence or an unwelcome display of selfishness and social disengagement. Babies in turn adjust to parents' culturally conditioned responses. Thus, certain relational adjustments are cultivated at the expense of others. More generally, infants' participation in interactions with caregivers accommodates to an articulated social world even before they are capable of understanding or internalising any of the associated meanings and prescriptions. Enculturation starts long before children explicitly appreciate the nature of the rules guiding their behaviour.

Caregivers need not be aware that they are indoctrinating their children either. Their perceptions and interpretations are shaped by habitual scripts, schemas and embodied simulations. For example, registering an active threat may lead parents to categorise a child's generic distress face (e.g., Camras, 1992) as 'fear'. This emotional interpretation may even alter parents' perceptions of its configural characteristics making them appear more similar to a stereotypical gasping pattern (Aviezer et al., 2012; Fernández-Dols et al., 2008; and see Chapter 3). In any case, parents' inclinations to engage and empathise with their offspring often encourage them to produce facial movements that match and emphasise their interpretation of the child's communicated emotional meaning. Their facial responses specifically accentuate the distinctive characteristics of the socially prescribed facial expression associated with the relevant emotion script. Thus, what infants often see when displaying a generic distress configuration is a representation of what a 'fear' face is supposed to look like in their society. Infants thereby become attuned to aspects of their own facial display that are culturally recognisable in emotional terms (e.g., Gergely & Watson, 1996; Holodynski & Friedlmeier, 2006). And they learn that adopting similar facial configurations themselves can lead to specific interpersonal effects.

Symbolic Orientational Movements

The displays and gestures that infants and toddlers first use to calibrate their orientations with those of caregivers derive their meaning and function from the local contexts in which they are deployed. They signal specific lines of action with respect to objects and people in the immediate environment. For example, the directed stare of a scowling face indicates a particular obstacle that the child is trying to push against. A nose-scrunch shows an urge to block off a nearby noxious smell. However, both kinds of display have also acquired wider significance in many societies as a consequence of their clear relational implications.

Because both scowling and nose-scrunching economically signal articulated lines of action relating to resistance and rejection they also provide a possible basis for more abstract and generic communicative functions. Thus, a scowling display that directly conveys a specific behavioural threat may be culturally co-opted as a warning about the imminent readiness to intervene in other ways. Similarly, the directed warning about a foul-smelling object delivered by nose-scrunching offers a means of indicating that any object, person or idea is something that needs to be held at metaphorical arm's length.

Many societies codify the extended pragmatic functions performed by these culturally elaborated signals in more abstract emotional concepts. Sounds and movements acquire the symbolic function of representing relational themes and agendas. Thus, a nose-scrunch may come to stand not only for all kinds of warning about literally and metaphorically malodorous objects but also for a more articulated concept of 'disgust'. Indeed, the behavioural trajectory signalled by the display may constitute a prototypical instance of the episodic script associated with this concept. The display can then be used to communicate a rejecting orientation to whatever is happening, and not just bad smells.

Elaborated emotion concepts do not consolidate around signalled behavioural trajectories in equivalent ways across all societies. Indeed, many displays may simply maintain their original specific functions and meanings. Nose-scrunching may remain a signal about something smelling bad and nothing more. However, the utility of stimulus-rejecting displays for communicating moral judgements and demands means that concepts overlapping with the Anglo-American idea of 'disgust' are also likely to have developed elsewhere in the world.

However, the extent of conceptual overlap is rarely if ever total. For example, cross-cultural variations in moral concerns affect the connotations of smelling bad or being off. Different kinds of things are beyond the pale in different kinds of community. Thus, individualistic societies are likely to develop nose-scrunch concepts that cluster around freedom and personal rights, whereas collectivist societies may include a greater proportion of relational and communal concerns (e.g., Markus & Kitayama, 1991). Similarly, the kinds of behaviour change demanded by scowling faces likely reflect the most hypercognised targets of disapproval in any given society (Levy, 1974).

No society's emotion concepts exhaust the full range of relation-alignment patterns that characterise social life. Some contextually embedded orientational adjustments are never allocated to culturally codified categories. They may persist as useful local influence strategies without acquiring more general symbolic functions. And other culturally extended concepts may slip in and out of contemporary relevance depending on prevailing historical conditions (e.g., Harré & Finlay-Jones, 1986). This means that the boundaries of the conceptual territory are always shifting and indeterminate. What counts as an instance of any emotion cannot be pinned down by settling on a few representative examples with fixed functions and meanings. However, within any particular cultural context in any given era, some faces and words achieve special significance as means of invoking more articulated relational meanings. Children growing up in a world where their sounds and movements carry these implications cannot avoid being influenced by them.

When an Anglo-American child displays a scowling 'anger' face, the various connotations of the associated emotion concept are implicitly activated in adult perceivers. They anticipate that the child's behaviour will unfold in accordance with a culturally familiar script (e.g., Kövecses, 1990). There will be a struggle against any resistance. Impulses may be difficult to contain. If the child's 'anger' is directed specifically at the perceiver, they may also read it as a form of threat, and respond to the performative force of such a pragmatic move. This may lead caregivers to concede to the child's demands or to resist them in an attempt to socialise appropriate regulatory capacities. In either case, the child learns something about the functionality of their facial communication in the local cultural context.

Here again, learning to use orientational cues and displays to solicit conceptually mediated interpersonal responses does not depend on prior understanding of their cultural meaning or function. Instead, children's attunement to the local possibilities for relational recalibration coupled with their growing ability to anticipate the changing course of interpersonal episodes allows them to deploy pragmatically effective symbolic movements in implicitly strategic ways. When more explicit linguistic knowledge ultimately does develop, it links up with a pre-established set of associations, habits and functional actions. Indeed, many of the earliest uses of emotional language simply extend the nonverbal displays that already serve the purpose of influencing other people (e.g., Coulter, 1979; Wittgenstein, 1953).

Layered Development

In previous sections, I have considered a variety of emotional capacities that children acquire over the course of socialisation and enculturation, ranging from dynamic adjustment to relational affordances to the deployment of pragmatically effective conversational demands. It is tempting to see each stage of emotional development as a rung on a ladder that takes the child forever upwards. Capacities that are increasingly more sophisticated replace more basic ones, ultimately producing a fully rational, strategic and independent adult agent; someone unencumbered by the direct pressures imposed by the social and material world and able to exert control over any unwanted impulses. However, the original relation-alignment processes that provide the foundations for more articulated modes of interpersonal influence never get fully left behind. Instead of superseding previous capacities, subsequent skills, routines and control processes get superimposed upon them. Adult emotional influence involves a complex layering of relational accommodation, orientation cuing, signalling, concept-mediated communication and regulated strategic manipulation.

Different levels of influence can take priority at different times and in different contexts. Sometimes the layers align and the processes work together. At other times, there are tensions between them. I may be implicitly resisting the demands you are making, while explicitly communicating that all is well. I may refuse to represent my emotional position as an angry one, even when I am pushing persistently against whatever is blocking my progress. I may be trying to regulate something that does not accurately reflect either your or my current orientation.

What happens when we peel away the layers? Is there an encapsulated meaning or integrated relation-alignment strategy somewhere at the core of emotional influence? Are there innate socially functional basic emotions that get distorted by the various cultural processes that are subsequently imposed on them? Instead, I have argued that the integrity of emotional influence derives from external factors that push and pull the relation alignment process in certain established directions from the outset, and not only over the course of development, but also as the immediate situation unfolds. The socialised responses of other people and the societal arrangements in which they operate channel emotions along premapped lines. According to this view, emotional structures depend on socially distributed processes that attain a kind of dynamic equilibrium. However, the interlocking forces that sustain this evolving structure also carry their own momentum that can take them beyond any familiar categories.

Conclusion

If emotions start out wholly inside an individual's mind or brain, then their impact on the social world is necessarily indirect. According to a popular view, babies are born with hard-wired neural programs that produce the experience and expression of a number of discrete affective states. The expression of these states can then be registered by others who respond to their recognisable meanings. At some later stage of development, children acquire the capacity to represent these emotions in words, although those words may not fully capture the underlying qualities of their subjective feelings. Because the emotions themselves remain private, any functional effects on other people depend on their imperfect translation into publicly available movements, signals and symbols.

I have suggested instead that patterns of relation alignment emerge from interactions between infants and caregivers and only achieve specific significance as emotional influence strategies after several successive stages of cultural socialisation. In this view, emotion words and faces are not representations of prior internal states but means of achieving interpersonal influence whose various functions consolidate in piecemeal ways over the course of development. In adults, some influence processes depend on emotional meaning and inference while others result from the dynamic calibration of orientational movements and cues. Strategic regulation of other people's responses may similarly involve a wide range of operations that need to be flexibly responsive to the other person's changing orientation to be effective.

Where does emotion itself fit into this picture? In my view, there is no distinctive set of internal sensations or perceptions that define the quality of what we experience when we get emotional. Instead, emotion emerges from the unfolding process of engaging with social events. We do not need to be conscious of bodily symptoms of any kind in order to orient to the world in an emotional way. What it feels like to be emotional, then, is usually the sense of things pressing against us or pulling us along as we navigate our way through (e.g., Frijda, 2005). Any emotional meaning that we or others attribute to our relational orientation is secondary to its central function as a mode of influence. We can't get to the heart of the phenomenon by looking ever deeper inside.

According to this reoriented perspective, there's no problem in getting from heart to heart, from one person's private experience to another's, because emotions already span any boundaries between us. This does not mean that we never conceal aspects of our relational orientation from someone else. However, this ability derives from our capacity to regulate something that was originally public, not from the inherent interiority of some putative primary process. We keep things to ourselves because we have learned their typical social consequences.

How, then, do your emotions affect other people? Let me count the ways. First, the practical parameters of an embodied relational stance impede or facilitate another person's physical progress. Second, orientational cues allow anticipatory adjustments to someone else's developing line of action. Third, many of these cues start to function as signals which are deployed to indicate the subsequent course of the behavioural trajectory, allowing a more strategic kind of mutual regulation. Fourth, certain hypercognised signals come to encapsulate more generalised pragmatic meanings associated with the norms and values of the surrounding culture, thus extending the range of their communicative influence. Fifth, people learn to make inferences based on the cultural meanings of emotional symbols, which permit them to make strategic changes to their own behaviour based on the implied consequences of the communicated emotion, factoring in appraisals, action tendencies and relational agendas. Sixth, people's engagement with collective practices allows them to participate in reciprocal processes of mutual entrainment where emotional influence flows in many directions at once. Seventh, organisational practices provide additional tools for the active regulation of other people's emotions, including deep-acting techniques and collaborative staging of emotional events. Eighth, people learn to exploit many of these social influence processes by selectively targeting different aspects of their own and other people's orientations, communications and actions during interpersonal or intergroup negotiations and conflicts.

The concept of relation alignment links these processes together at an abstract level, reminding us that emotions are relational rather than internal, social rather than individual and active rather than passive. However, no single unifying idea can fully capture the intricacies and specificities of the multifarious varieties of emotional influence that operate at different phases of development in different interpersonal, intergroup and organisational contexts across the different local, national and international societies of the world. I have tried to provide a taste of their complexity, flexibility and dynamism in this book, but we need to focus more closely on the details before we can properly appreciate the bigger picture.

References

Abelson, R. P., & Sermat, V. (1962). Multidimensional scaling of facial expressions. *Journal of Experimental Psychology*, *63*, 546–64.

Adams, R. B., Jr., Albohn, D. N., & Kveraga, K. (2017). A social vision account of facial expression perception. In J.-M. Fernandez-Dols & J. A. Russell (Eds.), *The science of facial expression* (pp. 315–32). Oxford: Oxford University Press.

Adams, R. B., Jr., & Franklin, R. G. (2009). Influence of emotional expression on the processing of gaze direction. *Motivation and Emotion*, *33,* 106–112.

Adams, R. B., Jr., Hess, U., & Kleck, R. E. (2015). The intersection of gender-related facial appearance and facial displays of emotion. *Emotion Review*, *7*, 5–13.

Adams, R. B., Jr., & Kleck, R. E. (2003). Perceived gaze direction and the processing of facial displays of emotion. *Psychological Science*, *14*, 644–7.

Adams, R. B., Jr., & Kleck, R. E. (2005). Effects of direct and averted gaze on the perception of facially communicated emotion. *Emotion*, *5*, 3–11.

Aldao, A. (2013). The future of emotion regulation research: Capturing context. *Perspectives on Psychological Science*, *8*, 155–72.

Aldao, A., Nolen-Hoeksema, S., & Schweizer, S. (2010). Emotion regulation strategies across psychopathology: A meta-analytic review. *Clinical Psychology Review*, *30*, 217–37.

Alexander, M. G., Brewer, M. B., & Herrmann, R. K. (1999). Images and affect: A functional analysis of out-group stereotypes. *Journal of Personality and Social Psychology*, *77*, 78–93.

Ambadar, Z., Schooler, J., & Cohn, J. (2005). Deciphering the enigmatic face: The importance of facial dynamics in interpreting subtle facial expressions. *Psychological Science*, *16*, 403–10.

American Psychiatric Association (2013). *DSM-V: Diagnostic and Statistical Manual of Mental Disorders* (5th edition). Arlington, VA: American Psychiatric Publishing.

Andersen, S. M., & Chen, S. (2002). The relational self: An interpersonal social-cognitive theory. *Psychological Review*, *109*, 619–45.

Anderson, C., Keltner, D., & John, O. P. (2003). Emotional convergence between people over time. *Journal of Personality and Social Psychology*, *84*, 1054–68.

Andreasson, P., & Dimberg, U. (2008). Emotional empathy and facial feedback. *Journal of Nonverbal Behavior*, *32*, 215–24.

Andrew, R. J. (1963). Evolution of facial expression. *Science*, *142*, 1034–41.

Anshel, A., & Kipper, D. A. (1988). The influence of group singing on trust and cooperation. *Journal of Music Therapy*, *25*, 145–55.

Aristotle (1991). *On rhetoric: A theory of civic discourse* (tr. G. A. Kennedy). Oxford: Oxford University Press.

Armstrong, S. L., Gleitman, H., & Gleitman, L. R. (1983). What some concepts might not be. *Cognition*, *13*, 263–308.

Arnold, M. B. (1960). *Emotion and personality: (Vol. 1) Psychological aspects*. New York: Columbia University Press.

Ashforth, B. E., & Humphrey, R. H. (1993). Emotional labor in service roles: The influence of identity. *Academy of Management Review*, *18*, 88–115.

Augustine, A. A., & Hemenover, S. H. (2009). On the relative effectiveness of affect regulation strategies: A meta-analysis. *Cognition and Emotion*, *23*, 1181–220.

Austin, J. L. (1962). *How to do things with words*. Oxford: Clarendon Press.

Averill, J. R. (1975). A semantic atlas of emotional concepts. *JSAS Catalog of Selected Documents in Psychology*, *5*, 330 (Ms. No. 421).

Averill, J. R. (1980). A constructivist view of emotion. In R. Plutchik & H. Kellerman (Eds.), *Theories of emotion* (pp. 305–40). New York: Academic Press.

Averill, J. R. (1982). *Anger and aggression: An essay on emotion*. New York: Springer.

Averill, J. R. (1985). The social construction of emotion: With special reference to love. In K. J. Gergen & K. Davis (Eds.), *The social construction of the person* (pp. 89–109). New York: Springer.

Averill, J. R., & Boothroyd, P. (1977). On falling in love in conformance with the romantic ideal. *Motivation and Emotion*, *1*, 235–47.

Averill, J. R., Catlin, G., & Chon, K. K. (1990). *Rules of hope*. New York: Springer.

Averill, J. R., & Nunley, E. P. (1988). Grief as an emotion and as a disease: A social-constructionist perspective. *Journal of Social Issues*, *44*, 79–95.

Averill, J. R., & Nunley, E. P. (1992). *Voyages of the heart: Living an emotionally creative life*. New York: Macmillan.

Aviezer, H., & Hassin, R. R. (2017). Inherently ambiguous: An argument for contextualized emotion perception. In J.-M. Fernandez-Dols & J. A. Russell (Eds.), *The science of facial expression* (pp. 333–49). Oxford: Oxford University Press.

Aviezer, H., Hassin, R. R., Ryan, J., Grady, C., Susskind, J., Anderson, A., Moscovitch, M., & Bentin, S. (2008). Angry, disgusted, or afraid? Studies on the malleability of emotion perception. *Psychological Science*, *19*, 724–32.

Aviezer, H., Trope, Y., & Todorov, A. (2012). Holistic person processing: Faces with bodies tell the whole story. *Journal of Personality and Social Psychology*, *103*, 20–37.

Ax, A. F. (1953). The physiological differentiation between fear and anger in humans. *Psychosomatic Medicine*, *15*, 433–42.

Baile, W. F., Buckman, R., Lenzi, R., Glober, G., Beale, E. A., & Kudelka, A. P. (2000). SPIKES – A six-step protocol for delivering bad news: Application to the patient with cancer. *The Oncologist*, *5*, 302–11.

Baker, S. D. (2007). Followership: The theoretical foundation of a contemporary construct. *Journal of Leadership and Organizational Studies*, *14*, 50–60.

Bakker, A. B., Schaufeli, W. B., Demerouti, E., Janssen, P. M. P., Van der Hulst, R., & Brouwer, J. (2000). Using equity theory to examine the difference between burnout and depression. *Anxiety, Stress and Coping*, 13, 247–68.

Barger, P., & Grandey, A. (2006). 'Service with a smile' and encounter satisfaction: Emotional contagion and appraisal mechanisms. *Academy of Management Journal*, 49, 1229–38.

Barr, C. L., & Kleck, R. E. (1995). Self-other perception of the intensity of facial expressions of emotion: Do we know what we show? *Journal of Personality and Social Psychology*, 68, 608–18.

Barrett, L. F. (2006). Are emotions natural kinds? *Perspectives on Psychological Science*, 1, 28–58.

Barrett, L. F. (2017). *How emotions are made: The secret life of the brain*. London: Macmillan.

Barsade, S. G. (2002). The ripple effect: Emotional contagion and its influence on group behavior. *Administrative Science Quarterly*, 47, 644–75.

Barsade, S. G., & Gibson, D. E. (1998). Group emotion: A view from top and bottom. In M. A. Neale & E. A. Mannix (Eds.), *Research on managing groups and teams* (Vol. 1, pp. 81–102). Stamford, CT: JAI Press.

Barsade, S. G., & Gibson, D. E. (2012). Group affect: Its influence on individual and group outcomes. *Current Directions in Psychological Science*, 21, 119–23.

Barsalou, L. W. (1985). Ideals, central tendency, and frequency of instantiation. *Journal of Experimental Psychology: Learning, Memory, and Cognition*, 11, 629–54.

Barsalou, L.W. (1999). Perceptual symbol systems. *Behavioral and Brain Sciences*, 22, 577–660.

Barsalou, L. W. (2005). Abstraction as dynamic interpretation in perceptual symbol systems. In L. Gershkoff-Stowe & D. Rakison (Eds.), *Building object categories* (pp. 389–431). Carnegie Symposium Series. Mahwah, NJ: Erlbaum.

Bartel, C., & Saavedra, R. (2000). The collective construction of work group moods. *Administrative Science Quarterly*, 45, 197–231.

Bass, B. M., & Riggio, R. E. (2006). *Transformational leadership* (2nd edition). Mahwah, NJ: Lawrence Erlbaum.

Baudrillard, J. (1988). *America*. New York: Verso.

Baumeister, R. F., Stillwell, A. M., & Heatherton, T. F. (1994). Guilt: An interpersonal approach. *Psychological Bulletin*, 115, 243–67.

Baumeister, R. F., Stillwell, A. M., & Heatherton, T. F. (1995). Personal narratives about guilt: Role in action control and interpersonal relationships. *Basic and Applied Social Psychology*, 17, 173–98.

Bavelas, J. B., Black, A., Chovil, N., Lemery, C. R., & Mullett, J. (1988). Form and function in motor mimicry: Topographic evidence that the primary function is communicative. *Human Communication Research*, 14, 275–99.

Bavelas, J. B., Black, A., Lemery, C. R., & Mullett, J. (1986). 'I show how you feel': Motor mimicry as a communicative act. *Journal of Personality and Social Psychology*, 50, 322–9.

Bavelas, J., Coates, L., & Johnson, T. (2004). Listener responses as a collaborative process: The role of gaze. *Journal of Communication*, *52*, 566–80.

Bayliss, A. P., Frischen, A., Fenske, M. J., & Tipper, S. P. (2007). Affective evaluations of objects are influenced by observed gaze direction and emotion expression. *Cognition*, *104*, 644–53.

Beal, D., & Trougakos, J. (2013). Episodic intrapersonal emotion regulation: Or, dealing with life as it happens. In A. A. Grandey, J. M. Diefendorff & D. Rupp (Eds.), *Emotional labor in the 21st century: Diverse perspectives on emotion regulation at work* (pp. 31–55). New York: Psychology Press/Routledge.

Beal, D. J., Trougakos, J. P., Weiss, H. M., & Green, S. G. (2006). Episodic processes in emotional labor: Perceptions of affective delivery and regulation strategies. *Journal of Applied Psychology*, *91*, 1053–65.

Bedford, E. (1957). Emotions. *Proceedings of the Aristotelian Society*, *57*, 281–304.

Beebe, B., Gerstman, L., Carson, B., Dolins, M., Zigman, A., Rosenzweig, H., Faughey, K., & Korman, M. (1982). Rhythmic communication in the mother-infant dyad. In M. Davis (Ed.), *Interaction rhythms: Periodicity in communicative behaviour* (pp. 77–100). New York: Human Sciences Press.

Benbassat, J., & Baumal, R. (2004). What is empathy, and how can it be promoted during clinical clerkships? *Academic Medicine*, *79*, 832–9.

Benitez-Quiroz, C. F., Srinivasan, R., & Martinez, A. M. (2018). Facial color is an efficient mechanism to visually transmit emotion. *Proceedings of the National Academy of Sciences of the United States of America*, *115*, 3581–6.

Bernardi, N. F., Bellemare-Pepin, A., & Peretz, I. (2017). Enhancement of pleasure during spontaneous dance. *Frontiers in Neuroscience*, *11*, article 572.

Berndsen, M., Hornsey, M. J., & Wohl, M. J. A. (2015). The impact of a victim-focused apology on forgiveness in an intergroup context. *Group Processes and Intergroup Relations*, *18*, 726–39.

Bernieri, F. J., Davis, J. M., Rosenthal, R., & Knee, C. R. (1994). Interactional synchrony and rapport: Measuring synchrony in displays devoid of sound and facial affect. *Personality and Social Psychology Bulletin*, *20*, 303–11.

Bernieri, F., Reznick, J. S., & Rosenthal, R. (1988). Synchrony, pseudo-synchrony, and dissynchrony: Measuring the entrainment process in mother-infant interactions. *Journal of Personality and Social Psychology*, *54*, 243–53.

Berry, D. S., & McArthur, L. A. (1982). Perceiving character in faces: The impact of age-related craniofacial changes on social perception. *Psychological Bulletin*, *100*, 3–18.

Biglan, A. A., Hops, H., Sherman, L., Friedman, L. S., Arthur, J., & Osteen, V. (1985). Problem-solving interactions of depressed women and their husbands. *Behavior Therapy*, *16*, 431–51.

Billig, M. (1987). *Arguing and thinking: A rhetorical approach to social psychology*. Cambridge: Cambridge University Press.

Billig, M., & Tajfel, H. (1973). Social categorization and similarity in intergroup behaviour. *European Journal of Social Psychology*, *3*, 27–52.

Birdwhistell, R. (1970). *Kinesics and context*. Philadelphia: University of Pennsylvania Press.

Blackmore, J., & Sachs, J. (1998). You never show you can't cope: Women in school leadership roles managing their emotions. *Gender and Education, 10*, 265–79.

Blairy, S., Herrera, P., & Hess, U. (1999). Mimicry and the judgment of emotional facial expressions. *Journal of Nonverbal Behavior, 23*, 5–41.

Blascovich, J., Ginsburg, G. P., & Howe, R. C. (1975). Blackjack and the risky shift, II: Monetary stakes. *Journal of Experimental Social Psychology, 11*, 224–32.

Block, J. (1957). Studies in the phenomenology of emotions. *Journal of Abnormal and Social Psychology, 54*, 358–63.

Boerebach, B. C., Scheepers, R. A., van der Leeuw, R. M., Heineman, M. J., Arah, O. A., & Lombarts, K. M. (2014). The impact of clinicians' personality and their interpersonal behaviors on the quality of patient care: A systematic review. *International Journal for Quality in Health Care, 26*, 426–81.

Bonanno, G. A., & Burton, C. L. (2013). Regulatory flexibility: An individual differences perspective on coping and emotion regulation. *Perspectives on Psychological Science, 8*, 591–612.

Bono, J. E., & Ilies, R. (2006). Charisma, positive emotions and mood contagion. *Leadership Quarterly, 17*, 317–34.

Bornstein, M. H., Kessen, W., & Weiskopf, S. (1976). Color vision and hue categorization in young human infants. *Journal of the Experimental Psychology: Human Performance, 1*, 115–29.

Bould, E., Morris, N., & Wink, B. (2008). Recognising subtle emotional expressions: The role of facial movements. *Cognition and Emotion, 22*, 1569–87.

Bourgeois, P., & Hess, U. (2008). The impact of social context on mimicry. *Biological Psychology, 77*, 343–52.

Bowlby, J. (1973). *Attachment and loss (Vol. 2) Separation: Anxiety and anger*. London: Hogarth Press.

Brand, R. J., Baldwin, D. A., & Ashburn, L. A. (2002). Evidence for 'motionese': Modifications in mothers' infant-directed action. *Developmental Science, 5*, 72–83.

Branscombe, N. R., & Doosje, B. (Eds.). (2004). *Collective guilt: International perspectives*. New York: Cambridge University Press.

Branscombe, N. R., & Miron, A. M. (2004). Interpreting the ingroup's negative actions toward another group: Emotional reactions to appraised harm. In L. Z. Tiedens & C. W. Leach (Eds.), *The social life of emotions* (pp. 314–35). Cambridge: Cambridge University Press.

Brauer, M., & Judd, C. M. (1996). Group polarization and repeated attitude expressions: A new take on an old topic. *European Review of Social Psychology, 7*, 174–207.

Braunstein, L. M., Gross, J. J., & Ochsner, K. N. (2017). Explicit and implicit emotion regulation: A multi-level framework. *Social Cognitive and Affective Neuroscience, 12*, 1545–57.

Brewer, M. B. (1991). The social self: On being the same and different at the same time. *Personality and Social Psychology Bulletin, 17*, 475–82.

Brewer, M. B., & Alexander, M. G. (2002). Intergroup emotions and images. In D. M. Mackie & E. R. Smith (Eds.), *From prejudice to intergroup emotions:*

Differentiated reactions to social groups (pp. 209–25). New York: Psychology Press.

Brotheridge, C., & Lee, R. T. (2003). Development and validation of the Emotional Labour Scale. *Journal of Occupational and Organizational Psychology*, *76*, 365–79.

Brotheridge, C., & Lee, R. T. (2008). The emotions of managing: An introduction to the special issue. *Journal of Managerial Psychology*, *23*, 108–17.

Brown, P., & Levinson, S. C. (1987). *Politeness: Some universals in language usage*. Cambridge: Cambridge University Press.

Bruder, M., Dosmukhambetova, D., Nerb, J., & Manstead, A. S. R. (2012). Emotional signals in nonverbal interaction: Dyadic facilitation and convergence in expressions, appraisals, and feelings. *Cognition and Emotion*, *26*, 480–502.

Bush, K. A., Inman, C. S., Hamann, S., Kilts, C. D., & James, G. A. (2017). Distributed neural processing predictors of multi-dimensional properties of affect. *Frontiers in Human Neuroscience*, *11*, article 49.

Bush, L. K., Barr, C. L., McHugo, G. J., & Lanzetta, J. T. (1989). The effects of facial control and facial mimicry on subjective reactions to comedy routines. *Motivation and Emotion*, *13*, 31–52.

Buss, D. M., & Schmidt, D. P. (1993). Sexual strategies theory: An evolutionary perspective on human mating. *Psychological Review*, *100*, 204–32.

Butalid, L., Bensing, J. M., & Verhaak, P. F. (2014). Talking about psychosocial problems: An observational study on changes in doctor-patient communication in general practice between 1977 and 2008. *Patient Education and Counseling*, *94*, 314–21.

Butler, E. A., Egloff, B., Wilhelm, F. H., Smith, N. C., Erickson, E. A., & Gross, J. J. (2003). The social consequences of expressive suppression. *Emotion*, *3*, 48–67.

Butler, E. A., & Randall, A. K. (2013). Emotional coregulation in close relationships. *Emotion Review*, *5*, 202–210.

Byrne, D. (1961). Interpersonal attraction and attitude similarity. *Journal of Abnormal and Social Psychology*, *62*, 713–15.

Cacioppo, J. T., Berntson, G. G., & Klein, D. J. (1992). What is an emotion?: The role of somatovisceral afference, with special emphasis on somatovisceral 'illusions'. *Review of Personality and Social Psychology*, *14*, 63–98.

Campos, J. J., Frankel, C. B., & Camras, L. (2004). On the nature of emotion regulation. *Child Development*, *75*, 377–94.

Campos, J. J., Mumme, D., Kermoian, R., & Campos, R. (1994). A functionalist perspective on the nature of emotion. In N. Fox (Ed.), *The development of emotion regulation: Biological and behavioral considerations. Monographs of the Society for Research in Child Development*, *59*, (2–3, Serial No. 240), 284–303.

Campos, J. J., & Stenberg, C. (1981). Perception, appraisal, and emotion: The onset of social referencing. In M. E. Lamb & L. R. Sherrod (Eds.), *Infant social cognition: Empirical and theoretical considerations* (pp. 273–314). Hillsdale, NJ: Erlbaum.

Camras, L. A. (1992). Expressive development and basic emotions. *Cognition and Emotion*, *6*, 269–83.

Camras, L. A., Campos, J. J., Oster, H., Miyake, K., & Bradshaw, D. (1992). Japanese and American infants' responses to arm restraint. *Developmental Psychology, 28*, 578–83.

Cannon, W. B. (1927). The James-Lange theory of emotions: A critical examination and an alternative theory. *American Journal of Psychology, 39*, 106–24.

Carlson, D., Ferguson, M., Hunter, E., & Whitten, D. (2012). Abusive supervision and work-family conflict: The path through emotional labor and burnout. *The Leadership Quarterly, 23*, 849–59.

Carpenter, M., Nagell, K., & Tomasello, M. (1998). Social cognition, joint attention, and communicative competence from 9 to 15 months of age. *Monographs of the Society for Research in Child Development, 63*, 1–143.

Carroll, J. M., & Russell, J. A. (1996). Do facial expressions signal specific emotions? Judging emotion from the face in context. *Journal of Personality and Social Psychology, 70*, 205–218.

Chaiken, S. (1979). Communicator physical attractiveness and persuasion. *Journal of Personality and Social Psychology, 37*, 1387–97.

Chang, L. J., Gianaros, P. J., Manuck, S. B., Krishnan, A., & Wager, T. D. (2015). A sensitive and specific neural signature for picture-induced negative affect. *PLOS Biology, 13*, e1002180.

Chartrand, T. L., & Bargh, J. A. (1999). The chameleon effect: The perception-behavior link and social interaction. *Journal of Personality and Social Psychology, 76*, 893–910.

Chen, C. N., Crivelli, C., Garrod, O. G. B., Schyns, P. G., Fernández-Dols, J.-M., & Jack, R. E. (2018). Distinct facial expressions represent pain and pleasure across cultures. *Proceedings of the National Academy of Sciences of the United States of America, 115*, e10013–e10021.

Cheshin, A., Amit, A., & van Kleef, G. A. (2018). The interpersonal effects of emotion intensity in customer service: Perceived appropriateness and authenticity of attendants' emotional displays shape customer trust and satisfaction. *Organizational Behavior and Human Decision Processes, 144*, 97–111.

Chi, N.-W., Grandey, A., Diamond, J., & Krimmel, K. (2011). Want a tip? Service performance as a function of emotion regulation and extraversion. *Journal of Applied Psychology, 96*, 1337–46.

Chi, N.-W., Yang, J. X., & Lin, C. Y. (2018). Service workers' chain reactions to daily customer mistreatment: Behavioral linkages, mechanisms, and boundary conditions. *Journal of Occupational Health Psychology, 23*, 58–70.

Chovil, N. (1997). Facing others: A social communicative perspective on facial displays. In J. A. Russell & J.-M. Fernández-Dols (Eds.), *The psychology of facial expression* (pp. 321–33). New York: Cambridge University Press.

Clark, H. H. (1985). Language use and language users. In G. Lindzey & E. Aronson (Eds.), *Handbook of social psychology* (3rd edition, pp. 179–231). New York: Harper and Row.

Clayton, M., Sager, R., & Will, U. (2004). In time with the music: The concept of entrainment and its significance for ethnomusicology. *ESEM CounterPoint, 1*, 1–84.

Clément, F., & Dukes, D. (2017). Social appraisal and social referencing: Two components of affective social learning. *Emotion Review, 9,* 253–61.

Clift, S., & Hancox, G. (2001). The perceived benefits of singing: Findings from preliminary surveys of a university college choral society. *Journal of the Royal Society for the Promotion of Health, 121,* 248–56.

Clore, G. L., & Ortony, A. (1991). What more is there to emotion concepts than prototypes? *Journal of Personality and Social Psychology, 60,* 48–50.

Clore, G. L., Ortony, A., & Foss, M. A. (1987). The psychological foundation of the affective lexicon. *Journal of Personality and Social Psychology, 53,* 751–66.

Cohen, J. B., & Andrade, E. B. (2004). Affective intuition and task-contingent affect regulation. *Journal of Consumer Research, 31,* 358–67.

Collins, R. (2004). *Interaction ritual chains.* Princeton: Princeton University Press.

Collins, R. (2014). Interaction ritual chains and collective effervescence. In C. von Scheve & M. Salmela (Eds.), *Collective emotions* (pp. 299–311). Oxford: University of Oxford Press.

Conger, J. A., & Kanungo, R. N. (1987). Toward a behavioral theory of charismatic leadership in organizational settings. *Academy of Management Review, 12,* 637–47.

Connelly, S., & Ruark, G. (2010). Leadership style and activating potential moderators of the relationships among leader emotional displays and outcomes. *Leadership Quarterly, 21,* 745–64.

Cossette, M., & Hess, U. (2015). Service with style and smile: How and why employees are performing emotional labor. *European Review of Applied Psychology, 65,* 71–82.

Costa, P., Magalhaes, E., & Costa, M. J. (2013). A latent growth model suggests that empathy of medical students does not decline over time. *Advances in Health Sciences Education: Theory and Practice, 18,* 509–22.

Côté, S. (2005). A social interaction model of the effects of emotion regulation on work strain. *Academy of Management Review, 30,* 509–30.

Coulter, J. (1979). *The social construction of mind: Studies in ethnomethodology and linguistic philosophy.* London: Macmillan.

Cowen, A. S., & Keltner, D. (2017). Self-report captures 27 distinct categories of emotion bridged by continuous gradients. *Proceedings of the National Academy of Sciences of the United States of America, 114,* E7900–E7909.

Cowen, A. S., & Keltner, D. (2018). Clarifying the conceptualization, dimensionality, and structure of emotion: Response to Barrett and colleagues. *Trends in Cognitive Sciences, 22,* 274–6.

Coyne, J. C. (1976). Toward an interactional description of depression. *Psychiatry, 39,* 28–40.

Crivelli, C. (2016). Facial expressions and emotions in small-scale societies. Ph.D. dissertation, Universita Autonóma de Madrid, Spain.

Crivelli, C., Carrera, P., & Fernández-Dols, J.-M. (2015). Are smiles a sign of happiness? Spontaneous expressions of judo winners. *Evolution and Human Behavior, 33,* 52–8.

Crivelli, C., & Fridlund, A. J. (2018). Facial displays are tools for social influence. *Trends in Cognitive Sciences*, *22*, 388–399.

Crivelli, C., & Fridlund, A. J. (2019). Inside-out: From basic emotions theory to the behavioral ecology view. *Journal of Nonverbal Behavior*, *43*, 161–94.

Crivelli, C., Jarillo, S., Russell, J. A., & Fernández-Dols, J.-M. (2016a). Reading emotions from faces in two indigenous societies. *Journal of Experimental Psychology: General*, *145*, 830–43.

Crivelli, C., Russell, J. A., Jarillo, S., & Fernández-Dols, J.-M. (2016b). The fear gasping face as a threat display in a Melanesian society. *Proceedings of the National Academy of Sciences of the United States of America*, *113*, 12403–7.

Crivelli, C., Russell, J. A., Jarillo, S., & Fernández-Dols, J.-M. (2017). Recognizing spontaneous facial expressions of emotion in a small-scale society in Papua New Guinea. *Emotion*, *17*, 337–47.

Csibra, G., & Gergely, G. (2009). Natural pedagogy. *Trends in Cognitive Science*, *13*, 148–53.

Csíkszentmihályi, M. (1990). *Flow: The psychology of optimal experience*. New York: Harper & Row.

Damen, F., van Knippenberg, B., & van Knippenberg, D. (2008). Affective match in leadership: Leader emotional displays, follower positive affect, and follower performance. *Journal of Applied Social Psychology*, *38*, 868–902.

Daniels, M. J. (1960). Affect and its control in the medical intern. *American Journal of Sociology*, *66*, 259–67.

Darwin, C. (1872/1998). *The expression of the emotions in man and animals* (3rd edition). London: HarperCollins.

Dasborough, M. T., Ashkanasy, N. M., Tee, E. Y. J., & Tse, H. M. (2009). What goes around comes around: How meso-level negative emotional contagion can ultimately determine organizational attitudes toward leaders. *Leadership Quarterly*, *20*, 571–85.

Davis, J. I., Senghas, A., Brandt, F., & Ochsner, K.N. (2010). The effects of BOTOX injections on emotional experience. *Emotion*, *10*, 433–40.

Dawkins, R., & Krebs, J. R. (1978). Animal signals: Information or manipulation. In J. R. Krebs & N. B. Davies (Eds.), *Behavioural ecology: An evolutionary approach* (pp. 282–309). Oxford, UK: Blackwell Scientific.

Decety, J., Yang, C.Y., & Cheng, Y. (2010). Physicians down-regulate their pain empathy response: An event-related brain potential study. *NeuroImage*, *50*, 1676–82.

De Hoogh, A. H. B., Den Hartog, D. N., & Koopman, P. L. (2005). Linking the Big Five-Factors of personality to charismatic and transactional leadership; perceived dynamic work environment as a moderator. *Journal of Organizational Behavior*, *26*, 839–65.

De Jong, P. (1999). Communicative and remedial effects of social blushing. *Journal of Nonverbal Behavior*, *23*, 197–217.

De Klerk, C. J. M., Hamilton, A. F. de C., & Southgate, V. (2018). Eye contact modulates facial mimicry in 4-month-old infants: An EMG and fNIRS study. *Cortex*, *106*, 93–103.

Del Piccolo, L., & Finset, A. (2018). Patients' autonomic activation during clinical interaction: A review of empirical studies. *Patient Education and Counseling*, *101*, 195–208.

Delvaux, E., Meeussen, L., & Mesquita, B. (2016). Emotions are not always contagious: Longitudinal spreading of self-pride and group pride in homogeneous and status-differentiated groups. *Cognition and Emotion*, *30*, 101–16.

Delvaux, E., Vanbeselaere, N., & Mesquita, B. (2015). Dynamic interplay between norms and experiences of anger and gratitude in groups. *Small Group Research*, *46*, 300–23.

De Melo, C. M., Carnevale, P. J., Read, S. J., & Gratch, J. (2014). Reading people's minds from emotion expressions in interdependent decision making. *Journal of Personality and Social Psychology*, *106*, 73–88.

De Rivera, J. (1977). *A structural theory of emotions*. New York: International Universities Press.

De Rivera, J. (2014). Emotion and the formation of social identities. In C. von Scheve & M. Salmela (Eds.), *Collective emotions* (pp. 217–31). Oxford: University of Oxford Press.

De Rivera, J., & Grinkis, C. (1986). Emotions as social relationships. *Motivation and Emotion*, *10*, 351–69.

Derksen, F. A., olde Hartman, T. C., Bensing, J. M., & Lagro-Janssen, A. L. (2016). Managing barriers to empathy in the clinical encounter: A qualitative interview study with GPs. *The British Journal of General Practice*, *66*, 653, e887–e895.

Descartes, R. (1649/1911). The passions of the soul. In *The philosophical works of Descartes* (tr. E. S. Haldane & G. R. T. Ross, Vol. 1, pp. 329–427). Cambridge: Cambridge University Press.

De Vos, B., van Zomeren, M., Gordijn, E., & Postmes, T. (2013). The communication of 'pure' group-based anger reduces tendencies toward intergroup conflict because it increases out-group empathy. *Personality and Social Psychology Bulletin*, *39*, 1043–52.

Dewey, J. (1894). The theory of emotion I: Emotional attitudes. *Psychological Review*, *1*, 553–69.

Diefendorff, J. M., Croyle, M. H., & Gosserand, R. H. (2005). The dimensionality and antecedents of emotional labor strategies. *Journal of Vocational Behavior*, *66*, 339–57.

Diefendorff, J. M., & Gosserand, R. (2003). Understanding the emotional labor process: A control theory perspective. *Journal of Organizational Behavior*, *24*, 945–59.

Dijker, A. J. M. (1987). Emotional reactions to ethnic minorities. *European Journal of Social Psychology*, *47*, 1105–17.

Dimberg, U., & Öhman, A. (1983). The effects of directional facial cues on electrodermal conditioning to facial stimuli. *Psychophysiology*, *20*, 160–7.

Dixon, T. (2012). 'Emotion': The history of a keyword in crisis. *Emotion Review*, *4*, 338–44.

Dogan, K., & Vecchio, R. P. (2001). Managing envy and jealousy in the workplace. *Compensation & Benefits Review*, *33*, 57–64.

Doosje, B., Branscombe, N., Spears, R., & Manstead, A. S. R. (1998). Guilty by association: When one's group has a negative history. *Journal of Personality and Social Psychology, 75*, 872–86.

Doré, B. P., Silvers, J. A., & Ochsner, K. N. (2016). Toward a personalized science of emotion regulation. *Social & Personality Psychology Compass, 10*, 171–87.

Draghi-Lorenz, R., Reddy, V., & Morris, P. (2005). Young infants can be perceived as shy, coy, bashful, embarrassed. *Infant and Child Development, 14*, 63–83.

Driver, J., Davis, G., Ricciardelli, P., Kidd, P., Maxwell, E., & Baron-Cohen, S. (1999). Gaze perception triggers reflexive visuospatial orienting. *Visual Cognition, 6*, 509–40.

Drury, J., Cocking, C., Beale, J., Hanson, C., & Rapley, F. (2005). The phenomenology of empowerment in collective action. *British Journal of Social Psychology, 44*, 309–28.

Duchenne de Boulogne, G-B. (1862, tr. 1990, R. A. Cuthbertson). *The mechanism of human facial expression*. Cambridge: Cambridge University Press.

Duffy, M. K., & Shaw, J. D. (2000). The Salieri syndrome: Consequences of envy in groups. *Small Group Research, 31*, 3–23.

Dunn, B. D., Billotti, D., Murphy, V., & Dalgleish, T. (2009). The consequences of effortful emotion regulation when processing distressing material: A comparison of suppression and acceptance. *Behaviour Research and Therapy, 47*, 761–73.

Durán, J. I., Reisenzein, R., & Fernández-Dols, J.-M. (2017). Coherence between emotions and facial expressions: A research synthesis. In J.-M. Fernández-Dols & J. A. Russell (Eds.), *The science of facial expression* (pp. 107–29). New York: Oxford University Press.

Durkheim, É. (1893, tr. 1997). *The division of labour in society*. New York: Free Press.

Durkheim, É. (1912, tr. 1995). *The elementary forms of religious life*. (tr. K. E. Fields). New York: Free Press.

Dyrbye, L. N., Thomas, M. R., Harper, W., Massie, F. S. Jr., Power, D. V., Eacker, A., Szydlo, D. W., Novotny, P. J., Sloan, J. A., & Shanafelt, T. D. (2009). The learning environment and medical student burnout: a multicentre study. *Medical Education, 43*, 274–82.

Edwards, D. (1999). Emotion discourse. *Cultural Psychology, 5*, 271–91.

Edwards, D., & Potter, J. (1992). *Discursive psychology*. London: Sage.

Eggly, S., Penner, L., Albrecht, T. L., Cline, R. J., Foster, T., Naughton, M., Peterson, A., & Ruckdeschel, J. C. (2006). Discussing bad news in the outpatient oncology clinic: Rethinking current communication guidelines. *Journal of Clinical Oncology, 24*, 716–19.

Ekman, P. (1972). Universals and cultural differences in facial expressions of emotion. In J. Cole (Ed.), *Nebraska Symposium on Motivation* (pp. 207–83). Lincoln: University of Nebraska Press.

Ekman, P. (1979). About brows: Emotional and conversational signals. In M. von Cranach, K. Foppa, W. Lepenies & D. Ploog (Eds.), *Human ethology:*

Claims and limits of a new discipline (pp. 169–202). New York: Cambridge University Press.

Ekman, P. (1989). The argument and evidence about universals in facial expressions of emotion. In H. Wagner & A. Manstead (Eds.), *Handbook of psychophysiology: The biological psychology of emotions and social processes* (pp. 143–164). London: Wiley.

Ekman, P. (1997). Should we call it expression or communication? *Innovations in Social Science Research*, *10*, 333–44.

Ekman, P. (2003). *Emotions revealed: Understanding faces and feeling*. London: Weidenfeld and Nicolson.

Ekman, P. (2009). Darwin's contributions to our understanding of facial expressions. *Philosophical Transactions of the Royal Society, Series B*, *364*, 3449–51.

Ekman, P. (2017). Facial expression. In J.-M. Fernandez-Dols & J. A. Russell (Eds.), *The science of facial expression* (pp. 39–56). Oxford: Oxford University Press.

Ekman, P., & Friesen, W. V. (1975). *Unmasking the face: A guide to recognizing emotions from facial clues*. Englewood Cliffs, NJ: Prentice-Hall.

Ekman, P., & Friesen, W. V. (1976). *Pictures of facial affect*. Palo Alto, CA: Consulting Psychologists Press.

Ekman, P., & Friesen, W. V. (1982). Felt, false, and miserable smiles. *Journal of Nonverbal Behavior*, *6*, 238–58.

Ekman, P., Friesen, W. V., & Ellsworth, P. (1972). *Emotion in the human face: Guidelines for research and an integration of findings*. New York: Pergamon Press.

Ekman, P., Friesen, W. V. and Ellsworth, P. (1982). What are the relative contributions of facial behavior and contextual information to the judgment of emotion? In P. Ekman (Ed.), *Emotion in the human face* (2nd edition, pp. 111–27). New York: Cambridge University Press.

Ekman, P., Friesen, W. V., & Simons, R. C. (1985). Is the startle reaction an emotion? *Journal of Personality and Social Psychology*, *49*, 1416–26.

Ekman, P., Levenson, R. W., & Friesen, W. V. (1983). Autonomic nervous system activity distinguishing among emotions. *Science*, *221*, 1208–10.

Ekman, P., Sorensen, E. R., & Friesen, W. V. (1969). Pan-cultural elements in facial displays of emotions. *Science*, *164*, 86–8.

Elfenbein, H. A. (2007). Emotion in organizations: A review and theoretical integration. *Academy of Management Annals*, *1*, 371–457.

Elfenbein, H. A. (2014). The many faces of emotional contagion: An affective process theory for affective linkage. *Organizational Psychology Review*, *4*, 326–62.

Elfenbein, H. A., & Ambady, N. (2002). On the universality and cultural specificity of emotion recognition: A meta-analysis. *Psychological Bulletin*, *128*, 203–35.

Elfenbein, H. A., Beaupré, M. G., Lévesque, M., & Hess, U. (2007). Toward a dialect theory: Cultural differences in the expression and recognition of posed facial expressions. *Emotion*, *7*, 131–46.

Elfenbein, H. A., Marsh, A. A., & Ambady, N. (2002). Emotional intelligence and the recognition of emotion from facial expressions. In L. F. Barrett &

P. Salovey (Eds.), *The wisdom in feeling: Psychological processes in emotional intelligence* (pp. 37–58). New York: Guilford Press.

Ellsworth, P. C. (2013). Appraisal theory: Old and new questions. *Emotion Review, 5*, 125–31.

Ellsworth, P. C., & Tourangeau, R. (1981). On our failure to disconfirm what nobody ever said. *Journal of Personality and Social Psychology, 40*, 363–69.

Erdmann, G., & Janke, W. (1978). Interaction between physiological and cognitive determinants of emotions. *Biological Psychology, 6*, 61–74.

Etcoff, N. L., & Magee, J. J. (1992). Categorical perception of facial expressions. *Cognition, 44*, 227–40.

Evaldsson, A.-C., & Melander, H. (2017). Managing disruptive student conduct: Negative emotions and accountability in reproach-response sequences. *Linguistics and Education, 37*, 73–86.

Fehr, B., & Russell, J. A. (1984). Concept of emotion viewed from a prototype perspective. *Journal of Experimental Psychology: General, 113*, 464–86.

Ferguson, C. A. (1977). Baby talk as a simplified register. In C. Snow & C. Ferguson (Eds.), *Talking to children: Language input and acquisition* (pp. 209–35). Cambridge: Cambridge University Press.

Fernández-Dols, J.-M. (2017). Natural facial expression: A view from psychological constructionism and pragmatics. In J.-M. Fernández-Dols & J. A. Russell (Eds.), *The science of facial expression* (pp. 457–75). Oxford: Oxford University Press.

Fernández-Dols, J.-M., Carrera, P., & Crivelli, C. (2011). Facial behavior while experiencing sexual excitement. *Journal of Nonverbal Behavior, 35*, 63–71.

Fernández-Dols, J.-M., Carrera, P., Barchard, K., & Gacitua, M. (2008). False recognition of facial expressions of emotion: Causes and consequences. *Emotion, 8*, 530–9.

Fernández-Dols, J.-M., & Crivelli, C. (2013). Emotion and expression: Naturalistic studies. *Emotion Review, 5*, 24–9.

Fernández-Dols, J.-M., & Russell, J. A. (2017). Introduction. In J.-M. Fernández-Dols & J. A. Russell (Eds.), *The science of facial expression* (pp. 3–14). Oxford: Oxford University Press.

Fernández-Dols, J.-M., Sierra, B., & Ruiz-Belda, M. A. (1993). On the clarity of expressive and contextual information in the recognition of emotions: A methodological critique. *European Journal of Social Psychology, 23*, 195–202.

Fernández-Dols, J.-M., & Ruiz-Belda, M. A. (1995). Are smiles a sign of happiness? Gold medal winners at the Olympic Games. *Journal of Personality and Social Psychology, 69*, 1113–19.

Festinger, L. (1957). *A theory of cognitive dissonance*. Stanford: Stanford University Press.

Field, T. M., Woodson, R., Greenberg, R., & Cohen, D. (1982). Discrimination and imitation of facial expressions by neonates. *Science, 278*, 179–81.

Figley, C. (Ed.). (1995). *Compassion fatigue: Coping with secondary traumatic stress disorder in those who treat the traumatized*. New York: Brunner/Mazel.

Finzi, E., & Rosenthal, N. E. (2014). Treatment of depression with onabotulinumtoxinA: A randomized, double-blind, placebo controlled trial. *Journal of Psychiatric Research*, *52*, 1–6.

Finzi, E., & Wasserman, E. (2006). Treatment of depression with botulinum toxin A: A case series. *Dermatological Surgery*, *32*, 645–9.

Fischer, A. H., & Evers, C. (2011). The social costs and benefits of anger as a function of gender and relationship context. *Sex Roles*, *65*, 23–34.

Fischer, A. H., Rotteveel, M., Evers, C., & Manstead, A. S. R. (2004). Emotional assimilation: How we are influenced by others' emotions. *Cahier de Psychologie Cognitive*, *22*, 223–45.

Fischer, A. H., & Giner-Sorolla, R. (2016). Contempt: Derogating others while keeping calm. *Emotion Review*, *8*, 346–57.

Fischer, A. H., & Manstead, A. S. R. (2008). Social functions of emotion. In M. Lewis, J. M. Haviland-Jones & L. F. Barrett, (Eds.), *Handbook of emotions* (3rd edition, pp. 456–68). New York: Guilford Press.

Fischer, A. H., & Manstead, A. S. R. (2016). Social functions of emotion and emotion regulation. In L. F. Barrett, M. Lewis & J. M. Haviland-Jones (Eds.), *Handbook of emotions* (4th edition, pp. 424–39). New York: Guilford Press.

Fischer, A. H., Manstead, A. S. R., & Zaalberg, R. (2003). Social influences on the emotion process. *European Review of Social Psychology*, *14*, 171–201.

Fischer, A. H., & Roseman, I. J. (2007). Beat them or ban them: The characteristics and social functions of anger and contempt. *Journal of Personality and Social Psychology*, *93*, 103–15.

Fischer, R., Xygalatas, D., Mitkidis, P., Reddish, P., Tok, P., Konvalinka, I., & Bulbulia, J. (2014). The fire-walker's high: Affect and physiological responses in an extreme collective ritual. *PLoS ONE*, *9*, e88355.

Fiske, S. T., Cuddy, A. J. C., & Glick, P. (2002). Emotions up and down: Intergroup emotions result from perceived status and competition. In D. M. Mackie & E. R. Smith (Eds.), *From prejudice to intergroup emotions: Differentiated reactions to social groups* (pp. 247–64). New York: Psychology Press.

Fleming, J. H. (1994). Multiple audience problems, tactical communication, and social interaction: A relational-regulation perspective. *Advances in Experimental Social Psychology 26*, 215–92.

Fodor, J. A. (1975). *The language of thought*. Boston: Harvard University Press.

Fogarty, L. A., Curbow, B. A., Wingard, J. R., McDonnell, K., & Somerfield, M. R. (1999). Can 40 seconds of compassion reduce patient anxiety? *Journal of Clinical Oncology*, *17*, 371–9.

Folkow, B. (2000). Perspectives on the integrative functions of the 'sympathoadrenomedullary system'. *Autonomic Neuroscience: Basic and Clinical*, *83*, 101–15.

Fontaine, J. R. J., Scherer, K. R., & Soriano, C. (Eds.). (2013). *Components of emotional meaning: A sourcebook*. Oxford: Oxford University Press.

Fransen, K., Steffens, N. K., Haslam, S. A., Vanbeselaere, N., Van de Broek, G., & Boen, F. (2016). We will be champions: Leaders' confidence in 'us' inspires team members' team confidence and performance. *Scandinavian Journal of Medicine and Science in Sports*, *26*, 1455–69.

Fredrickson, B. L. (2001). The role of positive emotions in positive psychology: The broaden-and-build theory of positive emotions. *American Psychologist*, *56*, 218–26.

Freeman, J. B., & Ambady, N. (2011). A dynamic interactive theory of person construal. *Psychological Review*, *118*, 247–79.

Freudenberger, H. J. (1974). Staff burnout. *Journal of Social Issues*, *30*, 159–65.

Freudenberger, H. J. (1975). The staff burn-out syndrome in alternative institutions. *Psychotherapy: Theory, Research and Practice*, *12*, 73–82.

Fridlund, A. J. (1991). Sociality of solitary smiling: Potentiation by an implicit audience. *Journal of Personality and Social Psychology*, *60*, 229–40.

Fridlund, A. J. (1994). *Human facial expression: An evolutionary view*. San Diego, CA: Academic Press.

Friedman, R., Anderson, C., Brett, J., Olekalns, M., Goates, N., & Lisco, C. C. (2004). The positive and negative effects of anger in dispute resolution: Evidence from electronically mediated disputes. *Journal of Applied Psychology*, *89*, 369–76.

Friesen, W. V. (1972). *Cultural differences in facial expressions in a social situation: An experimental test of the concept of display rules*. Unpublished doctoral dissertation. University of California, San Francisco.

Frijda, N. H. (1953). The understanding of facial expression of emotion. *Acta Psychologica*, *9*, 294–362.

Frijda, N. H. (1986). *The emotions*. Cambridge: Cambridge University Press.

Frijda, N. H. (1993). The place of appraisal in emotion. *Cognition and Emotion*, *7*, 357–87.

Frijda, N. H. (2005). Emotion experience. *Cognition and Emotion*, *19*, 473–97.

Frijda, N. H., Kuipers, P., & ter Schure, E. (1989). Relations among emotion, appraisal, and emotional action readiness. *Journal of Personality and Social Psychology*, *57*, 212–28.

Frijda, N. H., & Tcherkassof, A. (1997). Facial expressions as modes of action readiness. In J. A. Russell & J. M. Fernández-Dols (Eds.), *The psychology of facial expression* (pp. 78–102). New York: Cambridge University Press.

Frost, P. (2003). *Toxic emotions at work: How compassionate managers handle pain and conflict*. Boston: HBS Press.

Fugate, J. M. B. (2013). Categorical perception for emotional faces. *Emotion Review*, *5*, 84–9.

Gabriel, A. S., & Diefendorff, J. (2015). Emotional labor dynamics: A momentary approach. *Academy of Management Journal*, *58*, 1804–25.

Gausel, N., Leach, C. W., Mazziotta, A., & Feuchte, F. (2018). Seeking revenge or seeking reconciliation? How concern for social-image and felt shame helps explain responses in reciprocal intergroup conflict. *European Journal of Social Psychology*, *48*, 62–72.

Gemmiti, M., Hamed, S., Lauber-Biason, A., Wildhaber, J., Pharisa, C., & Klumb, P. L. (2017). Pediatricians' affective communication behavior attenuates parents' stress response during the medical interview. *Patient Education and Counseling*, *100*, 480–6.

Gendron, M., Crivelli, C., & Barrett, L. F. (2018). Universality reconsidered: Diversity in meaning making about facial expressions. *Current Directions in Psychological Science*, *27*, 211–19.

Gendron, M., Lindquist, K. A., Barsalou, L., & Barrett, L. F. (2012). Emotion words shape emotion percepts. *Emotion*, *12*, 314–25.

Gendron, M., Roberson, D., van der Vyver, J. M., & Barrett, L. F. (2014). Perceptions of emotion from facial expressions are not culturally universal: Evidence from a remote culture. *Emotion*, *14*, 251–62.

George, J. M. (1990). Personality, affect, and behavior in groups. *Journal of Applied Psychology*, *75*, 107–16.

George, M. (2008). Interactions in expert service work. *Journal of Contemporary Ethnography*, *37*, 108–31.

Gergely, G., & Watson, J. (1996). The social biofeedback theory of parental affect-mirroring: The development of emotional self-awareness and self-control in infancy. *International Journal of Psychoanalysis*, *77*, 1181–212.

Gibson, J. J. (1979). *The ecological approach to visual perception*. Boston: Houghton Mifflin.

Gilbert, D. T., & Malone, P. S. (1995). The correspondence bias. *Psychological Bulletin*, *117*, 21–38.

Gilbert, D. T, Pelham, B. W., & Krull, D. S. (1988). On cognitive busyness: When person perceivers meet persons perceived. *Journal of Personality and Social Psychology*, *54*, 733–40.

Ginsburg, S. G. (1974). The problem of the burned-out executive. *Personnel Journal*, *48*, 598–600.

Gladstones, W. H. (1962). A multidimensional scaling study of facial expression of emotion. *Australian Journal of Psychology*, *14*, 95–100.

Gleichgerrcht, E., & Decety, J. (2012). The costs of empathy among health professionals. In J. Decety (Ed.), *Empathy: From bench to bedside* (pp. 245–61). Cambridge, MA: MIT Press.

Gleichgerrcht E., & Decety J. (2013). Empathy in clinical practice: How individual dispositions, gender, and experience moderate empathic concern, burnout, and emotional distress in physicians. *PLoS ONE*, *8*, e61526.

Gleichgerrcht, E., & Decety, J. (2014). The relationship between different facets of empathy, pain perception and compassion fatigue among physicians. *Frontiers in Behavioral Neuroscience*, *8*, 1–9.

Glomb, T. M., & Tews, M. J. (2004). Emotional labor: A conceptualization and scale development. *Journal of Vocational Behavior*, *64*, 1–23.

Godinho, R. M., Spikins, P., & O'Higgins, P. (2018). Supraorbital morphology and social dynamics in human evolution. *Nature Ecology & Evolution*, *2*, 956–61.

Goffman, E. (1959). *The presentation of self in everyday life*. New York: Doubleday.

Goffman, E. (1961). *Encounters: Two studies in the sociology of interaction*. Indianapolis, IN: The Bobbs-Merrill Company.

Goldenberg, A., Halperin, E., van Zomeren, M., & Gross, J. J. (2016). The process model of group-based emotion: Integrating intergroup emotion and emotion regulation perspectives. *Personality and Social Psychology Review*, *20*, 118–41.

Goodwin, M. H., Cekaite, A., & Goodwin, C. (2012). Emotion as stance. In A. Peräkylä, & M.-L. Sorjonen (Eds.), *Emotion in interaction* (pp. 16–41). Oxford: Oxford University Press.

Gordon, R. M. (1974). The aboutness of emotions. *American Philosophical Quarterly*, *11*, 17–36.

Grandey, A. A. (2000). Emotion regulation in the workplace: A new way to conceptualize emotional labor. *Journal of Occupational Health Psychology*, *5*, 95–110.

Grandey, A. (2003). When 'the show must go on': Surface acting and deep acting as predictors of emotional exhaustion and peer-rated service delivery. *Academy of Management Journal*, *46*, 86–96.

Grandey, A., Dickter, D. N., & Sin, H. P. (2004). The customer is not always right: Customer aggression and emotion regulation of service employees. *Journal of Organizational Behavior*, *25*, 397–418.

Grandey, A., Fisk, G., Mattila, A., Jansen, K. J., & Sideman, L. (2005). Is service with a smile enough? Authenticity of positive displays during service encounters. *Organizational Behavior and Human Decision Processes*, *96*, 38–55.

Grandey, A. A., & Melloy, R. C. (2017). The state of the heart: Emotional labor as emotion regulation reviewed and revised. *Journal of Occupational Health Psychology*, *22*, 407–22.

Granström, K. (2011). Cheering as an indicator of social identity and self regulation in Swedish ice hockey supporter groups. *International Review for the Sociology of Sport*, *47*, 133–48.

Greene, G. (1961). *A burnt out case*. London: Heinemann.

Grice, H. P. (1975). Logic and conversation. In P. Cole & J. Morgan (Eds.), *Syntax and semantics 3: Speech acts* (pp. 41–58). New York: Academic Press.

Griffith, J., Connelly, S., Thiel, C., & Johnson, G. (2015). How outstanding leaders lead with affect: An examination of charismatic, ideological, and pragmatic leaders. *Leadership Quarterly*, *26*, 502–17.

Griffiths, P.E. (1997). *What emotions really are*. Chicago: University of Chicago Press.

Griffiths, P. E., & Scarantino, A. (2009). Emotions in the wild: The situated perspective on emotion. In P. Robbins & M. Aydede (Eds.), *Cambridge handbook of situated cognition* (pp. 437–53). Cambridge: Cambridge University Press.

Gross, J. J. (1998a). The emerging field of emotion regulation: An integrative review. *Review of General Psychology*, *3*, 271–99.

Gross, J. J. (1998b). Antecedent- and response-focused emotion regulation: Divergent consequences for experience, expression, and physiology. *Journal of Personality and Social Psychology*, *74*, 224–37.

Gross, J. J. (2015). Emotion regulation: Current status and future prospects. *Psychological Inquiry*, *26*, 1–26.

Gross, J. J., & John, O. P. (2003). Individual differences in two emotion regulation processes: Implications for affect, relationships, and well-being. *Journal of Personality and Social Psychology*, *85*, 348–62.

Gross, J. J., & Levenson, R. W. (1993). Emotional suppression: Physiology, self-report, and expressive behavior. *Journal of Personality and Social Psychology*, *64*, 970–86.

Gross, J. J., Richards, J. M., & John, O. P. (2006). Emotion regulation in everyday life. In D. K. Snyder, J. A. Simpson & J. N. Hughes (Eds.), *Emotion regulation in families: Pathways to dysfunction and health* (pp. 13–35). Washington, DC: American Psychological Association.

Groth, M., & Grandey, A. A. (2012). From bad to worse: Negative exchange spirals in employee-customer service interactions. *Organizational Psychology Review*, *2*, 208–33.

Groth, M., Hennig-Thurau, T., & Walsh, G. (2009). Customer reactions to emotional labor: The roles of employee acting strategy and customer detection accuracy. *Academy of Management Journal*, *52*, 958–74.

Gump, B. B., & Kulik, J. A. (1997). Stress, affiliation, and emotional contagion. *Journal of Personality and Social Psychology*, *72*, 305–19.

Gunnery, S., Hall, J., and Ruben, M. (2013). The deliberate Duchenne smile: Individual differences in expressive control. *Journal of Nonverbal Behavior*, *37*, 29–41.

Gyurak, A., Gross, J. J., & Etkin, A. (2011). Explicit and implicit emotion regulation: A dual-process framework. *Cognition and Emotion*, *25*, 400–12.

Hackenbracht, J., & Tamir, M. (2010). Preferences for sadness when eliciting help: Instrumental motives in sadness regulation. *Motivation and Emotion*, *34*, 306–15.

Hadjikhani, N., Hoge, R., Snyder, J., & de Gelder, B. (2008). Pointing with the eyes: The role of gaze in communicating danger. *Brain and Cognition*, *68*, 1–8.

Hagen, E. H., & Bryant, G. A. (2003). Music and dance as a coalition signaling system. *Human Nature*, *14*, 21–51.

Hains, S. C., Hogg, M. A., & Duck, J. M. (1997). Self-categorization and leadership: Effects of group prototypicality and leader stereotypicality. *Personality and Social Psychology Bulletin*, *23*, 1087–99.

Halberstadt, A. G., & Green, L. R. (1993). Social attention and placation theories of blushing. *Motivation and Emotion*, *17*, 53–64.

Halberstadt, J., Winkielmann, P., Niedenthal, P. M., & Dalle, N. (2009). Emotional conception: How embodied emotion concepts guide perception and facial action. *Psychological Science*, *20*, 1254–61.

Halperin, E. (2016). *Emotions in conflict: Inhibitors and facilitators of peace making*. New York: Routledge.

Halpern, J. (2001). *From detached concern to empathy: Humanizing medical practice*. New York: Oxford University Press.

Handford, C., Lemon, J., Grimm, M. C., & Vollmer-Conna, U. (2013). Empathy as a function of clinical exposure: Reading emotion in the eyes. *PLoS ONE*, *8*, e65159.

Hansen, C. H., & Hansen, R. D. (1988). Finding the face-in-the-crowd: An anger superiority effect. *Journal of Personality and Social Psychology*, *54*, 917–24.

Hareli, S. (2014). Making sense of the social world and influencing it by using a naïve attribution theory of emotions. *Emotion Review*, *6*, 336–43.

Hareli, S., & Hess, U. (2010). What emotional reactions can tell us about the nature of others: An appraisal perspective on person perception. *Cognition and Emotion, 24*, 128–40.

Hareli, S., & Parkinson, B. (2008). What's social about social emotions? *Journal for the Theory of Social Behavior, 38*, 131–56.

Hareli, S., & Rafaeli, A. (2008). Emotion cycles: On the social influence of emotions in organizations. *Research in Organizational Behavior, 28*, 35–59.

Harré, R., & Finlay-Jones, R. (1986). Emotion talk across times. In R. Harré (Ed.), *The social construction of emotions* (pp. 220–33). Oxford: Blackwell.

Harris, C. R., & Alvarado, N. (2005). Facial expressions, smile types, and self-report during humour, tickle, and pain. *Cognition and Emotion, 19*, 655–69.

Hassin, R. R., Aviezer, H., & Bentin, S. (2013). Inherently ambiguous: Facial expressions of emotions, in context. *Emotion Review, 5*, 60–5.

Hatfield, E., Cacioppo, J. T., & Rapson, R. L. (1994). *Emotional contagion.* New York: Cambridge University Press.

Hayes, S. C., Wilson, K. G., Gifford, E. V., Follette, V. M., & Strosahl, K. (1996). Experiential avoidance and behavioral disorders: A functional dimensional approach to diagnosis and treatment. *Journal of Consulting and Clinical Psychology, 64*, 1152–68.

Heider, A., & Warner, R. S. (2010). Bodies in sync: Interaction Ritual Theory applied to Sacred Harp singing. *Sociology of Religion, 71*, 76–97.

Heider, F. (1958). *The psychology of interpersonal relations.* New York: John Wiley.

Heinemann, L. V., & Heinemann, T. (2017). Burnout research: Emergence and scientific investigation of a contested diagnosis. *Sage Open, 7*, article 2158244017697154.

Henkel, A. P., Boegershausen, J., Rafaeli, A., & Lemmink, J. (2017). The social dimension of service interactions: Observer reactions to customer incivility. *Journal of Service Research, 20*, 120–34.

Hennig-Thurau, T., Groth, M., Paul, M., & Gremler, D. D. (2006). Are all smiles created equal? How emotional contagion and emotional labor affect service relationships. *Journal of Marketing, 70*, 58–73.

Henriques, J. (2010). The vibrations of affect and their propagation on a night out on Kingston's dancehall scene. *Body & Society, 16*, 57–89.

Hepburn, A., & Potter, J. (2012). Crying and crying responses. In A. Peräkylä, & M.-L. Sorjonen (Eds.), *Emotion in interaction* (pp. 195–211). Oxford: Oxford University Press.

Hess, U. (2014). Anger is a positive emotion. In W. G. Parrott (Ed.), *The positive side of negative emotions* (pp. 55–75). New York: Guilford Press.

Hess, U., Adams, R. B., Grammer, K., & Kleck, R. E. (2009). Face gender and emotion expression: Are angry women more like men? *Journal of Vision, 9*, 1–8.

Hess, U., Adams, R. B., Jr., & Kleck, R. E. (2005). Who may frown and who should smile? Dominance, affiliation, and the display of happiness and anger. *Cognition and Emotion, 19*, 515–36.

Hess, U., Adams, R. B., Jr., & Kleck, R. E. (2009). The face is not an empty canvas: How facial expressions interact with facial appearance. *Philosophical Transactions of the Royal Society London B, 364*, 3497–504.

Hess, U., Banse, R., & Kappas, A. (1995). The intensity of facial expression is determined by underlying affective state and social situation. *Journal of Personality and Social Psychology*, *69*, 280–8.

Hess, U., & Blairy, S. (2001). Facial mimicry and emotional contagion to dynamic emotional facial expressions and their influence on decoding accuracy. *International Journal of Psychophysiology*, *40*, 129–41.

Hess, U., Blaison, C., & Kafetsios, K., (2016). Judging facial emotion expressions in context: The influence of culture and self-construal orientation. *Journal of Nonverbal Behavior*, *40*, 55–64.

Hess, U., & Fischer, A. (2013). Emotional mimicry as social regulation. *Personality and Social Psychology Review*, *17*, 142–57.

Hess, U., & Fischer, A. (2016). *Emotional mimicry in social context*. Cambridge: Cambridge University Press.

Hess, U., & Hareli, S. (2018). On the malleability of the meaning of contexts: The influence of another person's emotion expressions on situation perception. *Cognition and Emotion*, *32*, 185–91.

Heyes, C. M. (2005). Imitation by association. In S. Hurley & N. Chater (Eds.), *Perspectives on imitation: From neuroscience to social science* (pp. 157–76). Cambridge, MA: MIT Press.

Hinde, R. A. (1981). Animal signals: Ethological and games-theory approaches are not incompatible. *Animal Behaviour*, *29*, 535–42.

Hinde, R. A. (1985). Was 'the expression of the emotions' a misleading phrase? *Animal Behavior*, *33*, 985–92.

Hobson, P. (2002). *The cradle of thought: Exploring the origins of thinking*. London: Macmillan.

Hochschild, A. R. (1979). Emotion work, feeling rules, and social structure. *American Journal of Sociology*, *85*, 551–75.

Hochschild, A. R. (1983). *The managed heart: Commercialization of human feeling*. Berkeley: University of California Press.

Hodges, S. D., & Biswas-Diener, R. (2007). Balancing the empathy expense account: Strategies for regulating empathic response. In T. F. D. Farrow & P. W. R. Woodruff (Eds.), *Empathy in mental illness* (pp. 389–405). Cambridge: Cambridge University Press.

Hofmann, W., De Houwer, J., Perugini, M., Baeyens, F., & Crombez, G. (2010). Evaluative conditioning in humans: A meta-analysis. *Psychological Bulletin*, *136*, 390–421.

Hogg, M. (2001). A social identity theory of leadership. *Personality and Social Psychology Review*, *5*, 184–200.

Hogg, M. A., Turner, J. C., & Davidson, B. (1990). Polarized norms and social frames of reference: A test of the self-categorization theory of group polarization. *Basic and Applied Social Psychology*, *11*, 77–100.

Hogg, M., & Van Knippenberg, D. (2003). Social identity and leadership processes in groups. *Advances in Experimental Social Psychology*, *35*, 1–52.

Holman, D. (2016). How does customer affiliative behaviour shape the outcomes of employee emotion regulation? A daily diary study of supermarket checkout operators. *Human Relations*, *69*, 1139–62.

Holodynski, M., & Friedlmeier, W. (2006). *Development of emotions and emotion regulation*. New York: Springer.

Hoogland, C. E., Schurtz, D. R., Cooper, C. M., Combs, D. J., Brown, E. G., & Smith, R. H. (2015). The joy of pain and the pain of joy: In-group identification predicts schadenfreude and gluckschmerz following rival groups' fortunes. *Motivation and Emotion*, *39*, 260–81.

Hopkins, N., Reicher, S., Khan, S. S., Tewari, S., Srinivasan, N., & Stevenson, C. (2016). Explaining effervescence: Investigating the relationship between shared social identity and positive experience in crowds. *Cognition and Emotion*, *30*, 20–32.

Hornsey, M. J., Okimoto, T. G., & Wenzel, M. (2017). The appraisal gap: Why victim and transgressor groups disagree on the need for a collective apology. *European Journal of Social Psychology*, *47*, 135–47.

Houston, L., III, Grandey, A., & Sawyer, K. (2018). Who cares if 'service with a smile' is authentic? An expectancy-based model of customer race and differential service reactions. *Organizational Behavior and Human Decision Processes*, *144*, 85–96.

Howell, A. J., Turowski, J. B., & Buro, K. (2012). Guilt, empathy, and apology. *Personality and Individual Differences*, *53*, 917–22.

Howell, J. M., & Shamir, B. (2005). The role of followers in the charismatic leadership process: Relationships and their consequences. *Academy of Management Review*, *30*, 96–112.

Hülsheger, U. R., Lang, J. W. B., & Maier, G. W. (2010). Emotional labor, strain, and performance: Testing reciprocal relationships in a longitudinal panel study. *Journal of Occupational Health Psychology*, *15*, 505–21.

Hülsheger, U. R., & Schewe, A. F. (2011). On the costs and benefits of emotional labor: A meta-analysis of three decades of research. *Journal of Occupational Health Psychology*, *16*, 361–89.

Hulsman, R. L., Pranger, S., Koot, S., Fabriek, M., Karemaker, J. M., & Smets, E. M. A. (2010). How stressful is doctor-patient communication? Physiological and psychological stress of medical students in simulated history taking and bad-news consultations. *International Journal of Psychophysiology*, *77*, 26–34.

Humphrey, R. H., Burch, G. F., and Adams, L. L. (2016). The benefits of merging leadership research and emotions research. *Frontiers in Psychology*, *7*, article 1022.

Humphrey, R. H., Pollack, J. M., & Hawver, T. (2008). Leading with emotional labor. *Journal of Managerial Psychology*, *23*, 151–68.

Huntsinger, J. R., Isbell, L. M., & Clore, G. L. (2014). The affective control of thought: Malleable, not fixed. *Psychological Review*, *121*, 600–18.

Huntsinger, J. R., & Ray, C. (2016). A flexible influence of affective feelings on creative and analytic performance. *Emotion*, *16*, 826–37.

Hutcherson, C. A., & Gross, J. J. (2011). The moral emotions: A social-functionalist account of anger, disgust, and contempt. *Journal of Personality and Social Psychology*, *100*, 719–37.

Hutchins, E. (1995). *Cognition in the wild*. Cambridge, MA: MIT Press.

Hutson, S. P., Hall, J. M., & Pack, F. L. (2015). Survivor guilt: Analyzing the concept and its contexts. *ANS Advances in Nursing Science*, *38*, 20–33.

Huttenlocher, J., Hedges, L. V., & Vevea, J. L. (2000). Why do categories affect stimulus judgment? *Journal of Experimental Psychology: General*, *129*, 220–41.

Ioannou, M., Al-Ramiah, A., & Hewstone, M. (2017). An experimental comparison of direct and indirect intergroup contact. *Journal of Experimental Social Psychology*, *76*, 393–403.

Isen, A. M., Daubman, K. A., & Nowicki, G. P. (1987). Positive affect facilitates creative problem solving. *Journal of Personality and Social Psychology*, *52*, 1122–31.

Ito, T. A., Chino, K. W., Devine, P. G., Lorig, T. S., & Cacioppo, J. T. (2006). The influence of facial feedback on race bias. *Psychological Science*, *17*, 256–61.

Iyer, A., & Leach, C. W. (2008). Emotion in intergroup relations. *European Review of Social Psychology*, *19*, 86–125.

Iyer, A., Schmader, T., & Lickel, B. (2007). Why individuals protest the perceived transgressions of their country: The role of anger, shame, and guilt. *Personality and Social Psychology Bulletin*, *33*, 572–87.

Izard, C. (1971). *The face of emotion*. New York: Appleton-Century-Crofts.

Jack, R. E., Garrod, O. G. B., Yu, H., Caldara, R., & Schyns, P. G. (2012). Facial expressions of emotion are not culturally universal. *Proceedings of the National Academy of Sciences of the United States of America*, *109*, 7241–4.

Jahoda, M. (1989). Why a non-reductionist social psychology is almost too difficult to be tackled but too fascinating to be left alone. *British Journal of Social Psychology*, *28*, 71–8.

Jakobs, E., Manstead, A. S. R., & Fischer, A. H. (1999). Social motives and emotional feelings as determinants of facial displays: The case of smiling. *Personality and Social Psychology Bulletin*, *25*, 424–35.

Jakobs, E., Manstead, A. S. R., & Fischer, A. H. (2001). Social context effects on acial activity in a negative emotional setting. *Emotion*, *1*, 51–69.

James, W. (1884). What is an emotion? *Mind*, *9*, 188–205.

James, W. (1898). *The principles of psychology* (Vol. 2). London: Macmillan.

Jäncke, L., & Kaufmann, N. (1994). Facial EMG responses to odors in solitude and with an audience. *Chemical Senses*, *19*, 99–111.

Jänig, W. (2006). *The integrative action of the autonomic nervous system: Neurobiology of homeostasis*. Cambridge: Cambridge University Press.

Jefferson, G. (1985). An exercise in the transcription and analysis of laughter. In A. Van Dijk & A. Teun (Eds.), *Handbook of discourse analysis* (Vol. 3, pp. 25–34). London: Academic Press.

Jefferson, G. (2004). Glossary of transcript symbols with an introduction. In G. H. Lerner (Ed.), *Conversation analysis: Studies from the first generation* (pp. 13–31). Amsterdam: John Benjamins.

Johnson, S., & Jacob, T. (2000). Sequential interactions in the marital communication of depressed men and women. *Journal of Consulting and Clinical Psychology*, *68*, 4–12.

Johnson-Laird, P. N., & Oatley, K. (1989). The language of emotions: An analysis of a semantic field. *Cognition and Emotion, 3*, 81–123.

Joinson, C. (1992). Coping with compassion fatigue. *Nursing, 22*, 116–22.

Jones, E. E., Wood, G. C., & Quattrone, G. A. (1981). Perceived variability of personal characteristics in ingroups and outgroups: The role of knowledge and evaluation. *Personality and Social Psychology Bulletin, 7*, 523–8.

Jones, S. (1996). Imitation or exploration? Young infants' matching of adults' oral gestures. *Child Development, 67*, 1952–69.

Judge, T. A., & Bono, J. E. (2000). Five-factor model of personality and transformational leadership. *Journal of Applied Psychology, 85*, 751–65.

Judge, T. A., Piccolo, R. F., & Kosalka, T. (2009). The bright and dark sides of leader traits: A review and theoretical extension of the leader trait paradigm. *Leadership Quarterly, 20*, 855–75.

Judge, T. A., Woolf, E. F., & Hurst, C. (2009). Is emotional labor more difficult for some than for others? A multi-level, experience sampling study. *Personnel Psychology, 62*, 57–88.

Kafetsios, K., Hantzara, K., Anagnostopoulos, F., & Niakas, D. (2016). Doctors' attachment orientations, emotion regulation strategies, and patient satisfaction: A multilevel analysis. *Health Communication, 31*, 772–7.

Kalokerinos, E. K., Tamir, M., & Kuppens, P. (2017). Instrumental motives in negative emotion regulation in daily life: Frequency, consistency, and predictors. *Emotion, 17*, 648–57.

Kamachi, M., Bruce, V., Mukaida, S., Gyoba, J., Yoshikawa, S., & Akamatsu, S. (2001). Dynamic properties influence the perception of facial expressions. *Perception, 30*, 875–87.

Kameda, T., Ohtsubo, Y., & Takezawa, M. (1997). Centrality in socio-cognitive networks and social influence: An illustration in a group decision-making context. *Journal of Personality and Social Psychology, 73*, 296–309.

Kammeyer-Mueller, J. D., Rubenstein, A. L., Long, D. M., Odio, M. A., Buckman, B. R., Zhang, Y., & Halvorsen-Ganepola, M. D. K. (2013). A meta-analytic structural model of dispositional affectivity and emotional labor. *Personnel Psychology, 66*, 47–90.

Kampfe, N., & Mitte, K. (2009). What you wish is what you get? The meaning of individual variability in desired affect and affective discrepancy. *Journal of Research in Personality, 43*, 409–18.

Kappas, A. (2011). Emotion and regulation are one! *Emotion Review, 3*, 17–25.

Kayyal, M., Widen, S., & Russell, J. A. (2015). Context is more powerful than we think: Contextual cues override facial cues even for valence. *Emotion, 15*, 287–91.

Keating, C. F., & Doyle, J. (2002). The faces of desirable mates and dates contain mixed social status cues. *Journal of Experimental Social Psychology, 38*, 414–24.

Keltner, D. (1995). Signs of appeasement: Evidence for the distinct displays of embarrassment, amusement, and shame. *Journal of Personality and Social Psychology, 68*, 441–54.

Keltner, D., & Buswell, B. N. (1997). Embarrassment: Its distinct form and appeasement function. *Psychological Bulletin, 122*, 250–70.

Keltner, D., & Cordaro, D. T. (2017). Understanding multimodal emotional expressions. In J.-M. Fernandez-Dols & J. A. Russell (Eds.), *The science of facial expression* (pp. 57–75). Oxford: Oxford University Press.

Keltner, D., Gruenfeld, D. H., & Anderson, C. (2003). Power, approach, and inhibition. *Psychological Bulletin, 110,* 265–84.

Keltner, D., & Haidt, J. (1999). Social functions of emotions at four levels of analysis. *Cognition and Emotion, 13,* 505–21.

Keltner, D., & Haidt, J. (2003). Approaching awe, a moral, spiritual, and aesthetic emotion. *Cognition and Emotion, 17,* 297–314.

Keltner, D., Haidt, J., & Shiota, M. N. (2006). Social functionalism and the evolution of emotions. In M. Schaller, J. A. Simpson & D. T. Kenrick (Eds.), *Evolution and social psychology* (pp. 115–42). New York: Psychology Press.

Keltner, D., Van Kleef, G. A., Chen, S., & Kraus, M. (2008). A reciprocal influence model of social power: Emerging principles and lines of inquiry. *Advances in Experimental Social Psychology, 40,* 151–92.

Kendon, A. (1967). Some functions of gaze direction in social interaction. *Acta Psychologica, 32,* 1–25.

Kiesler, S., Siegel, J., & McGuire, T. W. (1984). Social psychological aspects of computer-mediated communication. *American Psychologist, 39,* 1123–34.

Kim, E., & Yoon, D. J. (2012). Why does service with a smile make employees happy? A social interaction model. *Journal of Applied Psychology, 97,* 1059–67.

Kim, P. H., Mislin, A., Tuncel, E., Fehr, R., Cheshin, A., & van Kleef, G. A. (2017). Power as an emotional liability: Implications for perceived authenticity and trust after a transgression. *Journal of Experimental Psychology: General, 146,* 1379–401.

Klineberg, O. (1940). *Social psychology.* New York: Holt.

Klinnert, M. D., Campos, J. J., Sorce, J. F., Emde, R. N., & Svejda, M. (1983). Emotions as behavior regulators: Social referencing in infancy. In R. Plutchik & H. Kellerman (Eds.), *Emotions: Theory, research and experience* (Vol. 2, pp. 57–86). New York: Academic Press.

Kobayashi, H., & Kohshima, S. (1997). Unique morphology of the human eye. *Nature, 387,* 767–8.

Kokkinaki, T. S., Vasdekis, V. G. S., Koufaki, Z. E., & Trevarthen, C. B. (2017). Coordination of emotions in mother-infant dialogues. *Infant and Child Development, 26,* e1973.

Kölliker, M., Brodie III, E. D., & Moore, A. J. (2005). The coadaptation of parental supply and offspring demand. *The American Naturalist, 166,* 506–16.

Konvalinka, I., Xygalatas, D., Bulbulia, J., Schjødt, U., Jegindø, E-M., Wallot, S., Van Ordend, G., & Roepstorff, A. (2011). Synchronized arousal between performers and related spectators in a fire-walking ritual. *Proceedings of the National Academy of Sciences of the United States of America, 108,* 8514–19.

Koole, S. (2009). The psychology of emotion regulation: An integrative review. *Cognition and Emotion, 23,* 4–41.

Korb, S., Grandjean, D., & Scherer, K. R. (2010). Timing and voluntary suppression of facial mimicry to smiling faces in a go/nogo task: An EMG study. *Biological Psychology, 85,* 347–9.

Korsvold, L., Lie, H. C., Mellblom, A. V., Ruud, E., Loge, J. H., & Finset, A. (2016). Tailoring the delivery of cancer diagnosis to adolescent and young adult patients displaying strong emotions: An observational study of two cases. *International Journal of Qualitative Studies on Health and Well-Being, 11,* article 30763.

Kotsoni, E., de Haan, M., & Johnson, M. H. (2001). Categorical perception of facial expressions by 7-month-old infants. *Perception, 30,* 1115–25.

Kövecses, Z. (1990). *Emotion concepts.* New York: Springer-Verlag.

Kragel, P. A., & LaBar, K. S. (2016). Decoding the nature of emotion in the brain. *Trends in Cognitive Science, 20,* 444–55.

Kramer, A. D. I., Guillory, J. E., & Hancock, J. T. (2014). Experimental evidence of massive-scale emotional contagion through social networks. *Proceedings of the National Academy of Sciences of the United States of America, 111,* 8788–90.

Kraut, R. E., & Johnston, R. E. (1979). Social and emotional messages of smiling: An ethological approach. *Journal of Personality and Social Psychology, 37,* 1539–53.

Kreibig, S. D. (2010). Autonomic nervous system activity in emotion: A review. *Biological Psychology, 84,* 394–421.

Kristensen, T. S., Borritz, M., Villadsen, E., & Christensen, K. B. (2005). The Copenhagen burnout inventory: A new tool for the assessment of burnout. *Work and Stress, 19,* 192–207.

Kross, E., & Ayduk, Ö. (2011). Making meaning out of negative experiences by self-distancing. *Current Directions in Psychological Science, 20,* 187–91.

Krull, D. S. (1993). Does the grist change the mill? The effect of the perceiver's inferential goal on the process of social inference. *Personality and Social Psychology Bulletin, 19,* 340–8.

Krumhuber, E. G., Kappas, A., & Manstead, A. S. R. (2013). Effects of dynamic aspects of facial expressions: A review. *Emotion Review, 5,* 41–6.

Krumhuber, E. G., & Manstead, A. S. R. (2009). Can Duchenne smiles be feigned? New evidence on felt and false smiles. *Emotion, 9,* 807–20.

Kuppens, P., Van Mechelen, I., Smits, D. J. M., & De Boeck, P. (2003). The appraisal basis of anger: Specificity, necessity and sufficiency of components. *Emotion, 3,* 254–69.

Kuppens, T., Yzerbyt, V. Y., Dandache, S., Fischer, A. H., & van der Schalk, J. (2013). Social identity salience shapes group-based emotions through group-based appraisals. *Cognition and Emotion, 27,* 1359–77.

Laird, J. D. (1974). Self-attribution of emotion: The effects of expressive behavior on the quality of emotional experience. *Journal of Personality and Social Psychology, 29,* 473–86.

Laird, J. D., & Bresler, C. (1992). The process of emotional experience: A self-perception theory. In M. S. Clark (Ed.), *Review of personality and social psychology 13: Emotion* (pp. 213–34). Newbury Park, CA: Sage.

Lakin, J. L., Chartrand, T. L., & Arkin, R. M. (2008). I am too just like you: The effects of ostracism on nonconscious mimicry. *Psychological Science, 19,* 816–22.

Lakoff, G. (1987). *Women, fire, and dangerous things: What categories reveal about the mind*. Chicago: University of Chicago Press.

Lakoff, G., & Kövecses, Z. (1987). The cognitive model of anger inherent in American English. In D. Holland & N. Quinn (Eds.), *Cultural models in language and thought* (pp. 195–221). Cambridge: Cambridge University Press.

Lambie, J., & Marcel, A. (2002). Consciousness and emotion experience: A theoretical framework. *Psychological Review*, *109*, 219–59.

Lamm, H., & Myers, D. G. (1978). Group-induced polarization of attitudes and behavior. *Advances in Experimental Social Psychology*, *11*, 145–95.

Lammers, J., Galinsky, A. D., Gordijn, E. H., & Otten, S. (2008). Illegitimacy moderates the effects of power on approach. *Psychological Science*, *19*, 557–64.

Lane, A. M., Beedie, C. J., Davenport, T. J., & Stanley, D. M. (2011). Instrumental emotion regulation in sport: Relationships between beliefs about emotion and emotion regulation strategies used by athletes. *Scandinavian Journal of Medicine and Science in Sports*, *21*, 445–51.

Larsen, R. J. (2000). Toward a science of mood regulation. *Psychological Inquiry*, *11*, 129–41.

Latané, B., & Darley, J. M. (1968). Group inhibition of bystander intervention in emergencies. *Journal of Personality and Social Psychology*, *10*, 215–21.

Lazarus, R. S. (1966). *Psychological stress and the coping process*. New York: McGraw-Hill.

Lazarus, R.S. (1984). On the primacy of cognition. *American Psychologist*, *39*, 124–9.

Lazarus, R.S. (1991a). *Emotion and adaptation*. New York: Oxford University Press.

Lazarus, R.S. (1991b). Cognition and motivation in emotion. *American Psychologist*, *46*, 352–67.

Lazarus, R.S., & Folkman, S. (1984). *Stress, appraisal, and coping*. New York: Springer-Verlag.

Leach, C. W., Iyer, A., & Pedersen, A. (2006). Guilt and anger about in-group advantage as explanations of the willingness for political action. *Personality and Social Psychology Bulletin*, *32*, 1232–45.

Leach, C. W., & Spears, R. (2009). Dejection at in-group defeat and schadenfreude toward second-and third-party out-groups. *Emotion*, *9*, 659–65.

Leach, C. W., Spears, R., Branscombe, N. R., & Doosje, B. (2003). Malicious pleasure: Schadenfreude at the suffering of an outgroup. *Journal of Personality and Social Psychology*, *84*, 932–43.

Leary, M. R. (1983). A brief version of the Fear of Negative Evaluation Scale. *Personality and Social Psychology Bulletin*, *9*, 371–5.

Leary, M. R., Britt, T. W., Cutlip , W. D., & Templeton, J. L. (1992). Social blushing. *Psychological Bulletin*, *112*, 446–60.

Leary, M. R, Landel, J. L., & Patton, K. M. (1996). The motivated expression of embarrassment following a self-presentational predicament. *Journal of Personality*, *64*, 619–36.

Le Bon, G. (1895, tr. 1947). *The crowd: A study of the popular mind*. London: Ernest Benn.

Lee, D. H., Susskind, J. M., & Anderson, A. K. (2013). Social transmission of the sensory benefits of eye widening in fear expression. *Psychological Science, 24,* 957–65.

Leighton, J., Bird, G., Orsini, C., & Heyes, C. M. (2010). Social attitudes modulate automatic imitation. *Journal of Experimental Social Psychology, 46,* 905–10.

Lejuez, C. W., Read, J. P., Kahler, C. W., Richards, J. B., Ramsey, S. E., Stuart, G. L., Strong, D. R., & Brown, R. A. (2002). Evaluation of a behavioral measure of risk taking: The Balloon Analogue Risk Task (BART). *Journal of Experimental Psychology: Applied, 8,* 75–84.

Lelieveld, G.-J., Van Dijk, E., Van Beest, I., Steinel, W., & Van Kleef, G. A. (2011). Disappointed in you, angry about your offer: Distinct negative emotions induce concessions via different mechanisms. *Journal of Experimental Social Psychology, 47,* 635–41.

Lelieveld, G.-J., Van Dijk, E., Van Beest, I., & Van Kleef, G. A. (2012). Why anger and disappointment affect others' bargaining behavior differently: The moderating role of power and the mediating role of reciprocal and complementary emotions. *Personality and Social Psychology Bulletin, 38,* 1209–21.

Lelieveld, G.-J., Van Dijk, E., Van Beest, I., & Van Kleef, G. A. (2013). Does communicating disappointment in negotiations help or hurt? Solving an apparent inconsistency in the social-functional approach to emotions. *Journal of Personality and Social Psychology, 105,* 605–20.

Levenson, R. W. (1988). Emotion and the autonomic nervous system: A prospectus for research on autonomic specificity. In H. L. Wagner (Ed.), *Social psychophysiology and emotion: Theory and clinical applications* (pp. 17–42). Chichester: Wiley.

Levenson, R. W., & Gottman, J. M. (1983). Marital interaction: Physiological linkage and affective exchange. *Journal of Personality and Social Psychology, 45,* 587–97.

Leventhal, H., & Mace, W. (1970). The effect of laughter on evaluation of a slapstick movie. *Journal of Personality, 38,* 16–30.

Leventhal, H., & Scherer, K. R. (1987). The relationship of emotion and cognition: A functional approach to a semantic controversy. *Cognition and Emotion, 1,* 3–28.

Levinson, S. C. (1983). *Pragmatics*. Cambridge: Cambridge University Press.

Levy, R. (1973). *Tahitians*. Chicago, IL: Chicago University Press.

Lewis, K. M. (2000). When leaders display emotion: How followers respond to negative emotional expression of male and female leaders. *Journal of Organizational Behavior, 21,* 221–34.

Lewis, M. D., & Liu, Z. (2011). Three time-scales of neural self-organization underlying human basic and non-basic emotions. *Emotion Review, 3,* 416–23.

Leyens, J.-P., Paladino, P. M., Rodriguez-Torres, R., Vaes, J., Demoulin, S., Rodriguez-Perez, A., & Gaunt, R. (2000). The emotional side of prejudice: The role of secondary emotions. *Personality and Social Psychology Review, 4,* 186–97.

Leyens, J.-P., Rodriguez-Perez, A., Rodriguez-Torres, R., Gaunt, R., Paladino, M. P., Vaes, J., & Demoulin, S. (2001). Psychological essentialism and the differential attribution of uniquely human emotions to ingroups and outgroups. *European Journal of Social Psychology, 31*, 395–411.

Lipps, T. (1907). *Das Wissen von fremden Ichen.* In T. Lipps (Ed.), *Psychologische Untersuchungen* (Band 1, pp. 694–722). Leipzig: Engelmann.

Lief, H. I., & Fox, R. C. (1963). Training for 'detached concern' in medical students. In H. I. Lief, V. F. Lief & N. R. Lief (Eds.), *The psychological basis of medical practice* (pp. 12–35). New York: Harper & Row.

Little, L. M., Gooty, J., & Williams, M. (2016). The role of leader emotion management in leader-member exchange and follower outcomes. *Leadership Quarterly, 27*, 85–97.

Lively, K. J. (2000). Reciprocal emotion management: Working together to maintain stratification in private law firms. *Work and Occupations, 27*, 32–63.

Livingstone, A. G., Spears, R., Manstead, A. S. R., Bruder, M., & Shepherd, L. (2011). We feel, therefore we are: Emotion as a basis for self-categorization and social action. *Emotion, 11*, 754–67.

Livingstone, A. G., Shepherd, L., Spears, R., & Manstead, A. S. R. (2016). 'Fury, us': Anger as a basis for new group self-categories. *Cognition and Emotion, 30*, 183–92.

Lukács, G. (1971). *History and class consciousness: Studies in Marxist dialectics.* Cambridge, MA: MIT Press.

Lutz, C. A. (1982). The domain of emotion words on Ifaluk. *American Ethnologist, 9*, 113–28.

Lutz, C. A. (1988). *Unnatural emotions: Everyday sentiments on a micronesian atoll and their challenge to western theory.* Chicago, IL: University of Chicago Press.

Lutz, C. A., & Abu-Lughod, L. (1990). *Language and the politics of emotion.* New York: Cambridge University Press.

Mackie, D. M. (1986). Social identification effects in group polarization. *Journal of Personality and Social Psychology, 50*, 720–8.

Mackie, D. M., & Cooper, J. (1984). Attitude polarization: Effects of group membership. *Journal of Personality and Social Psychology, 46*, 575–86.

Mackie, D. M., Devos, T., & Smith, E. R. (2000). Intergroup emotions: Explaining offensive action tendencies in an intergroup context. *Journal of Personality and Social Psychology, 79*, 602–16.

Mackintosh, N. J. (2011). *IQ and human intelligence* (2nd edition). Oxford: Oxford University Press.

Mahoney, S., Sladek, R. M., & Neild, T. (2016). A longitudinal study of empathy in preclinical and clinical medical students and clinical supervisors. *BMC Medical Education, 16*, 270.

Mann, L., Feddes, A. R., Doosje, B., & Fischer, A. H. (2016). Withdraw or affiliate? The role of humiliation during initiation rituals. *Cognition and Emotion, 30*, 80–100.

Manstead, A. S. R., & Fischer, A. H. (2001). Social appraisal: The social world as object of and influence on appraisal processes. In K. R. Scherer, A. Schorr &

T. Johnstone (Eds.), *Appraisal processes in emotion: Theory, methods, research* (pp. 221–32). New York: Oxford University Press.

Manstead, A. S. R., & Wagner, H. L. (1981). Arousal, cognition and emotion: An appraisal of two-factor theory. *Current Psychological Reviews, 1*, 35–54.

Maringer, M., Krumhuber, E. G., Fischer, A. H., & Niedenthal, P. M. (2011). Beyond smile dynamics: Mimicry and beliefs in judgments of smiles. *Emotion, 11*, 181–7.

Markus, H. R., & Kitayama, S. (1991). Culture and the self: Implications for cognition, emotion, and motivation. *Psychological Review, 98*, 224–53.

Marsh, A. A., Elfenbein, H. A., & Ambady, N. (2003). Nonverbal 'accents': Cultural differences in facial expressions of emotion. *Psychological Science, 14*, 373–6.

Marshall, G., & Zimbardo, P. G. (1979). Affective consequences of inadequately explained physiological arousal. *Journal of Personality and Social Psychology, 37*, 970–88.

Martin, J., Rychlowska, M., Wood, A., & Niedenthal, P. (2017). Smiles as multi-purpose social signals. *Trends in Cognitive Science, 21*, 864–77.

Maslach, C. (1978). The client role in staff burn-out. *Journal of Social Issues, 34*, 111–24.

Maslach, C. (1979). Negative emotional biasing of unexplained arousal. *Journal of Personality and Social Psychology, 37*, 953–69.

Maslach, C. (1982). *Burnout: The cost of caring*. Englewood Cliffs, NJ: Prentice Hall.

Maslach, C., & Jackson, S. E. (1981). The measurement of experienced burnout. *Journal of Occupational Behavior, 2*, 99–113.

Maslach, C., Jackson, S. E., & Leiter, M. P. (1996). *MBI: The Maslach Burnout Inventory: Manual*. Palo Alto, CA: Consulting Psychologists Press.

Maslach, C., & Leiter, M. P. (1997). *The truth about burnout*. San Francisco: Jossey-Bass.

Maslach, C., & Pines, A. (1977). The burn-out syndrome in the day care setting. *Child Care Quarterly, 6*, 100–13.

Masters, W. H., & Johnson, V. E. (1966). *Human sexual response*. Boston: Little, Brown and Co.

Masuda, T., Ellsworth, P. C., Mesquita, B., Leu, J., Tanida, S., & Van de Veerdonk, E. (2008). Placing the face in context: Cultural differences in the perception of facial emotion. *Journal of Personality and Social Psychology, 94*, 365–81.

Masuda, T., Wang, H., Ishii, K., & Ito, K. (2012). Do surrounding figures' emotions affect judgment of the target figure's emotion? Comparing the eye-movement patterns of European Canadians, Asian Canadians, Asian international students, and Japanese. *Frontiers in Integrative Neuroscience, 6*, article 72.

Matsumoto, D., & Ekman, P. (1988). *Japanese and Caucasian facial expressions of emotion (JACFEE)* [Slides]. San Francisco: San Francisco State University, Department of Psychology, Intercultural and Emotion Research Laboratory.

Matsumoto, D., & Hwang, H. C. (2017). Methodological issues regarding cross-cultural studies of judgments of facial expressions. *Emotion Review, 9,* 375–82.

Matsumoto, D., & Willingham, B. (2006). The thrill of victory and the agony of defeat: Spontaneous expressions of medal winners of the 2004 Athens Olympic Games. *Journal of Personality and Social Psychology, 91,* 568–81.

Matsumoto, D., & Willingham, B. (2009). Spontaneous facial expressions of emotion of blind individuals. *Journal of Personality and Social Psychology, 96,* 1–10.

Mayer, A., & Traüble, B. E. (2012). Synchrony in the onset of mental state understanding across cultures: A study among children in Samoa. *International Journal of Behavioral Development, 37,* 21–8.

Mazziotta, A., Mummendey, A., & Wright, S. C. (2011). Vicarious intergroup contact effects: Applying social-cognitive theory to intergroup contact research. *Group Processes and Intergroup Relations, 14,* 255–74.

McGrath J. E., & Kelly, J. R. (1986). *Time and human interaction: Toward a social psychology of time.* New York: Guilford Press.

McGuire, G. M. (2007). Intimate work: A typology of the social support that workers provide to their network members. *Work and Occupations, 34,* 125–47.

McIntosh, D. M. (1996). Facial feedback hypothesis: Evidence, implications, and directions. *Motivation and Emotion, 20,* 121–47.

McNeill, A., Pehrson, S., & Stevenson, C. (2017). The rhetorical complexity of competitive and common victimhood in conversational discourse. *European Journal of Social Psychology, 47,* 167–79.

McNeill, W. (1995). *Keeping together in time.* Cambridge, MA: Harvard University Press.

Mead, G. H. (1934). *Mind, self, and society.* Chicago, IL: University of Chicago Press.

Medler-Liraz, H., & Seger-Guttmann, T. (2018). Authentic emotional displays, leader-member exchange, and emotional exhaustion. *Journal of Leadership and Organization Studies, 25,* 76–84.

Meltzoff, A. N., & Moore, M. K. (1977). Imitation of facial and manual gestures by human neonates. *Science, 198,* 75–78.

Meltzoff, A. N., & Moore, M. K. (1983). Newborn infants imitate adult facial gestures. *Child Development, 54,* 702–9.

Meltzoff, A. N., & Moore, M. K. (1997). Explaining facial imitation: a theoretical model. *Early Development and Parenting, 6,* 179–92.

Mesmer-Magnus, J. R., DeChurch, L. A., & Wax, A. (2012). Moving emotional labor beyond surface and deep acting: A discordance-congruence perspective. *Organizational Psychology Review, 2,* 6–53.

Messinger, D. S., Fogel, A., & Dickson, K. L. (1999). What's in a smile? *Developmental Psychology, 33,* 701–8.

Miller, R. S. (1992). The nature and severity of self-reported embarrassing circumstances. *Personality and Social Psychology Bulletin, 18,* 190–8.

Miller, R. S. (2004). Emotion as adaptive interpersonal communication: The case of embarrassment. In L. Z. Tiedens & C. W. Leach (Eds.), *The social life of emotions* (pp. 87–104). Cambridge: Cambridge University Press.

Mori, M. (1970, tr. 2012, K. F. MacDorman & N. Kageki).The uncanny valley (Bukimi no tani). *IEEE Robotics and Automation, 19,* 98–100.

Morris, J. A., & Feldman, D. C. (1996). The dimensions, antecedents, and consequences of emotional labor. *Academy of Management Review, 21,* 986–1010.

Morsbach, H., & Tyler, W. J. (1986). A Japanese emotion: Amae. In R. Harré (Ed.), *The social construction of emotion* (pp. 289–308). New York: Blackwell.

Moscovici, S., & Zavalloni, M. (1969). The group as a polarizer of attitudes. *Journal of Personality and Social Psychology, 12,* 125–35.

Mowrer, O. H. (1947). On the dual nature of learning: A reinterpretation of conditioning and problem solving. *Harvard Educational Review, 17,* 102–48.

Mumenthaler, C., & Sander, D. (2012). Social appraisal influences recognition of emotions. *Journal of Personality and Social Psychology, 102,* 1118–35.

Mumenthaler, C., & Sander, D. (2015). Automatic integration of social information in emotion recognition. *Journal of Experimental Psychology: General, 144,* 392–9.

Munn, N. L. (1940). The effect of knowledge of the situation upon judgment of emotion from facial expressions. *The Journal of Abnormal and Social Psychology, 35,* 324–38.

Murray, L., & Trevarthen, C. (1985). Emotional regulation on interactions between two-month-olds and their mothers. In T. M. Field & N. A. Fox (Eds.), *Social perception in infants* (pp. 177–97). Norwood, NJ: Ablex.

Myers, D. G., Bach, P. J., & Schreiber, B. V. (1974). Normative and informational effects of group interaction. *Sociometry, 37,* 275–86.

Nadler, A., & Shnabel, N. (2015). Intergroup reconciliation: Instrumental and socio-emotional processes and the needs-based model. *European Review of Social Psychology, 26,* 93–125.

Nagy, E., & Molnár, P. (2004). Homo imitans or homo provocans? Human imprinting model of neonatal imitation. *Infant Behavior and Development, 27,* 54–63.

Nakamura, M., Buck, R., & Kenny, D. A. (1990). Relative contributions of expressive behavior and contextual information to the judgment of the emotional state of another. *Journal of Personality and Social Psychology, 59,* 1032–9.

Negishi, K. (2012). Smiling in the post-Fordist 'affective' economy. *Transformations, 22.*

Nelissen, R. M. A., & Zeelenberg, M. (2009). When guilt evokes self-punishment: evidence for the existence of a Dobby Effect. *Emotion, 9,* 118–22.

Nelson, G. M., & Beach, S. R. H. (1990). Sequential interaction in depression: Effects of depressive behavior on spousal aggression. *Behavior Therapy, 21,* 167–82.

Nelson, N. L., & Russell, J. A. (2013). Universality revisited. *Emotion Review, 5,* 8–15.

Netzer, L., van Kleef, G. A., & Tamir, M. (2015). Interpersonal instrumental emotion regulation. *Journal of Experimental Social Psychology, 58*, 124–135.

Neumann, M., Edelhäuser, F., Tauschel, D., Fischer, M. R., Wirtz, M., Woopen, C., Haramati, A., & Scheffer, C. (2011). Empathy decline and its reasons: A systematic review of studies with medical students and residents. *Academic Medicine, 86*, 996–1009.

Neville, F., & Reicher, S. (2011). The experience of collective participation: Shared identity, relatedness and emotionality. *Contemporary Social Science, 6*, 377–96.

Newcombe, M. J., & Ashkanasy, N. M. (2002). The role of affect and affective congruence in perceptions of leaders: An experimental study. *Leadership Quarterly, 13*, 601–14.

Nezlek, J. B., Vansteelandt, K., Van Mechelen, I., & Kuppens, P. (2008). Appraisal-emotion relationships in everyday life. *Emotion, 8*, 145–50.

Niedenthal, P. M., Mermillod, M., Maringer, M., & Hess, U. (2010). The Simulation of Smiles (SIMS) model: Embodied simulation and the meaning of facial expression. *Behavioral and Brain Sciences, 33*, 417–33.

Niedenthal, P. M., Wood, A., Rychlowska, M., & Korb, S. (2017). Embodied simulation in decoding facial expression. In J.-M. Fernández-Dols & J. A. Russell (Eds.), *The science of facial expression* (pp. 397–413). Oxford: Oxford University Press.

Niederland, W. G. (1961). The problem of the survivor. *Journal of the Hillside Hospital, 10*, 233–47.

Niven, K. (2016). Why do people engage in interpersonal emotion regulation at work? *Organizational Psychology Review, 6*, 305–23.

Niven, K. (2017). The four key characteristics of interpersonal emotion regulation. *Current Opinion in Psychology, 17*, 89–93.

Niven, K., Totterdell, P. A., & Holman D. (2009). A classification of controlled interpersonal affect regulation strategies. *Emotion, 9*, 498–509.

Nolen-Hoeksema, S., Wisco, B. E., & Lyubomirsky, S. (2008). Rethinking rumination. *Perspectives on Psychological Science, 3*, 400–24.

Noor, M., Vollhardt, J. R., Mari, S., & Nadler, A. (2017). The social psychology of collective victimhood. *European Journal of Social Psychology, 47*, 121–34.

Novelli, D., Drury, J., Reicher, S., & Stott, C. (2013). Crowdedness mediates the effect of social identification on positive emotion in a crowd: A survey of two crowd events. *PLoS One, 8*, e78983.

Oakes, P. J. (1987). The salience of social categories. In J. C. Turner, M. A. Hogg, P. J. Oakes, S. D., Reicher & M. S. Wetherell (Eds.), *Rediscovering the social group: A self-categorisation theory* (pp. 117–41). Oxford: Basil Blackwell.

Oatley, K., & Johnson-Laird, P. N. (1987). Towards a cognitive theory of emotions. *Cognition and Emotion, 1*, 29–50.

Öhman, A., Eriksson, A., & Olofsson, C. (1975). One-trial learning and superior resistance to extinction of autonomic responses conditioned to potentially phobic stimuli. *Journal of Comparative and Physiological Psychology, 88*, 619–27.

O'Malley, M. N., & Greenberg, J. (1983). Sex differences in restoring justice: The down payment effect. *Journal of Research in Personality, 17*, 174–85.

Oostenbroek, J., Suddendorf, T., Nielsen, M., Redshaw, J., Kennedy-Costantini, S., Davis, J., et al. (2016). Comprehensive longitudinal study challenges the existence of neonatal imitation in humans. *Current Biology, 26*, 1334–8.

Orne, M. T. (1962). On the social psychology of the psychology experiment: With particular reference to demand characteristics and their implications. *American Psychologist, 17*, 776–83.

Ortony, A., Clore, G. L., & Collins, A. (1988). *The cognitive structure of emotions.* New York: Cambridge University Press.

Ortony, A., Clore, G. L., & Foss, M. (1987). The referential structure of the affective lexicon. *Cognitive Science, 11*, 361–84.

Osgood, C. E. (1962). Studies on the generality of affective meaning systems. *American Psychologist, 17*, 10–28.

Osgood, C. E. (1969). On the whys and wherefores of E, P, and A. *Journal of Personality and Social Psychology, 12*, 194–9.

Osgood, C. E., Suci, G. J., & Tannebaum, P. H. (1957). *The measurement of meaning.* Urbana: University of Illinois Press.

Overall, N. C., Girme, Y. U., Lemay, E. P., Jr., & Hammond, M. D. (2014). Attachment anxiety and reactions to relationship threat: The benefits and costs of inducing guilt in romantic partners. *Journal of Personality and Social Psychology, 106*, 235–56.

Overbeck, J. R., Neale, M. A., & Govan, C. L. (2010). I feel, therefore you act: Intrapersonal and interpersonal effects of emotion on negotiation as a function of social power. *Organizational Behavior & Human Decision Processes, 112*, 126–39.

Oyama, S. (1985). *The ontogeny of information: Developmental systems and evolution.* Cambridge: Cambridge University Press.

Páez, D., Rimé, B., Basabe, N., Wlodarczyk, A., & Zumeta, L. (2015). Psychosocial effects of perceived emotional synchrony in collective gatherings. *Journal of Personality and Social Psychology, 108*, 711–29.

Parkinson, B. (1991). Emotional stylists: Strategies of expressive management among trainee hairdressers. *Cognition and Emotion, 5*, 419–34.

Parkinson, B. (1995). *Ideas and realities of emotion.* London: Routledge.

Parkinson, B. (1996). Emotions are social. *British Journal of Psychology, 87*, 663–83.

Parkinson, B. (1997). Untangling the appraisal-emotion connection. *Personality and Social Psychology Review, 1*, 62–79.

Parkinson, B. (1999). Relations and dissociations between appraisal and emotion ratings in reasonable and unreasonable anger and guilt. *Cognition and Emotion, 13*, 347–85.

Parkinson, B. (2001a). Putting appraisal in context. In K. R. Scherer, A. Schorr & T. Johnstone (Eds.), *Appraisal processes in emotion: Theory, research, application* (pp. 173–86). Oxford University Press.

Parkinson, B. (2001b). Anger on and off the road. *British Journal of Psychology, 92*, 507–26.

Parkinson, B. (2011). Interpersonal emotion transfer: Contagion and social appraisal. *Personality and Social Psychology Compass, 5*, 428–39.

Parkinson, B. (2012). Piecing together emotion: Sites and time-scales for social construction. *Emotion Review, 4*, 290–8.

Parkinson, B. (2013). Journeys to the center of emotion. *Emotion Review, 5*, 180–4.

Parkinson, B. (2017). Interpersonal effects and functions of facial activity. In J.-M. Fernández-Dols & J. A. Russell (Eds.), *The science of facial expression* (pp. 435–56). Oxford: Oxford University Press.

Parkinson, B. (2018). Emotion. In G. Davey (Ed.), *Psychology* (pp. 479–528). Chichester: Wiley.

Parkinson, B. (2019). Calibrating emotional orientations: Social appraisal and other kinds of relation alignment. In D. Dukes & F. Clément (Eds.), *Foundations of affective social learning: Conceptualising the transmission of social value* (pp. 117–141). Cambridge: Cambridge University Press.

Parkinson, B., Fischer, A., & Manstead, A. S. R. (2005). *Emotion in social relations: Cultural, group, and interpersonal processes*. Philadelphia, PA: Psychology Press.

Parkinson, B., & Illingworth, S. (2009). Guilt in response to blame from others. *Cognition and Emotion, 23*, 1589–614.

Parkinson, B., & Lea, M. F. (1991). Investigating personal constructs of emotion, *British Journal of Psychology, 82*, 73–86.

Parkinson, B., & Lea, M. (2011). Video-linking emotions. In A. Kappas & N. Krämer (Eds.), *Face-to-face communication over the internet: Issues, research, challenges* (pp. 100–26). Cambridge: Cambridge University Press.

Parkinson, B., & Manstead A. S. R. (1992). Appraisal as a cause of emotion. *Review of Personality and Social Psychology, 13*, 122–49.

Parkinson, B., & Manstead, A. S. R. (1993). Making sense of emotion in stories and social life. *Cognition and Emotion, 7*, 295–323.

Parkinson, B., Phiri, N., & Simons, G. (2012). Bursting with anxiety: Adult social referencing in an interpersonal Balloon Analogue Risk Task (BART). *Emotion, 12*, 817–26.

Parkinson, B., Roper, A., & Simons, G. (2008). Appraisal ratings in diary reports of reasonable and unreasonable anger. *European Journal of Social Psychology, 38*, 82–7.

Parkinson, B., & Simons, G. (2009). Affecting others: Social appraisal and emotion contagion in everyday decision-making. *Personality and Social Psychology Bulletin, 35*, 1071–84.

Parkinson, B., & Simons, G. (2012). Worry spreads: Interpersonal transfer of problem-related anxiety. *Cognition and Emotion, 26*, 462–79.

Parkinson, B., Simons, G., & Niven, K. (2016). Sharing concerns: Interpersonal worry regulation in romantic couples. *Emotion, 16*, 449–58.

Parkinson, B., & Totterdell, P. (1997). Deliberate affect-regulation strategies: Preliminary data concerning reported effectiveness and frequency of use. In N. H. Frijda (Ed.), *Proceedings of the 9th Meeting of the International Society for Research on Emotions* (pp. 401–5). Storrs, CT: ISRE publications.

Parkinson, B., & Totterdell, P. (1999). Classifying affect-regulation strategies. *Cognition and Emotion, 13*, 277–303.

Parrott, W. G. (1993). Beyond hedonism: Motives for inhibiting good moods and for maintaining bad moods. In D. M. Wegner & J. W. Pennebaker (Eds.),

Handbook of mental control (pp. 278–305). Upper Saddle River, NJ: Prentice Hall.

Parrott, W. (2001). Implications of dysfunctional emotion for understanding how emotions function. *Review of General Psychology, 5*, 180–6.

Pasquarelli, B., & Bull, N. (1951). Experimental investigation of the body-mind continuum in affective states. *Journal of Nervous and Mental Disease, 113*, 512–21.

Pearce, E., Launay, J., & Dunbar, R. I. M. (2015). The ice-breaker effect: Singing mediates fast social bonding. *Royal Society Open Science, 2*, 150–221.

Pehrson, S., Stevenson, C., Muldoon, O. T., & Reicher, S. D. (2013). Is everyone Irish on St Patrick's Day? Divergent expectations and experiences of collective self-objectification at a multicultural parade. *British Journal of Social Psychology, 53*, 249–64.

Pescosolido, A. T. (2002). Emergent leaders as managers of group emotion. *Leadership Quarterly, 13*, 583–99.

Pines, A., & Aronson, E. (1981). *Burnout: From tedium to personal growth.* New York: Free Press.

Pollak, K. I., Arnold, R. M., Jeffreys, A. S., Alexander, S. C., Olsen, M. K., Abernethy, A. P., Sugg Skinner, C., Rodriguez, K. L., & Tulsky, J. A. (2007). Oncologist communication about emotion during visits with patients with advanced cancer. *Journal of Clinical Oncology, 25*, 5748–52.

Pomerantz, A. (1984). Agreeing and disagreeing with assessments: Some features of preferred/dispreferred turn shapes. In J. M. Atkinson & J. Heritage (Eds.), *Structures of social action: Studies in conversation analysis* (pp. 79–112). Cambridge: Cambridge University Press.

Porat, R., Halperin, E., Mannheim, I., & Tamir, M. (2015). Together we cry: Social motives and preferences for group-based sadness. *Cognition and Emotion, 30*, 66–79.

Porat, R., Halperin, E., & Tamir, M. (2016). What we want is what we get: Group-based emotional preferences and conflict resolution. *Journal of Personality and Social Psychology, 110*, 167–90.

Porter, S., & ten Brinke, L. (2008). Reading between the lies: Identifying concealed and falsified emotions in universal facial expressions. *Psychological Science, 19*, 508–14.

Porter, S., ten Brinke, L., & Wallace, B. (2012). Secrets and lies: Involuntary leakage in deceptive facial expressions as a function of emotional intensity. *Journal of Nonverbal Behavior, 36*, 23–37.

Posner, M. I., & Keele, S. W. (1968). On the genesis of abstract ideas. *Journal of Experimental Psychology, 77*, 353–63.

Potter, J., & Wetherell, M. (1987). *Discourse and social psychology: Beyond attitudes and behaviour.* London: Sage.

Provine, R. R. (1989). Faces as releasers of contagious yawning: An approach to face detection using normal human subjects. *Bulletin of the Psychonomic Society, 27*, 211–14.

Pugh, S. D. (2001). Service with a smile: Emotional contagion in the service encounter. *Academy of Management Journal, 44*, 1018–27.

Qu, F., Yan, W-J, Chen, Y-H, Li, K., Zhang, H., & Fu, X. (2017). 'You should have seen the look on your face. . .': Self-awareness of facial expressions. *Frontiers in Psychology*, *8*, article 832.

Rafaeli, A., & Sutton, R. I. (1987). Expression of emotion as part of the work role. *Academy of Management Review*, *12*, 23–37.

Rao, R. P. N., & Ballard, D. H. (1999). Predictive coding in the visual cortex: A functional interpretation of some extra-classical receptive-field effects. *Nature Neuroscience*, *2*, 79–87.

Ray, E., & Heyes, C. (2011). Imitation in infancy: The wealth of the stimulus. *Developmental Science*, *14*, 92–105.

Reddish, P., Fischer, R., & Bulbulia, J. (2013). Let's dance together: Synchrony, shared intentionality and cooperation. *PLoS ONE*, *8*, 1–13.

Reddy, V. (2000). Coyness in early infancy. *Developmental Science*, *3*, 186–92.

Reddy, V. (2008). *How infants know minds*. Cambridge, MA: Harvard University Press.

Reicher, S. D. (1987). Crowd behaviour as social action. In J. C. Turner, M. A. Hogg, P. J. Oakes, S. D. Reicher & M. S. Wetherell (Eds.), *Rediscovering the social group: A self-categorization theory* (pp. 171–205). Oxford: Blackwell.

Reisenzein, R. (1983). The Schachter theory of emotion: Two decades later. *Psychological Bulletin*, *94*, 239–64.

Reisenzein, R., Studtmann, M., & Horstmann, G. (2013). Coherence between emotion and facial expression: Evidence from laboratory experiments. *Emotion Review*, *5*, 16–23.

Riess, H., & Kraft-Todd, G. (2014). E.M.P.A.T.H.Y.: A tool to enhance nonverbal communication between clinicians and their patients. *Academic Medicine*, *89*, 1108–12.

Rimé, B. (2009). Emotion elicits the social sharing of emotion: Theory and empirical review. *Emotion Review*, *1*, 60–85.

Rizzolatti, G., & Craighero, L. (2004). The mirror-neuron system. *Annual Review of Neuroscience*, *27*, 169–92.

Robbins, J., & Rumsey, A. (Eds.). (2008). Introduction: Cultural and linguistic anthropology and the opacity of other minds. *Anthropological Quarterly*, *81*, 407–20.

Roberson, D., Damjanovic, L., & Pilling, M. (2007). Categorical perception of facial expressions: Evidence for a 'Category Adjustment' model. *Memory & Cognition*, *35*, 1814–29.

Roberson, D., & Davidoff, J. (2000). The categorical perception of colors and facial expressions: The effect of verbal interference. *Memory & Cognition*, *28*, 977–86.

Rodriguez Mosquera, P., Kahn, T., & Selya, A. (2017). American Muslims' anger and sadness about in-group social image. *Frontiers in Psychology*, *7*, article 2042.

Rolls, E. T. (1999). *The brain and emotion*. Oxford: Oxford University Press.

Rosch, E. (1973). Natural categories. *Cognitive Psychology*, *4*, 328–350.

Rose, A. J. (2002). Co-rumination in the friendships of girls and boys. *Child Development*, *73*, 1830–43.

Rose, A. J., Carlson, W., & Waller, E. M. (2007). Prospective associations of co-rumination with friendship and emotional adjustment: Considering the socioemotional trade-offs of co-rumination. *Developmental Psychology*, *43*, 1019–31.

Roseman, I. J., (1979). *Cognitive aspects of emotion and emotional behavior*. Paper presented at the 87th annual convention of the American Psychological Association, New York City.

Roseman, I. J., (1984). Cognitive determinants of emotions: A structural theory. In P. Shaver (Ed.), *Review of personality and social psychology* (Vol. 5, pp. 11–36). Beverly Hills, CA: Sage.

Roseman, I. J., & Evdokas, A. (2004). Appraisals cause experienced emotions: Experimental evidence. *Cognition and Emotion*, *18*, 1–28.

Roseman, I. J., & Smith, C. A. (2001). Appraisal theory: Overview, assumptions, varieties, controversies. In K. R. Scherer, A. Schorr & T. Johnstone (Eds.), *Appraisal processes in emotion: Theory, research, application* (pp. 3–19). Oxford University Press.

Ross E. D., & Pulusu V. K. (2013). Posed versus spontaneous facial expressions are modulated by opposite cerebral hemispheres. *Cortex*, *49*, 1280–91.

Rozin, P., & Fallon, A. E. (1987). A perspective on disgust. *Psychological Review*, *94*, 23–41.

Rozin, P., Lowery, L., Imada, S., & Haidt, J. (1999). The CAD triad hypothesis: A mapping between three moral emotions (contempt, anger, disgust) and three moral codes (community, autonomy, divinity). *Journal of Personality and Social Psychology*, *76*, 574–86.

Ruch, W. (1997). State and trait cheerfulness and the induction of exhilaration: A FACS study. *European Psychologist*, *2*, 328–41.

Ruiz-Belda, M. A., Fernández-Dols, J. M., Carrera, P., & Barchard, K. (2003). Spontaneous facial expressions of happy bowlers and soccer fans. *Cognition and Emotion*, *17*, 315–26.

Russell, C. L., Bard, K. A., & Adamson, L. B. (1997). Social referencing by young chimpanzees (Pan troglodytes). *Journal of Comparative Psychology*, *111*, 185–93.

Russell, J. A. (1978). Evidence of convergent validity on the dimensions of affect. *Journal of Personality and Social Psychology*, *36*, 1152–68.

Russell, J. A. (1980). A circumplex model of affect. *Journal of Personality and Social Psychology*, *39*, 1161–78.

Russell, J. A. (1983). Pancultural aspects of the human conceptual organization of emotions. *Journal of Personality and Social Psychology*, *45*, 1281–8.

Russell, J. A. (1991). In defense of a prototype approach to emotion concepts. *Journal of Personality and Social Psychology*, *60*, 37–47.

Russell, J. A. (1994). Is there universal recognition of emotion from facial expression? A review of the cross-cultural studies. *Psychological Bulletin*, *115*, 102–41.

Russell, J. A. (1995). Facial expressions of emotion: What lies beyond minimal universality? *Psychological Bulletin*, *118*, 379–91.

Russell, J. A. (1997). Reading emotions from and into faces: Resurrecting a dimensional contextual perspective. In J. A. Russell & J. M. Fernandez Dols (Eds.), *The psychology of facial expression* (pp. 295–320). New York: Cambridge University Press.

Russell, J. A. (2003). Core affect and the psychological construction of emotion. *Psychological Review, 110*, 145–72.

Russell, J. A. (2012). Introduction to special section: On defining emotion. *Emotion Review, 4*, 337.

Russell, J. A., & Fehr, B. (1994). Fuzzy concepts in a fuzzy hierarchy: Varieties of anger. *Journal of Personality and Social Psychology, 67*, 186–205.

Russell, J. A., & Fernández-Dols, J.-M. (1997). What does a facial expression mean? In J. A. Russell & J.-M. Fernández-Dols (Eds.), *The psychology of facial expression* (pp. 3–30). Cambridge: Cambridge University Press.

Russell, J. A., Lewicka, M., & Niit, T. (1989). A cross-cultural study of a circumplex model of affect. *Journal of Personality and Social Psychology, 57*, 848–56.

Rychlowska, M., Cañadas, E., Wood, A., Krumhuber, E. G., Fischer, A., & Niedenthal, P. M. (2014). Blocking mimicry makes true and false smiles look the same. *PLoS ONE, 9*, article e90876.

Sabini, J., Siepmann, M., Stein, J., & Meyerowitz, M. (2000). Who is embarrassed by what? *Cognition and Emotion, 14*, 213–40.

Sacks, H. (1992). *Lectures on conversation*, Vols. 1 and 2. Oxford: Blackwell.

Sander, D., Grandjean, D., Kaiser, S., Wehrle, T., & Scherer, K. R. (2007). Interaction effects of perceived gaze direction and dynamic facial expression: Evidence for appraisal theories of emotion. *European Journal of Cognitive Psychology, 19*, 470–80.

Sanders, G. S., & Baron, R. S. (1977). Is social comparison irrelevant for producing choice shifts? *Journal of Experimental Social Psychology, 13*, 303–14.

Sauter, D. A., LeGuen, O., & Haun, D. B. M. (2011). Categorical perception of emotional facial expressions does not require lexical categories. *Emotion, 11*, 1479–83.

Scarantino, A. (2010). Insights and blindspots of the cognitivist theory of emotions. *British Journal for the Philosophy of Science, 61*, 729–68.

Scarantino, A. (2017). How to do things with emotional expressions: The theory of affective pragmatics. *Psychological Inquiry, 28*, 165–85.

Schachter, S. (1959). *The psychology of affiliation*. Stanford, CA: Stanford University Press.

Schachter, S. (1964). The interaction of cognitive and physiological determinants of emotional state. *Advances in Experimental Social Psychology, 1*, 49–80.

Schachter, S., & Singer, J. E. (1962). Cognitive, social, and physiological determinants of emotional state. *Psychological Review, 69*, 379–99.

Schaubroeck, J. M., & Shao, P. (2012). The role of attribution in how followers respond to the emotional expression of male and female leaders. *Leadership Quarterly, 23*, 27–42.

Schaufeli, W. B., Leiter, M. P., & Maslach, C. (2009). Burnout: 35 years of research and practice. *The Career Development International, 14*, 204–20.

Scherer, K. R. (1984). Emotion as a multicomponent process: A model and some cross-cultural data. In P. Shaver (Ed.), *Review of personality and social psychology* (Vol. 5, pp. 37–63). Beverly Hills, CA: Sage.

Scherer, K. R. (1992). What does facial expression express? In K. T. Strongman (Ed.), *International review of studies in emotion* (Vol. 2, pp. 139–65). Chichester: Wiley.

Scherer, K. R. (1994). Toward a concept of 'modal emotions'. In P. Ekman & R. J. Davidson (Eds.), *The nature of emotion: Fundamental questions* (pp. 25–31). Oxford: Oxford University Press.

Scherer, K. R. (2001). Appraisal considered as a process of multi-level sequential checking. In K. R. Scherer, A. Schorr & T. Johnstone (Eds.), *Appraisal processes in emotion: Theory, Methods, Research* (pp. 92–120). New York and Oxford: Oxford University Press.

Scherer, K. R., & Grandjean, D. (2008). Facial expressions allow inference of both emotions and their components. *Cognition and Emotion*, *22*, 789–801.

Scherer, K. R., Mortillaro, M., & Mehu, M. (2017). Facial expression is driven by appraisal and generates appraisal inference. In J.-M. Fernandez-Dols & J. A. Russell (Eds.), *The science of facial expression* (pp. 353–73). Oxford: Oxford University Press.

Scherer, K. R., Mortillaro, M., Rotondi, I., Sergi, I., & Trznadel, S. (2018). Appraisal-driven facial actions as building blocks for emotion inference. *Journal of Personality and Social Psychology*, *114*, 358–79.

Schmidt, K.L., Bhattacharya, S., & Denlinger, R. (2009). Comparison of deliberate and spontaneous facial movement in smiles and eyebrow raises. *Journal of Nonverbal Behavior*, *33*, 35–45.

Schouten, B. C., & Meeuwesen, L. (2006). Cultural differences in medical communication: A review of the literature. *Patient Education and Counseling*, *64*, 21–34.

Schlosberg, H. (1952). The description of facial expression in terms of two dimensions. *Journal of Experimental Psychology*, *44*, 229–37.

Schofield, P. E., Butow, P. N., Thompson, J. F., Tattersall, M. H., Beeney, L. J., & Dunn, S. M. (2003). Psychological responses of patients receiving a diagnosis of cancer. *Annals of Oncology*, *14*, 48–56.

Schutte, N., Toppinen, S., Kalimo, R., & Schaufeli, W. (2000). The factorial validity of the Maslach Burnout Inventory: General Survey (MBI-GS) across occupational groups. *Journal of Occupational and Organizational Psychology*, *73*, 53–66.

Schwartz, B. (1974). Biological boundaries of learning. *Journal of the Experimental Analysis of Behavior*, *21*, 183–98.

Schwarz, N., & Bless, H. (1991). Happy and mindless, but sad and smart? The impact of affective states on analytic reasoning. In J. P. Forgas (Ed.), *Emotion and social judgments* (pp. 55–71). Oxford: Pergamon.

Sedikides, C., & Strube, M. J. (1997). Self-evaluation: To thine own self be good, to thine own self be sure, to thine own self be true, and to thine own self be better. *Advances in Experimental Social Psychology*, *29*, 209–69.

Sell, A., Tooby, J., & Cosmides, L. (2009). Formidability and the logic of human anger. *Proceedings of the National Academy of Sciences of the United States of America*, *106*, 15073–8.

Semin, G. R., & Manstead, A. S. R. (1982). The social implications of embarrassment displays and restitution behaviour. *European Journal of Social Psychology*, *12*, 367–77.

Sergi, I., Fiorentini, C., Trznadel, S., & Scherer, K. R. (2016). Appraisal inference from synthetic facial expressions. *International Journal of Synthetic Emotions*, *7*, 45–63.

Shackelford, T. K., Buss, D. M., & Bennett, K. (2002). Forgiveness or breakup: Sex differences in responses to a partner's infidelity. *Cognition and Emotion*, *16*, 299–307.

Shanafelt, T. D., Gradishar, W. J., Kosty, M., et al. (2014). Burnout and career satisfaction among US oncologists. *Journal of Clinical Oncology*, *51*, 678–86.

Shaver, P. R., Murdaya, U., & Fraley, R. C. (2001). Structure of the Indonesian emotion lexicon. *Asian Journal of Social Psychology*, *4*, 201–24.

Shaver, P., Schwartz, J., Kirson, D., & O'Connor, C. (1987). Emotion knowledge: Further exploration of a prototype approach. *Journal of Personality and Social Psychology*, *52*, 1061–86.

Shaw, J., Brown, R., & Dunn, S. (2015). The impact of delivery style on doctors' experience of stress during simulated bad news consultations. *Patient Education and Counseling*, *98*, 1255–9.

Sheppes, G., Catran, E., & Meiran, N. (2009). Reappraisal (but not distraction) is going to make you sweat: Physiological evidence for self-control effort. *International Journal of Psychophysiology*, *71*, 91–6.

Sheppes, G., Scheibe, S., Suri, G., & Gross, J. J. (2011). Emotion regulation choice. *Psychological Science*, *22*, 1391–6.

Shields, S. A., & MacDowell, K. A. (1987). 'Appropriate' emotion in politics: Judgments of a televised debate. *Journal of Communication*, *37*, 78–89.

Shirom, A., & Melamed, S. (2005). Does burnout affect physical health? A review of the evidence. In A. S. G. Antoniou & C. L. Cooper (Eds.), *Research companion to organizational health psychology* (pp. 599–622), Edward Elgar: Cheltenham.

Shnabel, N., Nadler, A., Ullrich, J., Dovidio, J. F., & Carmi, D. (2009). Promoting reconciliation through the satisfaction of the emotional needs of victimized and perpetrating group members: The needs-based model of reconciliation. *Personality and Social Psychology Bulletin*, *35*, 1021–30.

Shore, D. M., & Heerey, E. A. (2011). The value of genuine and polite smiles, *Emotion*, *11*, 169–74.

Shore, D. M., Katic, L., & Parkinson, B. (under review). *Making amends and mending things: Relationship repair and practical repair independently alleviate guilt*. University of Oxford, UK.

Shore, D. M., Rychlowska, M., van der Schalk, J., Parkinson, B., & Manstead, A. S. R. (2019). Intergroup emotional exchange: Ingroup guilt and outgroup anger increase resource allocation in trust games. *Emotion*, *19*, 605–616.

Shuman, V., Clark-Polner, E., Meuleman, B., Sander, D., & Scherer, K. R. (2017). Emotion perception from a componential perspective. *Cognition and Emotion*, *31*, 47–56.

Siegel, E. H., Sands, M. K., van den Noortgate, W., Condon, P., Chang, Y., Dy, J., Quigley, K. S., & Barrett, L. F. (2018). Emotion fingerprints or emotion populations? A meta-analytic investigation of autonomic features of emotion categories. *Psychological Bulletin*, *144*, 343–93.

Simner, M. L. (1971). Newborn's response to the cry of another infant. *Developmental Psychology*, *5*, 136–50.

Sinaceur, M., Kopelman, S., Vasiljevic, D., & Haag, C. (2015). Weep and get more: When and why sadness expression is effective in negotiations. *Journal of Applied Psychology*, *100*, 1847–71.

Sinaceur, M., & Tiedens, L. Z. (2006). Get mad and get more than even: When and why anger expression is effective in negotiations. *Journal of Experimental Social Psychology*, *42*, 314–22.

Slater, M. J., Haslam, S. A., & Steffens, N. K. (2018). Singing it for 'us': Team passion displayed during national anthems is associated with subsequent success. *European Journal of Sport Science*, *18*, 541–9.

Sliter, M., Jex, S., Wolford, K., & McInnerney, J. (2010). How rude! Emotional labor as a mediator between customer incivility and employee outcomes. *Journal of Occupational Health Psychology*, *15*, 468–81.

Smith, C. A. (1989). Dimensions of appraisal and physiological response in emotion. *Journal of Personality and Social Psychology*, *56*, 339–53.

Smith, C. A., & Ellsworth, P.C. (1985). Patterns of cognitive appraisal in emotion. *Journal of Personality and Social Psychology*, *48*, 813–38.

Smith, C. A., & Ellsworth, P. C. (1987). Patterns of appraisal and emotion related to taking an exam. *Journal of Personality and Social Psychology*, *52*, 475–88.

Smith, C. A., & Lazarus, R. S. (1993). Appraisal components, core relational themes, and the emotions. *Cognition and Emotion*, *7*, 233–69.

Smith, H., & Kessler, T. (2004). Group-based emotions and intergroup behavior. In L. Z. Tiedens & C. W. Leach (Eds.), *The social life of emotions* (pp. 292–313). Cambridge: Cambridge University Press.

Smith, E. R. (1993). Social identity and social emotions: Toward new conceptualizations of prejudice. In D. M. Mackie, D. Hamilton & D. Lewis (Eds.), *Affect, cognition, and stereotyping: Interactive processes in group perception* (pp. 297–315). San Diego, CA: Academic Press.

Smith, E. R., Seger, C. R., & Mackie, D. M. (2007). Can emotions be truly group level? Evidence regarding four conceptual criteria. *Journal of Personality and Social Psychology*, *93*, 431–46.

Smith, K. E., Norman, G. J., & Decety, J. (2017). The complexity of empathy during medical school training: evidence for positive changes. *Medical Education*, *51*, 1146–59.

Smith, R. H. (2013). *Schadenfreude and the dark side of human nature*. Oxford: Oxford University Press.

Snyder M., & Swann W. B. Jr. (1978). Behavioral confirmation in social interaction: From social perception to social reality. *Journal of Experimental Social Psychology*, *14*, 148–62.

Sorce, J. F., Emde, R. N., Campos, J., & Klinnert, M. D. (1985). Maternal emotional signaling: Its effect on the visual cliff behavior of 1 year olds. *Developmental Psychology*, *21*, 195–200.

Soussignan, R. (2002). Duchenne smile, emotional experience, and autonomic reactivity: A test of the facial feedback hypothesis. *Emotion*, *2*, 52–74.

Speisman, J. C., Lazarus, R. S., Mordkoff, A., & Davison, L. (1964). Experimental reduction of stress based on ego-defense theory. *Journal of Abnormal and Social Psychology*, *68*, 367–80.

Spencer, S., & Rupp, D. E. (2009). Angry, guilty, and conflicted: Injustice toward coworkers heightens emotional labor through cognitive and emotional mechanisms. *Journal of Applied Psychology*, *94*, 429–44.

Sperber, D., & Wilson, D. (1986). *Relevance: Communication and cognition*. Oxford: Blackwell.

Srinivasan, M. V., Laughlin, S. B., & Dubs, A. (1982). Predictive coding: A fresh view of inhibition in the retina. *Proceedings of the Royal Society of London. Series B, Containing Papers of a Biological Character*, *216*, 427–59.

Stamkou, E., van Kleef, G. A., Fischer, A. H., & Kret, M. E. (2016). Are the powerful really blind to the feelings of others? How hierarchical concerns shape attention to emotions. *Personality and Social Psychology Bulletin*, *42*, 755–68.

Stamm, B. H. (2008). *The ProQOL Test Manual* (2nd edition). Baltimore: Sidran Press.

Steinel, W., van Kleef, G. A., & Harinck, F. (2008). Are you talking to me?! Separating the people from the problem when expressing emotions in negotiation. *Journal of Experimental Social Psychology*, *44*, 362–69.

Stemmler, G. (1989). The autonomic differentiation of emotions revisited: Convergent and discriminant validation. *Psychophysiology*, *26*, 617–32.

Stemmler, G., Heldmann, M., Pauls, C. A., & Scherer, T. (2001). Constraints for emotion specificity in fear and anger: The context counts. *Psychophysiology 38*, 275–91.

Stern, D. N. (1999). Vitality contours: The temporal contour of feelings as a basic unit for constructing the infant's social experience. In P. Rochat (Ed.), *Early social cognition: Understanding others in the first months of life* (pp. 67–80). Mahwah, NJ: Lawrence Erlbaum Associates.

Stern, D. N., Hofer, L., Haft, W., & Dore, J. (1985). Affect attunement: The sharing of feeling states between mother and infant by means of intermodal fluency. In T. N. Field & N. Fox (Eds.), *Social perception in infants* (pp. 249–68). Norwood, NJ: Ablex.

Stoner, J. A. F. (1961). A comparison of individual and group decisions involving risk. Unpublished master's thesis. Massachusetts Institute of Technology, School of Industrial Management.

Stott, C., Hutchison, P., & Drury, J. (2001). 'Hooligans' abroad? Inter-group dynamics, social identity and participation in collective 'disorder' at the 1998 World Cup Finals. *British Journal of Social Psychology*, *40*, 359–84.

Stott, C., Adang, O., Livingstone, A., & Schreiber, M. (2007). Variability in the collective behaviour of England fans at Euro2004: *'Hooliganism', public order policing and social change European Journal of Social Psychology*, *37*, 75–100.

Strack, F., Martin, L. L., & Stepper, S. (1988). Inhibiting and facilitating conditions of the human smile: A non-obtrusive test of the facial feedback hypothesis. *Journal of Personality and Social Psychology*, *54*, 768–77.

Studer, R. K., Danuser, B., & Gomez, P. (2017). Physicians' psychophysiological stress reaction in medical communication of bad news: A critical literature review. *International Journal of Psychophysiology*, *120*, 14–22.

Su, L., & Levine, M. (2016). Does *'Lie to Me'* lie to you? An evaluation of facial clues to high-stakes deception. *Computer Vision and Image Understanding*, *147*, 52–68.

Suchman, A. L., Markakis, K., Beckman, H. B., & Frankel, R. (1997). A model of empathic communication in the medical interview. *Journal of the American Medical Association*. *277*, 678–82.

Suri, G., Sheppes, G., Young, G., Abraham, D., McRae, K., & Gross, J. J. (2018). Emotion regulation choice: The role of environmental affordances. *Cognition and Emotion*, *32*, 963–71.

Sutton, R. I. (1991). Maintaining norms about expressed emotions: The case of bill collectors. *Administrative Science Quarterly*, *36*, 245–68.

Sutton, R. I., & Rafaeli, A. (1988). Untangling the relationship between displayed emotions and organizational sales: The case of convenience stores. *Academy of Management Journal*, *31*, 461–87.

Swann, W. B., Jr., Gómez, A., Seyle, C. D., Morales, J. F., & Huici, C. (2009). Identity fusion: The interplay of personal and social identities in extreme group behavior. *Journal of Personality and Social Psychology*, *96*, 995–1011.

Swann, W. B., Jr., Jetten, J., Gómez, A., Whitehouse, H., & Bastian, B. (2012). When group membership gets personal: A theory of identity fusion. *Psychological Review*, *119*, 441–56.

Sy, T., & Choi, J. N. (2013). Contagious leaders and followers: Exploring multi-stage mood contagion in a leader activation and member propagation (LAMP) model. *Organizational Behavior and Human Decision Processes*, *122*, 127–40.

Sy, T., Côté, S., & Saavedra, R. (2005). The contagious leader: Impact of the leader's mood on the mood of group members, group affective tone, and group processes. *Journal of Applied Psychology*, *90*, 295–305.

Sy, T., Horton, C., & Riggio, R. (2018). Charismatic leadership: Eliciting and channeling follower emotions. *Leadership Quarterly*, *29*, 58–69.

Tabri, N., Wohl, M. J. A., & Caouette, J. (2018). Will we be harmed, will it be severe, can we protect ourselves? Threat appraisals predict collective angst (and its consequences). *European Journal of Social Psychology*, *48*, 72–85.

Tajfel, H., Flament, C., Billig, M. G., & Bundy, R. P. (1971). Social categorization and inter-group behavior. *European Journal of Social Psychology*, *1*, 149–77.

Tajfel, H., & Turner, J. C. (1979). An integrative theory of intergroup conflict. In S. Worchel & W. G. Austin (Eds.), *The psychology of intergroup relations* (pp. 33–47). Monterey, CA: Brooks-Cole.

Tajfel, H., & Wilkes, A. L. (1963). Classification and quantitative judgement. *British Journal of Psychology, 54*, 101–14.

Tamietto, M., Castelli, L., Vighetti, S., Perozzo, P., Geminiani, G., Weiskrantz, L., & de Gelder, B. (2009). Unseen facial and bodily expressions trigger fast emotional reactions. *Proceedings of the National Academy of Sciences of the United States of America, 106*, 17661–6.

Tamir, M. (2009). What do people want to feel and why? Pleasure and utility in emotion regulation. *Current Directions in Psychological Science, 18*, 101–5.

Tamir, M. (2016). Why do people regulate their emotions? A taxonomy of motives in emotion regulation. *Personality and Social Psychology Review, 20*, 199–222.

Tamir, M., Ford, B. Q., & Gilliam, M. (2013). Evidence for utilitarian motives in emotion regulation. *Cognition and Emotion, 27*, 483–91.

Tamir, M., Mitchell, C., & Gross, J. J. (2008). Hedonic and instrumental motives in anger regulation. *Psychological Science, 19*, 324–8.

Tarr, B., Launay, J., & Dunbar, R. I. M. (2016). Silent disco: Dancing in synchrony leads to elevated pain thresholds and social closeness. *Evolution and Human Behavior, 37*, 343–9.

Taylor, S. E., Fiske, S. T., Etcoff, N. L., & Ruderman, A. J. (1978). Categorical and contextual bases of person memory and stereotyping. *Journal of Personality and Social Psychology, 36*, 778–93.

Tetlock, P. E. (1986). Is self-categorization theory the solution to the level-of-analysis problem? *British Journal of Social Psychology, 25*, 255–6.

Thayer, R. E., Newman, J. R., & McClain, T. M. (1994). Self-regulation of mood: Strategies for changing a bad mood, raising energy, and reducing tension. *Journal of Personality and Social Psychology, 67*, 910–25.

Thirioux, B., Birault, F., & Jaafari, N. (2016). Empathy is a protective factor of burnout in physicians: New neuro-phenomenological hypotheses regarding empathy and sympathy in care relationship. *Frontiers in Psychology, 7*, article 763.

Thompson, R. A. (1987). Empathy and emotional understanding: The early development of empathy. In N. Eisenberg & J. Strayer (Eds.), *Empathy and its development* (pp. 119–43). New York: Cambridge University Press.

Thorstenson, C. A., Elliot, A. J., Pazda, A. D., Perrett, D. I., & Xiao, D. (2018). Emotion-color associations in the context of the face. *Emotion, 18*, 1032–42.

Tidd, K. L., & Lockard, J. S. (1978). Monetary significance of the affiliative smile: A case for reciprocal altruism. *Bulletin of the Psychonomic Society, 11*, 344–6.

Tiedens, L. Z. (2001). Anger and advancement versus sadness and subjugation: The effect of negative emotion expressions on social status conferral. *Journal of Personality and Social Psychology, 80*, 86–94.

Tomasello, M., & Call, J. (1997). *Primate cognition.* Oxford: Oxford University Press.

Tomasello, M., & Carpenter, M. (2007). Shared intentionality. *Developmental Science*, *10*, 121–5.

Tomkins, S. S. (1962). *Affect, imagery and consciousness. Vol. 1: The positive affects*. New York: Springer.

Tomkins, S. S., & McCarter, R. (1964). What and where are the primary affects? Some evidence for a theory. *Perceptual and Motor Skills*, *18*, 119–58.

Tomkins, S. S. (1981). The role of facial response in the experience of emotion: A reply to Tourangeau and Ellsworth. *Journal of Personality and Social Psychology*, *40*, 355–7.

Tooby, J., & Cosmides, L. (1990). The past explains the present: Emotional adaptations and the structure of ancestral environments. *Ethology and Sociobiology*, *11*, 375–424.

Tooby, J., & Cosmides, L. (2008). The evolutionary psychology of the emotions and their relationship to internal regulatory variables. In M. Lewis, J. M. Haviland-Jones & L. F. Barrett (Eds.), *Handbook of emotions* (3rd edition, pp. 114–37). New York: Guilford Pres.

Totterdell, P. (2000). Catching moods and hitting runs: Mood linkage and subjective performance in professional sport teams. *Journal of Applied Psychology*, *85*, 848–59.

Totterdell, P., & Holman, D. (2003). Emotion regulation in customer service roles: Testing a model of emotional labor. *Journal of Occupational Health Psychology*, *8*, 55–73.

Totterdell, P., Kellett, S., Teuchmann, K., & Briner, R. B. (1998). Evidence of mood linkage in work groups. *Journal of Personality and Social Psychology*, *74*, 1504–15.

Tourangeau, R., & Ellsworth, P. C. (1979). The role of facial response in the experience of emotion. *Journal of Personality and Social Psychology*, *37*, 1519–31.

Tracy, J. L., & Robins, R. W. (2004). Show your pride: Evidence for a discrete emotion expression. *Psychological Science*, *15*, 194–7.

Tracy, J. L., & Robins, R. W. (2008). The nonverbal expression of pride: Evidence for cross-cultural recognition. *Journal of Personality and Social Psychology*, *94*, 516–30.

Traut-Mattausch, E., Wagner, S., Pollatos, O., & Jonas, E. (2015). Complaints as starting point for vicious cycles in customer-employee-interactions. *Frontiers in Psychology*, *6*, article 1454.

Trevarthen, C. (1993). The function of emotions in early infant communication and development. In J. Nadel & L. Camaioni (Eds.), *New perspectives in early communicative development* (pp. 48–81). London: Routledge.

Tronick, E. Z. (1989). Emotions and emotional communication in infants. *American Psychologist*, *44*, 112–19.

Tsai, J. L., Knutson, B. K., & Fung, H. H. (2006). Cultural variation in affect valuation. *Journal of Personality and Social Psychology*, *90*, 288–307.

Tsai, W.-C., & Huang, Y.-M. (2002). Mechanisms linking employee affective delivery and customer behavioral intentions. *Journal of Applied Psychology*, *87*, 1001–08.

Tully, E. C., Ames, A. M., Garcia, S. E., & Donohue, M. R. (2016). Quadratic associations between empathy and depression as moderated by emotion dysregulation. *Journal of Psychology*, *150*, 15–35.

Turner, J. C. (1991). *Social influence*. Milton Keynes: Open University Press.

Turner, J. C., Hogg, M. A., Oakes, P. J., Reicher, S., & Wetherell, M. S. (1987). *Rediscovering the social group: A self-categorisation theory*. Oxford: Basil Blackwell.

Turner, J. C., & Oakes, P. J. (1986). The significance of the social identity concept for social psychology with reference to individualism, interactionism and social influence. *British Journal of Social Psychology*, *25*, 237–52.

Turner, J. C., Wetherell, M. S., & Hogg, M. A. (1989). Referent informational influence and group polarization. *British Journal of Social Psychology*, *28*, 135–47.

Tybur, J. M., Lieberman, D., & Griskevicius, V. (2009). Microbes, mating, and morality: Individual differences in three functional domains of disgust. *Journal of Personality and Social Psychology*, *97*, 103–22.

Van der Schalk, J., Kuppens, T., Bruder, M., & Manstead, A. S. R. (2015). The social power of regret: The effect of social appraisal and anticipated emotions on fair and unfair allocations in resource dilemmas. *Journal of Experimental Psychology: General*, *144*, 151–7.

Van Dijk, W. W., Ouwerkerk, J. W., Wesseling, Y. M., & Van Koningsbruggen, G. M. (2011). Towards understanding pleasure at the misfortunes of others: The impact of self-evaluation threat on schadenfreude. *Cognition and Emotion*, *25*, 360–8.

Van Doorn, E. A., van Kleef, G. A., & van der Pligt, J. (2015). Deriving meaning from others' emotions: Attribution, appraisal, and the use of emotions as social information. *Frontiers in Psychology*, *6*, 1077.

Van Dulmen, S., Tromp, F., Grosfeld, F., ten Cate, O., & Bensing, J. (2007). The impact of assessing simulated bad news consultations on medical students' stress response and communication performance. *Psychoneuroendocrinology*, *32*, 943–50.

Vangelisti, A. L., Daly, J. A., & Rudnick, J. R. (1991). Making people feel guilty in conversations: Techniques and correlates. *Human Communication Research*, *18*, 3–39.

Van Kleef, G. A. (2016). *The interpersonal dynamics of emotion: Toward an integrative theory of emotions as social information*. Cambridge: Cambridge University Press.

Van Kleef, G. A., & Côté, S. (2007). Expressing anger in conflict: When it helps and when it hurts. *Journal of Applied Psychology*, *92*, 1557–69.

Van Kleef, G. A., De Dreu, C. K. W., & Manstead, A. S. R. (2004a). The interpersonal effects of anger and happiness in negotiations. *Journal of Personality and Social Psychology*, *86*, 57–76.

Van Kleef, G. A., De Dreu, C. K. W., & Manstead, A. S. R. (2004b). The interpersonal effects of emotions in negotiations: A motivated information processing approach. *Journal of Personality and Social Psychology*, *87*, 510–28.

Van Kleef, G. A., De Dreu, C. W., Pietroni, D., & Manstead, A. S. R. (2006). Power and emotion in negotiation: Power moderates the interpersonal effects of anger and happiness on concession making. *European Journal of Social Psychology*, *36*, 557–81.

Van Kleef, G. A., Homan, A. C., Beersma, B., & van Knippenberg, D. (2010). On angry leaders and agreeable followers: How leaders' emotions and followers' personalities shape motivation and team performance. *Psychological Science*, *21*, 1827–34.

Van Kleef, G. A., Oveis, C., van der Löwe, I., & Keltner, D. (2008). Power, distress, and compassion: Turning a blind eye to the suffering of others. *Psychological Science*, *19*, 1315–22.

Van Vendeloo, S. N., Godderis, L., Brand, P. L. P., Verheyen, K. C. P. M., Rowell, S. A., & Hoekstra, H. (2018). Resident burnout: evaluating the role of the learning environment. *BMC Medical Education*, *18*, article 54.

Veil, C. (1959). Les états d'épuisement. *Le Concours Médical*, *23*, 2675–81.

Venkataramani, V., Green, S. G., & Schleicher, D. J. (2010). Well-connected leaders: The impact of leaders' social network ties on LMX and members' work attitudes. *Journal of Applied Psychology*, *95*, 1071–84.

Vergauwe, J., Wille, B., Hofmans, J., Kaiser, R. B., & De Fruyt, F. (2018). The double-edged sword of leader charisma: Understanding the curvilinear relationship between charismatic personality and leader effectiveness. *Journal of Personality and Social Psychology*, *114*, 110–30.

Viki, G. T., & Abrams, D. (2003). Infra humanization: Ambivalent sexism and the attribution of primary and secondary emotions to women. *Journal of Experimental Social Psychology*, *39*, 492–9.

Vygotsky, L. S. (1978). *Mind in society*. Cambridge, MA: Harvard University Press.

Wagenmakers, E.-J., Beek, T., Dijkhoff, L. et al. (2016). Registered replication report: Strack, Martin, & Stepper (1988). *Perspectives on Psychological Science*, *11*, 917–28.

Wagner, D. T., Barnes, C. M., & Scott, B. A. (2014). Driving it home: How workplace emotional labor harms employee home life. *Personnel Psychology*, *67*, 487–516.

Wagner, H. L., & Smith, J. (1991). Facial expression in the presence of friends and strangers. *Journal of Nonverbal Behavior*, *15*, 201–14.

Waldman, D. A., Ramirez, G. G., House, R. J., & Puranam, P. (2001). Does leadership matter? CEO leadership attributes and profitability under conditions of perceived environmental uncertainty. *Academy of Management Journal*, *44*, 134–43.

Wallach, M. A., Kogan, N., & Bem, D. J. (1962). Group influence on individual risk taking. *Journal of Abnormal and Social Psychology*, *65*, 75–86.

Walle, E., Reschke, P. J., & Knothe, J. M. (2017). Social referencing: Defining and delineating a basic process of emotion. *Emotion Review*, *9*, 245–52.

Wang, K. L., & Groth, M. (2014). Buffering the negative effects of employee surface acting: The moderating role of employee-customer relationship strength and personalized services. *Journal of Applied Psychology*, *99*, 341–50.

Webb, T. L., Miles, E., & Sheeran, P. (2012). Dealing with feeling: A meta-analysis of the effectiveness of strategies derived from the process model of emotion regulation. *Psychological Bulletin, 138*, 775–808.

Weber, M. (1924). *The theory of social and economic organizations.* New York: Free Press.

Weiner, B., Russell, D., & Lerman, D. (1979). The cognition-emotion process in achievement-related contexts. *Journal of Personality and Social Psychology, 37*, 1211–20.

Weisbuch, M., & Ambady, N. (2008). Affective divergence: Automatic responses to others' emotions depend on group membership. *Journal of Personality and Social Psychology, 95*, 1063–79.

Whitehouse, H. (1996). Rites of terror: Emotion, metaphor, and memory in Melanesian initiation cults. *Journal of the Royal Anthropological Institute, 2*, 703–15.

Williams, K. D. (2009). Ostracism: A temporal need–threat model. *Advances in Experimental Social Psychology, 41*, 275–314.

Wierzbicka, A. (1991). Talking about emotions: Semantics, culture, and cognition. *Cognition and Emotion, 6*, 285–319.

Wierzbicka, A. (1994). Emotion, language, and cultural scripts. In S. Kitayama & H. R. Markus (Eds.), *Emotion and culture: Empirical studies of mutual influence* (pp. 133–96). Washington, DC: APA.

Wierzbicka, A. (1999). *Emotions across languages and cultures: Diversity and universals.* New York: Cambridge University Press.

Wieser, M. J., & Brosch, T. (2012). Faces in context: a review and systematization of contextual influences on affective face processing. *Frontiers in Psychology, 3*, article 471.

Wiltermuth, S. S., & Heath, C. (2009). Synchrony and cooperation. *Psychological Science, 20*, 1–5.

Wittgenstein, L. (1953). *Philosophical investigations.* Oxford: Blackwell.

Wohl, M. J. A., Matheson, K., Branscombe, N. R., & Anisman, H. (2013). Victim and perpetrator groups' responses to the Canadian government's apology for the head tax on Chinese immigrants and the moderating influence of collective guilt. *Political Psychology, 34*, 713–29.

Wölfer, R., Faber, N. S., & Hewstone, M. (2015). Social network analysis in the science of groups. *Group Dynamics: Theory, Research, and Practice, 19*, 45–61.

Wondra, J. D., & Ellsworth, P. C. (2015). An appraisal theory of empathy and other vicarious emotional experiences. *Psychological Review, 122*, 411–28.

Wong, E., Tschan, F., & Semmer, N. K. (2017). Effort in emotion work and well-being: The role of goal attainment. *Emotion, 17*, 67–77.

Wood, A., Lupyan, G., Sherrin, S., & Niedenthal, P. (2016). Altering sensorimotor feedback disrupts visual discrimination of facial expressions. *Psychonomic Bulletin and Review, 23*, 1150–6.

Wright, S. C., Aron, A., McLaughlin-Volpe, T., & Ropp, S. A. (1997). The extended contact effect: Knowledge of cross-group friendships and prejudice. *Journal of Personality and Social Psychology, 73*, 73–90.

Wróbel, M., & Imbir, K. K. (2019). Broadening the perspective on emotional contagion and emotional mimicry: The correction hypothesis. *Perspectives on Psychological Science*, *14*, 437–51.

Wundt, W. (1897). *Outlines of psychology*. Leipzig: Wilhelm Engelmann.

Xygalatas, D., Konvalinka, I., Bulbulia, J., & Roepstorff, A. (2011). Quantifying collective effervescence: Heart-rate dynamics at a firewalking ritual. *Communicative and Integrative Biology*, *4*, 735–8.

Yam, P. C., & Parkinson, B. (under review). *Social functions of intergroup schadenfreude during and after an international soccer tournament*. University of Oxford, UK.

Yan, W., Wu, Q., Liang, J., Chen, Y., & Fu, X. (2013). How fast are the leaked facial expressions? The duration of micro-expressions. *Journal of Nonverbal Behavior*, *37*, 217–30.

Yik, M. S. M., & Russell, J. A. (1999). Interpretation of faces: A cross-cultural study of a prediction from Fridlund's theory. *Cognition and Emotion*, *13*, 93–104.

Yzerbyt, V., Dumont, M., Wigboldus, D., & Gordijn, E. (2003). I feel for us: The impact of categorization and identification on emotions and action tendencies. *British Journal of Social Psychology*, *42*, 533–49.

Yzerbyt, V., Kuppens, T., & Mathieu, B. (2016). When talking makes you feel like a group: The emergence of group-based emotions. *Cognition and Emotion*, *30*, 33–50.

Zajonc, R. B. (1980). Feeling and thinking: Preferences need no inferences. *American Psychologist*, *35*, 151–75.

Zaki, J., & Williams, W. C. (2013). Interpersonal emotion regulation. *Emotion*, *13*, 803-810.

Zajonc, R. B. (1984). On the primacy of affect. *American Psychologist*, *39*, 117–23.

Zhan, Y., Wang, M., & Shi, J. (2016). Interpersonal process of emotional labor: The role of negative and positive customer treatment. *Personnel Psychology*, *69*, 525–57.

Zimbardo, P. (1969). The human choice: Individuation, reason, and order versus deindividuation, impulse, and chaos. *Nebraska Symposium on Motivation*, *17*, 237–307.

Zimbardo, P. G., Ebbeson, E. B., & Maslach, C. (1977). *Influencing attitudes and changing behavior* (2nd edition). Reading, MA: Addison-Wesley.

Zimmermann, B. K., Dormann, C., & Dollard, M. F. (2011). On the positive aspects of customers: Customer-initiated support and affective crossover in employee-customer dyads. *Journal of Occupational and Organizational Psychology*, *20*, 31–57.

Zuckerman, M., Klorman, R., Larrance, D. T., & Spiegel, N. H. (1981). Facial, autonomic, and subjective components of emotion: The facial feedback hypothesis versus the externalizer-internalizer distinction. *Journal of Personality and Social Psychology*, *41*, 929–44.

Zwingmann, J., Baile, W. F., Schmier, J. W., Jürg, B., & Keller, M. (2017). Effects of patient-centered communication on anxiety, negative affect, and trust in the physician in delivering a cancer diagnosis: A randomized, experimental study. *Cancer*, *123*, 3167–75.

Index

"Aboutness." *See* Object-directedness
Accidie, 32, 240
Action readiness
    facial activity and, 115–16
    relational activity theory and, 18–19
Activation, 2–4, 5–6
Adams, R.B., Jr., 106–7
Adjacency pairs, 235–6
Adjustment, 140–1, 334
Admiration
    intergroup relations and, 266–7
    pride and, 135
Affective primacy, 12–14
Alexander, M.G., 267–8
Ambadar, Z., 104–5
Ambady, N., 90–1
Amusement, smiling and, 120–1, 124
Anger
    addressing targets and, 191–2
    appraisal theory and, 10–11
    categorical perception and, 109–11
    cluster analysis and, 33–5
    componential information and, 140
    conceptual differences between
        emotions, 25–6
    conceptual mapping of, 36–7, 39, 40–1
    contempt and, 228–9, 271
    defining, 30
    directionality of, 144
    disgust and, 228–9
    divergence and, 135
    emotion norms and, 255–6
    facial expressions and, 19, 82, 83, 86,
        100–1, 106–7, 166, 342
    fear and, 39, 186–7, 224, 279
    functions of, 224–6
    gaze direction and, 106–7
    groups and, 241–2
    induction of, 121
    intergroup relations and, 271, 273
    language regarding, 325
    leadership and, 285, 286–7
    meta-emotion and, 188–9
    neurocultural theory and, 74
    orientation of, 141–2
    regulation of, 199–200, 201–3, 208–10
    relation alignment approach and, 324
    reverse engineering model and, 172
    road rage, 225–6
    scowling and, 121, 154–5, 166, 203, 342
    scripts and, 48–50
    social appraisal and, 174–5, 185–6, 206
    social constructionist theory and, 238
    using others to regulate own
        emotions, 211
    while driving, 225–6
Anisman, H., 272
Appraisal theory, 9–10
    anger and, 10–11
    causal relation between appraisal and
        emotions, 12–14
    cumulative appraisal, 14–15
    dimensions of appraisal, 10–12
    distributed appraisal, 16–17
    facial activity and, 115
    group-based appraisal, 244–6
    implicit social appraisal, 173–5
    practical functions of emotions
        and, 217
    social appraisal (*See* Social appraisal)
Arkin, R.N., 152–3
Armstrong, S.L., 44–5
Arnold, M.B., 9–10, 17, 18
Arousal, 2–4, 5–6, 37–41

STUDIES IN EMOTION AND SOCIAL INTERACTION